Handbook of Frontier Markets

Handbook of Frontier Markets

The African, European and Asian Evidence

Edited by

P. Andrikopoulos
Coventry Business School
Coventry, United Kingdom

G.N. Gregoriou
State University of New York (Plattsburgh)
School of Business and Economics
Plattsburgh, NY, United States

V. Kallinterakis
University of Liverpool Management School
Liverpool, United Kingdom

AMSTERDAM • BOSTON • HEIDELBERG • LONDON
NEW YORK • OXFORD • PARIS • SAN DIEGO
SAN FRANCISCO • SINGAPORE • SYDNEY • TOKYO

Academic Press is an imprint of Elsevier

Academic Press is an imprint of Elsevier
125 London Wall, London EC2Y 5AS, United Kingdom
525 B Street, Suite 1800, San Diego, CA 92101-4495, United States
50 Hampshire Street, 5th Floor, Cambridge, MA 02139, United States
The Boulevard, Langford Lane, Kidlington, Oxford OX5 1GB, United Kingdom

Notices
Knowledge and best practice in this field are constantly changing. As new research and experience broad-
en our understanding, changes in research methods, professional practices, or medical treatment may
become necessary.

Practitioners and researchers must always rely on their own experience and knowledge in evaluating and
using any information, methods, compounds, or experiments described herein. In using such information
or methods they should be mindful of their own safety and the safety of others, including parties for whom
they have a professional responsibility.

To the fullest extent of the law, neither the Publisher nor the authors, contributors, or editors, assume any
liability for any injury and/or damage to persons or property as a matter of products liability, negligence
or otherwise, or from any use or operation of any methods, products, instructions, or ideas contained in
the material herein.

Library of Congress Cataloging-in-Publication Data
A catalog record for this book is available from the Library of Congress

British Library Cataloguing-in-Publication Data
A catalogue record for this book is available from the British Library

ISBN: 978-0-12-803776-8

For information on all Academic Press publications
visit our website at https://www.elsevier.com/

Working together
to grow libraries in
developing countries

www.elsevier.com • www.bookaid.org

Publisher: Nikki Levy
Acquisition Editor: Scott J. Bentley
Editorial Project Manager: Susan Ikeda
Production Project Manager: Jason Mitchell
Designer: Mark Rogers

Typeset by Thomson Digital

Contents

Section A
Africa

9. Another Look at Financial Analysts' Forecasts Accuracy: Recent Evidence From Eastern European Frontier Markets

A. Coën, A. Desfleurs

10. Are There Herding Patterns in the European Frontier Markets?

N. Blasco, P. Corredor, S. Ferreruela

Section C
Asia

List of Contributors

P. Andrikopoulos   Coventry Business School, Coventry, United Kingdom

D.L.T. Anh   School of Banking and Finance, National Economics University, Hanoi, Vietnam

K. Bangassa   University of Liverpool, Management School, Liverpool, United Kingdom

J. Ahmadu-Bello   School of Economics, Finance and Accounting, University of Coventry, Coventry, United Kingdom

N. Blasco   University of Zaragoza, Zaragoza, Spain

D. Bond   Ulster Business School, Ulster University, Londonderry, United Kingdom

D. Bozdog   Financial Engineering Division, Stevens Institute of Technology, Castle Point on Hudson, Hoboken, NJ, United States

S. Brahma   Glasgow Caledonian University Business School, Glasgow, United Kingdom

A. Calugaru   MarketAxess, New York City, NY, United States

T. Chaiyakul   Kasetsart University Sriracha Campus, Faculty of Management Sciences, Chonburi, Thailand

A. Coën   ESG-UQÀM, Graduate School of Business, University of Quebec in Montreal and Ivanhoe-Cambridge Real Estate Chair, Montreal, QC, Canada

P. Corredor   Public University of Navarre, Pamplona, Spain

A. Desfleurs   School of Accounting, Faculty of Administration, University of Sherbrooke, Sherbrooke, QC, Canada

K. Dyson   Ulster Business School, Ulster University, Londonderry, United Kingdom

F. Economou   Centre of Planning and Economic Research, Athens, Greece

A. Erdenetsogt   ABJYA LLC Brokerage Company, Ulaanbaatar, Mongolia

S. Ferreruela   University of Zaragoza, Zaragoza, Spain

K. Gavriilidis   University of Stirling Management School, Stirling, Scotland, United Kingdom

M.A. Georgescu   Faculty of Public Administration, National University of Political Studies and Public Administration, Bucharest, Romania

G.N. Gregoriou   State University of New York (Plattsburgh), School of Business and Economics, Plattsburgh, NY, United States

Y. Guney   University of Hull Business School, Hull, United Kingdom

M. Iskandrani University of Jordan, Faculty of Business, Amman, Jordan

V. Kallinterakis University of Liverpool, Management School, Liverpool, United Kingdom

D.S. Kambouroudis School of Management, University of Stirling, Stirling, Scotland, United Kingdom

E. Katsikas Kent Business School, University of Kent, United Kingdom

L.M. Kgari Bank of Botswana, Finance Department, Gaborone, Botswana

G. Komba Mzumbe University, School of Business, Morogoro, Tanzania

M.K. Newaz Coventry Business School, Coventry, United Kingdom

C. Pop Department of Business, Faculty of Business, Babeş-Bolyai University, Cluj-Napoca, Romania

T. Rodgers School of Economics, Finance and Accounting, University of Coventry, Coventry, United Kingdom

S.M. Wangeci Adam Smith Business School, University of Glasgow, Glasgow, United Kingdom

About the Editors

Dr Panagiotis Andrikopoulos is the Associate Head of School (Research) for the School of Economics, Finance and Accounting at Coventry Business School. Prior to joining Coventry University, Dr Andrikopoulos was a Reader in Finance at Leicester Business School (De Montfort University, United Kingdom) where he taught various finance courses such as investment theory and analysis, finance theory, corporate finance, and behavioral finance. During the period 2012–15, he has also been an Extraordinary (Adjunct) Associate Professor in Finance for the School of Accounting Sciences at North-West University of South Africa. He obtained his PhD in finance at the University of Portsmouth. Dr Andrikopoulos's research interests lie in the areas of corporate finance, market efficiency, empirical asset pricing, and behavioral finance, subjects on which he has widely published in various academic journals of international standing, such as the Journal of *Business, Finance and Accounting, the Accounting Forum, the European Journal of Finance, Review of Behavioral Finance and Journal of Economics and Business*. He currently serves as a panel member of various editorial and/or scientific advisory boards and has also been a frequent contributor to a wide range of international conferences.

Greg N. Gregoriou, a native of Montreal, obtained his joint PhD in finance at the University of Quebec at Montreal, which merges the resources of Montreal's four major universities—McGill, Concordia, UQAM, and HEC. Dr Gregoriou is Professor of Finance at the State University of New York (Plattsburgh) and has taught a variety of finance courses such as alternative investments, international finance, money and capital markets, portfolio management, and corporate finance. He has also lectured at the University of Vermont, the University of Navarra, and the University of Quebec at Montreal. Professor Gregoriou has published 50 books, 65 refereed publications in peer-reviewed journals, and 24 book chapters since his arrival at SUNY Plattsburgh in Aug. 2003. His books have been published by McGraw-Hill, John Wiley & Sons, Elsevier-Butterworth/Heinemann, Taylor and Francis/CRC Press, Palgrave-MacMillan, and Risk Books. Four of his books have been translated into Chinese and Russian. His academic articles have appeared in well-known peer-reviewed journals such as the *Review of Asset Pricing Studies, Journal of Portfolio Management, Journal of Futures Markets, European Journal of Operational Research, Annals of Operations Research*, and *Computers and Operations Research*. Professor Gregoriou is the derivatives editor and editorial board member for the *Journal of Asset Management* as well as an editorial board member for the *Journal of*

Wealth Management, the *Journal of Risk Management in Financial Institutions, Market Integrity, IEB International Journal of Finance,* and the *Brazilian Business Review.* His interests focus on hedge funds, funds of funds, commodity trading advisors, managed futures, venture capital, and private equity. He has also been quoted several times in the *New York Times, Barron's,* the *Financial Times of London, Le Temps* (Geneva), *Les Echos* (Paris), and *L'Observateur de Monaco.* He has done consulting work for numerous clients and investment firms in Montreal. He is a part-time lecturer in finance at McGill University, an advisory member of the Markets and Services Research Centre at Edith Cowan University in Joondalup (Australia), a senior advisor to the Ferrell Asset Management Group in Singapore, and a research associate with the University of Quebec at Montreal's CDP Capital Chair in Portfolio Management. In addition, he is a fellow at Hefei University of Technology at the Research Center for Operations & Productivity Management, in Hefei, China.

Vasileios (Bill) Kallinterakis is currently Lecturer of Finance at University of Liverpool Management School; he has also lectured at Durham University Business School (from where he also obtained his PhD) and Leeds University Business School. During his career, he has taught a variety of courses related to behavioral finance, corporate finance, and econometrics. His research interests focus on behavioral finance, institutional investors, market volatility, and emerging markets. To date, he has published a series of academic articles in peer-reviewed journals including the *European Financial Management Journal,* the *Journal of International Financial Markets, Institutions and Money,* the *International Review of Financial Analysis,* and the *Review of Behavioral Finance.* He has contributed to the *Wiley Encyclopedia of Management* and has served as ad hoc referee to research projects submitted to the National Stock Exchange of India. He is currently a member of the editorial board of several peer-reviewed journals (*Economic Analysis, International Business Research,* and *International Journal of Economics and Finance*).

About the Contributors

Dao Le Trang Anh is a lecturer in finance at the National Economics University of Vietnam (NEU). Her teaching and research interests focus on the field of equity markets and corporate finance management, while she is currently involved in relevant research projects for the Vietnamese government. She holds an MSc in financial forecasting and investment from the University of Glasgow.

Kenbata Bangassa holds a BA (honors) degree in accounting, MSc in finance, and PhD in finance. He has taught accounting and finance at the University of Liverpool, the University of Manchester, Strathclyde University, and Addis Ababa University at undergraduate and postgraduate levels. He has also supervised PhD theses and MSc dissertations of candidates who have successfully graduated. His research interests include developed, emerging, and frontier financial markets, as well as mutual fund performance, initial public offerings (IPOs), asset pricing, capital structure, value of analyst recommendations, and more. His work has been published in internationally refereed academic journals. He has held administrative positions up to the rank of head of finance department in government ministry. In connection to academic appointment at the universities he worked for, he held various administrative positions, including program director for undergraduate and postgraduate programs, external examiner, and referee for academic journals.

Jaliyyah Ahmadu-Bello teaches in the Department of Economics, Finance, and Accounting at Coventry University. Her undergraduate studies were at Federal University of Technology, Minna, Nigeria, and she has subsequently completed master's and PhD programs at Coventry University, United Kingdom. Her research interests include financial contagion effects in emerging and frontier African markets, and she has also worked as a research and development consultant in industry.

Natividad Blasco is Professor of Finance at the Department of Accounting and Finance (Faculty of Economics and Business Administration) at the University of Zaragoza. Her key research interests include market microstructure, corporate finance, and behavioral finance. Her research has been published in peer-reviewed journals such as the *Journal of Business Finance & Accounting*, *Journal of Accounting, Auditing and Finance*, *Journal of the Operational Research Society*, *Accounting and Finance*, *European Journal of Operational Research*, *Quantitative Finance*, *Applied Economics*, and *Journal of Behavioral Finance*. She is currently combining teaching and research with professional collaboration with companies and private and public institutions.

Derek Bond is a member of the academic staff at Ulster University. He is a former Principal Economist in the Northern Ireland Treasury and Director of the ESRC's Northern Ireland Regional Research Laboratory. He has acted as an advisor to many national and international organizations and held honorary offices in various international learned societies. He is currently a member of the Northern Ireland Statistical Advisory Committee and Associate Editor of the *Statistical Journal of the IAOS*. He has published widely in the areas of (financial) econometrics, geographic information systems (GIS), and innovation.

Dragos Bozdog, PhD, is the Deputy Director of the Hanlon Financial Systems Lab and Adjunct Professor in the Financial Engineering Division at Stevens Institute of Technology (United States). Dr Bozdog earned his PhD in financial engineering (Stevens Institute of Technology) and another PhD in mechanical engineering (University of Toledo). His research interests include mathematics of finance, high-frequency data analysis, rare events, emerging markets, algorithms and optimization, and tire mechanics. Previously, he was a postdoctoral fellow at Rutgers Center for Operations Research. In past years he worked as quantitative analyst for the financial industry and government. He published many research articles and book chapters, and he is regularly invited to give presentations at international conferences.

Sanjukta Brahma is Senior Lecturer in Finance at Glasgow Caledonian University Business School. Her research interest is in the area of corporate finance, particularly mergers and acquisitions, initial public offerings, and firm valuation. Her work has been published in peer-reviewed journals, and she has published a book on financial markets and institutions and has presented in various international conferences.

Adina Calugaru earned her PhD in finance from Babes-Bolyai University, Romania, and an MBA from Montclair State University (United States). She is working in the financial industry in New York City and is actively involved in investment funds research.

Thitima Chaiyakul is Lecturer at the Faculty of Management Sciences, Kasetsart University in Thailand. Her previous employments include placements with the Bank of Thailand and the Thai Airways International Public Company Limited. Her research interests include financial investment, credit management, and operations management, while her work has also been published in several books. She obtained her PhD from the University of Liverpool and holds an MBA from Kasetsart University.

Alain Coën is Full Professor of Finance at the Graduate School of Business (ESG) of the University of Quebec in Montreal (UQÀM). Before joining ESG–UQÀM, he was associate professor of finance at EDHEC School of Management. He obtained his PhD in finance from the University of Grenoble, and his PhD in economics from the University of Paris I Panthéon–Sorbonne. He holds an MA in economics with a major in macroeconomics from Laval University and accreditations to supervise research (HDR in management) from Paris-Dauphine University and (HDR in economics) from University of Paris

I Panthéon–Sorbonne. He has been visiting professor at Paris–Dauphine University, University of Paris-Ouest-Nanterre, EDHEC, Laval University, HEC–University of Liège, and University of Sherbrooke. His research interests focus on asset pricing, international finance, hedge funds, REITs, business cycles, and financial econometrics. He has published in several international leading journals, including the *Journal of Empirical Finance, Journal of Financial Research, Economics Letters, Finance Research Letters, Journal of Economics and Business, Finance, Journal of Alternative Investments*, and others, and has written a book in financial management. He is an associate researcher of the Ivanhoé Cambridge Real Estate Chair at ESG–UQÀM Graduate School of Business.

Pilar Corredor is Professor of Finance at the Department of Business Administration (Faculty of Economics and Business Administration) at the Public University of Navarre. Her key research interests are derivatives, corporate finance, and behavioral finance. Her research has appeared in peer-reviewed journals such as the *Journal of the Operational Research Society, Journal of Futures Markets, Technovation, Journal of Business Research, Accounting and Finance, Quantitative Finance, Applied Economics, European Journal of Operational Research, International Review of Financial Economics, International Business Research*, and *Journal of Behavioral Finance*.

Aurélie Desfleurs is Associate Professor in the Accounting Department at the University of Sherbrooke (Canada). She graduated from the EDHEC School of Management and obtained her PhD in finance from Laval University. She is also a Chartered Professional Accountant of Canada. She has published articles in the *Journal of Economics and Business* and the *Journal of Multinational Financial Management*. Her research focuses on financial analysts' forecasts, mergers and acquisitions, and International Financial Reporting Standards.

Ken Dyson is a member of academic staff at Ulster University. He has worked as an academic consultant for major international banks, including Citi. He is recognized for his applied research on behavioral finance and has published mainly in the area of financial theory and the functioning of financial markets.

Fotini Economou received her PhD from the Department of Business Administration at the University of Piraeus, Greece, supported by a scholarship from the Alexander S. Onassis Foundation. She is Research Fellow at the Center of Planning and Economic Research (KEPE), Athens, Greece, as well as Adjunct Lecturer at the Open University of Cyprus and the Hellenic Open University. Her research focuses on behavioral finance, herd behavior, investor sentiment, and international financial markets. She has published several papers in peer-reviewed financial journals (*Journal of International Financial Markets, Institutions and Money* and *International Review of Financial Analysis*, and others) and she has contributed to research projects for various public, private, and academic institutions.

Ariunjargal Erdenetsogt is the Director of ABJYA LLC brokerage in Mongolia. Her previous professional experience includes placements with the

Golomt Bank of Mongolia as treasury economist and product developer and at the Ministry of Mongolia as an analyst. She holds an MSc in finance and investment from Durham University.

Sandra Ferreruela is Lecturer at the Department of Accounting and Finance (Faculty of Economics and Business Administration) at the University of Zaragoza. Her research focuses on behavioral finance issues and market microstructure. She has published in peer-reviewed journals such as *Accounting and Finance*, *Journal of the Operational Research Society*, *Quantitative Finance*, and *Journal of Behavioral Finance*, and her research has been presented in a variety of academic conferences internationally (eg, EFMA, World Finance Conference, Behavioral Finance Working Group Conference, and Euro Working Group on Financial Modeling).

Konstantinos Gavriilidis teaches at the Stirling University Management School, United Kingdom. Before joining Stirling University, he held a position at Durham University Business School, and prior to joining academia he had an extensive work experience in the shipping industry. He has taught behavioral finance, corporate finance, and portfolio management, among other subjects, while his research area lies in behavioral finance. He holds an MSc in international money, finance, and investment and a PhD in finance, both from Durham University, United Kingdom.

Maria-Andrada Georgescu is an associate professor at the National University of Political Studies and Public Administration, Romania. She holds a PhD in finance from Babes-Bolyai University, Romania. Her main research interest is focused on European security markets, mainly bond segments. She has published several papers in this field in collaboration with Cornelia Pop, and she also the author of a number of Romanian books on financial analysis and public finance.

Yilmaz Guney is a senior lecturer and program leader for the MSc in financial management program at the Business School of the University of Hull, and was a lecturer at the School of Management of the University of Surrey. His main research area spans corporate finance, corporate governance, and behavioral finance. His work has been published in international journals, including the *Journal of Financial and Quantitative Analysis*, *European Financial Management*, *International Review of Financial Analysis*, *Journal of Multinational Financial Management*, and *Pacific-Basin Finance Journal*. Dr Guney holds a first degree in economics and MSc and PhD degrees in finance, and is the European editor of the *International Journal of Behavioural Accounting and Finance*.

Majd Iskandrani holds a BA (honours) in Finance, MBA in Finance and PhD in Management studies. He has taught Accounting and Finance at the University of Liverpool and the University of Jordan at undergraduate level and has participated in training courses at institute of banking studies. His research interests include: asset pricing, market liquidity, market microstructure, capital structure and trading mechanisms, etc. He is currently working as an Assistant to the Director of International Relations at the University of Jordan.

Dimos S. Kambouroudis is a lecturer in finance at the University of Stirling in Scotland. He previously held positions at the University of Edinburgh and

Durham University. His research interests are mainly in the area of empirical finance, modeling, and forecasting the volatility of stock markets with applications to risk management and socially responsible investing.

Epameinondas Katsikas is lecturer in accounting at Kent University Business School, United Kingdom. His research interests are in financial and management accounting, the effect of change in management accounting systems, performance measurement, accounting innovations, public sector management, institutional change, benchmarking, stock markets, and investment banking. He has published his work in international peer-reviewed journals and presented parts of his work at international conferences.

Lechedzani M. Kgari works in the finance department of the Bank of Botswana. She holds an MSc in financial forecasting and investment from Glasgow University, United Kingdom.

Gabriel Komba is a PhD candidate at the University of Hull Business School. For the past 15 years, he has been a lecturer in accounting and finance at the School of Business, Mzumbe University, Tanzania. He holds an advanced diploma in certified accountancy (ADCA) from the Institute of Development Management (IDM) in Tanzania, and an MSc in international banking and finance from Salford University (United Kingdom). He also holds a certified public accountant (CPA) professional qualification.

Mohammad K. Newaz is a Lecturer in Finance at Coventry Business School, Coventry University. His research interest includes international finance, corporate finance and behavioural finance especially in the areas of frontier and emerging markets. Mohammad is a frequent contributor to a wide range of local and international conferences.

Cornelia Pop is a full professor at Babes-Bolyai University, Romania. She received her PhD in finance in 1997 from the same university. The core of her research focuses on the Romanian security market, considering aspects related to its status as a frontier market, the internal growth potential of the equity market, and the development of its bond market segment. On these topics she published numerous papers in English and Romanian. She also has a collateral research interest in the hospitality industry and is coauthor of an international book, *Romania as a Tourist Destination and the Romanian Hotel Industry*, published in 2007 by Cambridge Scholars Publishing, United Kingdom.

Timothy Rodgers is a principal lecturer in economics and finance at Coventry University in the United Kingdom. He is currently academic course director of the MSc Investment Management program and also supervises a number of PhD students in the finance area. His personal research interests include financial contagion, portfolio theory, corporate capital structure, and Islamic finance, as well as, in the area of education, quality, ethnicity, and student performance in higher education.

Susan Maina Wangeci is an MSc financial risk management graduate from Adam Smith Business School at the University of Glasgow. Economics is a field that intrigues her, especially in the African context.

Acknowledgment

We would like to thank Dr J. Scott Bentley, Susan Ikeda, and Jason Mitchell at Elsevier for all their help and support throughout this process. In addition, we thank several anonymous referees in the selection of the papers for this book. Neither the publisher nor editors can guarantee the accuracy of each chapter in this book; each author/coauthor(s) is/are responsible for their own work.

Section A

Africa

Chapter 1

Testing for the Weak-Form Market Efficiency of the Dar es Salaam Stock Exchange

Y. Guney*, G. Komba**

*University of Hull Business School, Hull, United Kingdom;
**Mzumbe University, School of Business, Morogoro, Tanzania

Chapter Outline

1 INTRODUCTION

As a prominent theory in finance, the efficient market hypothesis (EMH) posits that if prices are determined rationally, then the arrival of new information will cause them to change. This means that the price of a security at any time reflects investors optimal use of all available information. By definition, though, information is understood to arise instantly, in an unpredictable manner, and ubiquitously to all investors. It follows that no single individual has a chance to

Handbook of Frontier Markets. http://dx.doi.org/10.1016/B978-0-12-803776-8.00001-X

outperform the market, as the current price of an asset is the best estimate of its fundamental value (Fama, 1970).

There are three types of efficiency: operational, allocational, and informational. Operational efficiency is concerned with the cost to buyers and sellers of securities on the exchange markets. Allocational (economic) efficiency refers to the supply of scarce resources to the most productive sectors of the economy. And finally, informational (pricing) efficiency is about the extent to which market prices accurately and instantly reflect all available and relevant information, hence implying a true representation of the fundamental value of the underlying asset. This is what the term "efficient" market hypothesis implies.

The EMH is normally defined and tested in three different forms, namely the weak form, the semistrong form, and the strong form (Fama, 1970, 1991). The purpose of this chapter is to investigate the weak-form efficiency of the Dar es Salaam Stock Exchange. A stock market is described as being weak-form efficient if market participants cannot predict the prices of securities and hence cannot generate abnormal returns (except by chance) by analyzing movements of past information (eg, prices and trading volumes). This means that various mechanical investment strategies such as technical analysis or fundamental analysis are of no value, since all investors already know any signal conveyed by the historical information about future performance. Therefore, security prices will always be at equilibrium.

Most of the research on market efficiency over the past decades has centered on the world's developed and emerging equity markets. Little attention is given to the African frontier markets despite their offering higher rates of return than mature markets and significantly attracting the interest of foreign investors. More specifically, in spite of their economic potential for efficient allocation of scarce resources, the weak-form efficiency studies of the East African stock exchanges are sparse. The evidence from the relatively few known studies is too old to explain the prevailing states of market developments that can be attributed to the benefits of globalization, industrialization, and technology. Moreover, the results offer contradicting conclusions (Dickinson and Muragu, 1994; Smith et al., 2002).

To the best of our knowledge, we offer for the first time an extensive examination of the behavior of stock prices and returns of the Dar es Salaam Stock Exchange (DSE) since its inception. The market was established in 1996 and started listing companies in 1998, when only one company was listed. Since then the total number of listed companies has increased to 21 by the end of 2014. Of these, 14 are domestic while the others are crosslisted, six from the Nairobi Stock Exchange and one from the London Stock Exchange. The DSE was also declared the best bourse in Africa in the same year in terms of market capitalization.

In this chapter, we extend the evidence on the weak-form efficiency in frontier markets by examining the data from the DSE in Tanzania. We use the All Share Index (DSEI), which includes both domestic and foreign firms, and the

Tanzania Share Index (TSI) covering only domestic firms, as well as the indices covering banks, finance, and investment companies (BI); commercial services (CS); and industrial and allied sectors (IA). We employ the augmented Dickey–Fuller test, variance ratio test, and ranks and signs test to determine whether the results are consistent. We find that returns series based on price indices for DSEI, BI, and CS indeed follow a random walk (RW), whereas the returns series for TSI and IA do not follow this pattern. However, findings on the same tests for the returns based on the return indices show that they are all not efficient.

The remainder of this chapter is organized as follows. In Section 2, we provide an overview of the random walk theory and the EMH. In Section 3, we present the empirical literature review on the random walk. Sections 4 and 5 describe the data and research methodology, respectively. Section 6 presents empirical findings. Section 7 concludes the chapter and provides some recommendations.

2   THE RANDOM WALK THEORY AND THE EFFICIENT MARKET HYPOTHESIS

The random walk (RW) theory is a version of the EMH. The EMH is built on the assumption that an efficient market is made up of a large number of active, rational, and profit-maximizing individuals who compete to predict the future market values of securities on the basis of freely available information (Fama, 1965, 1970, 1995). Fama further points out that the competition among the many participants and the instantaneous incorporation of both current and expected information make the actual prices good estimates of the intrinsic value of the securities.

Fama (1970) posits that the RW model should be regarded as an extension of the general expected return or fair-game efficient market model. The theory states that given all past information about the stock, the price P_{it} of a firm i today ($t = 0$) is expected to be equal to tomorrow's price P_{it+1}. The term "expected" means that the chance for the stock price to rise is the same as it is to fall. Hence, the change is equal to zero. The relationship can be summarized as follows:

$$P_{it} = P_{it-1} + \varepsilon_{it} \tag{1.1}$$

For $i = 1, 2, \ldots, N$ traded stocks; periods $t = 1, 2, \ldots, T$; and where P_{it-1} is the lagged price of the stock, and ε_{it} is an independent and identically distributed random variable with zero mean and unit variance [$\varepsilon_{it} \sim$ i.i.d., $N(0, \partial^2)$]. The RW model can econometrically be written as:

$$P_{it} = \beta P_{it-1} + \varepsilon_{it} \tag{1.2}$$

where β is the slope coefficient. This is a more restrictive definition of the RW than the martingale version because it requires the price P_{it+1} to be statistically independent. The martingale difference sequence (MDS) is less restrictive. It relaxes the independence restriction on the memory of the sequence (Gaussian random variable assumption). That is, while agreeing that the successive price changes are not predictable, it allows for the predictability of the conditional variances of price changes from past variances (Ntim et al., 2011). In other words, an asset's price series at time t is an MDS if it satisfies the following conditions: $E[P_t] < \infty$, and $E[P_{t+1} - P_t \mid P_t, P_{t-1}, ...] = 0$.

If β is equal to 1, then Eq. 1.2 can be written as $P_{it} - P_{it-1} = \Delta P_{it} = \varepsilon_{it}$. The model in this case is said to have a unit root problem or to be at a nonstationary situation. That is, ΔP_{it} is an RW or nonstationary, which means that the changes in price are explained by the error term. The term *unit root* is derived from the fact that the slope coefficient $\beta = 1$. This is a necessary condition for the random walk model to hold.

Since the establishment of the RW property of the stock return generating process, there has been a long-standing interest by researchers(see section 3) for testing the behavior of stock price changes. This is because the theory has obvious investment strategy and economic implications. For example, if a stock market does not follow a random walk, it may be considered inefficient, implying that the stocks are not appropriately priced. Thus, intelligent market participants may use the mispricings to predict the path by which the actual prices will move and thereby make a profit. The presence of the random walk is, therefore, essential if the stock markets are to generate the expected benefits such as improving availability and allocation of capital to a real economy.

3 EMPIRICAL LITERATURE REVIEW ON WEAK-FORM MARKET EFFICIENCY

The early tests of the EMH dealt with testing for the presence of the random walk on stock prices (Fama, 1965, 1970, 1991, 1995). Until the early 1970s, for example, there was little evidence against the EMH. In the mid-1980s, however, contradictory evidence began to emerge regarding the applicability of the EMH in explaining the functioning of the financial markets and their participants (De Bondt and Thaler, 1985, 1987; Pesaran and Timmermann, 1995). These scholars found that stock returns could be predicted by means of the available information. To many, this contradiction seemed to be evidence of market inefficiency, which in turn was interpreted as an indication of the invalidity of the EMH.

In the wake of this, scholars like Fama and French (1988a), Pesaran and Timmermann (1995), and Lander et al. (1997) have examined the performance of various investment strategies in predicting returns or timing the market. Their findings indicate that various financial variables, such as the price-to-earnings (P/E) ratio, dividends-to-price ratio, and short-term Treasury bills, can be used to forecast future movements of stock returns.

The discovery of the mean-reversion property in stock prices provides other evidence of returns' predictability. The mean-reversion hypothesis states that stock prices contain a predictable temporary component that is mean-reverting. That is, actual stock prices temporarily swing away from their fundamental values from time to time, but will then tend to go back to their mean. Using autocorrelation-based tests, Fama and French (1988b) show a slowly mean-reverting component of stock prices. They assert that their findings indicate that the returns are positively and negatively correlated for short and long horizons, respectively. They further indicate that the predictable variations of 3- to 5-year stock returns range from 25% to 40% for portfolios of large and small firms, respectively. Jegadeesh (1991), however, disputes these observations. He points out that although the equally weighted index of stocks traded on the New York Stock Exchange (NYSE) exhibited mean reversion over the 1926–88 period, the evidence shows that both the equally weighted and the value-weighted indices exhibited significant serial correlation after World War II. More specifically, the long-term mean reversions concentrated in January, and no evidence of the same was found when the entire sample period was included in the test.

Other studies on mean reversion and stock price predictability use the variance-estimator testing methodology. Poterba and Summers (1988) and Lo and MacKinlay (1989) contend that variance ratio tests are more powerful tests of the null hypothesis of market efficiency since they give more precise estimates of the relative predictability of returns over different horizons. In their study, Poterba and Summers (1988) report the existence of a transitory component in stock prices, with returns showing positive autocorrelation over a period of less than 1 year, and negative autocorrelation over longer periods of up to 8 years. Using the variance ratio test to analyze the importance of stationary components in stock prices, they report negative autocorrelations for both real and excess returns at long horizons. They further caution that nontrading effects can affect the interpretation of the positive serial correlation at a short horizon.

Lo and MacKinlay (1988) test the random walk hypothesis for weekly market returns from data sampled at different sampling frequencies. In contrast to Fama (1998), they find both statistically and economically significant positive serial correlation for the weekly and monthly stock returns. They further show that, during the period from 1962 to 1985, the weekly first-order autocorrelation coefficient of the equal-weighted return index was 30% while that of the value-weighted average was 8%. Their results provide evidence against the random walk model, though they do not support the mean reversion hypothesis. On the other hand, Mukherji (2011) uses a powerful nonparametric block bootstrap method, and finds evidence of the existence of weak mean reversion that persists for small-company stocks.

There are also numerous empirical studies on weak-form efficiency from emerging stock markets, but, like those conducted in developed markets, they provide conflicting evidence. Buguk and Brorsen (2003) examine the informational efficiency of the Istanbul Stock Exchange using its composite, industrial, and financial index weekly closing prices. Their findings indicate that all three series follow a random walk process. Urrutia (1995) tests the random walk and market efficiency for Latin American emerging equity markets. The findings from the runs test fail to reject the null hypothesis that the markets are weak-form efficient. However, consistent with those obtained by Lo and MacKinlay (1988), the variance ratio test rejects the null hypothesis, and the patterns of the test's rejection do not support the mean-reverting process.

Investigations on weak-form market efficiency in African markets have also attracted the interest of many researchers, but with inconclusive findings. One of the earliest studies on the efficiency of African stock markets was carried out by Dickinson and Muragu (1994). The results obtained from using the serial correlation and runs tests suggest that small markets may conform to the weak-form efficiency notion. Magnusson and Wydick (2002) carried out weak-form efficiency tests using 1989–98 data on eight African markets (including South Africa) listed in the International Finance Corporation (IFC) global composite index. The findings reveal that six out of the eight analyzed stock market indices are weak-form efficient. In contrast, Smith et al. (2002) used multiple variance ratios to examine the informational efficiency in stock indices of a group of the eight largest African markets covering 1990–98. Except for South Africa, the results in seven of these markets reject the random walk hypothesis due to autocorrelation. Despite using a different approach for a group of seven African markets, Jefferis and Smith (2005) obtained similar results to those of Smith et al. (2002).

In another study, Ntim et al. (2011) tested the efficiency of a set of 24 African continent-wide stock price indices and eight individual African national stock price indices using ranks and signs tests. The results show that, in comparison to the national indices, the African continent-wide stock price indices exhibit a reasonable normal distribution and have superior weak-form efficiency.

Another multi-country study was carried out by Mlambo and Biekpe (2007). They find sufficient evidence to conclude that the markets for Namibia, Kenya, and Zimbabwe are generally weak-form efficient. In all other markets, the majority of stocks rejected the random walk. In a recent study, Smith and Dyakova (2014) examined the weak-form efficiency of eight African markets. The results of variance ratio tests show that Kenya's and Zambia's markets are the most predictable and least informationally efficient. They further reveal that the least predictable stock market is that of Egypt, followed jointly by the South African and Tunisian markets.

In summary, the empirical evidence from the African stock markets is not only small but also still offers contradictory conclusions. Many of these studies, however, indicate that the South African and Egyptian stock markets are weak-form efficient (Jefferis and Smith, 2005; Smith and Dyakova, 2014). The Kenyan market is the most studied from the Eastern Africa region (Dickinson and Muragu, 1994; Ntim et al., 2011; Smith and Dyakova, 2014). The main reason could be that it is among the oldest markets in Africa, established in 1954. In comparison, the Tanzanian market, the DSE, is relatively new and small. The conflicting results from past studies in other markets make it appealing to undertake an empirical work for the DSE.

4   DATA SOURCES

The data used in this study are daily closing prices of the five DSE indices (ie, DSEI, TSI, BI, CS, and IA) in local currency, the Tanzanian shilling (TZS). All indices are value-weighted market capitalization. Given the small size and new-ness of the market, it was thought that daily stock prices would yield sufficient observations for meaningful statistical analyses and be representative of the true distribution characteristics of the market. The data set for testing the random walk hypothesis covered the period from Jan. 2007 to Dec. 2014. This choice of the starting time was dictated by the moment when the DSE began to compile electronically and maintain a computerized database. By Dec. 2006, there were 10 listed companies. Therefore, this was when the market had become more active. All data were provided by the DSE's market research and development department.

5   METHODOLOGY

To the best of our knowledge, this is the first and the only comprehensive study to test the weak-form market efficiency of the DSE. It was therefore considered worthwhile to employ a battery of tests to determine whether the conclusions obtained confirm the random walk hypothesis or are fragile. The following sections present the tests that were performed.

5.1   Augmented Dickey–Fuller Test

The augmented Dickey–Fuller (ADF) test is a popular approach used for testing the unit root null hypothesis. The tests were performed on raw price indices and logarithm-transformed data in both levels and first differences. The ADF test employs the following regression model:

$$\Delta Y_t = \beta_1 + \beta_2 t + \delta Y_{t-1} + \sum_{i=1}^{k} \infty_i \Delta Y_{t-i} + \varepsilon_t \tag{1.3}$$

where Δ = the first difference operator; ΔY_{t-i} = lagged values of the dependent variable, for example, $\Delta Y_{t-1} = (Y_{t-1} - Y_{t-2})$, $\Delta Y_{t-2} = (Y_{t-2} - Y_{t-3})$, and so forth; ε_t is a white noise error term; β_1 is a constant; β_2 is a slope coefficient on time trend t; δ is a coefficient of lagged Y_{t-1}; and Y_t is the logarithm of the stock price or market price index. Recall that under Eq. 1.2 it was asserted that there is a unit root if $\beta = 1$. Econometrically, however, it is argued that this regression equation cannot be estimated using the ordinary least squares (OLS) method. In addition, the hypothesis $\beta = 1$ cannot be tested using the standard t-distribution since the test is based on the residual terms, which may be highly autocor-related, and thus can lead to biased estimate of δ (Gujarati and Porter, 2009). Instead, the ADF test was used. The model in Eq. 1.3 was used to examine the returns (ΔY_t) in order to take into account the autocorrelation problem regarding the residual terms. In this specification, the tested unit root hypothesis was $\delta = 0$ (where $\delta = \beta - 1$). As the literature suggests, in order to attain the white-noise structure in ε_t and the unbiased estimate of δ, it is important to select the appropriate lag length by including enough terms. The choice of the lag length was based on the Schwarz information criterion (SIC). Following the previous discussion, it is hereby hypothesized that:

H_0: Stock price/returns indices at the DSE follow a random walk process (ie, $\delta = 0$).

5.2 The Variance Ratio Test

The major criticism against the ADF tests is that they have low power for testing the unit root null hypothesis. In addressing this problem, Lo and MacKinlay (1988) developed a variance ratio test for evaluating the RW properties of asset prices. One of such properties is the indefinite linear increase of the variance (σ^2) of a series (Y_t) over time (t) [ie, $\text{Var}(Y_t) = t\sigma^2$], which violates the condition of stationarity. The Lo and MacKinlay (1988) model exploited this property that variances of differences of time-series data computed over different time intervals are linearly related. Put differently, they assumed that, if a natural logarithm of a series of stock prices follows a random walk (with drift), then the variance of, say, monthly-period differences should be 4 times the variance of the weekly-period differences. Let $nq + 1$ denote observations consisting of $X_1, X_2, \ldots, X_{nq}$ of a time series. Then, the variance ratio of the qth difference, $\text{VR}(q)$, is defined as:

$$\text{VR}(q) = \frac{\sigma^2(q)}{\sigma^2(1)} \tag{1.4}$$

where $\sigma^2(q) = 1/q$ times the variance of the q-differences, and $\sigma^2(1)$ is the variance of the first differences. Lo and MacKinlay (1988) further provide the formula for computing the values of the estimator of the variance of q-period difference and of the first difference, $\sigma^2(q)$ and $\sigma^2(1)$, respectively, as follows:

$$\sigma^2(q) = \frac{1}{m} \sum_{k=q}^{nq} (X_k - X_{k-q} - q\hat{\mu})^2 \tag{1.5}$$

where

$$m = q(nq - q + 1)\left(1 - \frac{q}{nq}\right)$$

and

$$\sigma^2(1) = \frac{1}{nq-1} \sum_{k=1}^{nq} (X_k - X_{k-1} - \hat{\mu})^2 \tag{1.6}$$

where

$$\hat{\mu} = \frac{1}{nq}(X_{nq} - X_0)$$

The null hypothesis is VR(q) = 1. In principle, two reasons may lead to the rejection of the null of the RW. It could be due to either heteroscedasticity or autocorrelation in the asset's series (Lo and MacKinlay, 1988). Additionally, the authors point out that since volatilities do change over time, a rejection of the RW due to heteroscedasticity would have marginal interest. The VR(q) is formulated with two test statistics to examine the null hypotheses of random walk under the homoscedastic and heteroscedastic assumptions about the error term. The homoscedasticity-consistent test allows for the strict RW hypothesis, that is, $\varepsilon_{it} \sim$ i.i.d.; $N(0,\partial^2)$. The heteroscedasticity-consistent test, in contrast, relaxes the strict Gaussian assumption by considering that time-varying volatilities that might exist in a series. Put differently, the test statistic allows for some forms of conditional heteroscedasticity and dependence. It follows that the Lo and MacKinlay (1988) variance ratio is widely employed to test the RW and MDS hypotheses of the weak-form market efficiency (Urrutia, 1995; Buguk and Brorsen, 2003; Ntim et al., 2011). The homoscedasticity test statistic Z(q) is expressed as:

$$Z(q) = \frac{\text{VR}(q) - 1}{[\varnothing(q)]^{1/2}} \sim N(0,1) \tag{1.7}$$

where

$$\varnothing(q) = \frac{2(2q-1)(q-1)}{3q(nq)} \tag{1.8}$$

If we assume heteroscedastic increments, then the test static $Z^{\wedge}(q)$, that uses overlapping intervals, is more robust. This is expressed as:

$$Z^{\wedge}(q) = \frac{\text{VR}(q) - 1}{[\varnothing^{\wedge}(q)]^{1/2}} \sim N(0,1) \tag{1.9}$$

where

$$\varnothing^{\wedge}(q) = \sum_{j=1}^{q-1}\left[\frac{2(q-1)}{q}\right]^2 \hat{\delta}(j) \tag{1.10}$$

and

$$\hat{\delta} = \frac{\sum_{k=j+1}^{nq}(X_k - X_{k-1} - \hat{\mu})^2(X_{k-j} - X_{k-j-1} - \hat{\mu})^2}{\sum_{k=1}^{nq}[(X_k - X_{k-1} - \hat{\mu})^2]^2} \tag{1.11}$$

It should be noted, however, that the two test statistics derived by Lo and MacKinlay (1988) focus on testing individual variance ratios for a specific aggregation interval, q, and not for all periods (Smith et al., 2002). A procedure that Chow and Denning (1993) developed provides a means of comparing multiple sets of variance ratio estimates with unity. The decision criterion to reject the null hypothesis against the alternative hypothesis is based on whether any of the estimated variance ratios are significantly different from unity.

5.3 Ranks- and Signs-Based Variance Ratio Tests

The Lo and MacKinlay (1988) variance ratio test, like other parametric tests, is criticized for lacking power, particularly when the series of data are nonnormal. Wright (2000) argues against the assumption that a time series is independent and identically distributed (i.i.d.). The author contends that the hypothesis may not always hold when the data are serially correlated. He further points out that although Lo and MacKinlay showed that the test can be made robust against conditional heteroscedasticity, the finite-sample null distribution of the test statistic is asymmetric and nonnormal. As a remedy, Wright (2000) proposed an alternative nonparametric test that uses standardized ranks and signs instead of the underlying asset's returns differences. One advantage of the nonparametric statistical tests is that they are exact; they avoid making asymptotic approximation, and they have low size distortion. The other is that the tests are more powerful in the presence of highly nonnormal data compared to the conventional tests. The evidence in Table 1.1 (based on Jarque–Bera statistics) justifies the application of this method to analyze our data.

Wright's (2000) alternative model is described as follows. Letting $r(y_t)$ be the rank of y_t among $y_1, y_2, y_3, ..., y_T$, he defined:

$$r_{1t} = \left(r(y_t) - \frac{T+1}{2} \right) \Big/ \sqrt{\frac{(T-1)(T+1)}{12}} \qquad (1.12)$$

$$r_{2t} = \Phi^{-1}[r(y_t)/(T+1)] \qquad (1.13)$$

where ϕ is the standard normal cumulative distribution. Wright (2000) defines the series r_{1t} as a simple linear transformation of the ranks, standardized to have a sample mean 0 and sample variance 1. The same applies to series r_{2t} (the inverse normal or van der Waerden scores); it has a sample mean 0 except that it has a sample variance approximately equal to 1.

The ranks-based ratio tests are calculated by substituting r_{1t} and r_{2t} for y_t in the Lo and MacKinlay (1988) definition of variance ratio test statistic. Wright (2000) therefore proposed the following test statistics:

$$R_1 = \left(\frac{\frac{1}{Tk}\sum_{t=k+1}^{T}(r_{1t} + r_{1t-1} + ... + r_{1t-k})^2}{\frac{1}{T}\sum_{t=1}^{T}r_{1t}^2} - 1 \right)\left(\frac{2(2k-1)(k-1)}{3kT} \right)^{-1/2} \qquad (1.14)$$

TABLE 1.1 Descriptive Statistics and Diagnostics

		Mean	Std. dev.	Skewness	Kurtosis	Jarque–Bera	N
DSEI	Price index	1,373.053	388.374	1.709	5.390	1,439.677**	1,986
	Returns index	7.192	0.243	1.203	3.809	533.388**	1,986
	Returns (%)	0.050	0.572	8.189	170.412	2,247,083**	1,906
BI	Price index	1,418.895	898.351	2.247	8.467	4,145.724**	1,987
	Returns index	7.126	0.465	1.333	4.266	720.748**	1,987
	Returns (%)	0.065	9.253	−5.450	604.589	28,781,265**	1,908
CS	Price index	1,339.551	526.858	0.847	4.334	384.292**	1,982
	Returns index	7.082	0.646	−4.115	25.231	46,408.67**	1,982
	Returns (%)	0.057	10.196	−15.128	929.067	68,037,409**	1,902
IA	Price index	1,700.499	1,319.610	2.488	8.961	4,990.162**	1,986
	Returns index	7.255	0.550	1.031	4.747	604.257**	1,986
	Returns (%)	0.090	6.656	15.051	875.410	60,515,964**	1,906
TSI	Price index	1,487.536	1,014.086	2.385	8.129	4,061.442**	1,987
	Returns index	7.164	0.4702	1.652	4.611	1,118.730**	1,987
	Returns (%)	0.079	0.585	2.369	28.379	52,988.63**	1,908

Notes: The double asterisks (**) represent statistical significance at the 1% level.

$$R_2 = \left(\frac{\frac{1}{Tk} \sum_{t=k+1}^{T} (r_{2t} + r_{2t-1} + \ldots + r_{2t-k})^2}{\frac{1}{T} \sum_{t=1}^{T} r_{2t}^2} - 1 \right) \left(\frac{2(2k-1)(k-1)}{3kT} \right)^{-1/2} \quad (1.15)$$

According to Wright (2000), the tests based on ranks are exact under i.i.d. assumption. The rank $r(y_t)$ is a random permutation of the numbers 1, 2, ..., T, each with equal probability. The proposed modified test statistics based on the signs are as described hereafter. Wright (2000) shows that, for any series y_t, if $u(x_t, q) = 1(x_t > q) - 0.5$, then $u(x_t, 0)$ is 0.5 if x_t is positive and -0.5 otherwise. Also, if $S_t = 2u(y_t, 0) = 2u(\varepsilon_t, 0)$ and S_t is an i.i.d. series with mean 0 and variance 1, then each S_t is equal to 1 with probability 0.5 and is equal to -1 otherwise. The test statistic (S_t) is defined as:

$$S_1 = \left(\frac{\frac{1}{Tk} \sum_{t=k+1}^{T} (s_t + s_{t-1} \ldots + s_{t-k})^2}{\frac{1}{T} \sum_{t=1}^{T} s_t^2} - 1 \right) \left(\frac{2(2k-1)(k-1)}{3kT} \right)^{-1/2} \quad (1.16)$$

As with the ranks, Wright (2000) points out that the exact sampling distribution of S_1 can be simulated for different levels of T and k. Moreover, he also demonstrates in a Monte Carlo experiment that the tests based on ranks are consistent with the homoscedasticity assumption, while the signs are robust under the conditional heteroscedasticity assumption.

6   ANALYSES AND PRESENTATION OF THE RESULTS

The following subsections discuss the test results of the study.

6.1   Descriptive Statistics and Diagnostics

The analyses in these subsections were performed on the raw and the logarithm-transformed daily price indices. The daily returns (R_t) are computed from the logarithm transformation of the daily price data as follows:

$$R_t = \ln(P_t) - \ln(P_{t-1}) \quad (1.17)$$

where P_t is the value of the index at time t, P_{t-1} is the 1-day lagged daily value, and ln is the natural logarithm. Table 1.1 presents the descriptive statistics and diagnostics of the daily data for price indices, log of price indices, and returns of the five studied indices. For the period under consideration, all indices experienced positive mean returns, which are comparable to what Ntim et al. (2011) reports.

The lowest daily return in Table 1.1 is 0.05% for the DSEI, and the highest one is 0.09% for the IA series. The examination of the standard deviations, a measure of market risk, shows generally that volatility for the percentage returns is considerable for all indices. The lowest deviation, which implies lowest risk, is observed in the DSEI, with the TSI a close second. Furthermore, the results reveal that the CS has the highest standard deviation. This is followed closely by the BI and IA indices.

The measures of skewness and kurtosis for the perfectly normal distribution are supposed to be zero and 3, respectively. Considering the results for the log price index in Table 1.1, it is found that CS has extremely high negative skewness. Likewise, the returns for BI and CS are negatively skewed. This kind of returns distribution implies that the returns are characterized by regular small gains and few excessive losses. On the contrary, the returns for the remaining indices are positively skewed, suggesting that they are experiencing frequent small losses with lesser chances of extreme gains. The results for kurtosis tests show that the values for the price indices and percentage returns for all indices are positive and greater than 3. This means that the distributions are leptokurtic relative to the normal distribution. In other words, there is strong evidence that the data are highly concentrated around the mean because the variation within the observations is low. This observation signifies that the market exhibits unexpected moments of very low and high returns. It is therefore plausible to argue that these indices are more likely to attract risk-averse investors who avoid large return surprises that cause high variation in their stock holdings. This is supported by the fact that the annualized[a] daily returns appear to be reasonably high. The returns range from a low of 12.5% in the case of DSEI to a high of 22.5% in the case of IA. Correspondingly, the Jarque–Bera test statistic strongly rejects the normality hypothesis for all indices. This observation is consistent with the evidence in prior studies that nonnormality is a common phenomenon in African stock market price and return series (Jefferis and Smith, 2005; Ntim et al., 2011).

6.2 Augmented Dickey–Fuller Test Results

We employ Eq. 1.3 to test the null hypothesis that returns based on price indices and those based on returns indices at the DSE follow a random walk. The decision criterion is to reject the null hypothesis if the test statistic is greater than the critical values in absolute terms. Table 1.2 shows the results of the ADF test for the five indices. In the columns headed returns based on price indices, we find that, at the 5% significance level, we do not have sufficient evidence to reject the null hypothesis regarding levels in panel A for all indices. This suggests that all series are nonstationary.

Gujarati and Porter (2009) point out that the first differences of a random walk time series are stationary. Accordingly, we performed the ADF test with the first differences to examine the indices for the presence of a second unit root. The results are presented in panel B of Table 1.2 in the columns headed returns based on price indices. It is observed that the null hypothesis of a second unit root is rejected except with TSI. The findings reveal the absence of a second unit

---

a. We calculate the average daily return for each index and then multiply it by the number of trading days in a year (ie, 250 in our case) to obtain the annualized return.

root and confirm the contention in Gujarati and Porter (2009) for the four series. Hence, we can verify that all series under consideration satisfy the necessary condition for the random walk to hold.

Panel A in Table 1.2 also presents the results of the ADF test for the returns based on return indices. The examination of the findings provides strong evidence against the null of a unit root. Hence, we can confirm that all series under consideration are stationary in levels.

6.3 Variance Ratio Test Results

We employ the Lo and MacKinlay (1988) variance ratio test to test the random walk for each of the five DSE indices. We perform the tests using daily sampling intervals (q) of 2, 4, 8, and 16 days. As there is more than one specified period for each time series, EViews (the data processing package that we use) reports two sets of results. The "joint tests" output presents the results of the joint null hypothesis for all periods, whereas the output of the "individual tests" relates to the tests for individual periods. Table 1.3 reports the variance ratio estimations.

In panel A of the columns labeled returns based on price indices, we present the results assuming homoscedasticity in the error term. The findings provide strong evidence to reject the joint null hypothesis at a 5% significance level for all indices, except the DSEI series. A further analysis of the individual tests shows that the null of a random walk is strongly rejected for the indices BI, IA, and TSI. Moreover, we find that the null is rejected for the first two intervals of the CS, whereas it is not rejected with the DSEI.

We present the heteroscedasticity-consistent results in panel B of the columns labeled returns based on price indices. The findings reveal that the null of joint hypotheses cannot be rejected with all indices except with TSI. Similarly, the individual variance ratio tests fail to reject the null hypothesis that the stock price indices in the DSE follow a random walk process, except for periods 8 and 16, respectively, of the TSI. We fail to reject the random walk hypothesis in both panels for the DSEI series for all lags. The findings under returns based on price indices in Table 1.3 provide strong evidence against the null hypothesis in panel A but not in panel B with the BI, CS, and IA series. Accordingly, these rejections may be due to heteroscedasticity in the residuals. It therefore means that the respective indices meet some of the strict conditions of the random walk process. Furthermore, the results suggest strong rejection of the RW with TSI regardless of the type of increment assumption; this implies that the rejection is due to autocorrelation of the daily increments.

Under the null hypothesis suggesting a random walk, our interest is whether the value of the variance ratio equals 1, and the test statistics have an asymptotically standard normal distribution. The findings under returns based on price indices in Table 1.3 reveal that the majority of the variance ratios (except for TSI) are less than unity, and the $Z^\wedge$ scores are not significant (panel B). Moreover,

TABLE 1.2 ADF Unit Root Test Results

Model	Returns based on price indices					Returns based on return indices				
	DSEI	BI	CS	IA	TSI#	DSEI	BI	CS	IA	TSI
Panel A: level										
Intercept	2.837	1.514	0.353	3.097	5.999	−27.866**	−25.488**	−7.793**	−22.022**	−18.687**
Trend and intercept	0.548	2.140	−1.745	1.670	5.452	−27.997**	−25.482**	−7.794**	−22.296**	−25.489**
Panel B: first difference										
Intercept	−28.335**	−29.696**	−56.506**	−16.185**	3.497					
Trend and intercept	−28.561**	−29.681**	−56.546**	−16.443**	2.789					

Notes: ******* means significant at the 1 and 5% level, respectively. Critical values for the ADF test for 1, 5, and 10% significance levels with the constant model are −3.43, −2.87, and −2.57, respectively. For the trend and constant model, the critical values are −3.97, −3.42, and −3.13, respectively. # means stationary in second differences. DSE All Share Index (DSEI) consisting of home and foreign firms, and Tanzania Share Index (TSI) covering only domestic firms. It also includes the indices covering banks, finance, and investment companies (BI); commercial services (CS); and industrial and allied sectors (IA).

TABLE 1.3 Lo and MacKinlay Variance Ratio Test Results

Series		Sampling interval (q-days)							
		Returns based on price indices				Returns based on return indices			
		2	4	8	16	2	4	8	16
Panel A: variance ratios assuming homoscedasticity									
DSEI	VR$_{(q)}$	0.9683	0.9991	1.0052	0.9863	0.4499	0.2373	0.1140	0.0490
	Z$_{(q)}$	−1.3857[a]	−0.0202	0.0770	−0.1364	−23.5185***[a]	−17.4313**	−12.8066**	−9.2369**
BI	VR$_{(q)}$	0.5638	0.3807	0.2889	0.2168	0.3321	0.1560	0.0942	0.0436
	Z$_{(q)}$	−19.0518***[a]	−14.4589***[a]	−10.5009**	−7.7717**	−28.5776***[a]	−19.3041**	−13.1029**	−9.2976**
CS	VR$_{(q)}$	0.8324	0.9085	0.9392	0.9975	0.3419	0.4120	0.2395	0.0852
	Z$_{(q)}$	−7.3099***[a]	−2.13409*	−0.89729	−0.0253	−28.1066***[a]	−13.4236**	−10.9804**	−8.8756**
IA	VR$_{(q)}$	0.5644	0.3873	0.3057	0.2734	0.3292	0.1338	0.0980	0.0456
	Z$_{(q)}$	−19.0173***[a]	−14.2984**	−10.2468**	−7.2067**	−28.6783***[a]	−19.7951**	−13.0372**	−9.2707**
TSI	VR$_{(q)}$	0.9543	1.1368	1.5088	2.1505	0.3936	0.2182	0.1131	0.0549
	Z$_{(q)}$	−1.9947*	3.1945**	7.5136**	11.4172**[d]	−25.9491***[a]	−17.8806**	−12.8297**	−9.1876**
Panel B: heteroscedasticity-consistent variance ratios									
DSEI	VR$_{(q)}$	0.9683	0.9991	1.0052	0.9863	0.4499	0.2373	0.1140	0.0490
	Z^$_{(q)}$	−0.6471[a]	−0.0104	0.0469	−0.0970	−3.6069**[a]	−3.2777**	−3.1914**	−3.1038*
BI	VR$_{(q)}$	0.5638	0.3807	0.2889	0.2168	0.3321	0.1560	0.0942	0.0436
	Z^$_{(q)}$	−1.1604[a]	−1.0984	−1.0811	−1.1077	−1.6250[a]	−1.3332	−1.2062	−1.1790

CS	$VR_{(q)}$	0.8324	0.9085	0.9392	0.9975	0.3419	0.4120	0.2395	0.0852
	$\hat{Z}_{(q)}$	−1.0972[a]	−0.3995	−0.2276	−0.0089	−5.23440[a]	−2.4726	−2.4590	−2.6416
IA	$VR_{(q)}$	0.5644	0.3873	0.3057	0.2734	0.3292	0.1338	0.0980	0.0456
	$\hat{Z}_{(q)}$	−1.2245[a]	−1.1482	−1.1152	−1.0893	−1.5157[a]	−1.2770	−1.1245	−1.1036
TSI	$VR_{(q)}$	0.9543	1.1368	1.5088	2.1505	0.3936	0.2182	0.1131	0.0549
	$\hat{Z}_{(q)}$	−0.7608	1.3171	3.4315*	5.7070**[d]	−6.2750***[a]	−4.9937**	−4.3668**	−3.7685**

Notes: Test statistics with ** and * indicate 1 and 5% levels of significance, respectively. H_0: $VR(q) = 1$ (ie, the series follows a random walk process). Joint tests Max |z|; at periods 2[a], 4[b], 8[c], and 16[d]. In other terms, the notations "a, b, c, and d" imply the joint significance at 2, 4, 6, and 8 intervals, respectively. The DSE All Share Index (DSEI) consists of home and foreign firms, and the Tanzania Share Index (TSI) covers only domestic firms. The table also includes the indices covering banks, finance, and investment companies (BI), commercial services (CS), and industrial and allied sectors (IA).

only TSI series has its joint test statistics significantly different from 1 at the 1% level at lag 16. The individual tests are significant at all lags at the 5% level in panel A. The significance of the results, however, disappears at lag 2 and 4 when heteroscedasticity-consistent estimators are used. Generally, this observation indicates a mean-reversion across the lags of TSI (Lo and MacKinlay, 1988; Grieb and Reyes, 1999). Furthermore, notice also that the variance ratios' results obtained with the DSEI are consistent with the implication of ADF results.

Next, we use the variance ratio test to examine the behavior of the returns of stock price indices for all five indices. The findings under returns based on return indices in Table 1.3 present the results. The RW hypothesis is strongly rejected for all five indices under both joint and individual tests (panel A).

6.4 Ranks- and Signs-Based Variance Ratio Tests

In this section, we report the results the ranks- and signs-based variance ratio tests of Wright (2000) (Table 1.4). The tests are based on daily sampling intervals (q) equal to 2, 4, 8, and 16 days as before. EViews performs the Wright (2000) variance ratio test with ties replaced by the average of the tied ranks for the tied data (using the "tie handling" option). It uses the permutation bootstrap to obtain the probabilities for the joint and individual test statistics. The standard error estimates for the ranks (R_1, R_2) and signs assume no heteroscedasticity.

The findings under returns based on price indices in panel A reveal that the RW hypothesis cannot be rejected for the DSEI, BI, and CS indices for all intervals of q. In the case of the IA index, the RW is rejected only for $q = 2$. For the TSI, on the other hand, we fail to reject the null at periods 2 and 4. In contrast, the results obtained using the signs-based variance ratio test strongly reject the heteroscedasticity-consistent random walk for all indices for all intervals except the CS (panel B).

We also assess whether the Lo and MacKinlay (1988) and Wright (2000) variance ratio tests produce consistent results. The findings reveal that the two versions reach similar conclusions under the i.i.d. for all indices except the BI and CS. For these data series, the Lo and MacKinlay variance ratio rejects the null under the homoscedasticity assumption. Wright's ranks and rank scores, however, do not reject the same hypothesis. The opposite is true in the presence of heteroscedasticity. All indices except the TSI fail to reject the null of the random walk hypothesis under the Lo and MacKinlay test. However, only the CS and TSI indices produce consistent results when Wright's signs test is used. That is, all indices except the CS rejected the hypothesis that the series are random walk, which is also implied in Table 1.3 when we reject the null hypothesis that the variance ratio equals 1.

Table 1.4 presents the results of Wright's tests for the returns of the five stock price indices. The findings in panel A of the column labeled returns based on return indices indicate that R_1 and R_2 strongly reject the null hypothesis that the series follow the random walk process for all indices at the 1% significance

TABLE 1.4 Ranks- and Signs-Based Variance Ratio Test Results

Series		Returns based on price indices				Returns based on return indices			
		2	4	8	16	2	4	8	16
Panel A: ranks									
DSEI	R_1	0.0683	1.8678[b]	0.7736	0.1822	−20.5618**a	−15.2059**	−11.4662**	−8.3621**
	R_2	−0.7535	0.8851	−0.6153	−1.4370[d]	−21.7738**a	−16.0182**	−12.0034**	−8.6529**
BI	R_1	0.7253	3.1001	4.2282[c]	3.8826	−19.4633**a	−15.1128**	−11.4231**	−8.5815**
	R_2	0.7217	3.2266	4.3248[c]	3.8455	−20.8604**a	−16.0052**	−11.9907**	−8.8800**
CS	R_1	−2.3395[a]	−1.6912	−1.1391	−0.0348	−21.4935**a	−16.4489**	−12.2150**	−8.7777**
	R_2	−2.4778[a]	−1.8932	−1.7035	−0.5575	−21.7865**a	−16.7749**	−12.4560**	−8.9354**
IA	R_1	−3.9440*a	−1.2447	0.4351	0.1501	−22.4674**a	−16.1964**	−11.6697**	−8.3594**
	R_2	−4.9501**a	−2.1724	−0.1851	−0.0859	−23.5148**a	−16.8926**	−12.1644**	−8.6929**
TSI	R_1	1.1691	3.8551	5.7375**	6.7461**d	−19.7498**a	−15.1220**	−11.6126**	−8.6359**
	R_2	0.0214	3.1628	5.2309*	5.9696*d	−21.8065**a	−16.2755**	−12.2515**	−8.9441**
Panel B: signs									
DSEI	S	6.0928**	9.8193**	10.6589***c	8.9687**	−9.4024***a	−5.2383**	−2.6014**	−1.9421**
BI	S	20.8788**	31.4615**	39.6025**	41.6005**d	9.6985	18.9999**	26.3125**	28.0263***d
CS	S	28.4785	42.2599	52.2302	52.4674[d]	22.7590	35.1189*	44.2007*	45.0331[d]
IA	S	9.2538**	15.9165**	19.3160***c	16.5376**	−1.4033	5.5634	9.9548***c	9.5938*
TSI	S	15.6591**	23.6665**	29.2549**	30.9033***d	3.9495	11.6298**	17.7681**	20.4940***d

Notes: Test statistics with ** and * indicate 1 and 5% levels of significance, respectively. H_0: The series follow a random walk process. Joint tests Max $|z|$: at periods 2[a], 4[b], 8[c], and 16[d]. In other terms, the notations "a, b, c, and d" imply the joint significance at 2, 4, 6, and 8 intervals, respectively. The DSE All Share Index (DSEI) consists of home and foreign firms, and the Tanzania Share Index (TSI) covers only domestic firms. The table also includes the indices covering banks, finance, and investment companies (BI); commercial services (CS); and industrial and allied sectors (IA).

level. The signs-based tests slightly offer mixed results (panel B). For the DSEI index, the results are in agreement with those in the ranks-based tests. For the BI and TSI indices, the null hypothesis is rejected only for $q = 2$ with the signs test. For the IA index, the signs test rejects the null hypothesis of a random walk for $q > 4$, but fails to support the null hypothesis with $q = 2$ and 4 intervals at the 5% level. Prior studies have also observed that individual tests tend to provide contradictory results (Wright, 2000; Buguk and Brorsen, 2003; Ntim et al., 2011). That is, tests reject the null hypothesis for some periods of q but fail to reject the null for others. In the case of CS, the signs test rejects the random walk hypothesis at period 4 and 8 at the conventional significance level. Except for the CS index, the joint tests for all other cases provide strong evidence against the random walk hypothesis.

The individual interval results obtained from Wright's ranks-based tests for the returns of the stock price indices are all consistent with the Lo and MacKinlay (1988) results under the homoscedasticity assumption. Under the heteroscedasticity-consistent tests, however, only the DSEI and TSI indices' results are in agreement with each other. Specifically, we fail to reject the null hypothesis of the random walk for BI, CS, and IA under the Lo and MacKinlay variance ratio test in both cases; that is, the joint and individual tests. By contrast, the signs-based variance ratio test results are ambiguous. The joint test is strongly against the null hypothesis for the BI and IA series. The individual test results for the same index reject the hypothesis for $q > 2$. For the CS, we fail to reject the null hypothesis under the joint test at the 5% level of significance. The individual tests, however, reject the random walk hypothesis for $q = 2$ and 16.

6.5 Summary of the Findings

Wright (2000) shows that ranks and signs tests can be exact, and have better power properties than the conventional variance ratio tests. Moreover, he demonstrates that ranks-based variance ratio tests have, generally, more power than the signs-based variance ratio tests. Considering Lo and MacKinlay (1988) variance ratio tests, Wright (2000) demonstrates that the nonrobust $Z_{(q)}$ is more powerful than the heteroscedastic robust $Z^{\wedge}_{(q)}$. The summary presented in Table 1.5 is based on these rejection rules. This is because the data in this study are highly nonnormal (Table 1.1).

Panel A indicates that the results obtained from the three different tests are largely mixed. The ADF test shows that all five indices fail to be in line with the random walk hypothesis. However, the method is widely criticized for lacking power, particularly when data exhibit nonnormality. For the DSEI, BI, and CS indices, nevertheless, the results are supported by the powerful ranks-based variance ratio test results. In contrast, the ranks and signs tests do not support the findings of the ADF test for the IA and TSI indices. Specifically, ranks- and signs-based variance ratio test results are consistent with the homoscedastic random walk findings based on variance ratio tests.

TABLE 1.5 Summary of the Findings

Series	ADF	$Z(q)$	$Z^{\wedge}(q)$	R_1	R_2	S
Panel A: returns based on price indices						
DSEI	Fail	Fail	Fail	Fail	Fail	Reject
BI	Fail	Reject	Fail	Fail	Fail	Reject
CS	Fail	Reject	Fail	Fail	Fail	Fail
IA	Fail	Reject	Fail	Reject	Reject	Reject
TSI	Fail	Reject	Reject	Reject	Reject	Reject
Panel B: returns based on return indices						
DSEI	Reject	Reject	Reject	Reject	Reject	Reject
BI	Reject	Reject	Fail	Reject	Reject	Reject
CS	Reject	Reject	Fail	Reject	Reject	Fail
IA	Reject	Reject	Fail	Reject	Reject	Reject
TSI	Reject	Reject	Reject	Reject	Reject	Reject

Notes: "Fail" means the null hypothesis proposing the presence of random walk is not rejected, and "reject" means the null hypothesis is rejected. ADF is the augmented Dickey–Fuller test, $Z(q)$ is the Z-test based on the variance ratio test assuming homoscedasticity, $Z^{\wedge}(q)$ is the Z-test based on the variance ratio test that is robust to heteroscedasticity, R_1 is the ranks test based on the simple linear transformation of ranks, R_2 is the ranks test based on the inverse normal or van der Waerden scores, and S is the signs test.

The results in panel B seem to be more consistent under the three different tests. The ADF, $Z_{(q)}$, R_1, R_2, and S tests largely reject the random walk hypothesis. Three indices under $Z^{\wedge}_{(q)}$, on the other hand, fail to reject this hypothesis.

7   CONCLUSIONS AND RECOMMENDATIONS

Tanzania, like many other African countries, established its stock exchange in 1996, as part of the implementation of economic reforms that were sponsored by the International Monetary Fund and the World Bank. The DSE became operational in 1998. Since then, however, to the best knowledge of the researchers, there has been no study that has vigorously examined the behavior of stock prices and returns in the market from the efficiency point of view. The aim of this study is, therefore, to examine the price and return behavior of the DSE stock price indices using the ADF, conventional variance ratio, and ranks- and signs-based nonparametric variance ratio tests.

Our analysis shows that the distribution of the data used in the study is highly nonnormal. According to Wright (2000), with such characteristics the conventional tests yield ambiguous results. He further points out that the ranks- and signs-based tests have better power properties than the aforementioned tests. The conclusions derived from the latter may therefore be the most appropriate ones, as they represent the true underlying values of the series. Hence, we can conclude that the DSE's All Share Index, banking, finance and investment (BI) index, and the commercial services (CS) index tend to have patterns that are in line with the random walk hypothesis. In contrast, the industrial and allied sectors (IA) index and the Tanzania Share Index are conclusively not weak-form efficient. Moreover, the results show that the returns based on return indices do not follow a random walk process for all five indices at the DSE, implying the absence of the weak-form efficient markets.

The literature suggests a number of possible explanations for the rejection of weak-form efficiency in infant stock markets that can be squarely applicable to the DSE (Smith et al., 2002; Ntim et al., 2011). The first reason is the absence of derivatives trading. This is associated with lower speed, poorer quality, and increased costs related to information processing. As a result, any profit opportunity arising from price disagreement from traders may take a long time to be brought back to equilibrium levels. In other words, the absence of derivatives trading negatively impacts the DSE's objective of facilitating a price discovery process in the market.

Second, the DSE is considered to be a very small stock exchange in terms of market capitalization and number and size of individual stocks. The market has listed only 21 companies to date. However, the DSE has recorded impressive growth in market capitalization since its establishment. For instance, its market capitalization grew by 249% from USD 3.669 billion in Oct. 2011 to USD 12.800 billion in Dec. 2014 (DSE, quarterly updated reports). Again, the market topped the list in 2014 in terms of market capitalization among the African stock exchanges.

Low liquidity and nontrading at the DSE may also explain the rejection of weak-form efficiency. According to Demirguc-Kunt and Maksimovic (1996), liquid secondary capital markets lower informational asymmetry and transaction costs. Despite the fact that the market has grown rapidly, the DSE suffers from low liquidity. Its average stock turnover ratios in 2011 and 2012 were 2.5 and 1.6%, respectively (World Bank, 2015). A ratio of such small magnitude demonstrates an inability of the market to facilitate an active price formation process (Smith et al., 2002; Ntim et al., 2011). Related to liquidity is the behavior of the market participants. Many investors at the DSE may be classified as buy-and-hold investors. They are characterized by targeting dividends as the main source of investment return instead of trading on stock price fluctuations.

In addition, the majority of Tanzanians have not yet appreciated the importance of the stock exchange as an option for diversifying their investments. This is evidenced by the low involvement of individuals in the market, which is estimated to be less than 1% of the population. Indeed, with such a small number of investors, the country is not expected to have a vibrant capital market. The government has, however, lifted the restrictive 60% limit for foreigners' ownership in order to attract a critical mass of investors to enhance liquidity (CMSA, 2014).

Our results reveal that returns based on price indices for the IA and TSI series are not weak-form efficient. These indices are composed by domestic companies only. Moreover, due to the effects of home bias, the majority of their floating shares are locally owned. As mentioned earlier, since many individual investors tend to buy and hold these stocks, they cause thin trading in the market. This behavior causes a mismatch between the supply of and demand for a particular stock. Consequently, higher demand for these stocks pushes their prices up, and a greater supply of stocks pulls prices down. It is, therefore, potentially easy to speculate on the direction of prices for these stocks.

According to the EMH, stock pricing inefficiencies may be exploited by sophisticated investors (Fama, 1965). Our findings do not in any way provide evidence indicating whether exploitation of these inefficiencies is profitable. As a recommendation for further study, though, it appears that there is a need to examine whether investors at the DSE can systematically make abnormal returns.

The main policy implication from this evidence is that the market is still not informationally efficient. The regulatory authorities have to put in more effort to promote and develop the functioning of the capital markets sufficiently to produce significant informational efficiency. Successful implementation of this role is a vital incentive for attracting foreigners. The economic implication is that stocks at the DSE are not appropriately priced at their equilibrium values. This distortion in pricing may have repercussions on the ability of the market to play the crucial role of capital allocation and risk pricing.

REFERENCES

Buguk, C., Brorsen, B.W., 2003. Testing weak-form market efficiency: evidence from the Istanbul Stock Exchange. Int. Rev. Financ. Anal. 12, 579–590.

Chow, K.V., Denning, K., 1993. A simple multiple variance ratio test. J. Econometrics 58, 385–401.

CMSA, 2014. The Capital Market and Securities Act: the capital market and securities (foreign investors) regulations. Government Notice no. 338, Tanzania.

De Bondt, W.F.M., Thaler, R.H., 1985. Does the stock market overreact? J. Financ. 40, 793–805.

De Bondt, W.F.M., Thaler, R.H., 1987. Further evidence on investor overreaction and stock market seasonality. J. Financ. 42, 557–581.

Demirguc-Kunt, A., Maksimovic, V., 1996. Stock market development and financing choices of firms. World Bank Econ. Rev. 10, 341–369.

Dickinson, J.P., Muragu, K., 1994. Market efficiency in developing countries: a case study of the Nairobi Stock Exchange. J. Bus. Finan. Account. 21, 133–150.

DSE. Quarterly updated reports. Dar es Salaam Stock Exchange, Dar es Salaam, Tanzania.

Fama, E.F., 1965. The behavior of stock market prices. J. Bus. 38, 34–105.

Fama, E.F., 1970. Efficient capital markets: a review of theory and empirical work. J. Financ. 25, 383–417.

Fama, E.F., 1991. Efficient capital markets: II. J. Financ. 46, 1575–1617.

Fama, E.F., 1995. Random walks in stock market prices. Financ. Anal. J. 51, 75–80.

Fama, E.F., 1998. Market efficiency, long-term returns, and behavioral finance. J. Financ. Econ. 49, 283–306.

Fama, E.F., French, K.R., 1988a. Dividends yields and expected returns. J. Financ. Econ. 22, 3–25.

Fama, E.F., French, K.R., 1988b. Permanent and temporary components of stock prices. J. Polit. Econ. 96, 246–273.

Grieb, T., Reyes, M.G., 1999. Random walk tests for Latin American equity indexes and individual firms. J. Financ. Res. 22, 371–383.

Gujarati, D.N., Porter, D.C., 2009. Basic Econometrics. McGraw-Hill International Edition, New York.

Jefferis, K., Smith, G., 2005. The changing efficiency of African stock markets. S. Afr. J. Econ. 73, 54–67.

Jegadeesh, N., 1991. Seasonality in stock price mean reversion: evidence from the US and the UK. J. Financ. 46, 1427–1444.

Lander, J., Orphanides, A., Douvogiannis, M., 1997. Earnings forecasts and the predictability of stock returns. J. Portfolio Manage. 23, 24–35.

Lo, A.W., MacKinlay, A.C., 1988. Stock market prices do not follow random walks: evidence from a simple specification test. Rev. Financ. Stud. 1, 41–66.

Lo, A.W., MacKinlay, A.C., 1989. The size and power of the variance ratio test in finite samples: a Monte Carlo investigation. J. Econom. 40, 203–238.

Magnusson, M., Wydick, B., 2002. How efficient are Africa's emerging stock markets? J. Dev. Stud. 38, 141–156.

Mlambo, C., Biekpe, N., 2007. The efficient market hypothesis: evidence from ten African stock markets. Invest. Anal. J. 66, 5–18.

Mukherji, S., 2011. Are stock returns still mean-reverting? Rev. Financ. Econ. 20, 22–27.

Ntim, C.G., Opong, K.K., Danbolt, J., Dewotor, F.S., 2011. Testing the weak-form efficiency in African stock markets. Manage. Financ. 37, 195–218.

Pesaran, M.H., Timmermann, A., 1995. Predictability of stock returns: robustness and economic significance. J. Financ. 50, 1201–1228.

Poterba, J.M., Summers, L.H., 1988. Mean reversion in stock prices: evidence and implications. J. Financ. Econ. 22, 27–59.

Smith, G., Dyakova, A., 2014. African stock markets: efficiency and relative predictability. S. Afr. J. Econ. 82, 258–275.

Smith, G., Jefferis, K., Ryoo, H.J., 2002. African stock markets: multiple variance ratio tests of random walks. Appl. Financ. Econ. 12, 475–484.

Urrutia, J.L., 1995. Tests of random walk and market efficiency for Latin American emerging equity markets. J. Financ. Res. 18, 299–309.

World Bank, 2015. World development indicators: stock markets.

Wright, J.H., 2000. Alternative variance-ratio tests using ranks and signs. J. Bus. Econ. Stat. 18, 1–9.

Chapter 2

Stock Returns and Inflation: The Case of Botswana

K. Gavriilidis*, L.M. Kgari**

*University of Stirling Management School, Stirling, Scotland, United Kingdom;
**Bank of Botswana, Finance Department, Gaborone, Botswana

Chapter Outline

1 INTRODUCTION

The infamous "Fisher effect" postulated by Fisher (1930) suggests that the market interest rate comprises the real interest rate and the expected rate of inflation. Bodie (1976) extended the Fisher hypothesis to stock returns, suggesting that these can hedge against inflation. In other words, equity investments, as claims against real assets, should compensate investors for the loss in their purchasing power due to inflation. This proposition has attracted a considerable amount of research testing this without hypothesis, however, reaching a conclusive answer. In fact, while we would expect a positive relationship between stock returns and inflation, the bulk of the empirical studies find a negative relationship between them.

This study tests for the relationship between stock prices and inflation in the context of the Botswana market. Botswana is an African country, which is classified as a frontier market. This type of market is characterized by small market capitalization, weak regulatory framework, and investors' lack of experience. Frontier markets, in general, are considered tomorrow's emerging markets.

We find a positive relationship, though not a statistically significant one, between stock returns and inflation in Botswana. In addition, we test for the long-run relationship between stock market returns and inflation; however, no evidence of such relationship is supported by our results.

Handbook of Frontier Markets. http://dx.doi.org/10.1016/B978-0-12-803776-8.00002-1
27

This chapter is arranged as follows: Section 2 provides a literature review, Section 3 presents an outline of the economy of Botswana, Section 4 presents the data and the methodology employed; Section 5 presents the results, and finally, Section 6 concludes.

2   LITERATURE REVIEW

The Fisher effect, a hypothesis developed from an economic theory by Fisher (1930), expresses the real rate of interest as the difference between the nominal rate of interest and the expected rate of inflation. The most common form of this relationship expresses the expected nominal rates of return of assets as a summation of the expected rate of inflation and the expected rate of real return. The Fisher effect implies that the expected nominal returns on assets should provide a complete hedge against inflation; if this is the case, a positive relationship is expected between stock returns and inflation, which implies that investors are compensated for the loss in purchasing power due to inflation.

During the 1970s, new evidence contradicted the economic hypothesis by Fisher (1930). More specifically, Nelson (1976), Bodie (1976), Jaffe and Mandelker (1976), Fama and Schwert (1977), and Modigliani and Cohn (1979) report a negative relationship between stock returns and inflation. Furthermore, competing theories emerged which sought to explain the puzzling evidence on the relationship between stock returns and inflation. One of them is the proxy hypothesis put forward by Fama (1981). The argument by Fama (1981) rests on the negative relationship between inflation and real output growth, and considers the observed negative relationship between stock returns and inflation as spurious. Stock returns are positively related to measures of real activity, and measures of real activity are negatively related to inflation; hence stock returns are negatively related to inflation. The proxy hypothesis garnered substantial support in the 1980s and 1990s, most notably Gultekin (1983), Geske and Roll (1983), Kaul (1987, 1990), and Lee and Ni (1996). Nevertheless, Boudoukh and Richardson (1993) and Ely and Robinson (1997) provide evidence of a positive relationship between stock returns and inflation, and fail to find supporting evidence to the proxy hypothesis.

Feldstein (1980) proposes the tax-effect hypothesis, which attributes the negative relationship between stock returns and inflation to the high effective corporate tax rate on corporate income. He argues that artificial capital gains are created by inflation in valuing depreciation and inventories, which are subject to taxation. This increases the tax liability and reduces real after-tax earnings by investors, and affects the valuation of real assets. However, Fama (1981) and Friend and Hasbrouck (1982) do not find supporting evidence for the tax-effect hypothesis. Modigliani and Cohn (1979) document empirical evidence in support of the inflation illusion hypothesis, which explains the observed negative relationship between stock returns and inflation as a result of the use of nominal rates of return to discount real cash flows. They argue that using the nominal rates of return to discount real cash flows creates a distortion, and stock prices appear to be calculated in this way.

Geske and Roll (1983) propose that the negative relationship between stock returns and inflation can be explained through the fiscal and monetary linkage in what has come to be known as the reverse causality hypothesis. They show that changes in the stock prices that occur in anticipation of future economic activity are highly correlated with government revenue, and if economic activity declines and the government faces a deficit, the monetary base will be expanded to balance the budget, causing inflation. The negative relationship between stock returns and inflation is not universally supported. Boudoukh and Richardson (1993) suggest that examining the relationship between stock returns and inflation at long horizons may provide further information to explain the negative relationship observed between stock returns and both actual and expected inflation in the short run. They find that, in contrast to existing evidence in the short run, nominal stock returns have a positive relationship with both actual and expected inflation at long horizons. This finding is supported by Boudoukh et al. (1994) and Anari and Kolari (2001). Ely and Robinson (1997), Luintel and Paudyal (2006), and Adam and Frimpong (2010) also find a positive relationship between stock returns and inflation using tests for cointegration. Furthermore, Boudoukh et al. (1994) and Luintel and Paudyal (2006) find evidence of considerable heterogeneity across industries, and report that the relationship between stock returns and inflation varies across industries.

3 OVERVIEW OF THE ECONOMY OF BOTSWANA

The development of the economy of Botswana since its independence from Great Britain in 1966 has largely been propelled by revenues from diamond mining, which account for more than one-third of its gross domestic product (GDP). The tourism industry and beef production also constitute significant contributors to government revenues.

The Botswana Stock Exchange (BSE) is the national stock exchange of Botswana. Its origin can be traced back to 1989 when it started its operations as what was known as the Botswana Share Market. It operated as an informal market with only five listed companies and one stockbroking firm. Furthermore, it was led by a committee of officials who had the power to list and delist the stocks of entities. It became necessary to separate the functions of a stock exchange and a stockbroking firm. Hence, in Sep. 1994, the BSE was established by an act of Parliament as an independent exchange, and commenced trading in Nov. 1995. Ernst & Young initially held a secretariat role in the BSE when it was first established as an independent exchange, but this role was discontinued in Apr. 2003 and a full-time chief executive officer was appointed.

The BSE is pivotal to the financial system of Botswana as a platform on which private companies and the government raise capital. Currently, the products offered by the BSE include equities, government bonds, corporate bonds, and commercial paper. The introduction of the automated trading system (ATS) in Aug. 2012 enhanced trading in equity, debt, exchange-traded funds (ETFs), and global depositary receipts (GDRs). At year-end 2013, the BSE's total listing was reported to be 36, consisting of 23 domestic companies and 13 foreign companies. The listing in the BSE is mainly concentrated on the financial and service industries. In 1989, when the BSE was first established, it had only one performance index, the Botswana Share Market Index (BSI). Since then, the performance of the listed companies has been reported using three indexes, the Domestic Company Index (DCI), the Foreign Company Index (FCI), and the All Share Index (ALSI). Since its inception in 1989, the BSE has become one of the best-performing stock exchanges in Africa, with aggregate returns over the past decade averaging 24%. It is also the third largest stock exchange in sub-Saharan Africa in terms of market capitalization.

4 DATA AND METHODOLOGY

4.1 Data

The study employs monthly data on stock prices of the BSE ALSI. The ALSI is a weighted average of the Domestic Company Index and the Foreign Company Index; the data are obtained from the Bank of Botswana Financial Statistics Report. Moreover, the Consumer Price Index (CPI) is used to infer the rate of inflation in Botswana and is based on a basket of 384 items; the data are obtained from the Central Statistics Office (CSO) of Botswana.

Table 2.1 presents the descriptive statistics of the data. The average return of ALSI is 8.43% during the period of the study, while the maximum return is 9.40% and the minimum 6.87%. The ALSI returns appear to be quite volatile, with a standard deviation of 73%, while the CPI exhibits a standard deviation of 38%. The series of ALSI and INPR appear negatively skewed. Finally, the Jarque–Bera test confirms that the residuals are not normally distributed for both variables.

4.2 Methodology

The first step in processing the time-series data involves transforming the time-series data into natural logarithms in order for the data to become stationary. Brooks (2002) defines a stationary series in terms of constant mean, constant variance,

TABLE 2.1 Descriptive Statistics

Variable	Mean	Median	Std. dev.	Kurtosis	Skewness	Min	Max	Jarque–Bera
ALSI	8.4299	8.4744	0.7285	1.8302	−0.4085	6.8665	9.3954	16.29
CPI	4.5399	4.5379	0.3798	1.6968	0.0155	3.91	5.1457	13.4

and constant autocovariance at each lag. This study employs two unit root tests in order to test for the stationarity of the series: the augmented Dickey–Fuller (ADF) test developed by Dickey and Fuller (1979, 1981) and the Phillips–Perron (PP) test developed by Phillips and Perron (1988) to test for unit root.

To estimate the relationship between stock market returns and inflation, a simple ordinary least squares (OLS) linear regression is employed according to the following model:

$$\Delta P_t = \alpha_0 + \alpha_1 \Delta \text{CPI}_t \tag{2.1}$$

Where ΔP_t is the change in the All Share Index at time t and ΔCPI_t is the change in the Consumer Price Index at time t. The change in the All Share Index is adopted as a proxy for stock market returns, while the change in the CPI is adopted as a proxy for the rate of inflation.

Graham (1996) shows that this model yields the same qualitative evidence as the model employed by Fama and Schwert (1977), although it does not distinguish between expected and unexpected components of inflation. Spyrou (2001) also uses this model to estimate the relationship between stock returns and inflation in Greece for the period 1990–2000. Furthermore, in order to test for the impact of the recent global financial crisis, we split the sample period into two subperiods (1998M01–2008M08) and (2008M09–2013M12).

One of the objectives of this study is to examine whether a long-run relationship exists between stock returns and inflation. In order to do this, a test for cointegration is employed. Two variables are described as being cointegrated if they have a long-run or equilibrium relationship between them. Hendry (1995) describes a cointegrating process as defining a "long term equilibrium trajectory," departure from which induces corrections to the equilibrium designed to bring the economy to its normal path. Thomas (1997) also describes cointegration as the statistical equivalent of a long-run economic relationship between the same-order variables. Cointegration exists between two variables if they are integrated to the same order; that is, Y_t and X_t are integrated to the same order. Maddala and Kim (1998) note that if Y_t and X_t are cointegrated, there exists β such that $Y_t - \beta X_t$ is integrated to order I(0), denoted by saying that Y_t and X_t are CI(1,1).

To ascertain the long-run relationship between variables, the Johansen and Juselius (1990) method for cointegration is used. This method requires that we specify the optimal lag length since it is sensitive to the lag length employed. We select the lag length optimally using the Akaike information criterion and the Schwartz Bayesian criterion.

Johansen and Juselius (1990) developed a model concerned with the calculation of maximum likelihood estimators and likelihood ratio tests in the model for cointegration under linear restrictions of the cointegration vectors β and weights α. They show that starting with a VAR model (1.1) a hypothesis of cointegration can be constructed as a hypothesis of the long-run impact matrix $\Pi = \alpha\beta'$ with β indicating cointegrating vectors and α indicating the amount of each cointegrating vector included in the vector error correction model (VECM).

We start with a VAR with k lags, which can be expressed as follows:

$$y_t = \mu + \beta_1 y_{t-1} + \beta_2 y_{t-2} + \ldots + \beta_k y_{t-k} + u_t \qquad (2.2)$$

Where $t = 1, 2 \ldots, T$; y_t is an n-vector of I(1) variables; μ is an $N*1$ vector of intercept terms; and u_t is an $N*1$ vector of error terms at time t. Johansen and Juselius (1990) suggest that model 5 should be expressed in first differenced form. The first difference operator should also be applied to the error-correction process to avoid loss of information, hence applying $\Delta = 1 - L$, where L is the lag operator to model 2 and yields the following expression:

$$\Delta y_t = \mu + \Pi y_{t-k} + \Gamma_1 \Delta y_{t-1} + \Gamma_2 \Delta y_{t-2} + \ldots + \Gamma_{k-1} \Delta y_{t-(k-1)} + u_t \qquad (2.3)$$

where $\Pi = (\sum_{i=1}^{k} \beta_i) - I_g$ and $\Gamma_i = (\sum_{j=1}^{i} \beta_j) - I_g$

Model 3 can be interpreted as a vector error correction model (VECM). The VECM adjusts to both short-run changes in the variables as well as deviations from the equilibrium. Sims (1980) and Hendry (1995) strongly suggest the use of the VECM as a way of jointly estimating the relationships among variables without imposing a priori restrictions. Brooks (2002) describes the Johansen test as being centered on the examination of the Π matrix in model 6, which is commonly interpreted as the long-run coefficient matrix. In equilibrium, all the Δy_{t-i} will equal zero, and the error terms will also equal their expected value of zero; hence Πy_{t-k} will equal zero.

Testing for cointegration requires an examination of the Π matrix through its eigenvalues. To determine the number of cointegrating equations (r), three types of methods are applied, which are based on the Johansen's maximum likelihood estimator of the parameters of a cointegrating VECM. These methods are the Johansen's trace statistics method, the maximum eigenvalue statistic method, and a third method that chooses (r) to minimize an information criterion. The trace statistic (λ_{trace}) is a joint test of the null hypothesis that the number of cointegrating vectors is less than or equal to (r) against an alternative hypothesis that the number of cointegrating vectors is more than (r). The maximum eigenvalue statistic (λ_{max}) is a test of the null hypothesis that the number of cointegrating vectors is (r) against the alternative hypothesis that the number of cointegrating vectors is ($r + 1$). The distributions for λ_{trace} and λ_{max} are represented as follows:

$$\lambda_{\text{trace}}(r) = -T \sum_{i=r+1}^{g} \ln\left(1 - \hat{\lambda}_t\right)$$

$$\lambda_{\text{max}}(r, r+1) = -T \ln\left(1 - \hat{\lambda}_{r+1}\right)$$

Where r is the number of cointegrating vectors, and λ_i is the estimated value for the ith ordered eigenvalue from the Π matrix.

The critical values for the two statistics (λ_{trace} and λ_{max}) are provided by Johansen and Juselius (1990). If the statistic is found to be greater than the appropriate critical value from the tables, the null hypothesis that there are (r) cointegrating vectors is rejected against the null hypothesis that there are ($r + 1$) cointegrating vectors for λ_{trace} and more than (r) for λ_{max}. If the test statistic is found to be smaller than the critical value, the null hypothesis that there are (r) cointegrating vectors cannot be rejected. In this study the trace statistic is employed to determine the number of cointegrating equations.

5 RESULTS

Table 2.2 presents the results for testing the null hypothesis that a unit root exists on log series of the variables using the ADF (panel A) and the PP test (panel B). The results show that we cannot reject the null hypothesis of a unit root for the series of both variables (ALSI and CPI). We infer that the log series of the variables is nonstationary. Panel B presents the results for testing the null hypothesis that a unit root exists on log price series of the variables using the PP test. We deduce from the results that we cannot reject the null hypothesis of a unit root for all the variables (ALSI and CPI). These results confirm the conclusion reached by employing the ADF test that the log price series of the variables (ALSI and CPI) are nonstationary.

Panel A of Table 2.3 presents the results of employing the ADF test on the first differenced values of the variables. We conclude that the null hypothesis of unit root can be rejected at the 1% level for the first differenced series of both variables. We infer from the results that the series of first differenced values of the

TABLE 2.2 Unit Root Tests (Log Series)	
Panel A: ADF test	
Variable	**t-Statistic**
ALSI	−2.2515 (0.1890)
CPI	−0.6158 (0.8630)
Panel B: PP test	
Variable	**t-Statistic**
ALSI	−2.0622 (0.2604)
CPI	−0.5520 (0.8768)

H_0: Unit root exists.
P-values in parentheses.

TABLE 2.3 Unit Root Tests (First Differences)

Panel A: ADF test	
Variable	*t*-Statistic
ALSI	−13.0137 (0.0000)
CPI	−10.7199 (0.0000)
Panel B: PP test	
Variable	*t*-Statistic
ALSI	−13.2131 (0.0000)
CPI	−10.7171 (0.0000)

H_0: Unit root exists.
P-values in parentheses.

variables are stationary. Panel B presents the results of employing the PP test to test the null hypothesis of a unit root on first differenced values of the variables. The results show that we reject the null hypothesis of a unit root at the 1% level for both variables. The results reaffirm the conclusion reached by employing the ADF test that the series of first differenced values of variables are stationary.

Table 2.4 presents the results of estimating the relationship between stock market returns and inflation in accordance with model 1, as discussed in the previous section. The results of the linear regression show that the relationship between stock market returns and inflation is positive for all the subperiods and the whole sample period. However, the observed positive relationship between stock market returns and inflation is not statistically significant in any of the two subperiods or in the whole sample period. Thus, our results cannot support the hypothesis that stock returns can compensate investors for the loss of their purchasing power due to inflation.

Motivated by prior research suggesting that, even though there might not be a positive relationship in the short run between stock returns and inflation, there could be a positive relationship between them in the long run, we tested whether such a long-term relationship exists. Table 2.5 presents the results of testing for cointegration to ascertain the long-run relationship between ALSI and CPI. The lag length employed in each period is reported in the table. We employ the criteria discussed in the methodology section to interpret the trace statistic that is reported in the table.

We fail to reject the null hypothesis of no cointegration at any level of significance for the subperiod (1998M01–2008M08). We also fail to reject the null

TABLE 2.4 OLS Regression

Panel A: 1998M01–2008M08

Coefficient Estimates

α_0	0.0152
	(1.9519)**
α_1	0.4951
	(0.5777)
R^2	0.0027
DW	2.0017

Panel B: 2008M09–2013M12

Coefficient Estimates

α_0	−0.0018
	(−0.2812)
α_1	0.4253
	(0.4679)
R^2	0.0035
DW	1.4345

Panel C: 1998M01–2013M12

Coefficient Estimates

α_0	0.008
	(1.4334)
α_1	0.7118
	(0.6577)
R^2	0.0062
DW	1.8466

Estimation model: $\Delta P_t = \alpha_0 + \alpha_1 \Delta CPI_t$. Dependent variable: change in the All Share Index. Explanatory variable: change in the Consumer Price Index. * denotes significance at the 5% level; ** denotes significance at the 10% level; t-statistics appear in parentheses.

hypothesis of no cointegration for the subperiod (2008M09–2013M12). The trace test also indicates no cointegration at any significance level when the Johansen technique is applied to the whole sample period (1998M01–2013M12). We infer that there is no long-run relationship between stock market returns and inflation in the Botswana stock market.

Our findings of no long-run relationship between stock market returns and inflation in Botswana are consistent with those by Floros (2004), who reports that there is no long-run equilibrium relationship between stock returns and inflation in Greece using data from 1988 to 2002. Floros (2004) also suggests that

TABLE 2.5 Testing for Cointegration

Panel A: 1998M1–2008M8 (order of VAR = 1)				
Null	**Alternative**	**Statistic**	**95% Critical Value**	**90% Critical Value**
$r = 0$	$r \geq 1$	7.6489	15.4947	13.4288
$r \leq 1$	$r \geq 2$	2.3628	3.8414	2.7055
Panel B: 2008M9–2013M12 (order of VAR = 1)				
Null	**Alternative**	**Statistic**	**95% Critical Value**	**90% Critical Value**
$r = 0$	$r \geq 1$	11.9869	15.4947	13.4288
$r \leq 1$	$r \geq 2$	0.4497	3.8415	2.7055
Panel C: 1998M1–2013M12 (order of VAR = 1)				
Null	**Alternative**	**Statistic**	**95% Critical Value**	**90% Critical Value**
$r = 0$	$r \geq 1$	8.2983	15.4947	13.4288
$r \leq 1$	$r \geq 2$	3.1383	3.8414	2.7055

The Akaike information criterion and the Schwartz Bayesian criterion suggest taking 1 lag as the correct lag structure for all the subperiods and the whole sample period.

stock returns and inflation should be treated as independent factors in Greece. Our findings are also consistent with those by Jana (2013), who finds no evidence of a long-run relationship between the closing price of the Sensex and the Wholesale Price Index (measure of inflation) in India for the period 1982–2012.

6 CONCLUSIONS

This study examined the relationship between stock market returns and inflation in the Botswana stock market. In order to do so, we employed an OLS regression of the Consumer Price Index on the All Share Index using monthly data. We found evidence that the relationship between stock market returns and inflation is observed to be positive in all the subperiods and the whole sample period; however, this relationship is not statistically significant. We also found evidence that there is no long-run relationship between stock market returns and inflation in the Botswana stock market.

The findings of this study have shown that investing in the Botswana stock market does not compensate investors for the loss in purchasing power through inflation. This has important implications for policy makers and authorities charged with the responsibility to monitor and control inflation, since investors face diminished returns from their investments in the stock market when inflation increases. The findings of this study also have important implications for the government of Botswana in its continued efforts to attract foreign investment to the country, and for potential investors who want to invest in frontier markets such as Botswana.

REFERENCES

Adam, A.M., Frimpong, S., 2010. Can stocks hedge against inflation in the long run? evidence from Ghana stock market. Int. J. Bus. Manage. 5 (6), 188–194.

Anari, A., Kolari, J., 2001. Stock prices and inflation. J. Financ. Res. 24 (4), 587–602.

Bodie, Z., 1976. Common stock as a hedge against inflation. J. Finance 31 (2), 459–470.

Boudoukh, J., Richardson, M., 1993. Stock returns and inflation: a long-horizon perspective. Amer. Econ. Rev. 85 (5), 1346–1355.

Boudoukh, J., Richardson, M., Whitelaw, R.F., 1994. Industry returns and the Fisher effect. J. Finance 49 (5), 1595–1615.

Brooks, C., 2002. Introductory Econometrics for Finance. Cambridge University Press, Cambridge, UK.

Dickey, D.A., Fuller, W.A., 1979. Distribution of estimators for autoregressive time series with a unit root. J. Am. Stat. Assoc. 74 (366), 427–431.

Dickey, D.A., Fuller, W.A., 1981. Likelihood ratio statistics for autoregressive time series with a unit root. Econometrica 49 (4), 1057–1072.

Ely, D., Robinson, K.J., 1997. Are stocks a hedge against inflation? international evidence using a long run approach. J. Int. Money Finance 16 (1), 141–167.

Fama, E.F., 1981. Stock returns, real activity, inflation and money. Am. Econ. Rev. 71 (4), 545–565.

Fama, E.F., Schwert, G.W., 1977. Asset returns and inflation. J. Financial Econ. 5 (2), 115–146.

Feldstein, M., 1980. Inflation, tax rules and the stock market. J. Monetary Econ. 6, 309–331.

Fisher, R.A., 1930. The General Theory of Natural Selection. Oxford University Press, Oxford, UK.

Floros, C., 2004. Stock returns and inflation in Greece. Appl. Economet. Int. Dev. 4 (2), 1–14.

Friend, I., Hasbrouck, J., 1982. Inflation and the stock market: comment. Am. Econ. Rev. 72 (1), 237–242.

Geske, R., Roll, R., 1983. The fiscal and monetary linkages between stock returns and inflation. J. Finance 38, 1–33.

Graham, F.C., 1996. Inflation, real stock returns and monetary policy. Appl. Financial Econ. 6 (1), 29–35.

Gultekin, N.B., 1983. Stock market returns and inflation: evidence from other countries. J. Finance 38 (1), 49–65.

Hendry, D.F., 1995. Dynamic Econometrics. Oxford University Press, Oxford, UK.

Jaffe, J.F., Mandelker, G., 1976. The Fisher effect" for risky assets: an empirical investigation. J. Finance 31 (2), 447–458.

Jana, S., 2013. Applicability of Fisher hypothesis on pre and post reforms era of Indian capital market. Int. J. Manage. 2 (2), 1–11.

Johansen, S., Juselius, K., 1990. Maximum likelihood estimation and inference on cointegration—with applications to the demand for money. Oxford Bull. Econ. Stat. 52 (2), 169–210.

Kaul, G., 1987. Stock returns and inflation: the role of the monetary sector. J. Financial Econ. 18, 253–276.

Kaul, G., 1990. Monetary regimes and the relation between stock returns and inflationary expectation. J. Financial. Quant. Anal. 25 (3), 307–321.

Lee, K., Ni, S., 1996. Stock returns, real activities and temporary and persistent inflation. Appl. Financial Econ. 6 (5), 433–441.

Luintel, K.B., Paudyal, K., 2006. Are common stocks a hedge against inflation? J. Financial Res. 29 (1), 1–19.

Maddala, G.S., Kim, I., 1998. Unit Roots, Cointegration and Structural Change. Cambridge University Press, Cambridge, UK.

Modigliani, F., Cohn, R., 1979. Inflation, rational valuation and the markets. Financial Anal. J. 35 (2), 24–44.

Nelson, C.R., 1976. Inflation and rates of return on common stocks. J. Finance 31 (2), 471–483.

Phillips, P.C.B., Perron, P., 1988. Testing for a unit root in time series regression. Biometrika 75 (2), 335–346.

Sims, C.A., 1980. Comparison of interwar and post-war business cycles: monetarism reconsidered. Am. Econ. Rev. 70 (2), 250–257.

Spyrou, S.I., 2001. Stock returns and inflation: evidence from an emerging market. Appl. Econ. Lett. 8 (7), 447–450.

Thomas, R.L., 1997. Modern Econometrics. Addison-Wesley Longman, Essex, UK.

Chapter 3

Modeling and Forecasting Stock Market Volatility in Frontier Markets: Evidence From Four European and Four African Frontier Markets

D.S. Kambouroudis

School of Management, University of Stirling, Stirling, Scotland, United Kingdom

Chapter Outline

1 INTRODUCTION

The popular topic of volatility modeling and forecasting with the main aim of finding the best model for accurately forecasting volatility has mainly been based on samples consisting of developed and emerging economies, with little or no attention to frontier markets. Data availability no longer poses a problem due to advances in information technology on one hand; on the other hand, investors' increasing interest in small, less accessible but still investable markets

Handbook of Frontier Markets. http://dx.doi.org/10.1016/B978-0-12-803776-8.00003-3

has initiated a stream of research toward investigating the special characteristics of frontier markets. So far the focus of the academic literature has been on the integration, diversification, and interdependence of frontier markets, for which a considerable number of studies exist; however, in terms of stock market volatility very little is known.

The purpose of this chapter is to enter into the ongoing debate in the academic literature to identify the model that will give the most accurate forecast with the use of a sample consisting of frontier markets. Using a number of well-established forecasting models from the autoregressive conditional heteroscedasticity (ARCH) genre of models, it attempts to capture the characteristics found in stock market returns such as volatility clustering, asymmetry, and persistence, and performs a comparison exercise with the use of a number of statistical measures of forecasting accuracy in order to identify the model giving the most accurate forecast. The sample consists of four European and four African frontier markets, namely: Bulgaria, Croatia, Romania, Ukraine, Kenya, Mauritius, Nigeria, and Tunisia. In identifying the best model for forecasting the volatility of our sample of frontier markets, the component generalized ARCH (CGARCH) model capturing the long memory effect is the overall winner of the "horse race" exercise.

The rest of this chapter is structured as follows. In the next section some relevant background information is presented setting the scene and establishing the importance of this study. The data, methodology, and discussion of results sections follow, and finally some concluding remarks are made.

2 BACKGROUND INFORMATION

In this section, the importance of volatility forecasting is highlighted, followed by a literature review on forecasting volatility looking at the overall findings and modeling aspects of the topic.

2.1 Importance of Volatility Forecasting[a]

One of the most popular subjects within the academic finance literature has been the modeling and forecasting of stock market volatility. The topic of volatility modeling and forecasting has attracted the attention of academics, and as a result an enormous body of research exists, especially after the Oct. 19, 1987, stock market crashed when in a single day the Standard & Poor's (S&P) composite portfolio dropped by 20% (from 282.70 to 224.84 points) and the Dow Jones Industrial Average (DJIA) fell by 508 points the same day. According to Schwert (1990a,b), stock volatility jumped dramatically during and after the crash. Accurately modeling and forecasting volatility is of significant importance to anyone involved in the financial markets. The term *volatility* is associated with risk, and

---

a. This section is based on Kambouroudis (2012).

high volatility is thought of as a symptom of market disruption implying that assets and securities are unfairly priced (Figlewski, 1997). The topic of volatility forecasting is of interest not only to academics but also to practitioners and policy makers. For example, during periods of high volatility, practitioners may have to alter their investment strategies either by shifting their investment portfolios toward less risky short-term assets or by using immunization strategies for their portfolios. Furthermore, during periods of increased volatility, policy makers would pursue regulatory reforms either by trying to reduce volatility directly or by assisting financial markets and institutions to adapt to increased volatility (Becketti and Sellon, 1989).

Other activities such as risk management, portfolio management and selection, derivative pricing, and hedging are examples of activities that would suffer without accurate volatility predictions. More specifically, Engle and Patton (2001) observe: "A risk manager must know today the likelihood that his portfolio will decline in the future. An option trader will want to know the volatility that can be expected over the future of the life of the contract. To hedge this contract he will also want to know how volatile is this forecast volatility. A portfolio manager may want to sell a stock or a portfolio before it becomes more volatile. A market maker may want to set the bid ask spread wider when the future is believed to be more volatile" (p. 2).

The importance of accurately forecasting volatility is paramount for the functioning of the economy and everyone involved in finance activities. In periods of instability, volatility forecasting becomes even more important since governments, the banking system, and both institutional and individual investors are trying to cope with increased risk, uncertainty, and lack of resources. Knowledge, understanding, and the ability to forecast and proxy volatility accurately could be determining factors for survival not only during turbulent times but also during periods of economic growth, giving an advantage to whoever can successfully manage future volatility. There are many reasons why forecasting volatility is important, according to Walsh and Tsou (1998), for example, option pricing has traditionally suffered without accurate volatility forecasts. Controlling for estimation error in portfolios constructed to minimize ex ante risk, with accurate forecasts we have the ability to take advantage of the correlation structure between assets. Finally, when building and understanding asset pricing models, we must take into account the nature of volatility and its ability to be forecasted, since risk preferences will be based on market assessment of volatility.

2.2   Emerging Markets or Country Samples

At first the academic literature investigated the volatility of developed economies; however, more recently emerging economies have been included in the samples of studies for comparison purposes, due to their volatile nature and special characteristics. The main reason for focusing at first on developed economies and then on emerging economies was the availability of data; nevertheless, due to advances in information technology, data availability no longer poses a problem. The question initially addressed by the academic literature related primarily to finding the best and most suitable model for accurately forecasting volatility. By incorporating emerging markets into the samples of investigation, a number of additional elements were also addressed due to the volatile nature and idiosyncratic characteristics of emerging markets. Generally, emerging stock markets have been characterized by both high average volatility and a wide dispersion of volatility. Furthermore, both the magnitude and the range of volatility in emerging stock markets are much greater than what are found in developed stock markets. Based on these essential characteristics of emerging markets, empirical investigations have attempted to provide an understanding of the nature and the determinants of emerging market volatility (Fifield et al., 1998). Richards (1996) examined the proposition that emerging stock markets' returns have become more volatile in recent years. The reason for this is primarily the increased scale of institutional involvement. Richards (1996) also found that during the period between 1975 and 1992 there was no tendency for an increase in volatility, whereas the period between 1992 and 1995 was characterized by lower volatility than in the earlier sample period despite the increased foreign institutional investment. Results by Spyrou and Kassimatis (1999) suggest that the nature of volatility has not changed dramatically after financial liberalization and that volatility is more likely to be unaffected or reduced following liberalization, confirming the study of Kim and Singal (1993). On the other hand, Grabel (1995) presented evidence that volatility increased following financial liberalization. Arestis and Demetriades (1997) argue that there still is a relationship between financial liberalization and equity market volatility. More recent studies also failed to produce a generally accepted conclusion (Kim and Singal, 2000; Jayasuriya, 2005; Cunado et al., 2006).

Emerging stock markets appear to be more sensitive to information inflows compared to developed markets. This could be for various reasons such as the liberalization mentioned earlier, or the regulatory changes of the economies and markets, for example, foreign influences. An example of this could be the Istanbul Stock Exchange, which underwent regulatory changes in 1991 and as consequence an increase in volatility was reported (Antoniou et al., 1997).

Frontier markets have more recently been included in finance studies. This interest is not only from an academic point of view due to their special characteristics as smaller and less accessible but investable markets, but also from an investors' viewpoint, as can be seen by the recent launch of frontier market indices, for example by Standard & Poor's (S&P) and MSCI, Inc. Aspects investigated include integration and diversification (Berger et al., 2011), contagion and stock market interdependence (Samarakoon, 2011), and behavioral finance aspects such as fund manager herding (Economou et al., 2015). In contrast, volatility forecasting within frontier markets is a subject that has attracted little or no attention. This is the topic of this chapter.

2.3 Modeling of Volatility Forecasting

As mentioned previously, at first the academic literature focused on finding the type of model or models that would produce accurate volatility forecasts. Taking into account the different features found in the data sets used, however, this was not a straightforward task. In the beginning, time-series analysis was employed to model and to forecast volatility. A number of simple historical models were introduced such as moving averages and exponential smoothing and their extensions; nevertheless, it was only after the introduction of the autoregressive conditional heteroscedasticity (ARCH) model by Engle (1982) and its generalization (GARCH) by Bollerslev (1986) and Taylor (1986) that the characteristic of "volatility clustering"[b] was factored into the modeling process. Unlike the simple models, these more "sophisticated" time-series models belonging in the ARCH genre of models do not make use of the sample standard deviations but derive the conditional variance of the returns with the use of the maximum likelihood method, as stated in Poon and Granger (2003). Other data features were also successfully captured by the ARCH genre of models: more specifically, nonsymmetrical dependencies, also known as the "leverage effect," where negative shocks appear to have a bigger impact on volatility than positive shocks of the same magnitude, were successfully captured by, for example, the exponential GARCH (EGARCH) model by Nelson (1991) and the threshold GARCH (TGARCH) or GJR GARCH model by Glosten et al. (1993). The characteristic of "volatility persistence," where more recent shocks have a greater impact on volatility than past shocks, is also captured by the ARCH models. Examples of such models, known as "long memory" models, are the integrated GARCH (IGARCH) model by Engle and Bollerslev (1986) and the component GARCH (CGARCH) model by Engle and Lee (1999).[c] As expected, the ARCH genre of models found criticism and support by the academic literature, and today the debate is ongoing for finding which model is the best. A number of studies and reviews either reporting poor results or providing support for the ARCH models can be found; here just a few are mentioned: Andersen and Bollerslev (1998), Cumby et al. (1993), Jorion (1995), Franses and Dijk (1996), Figlewski (1997), Andersen et al. (1999), McMillan et al. (2000), Poon and Granger (2003), Hansen and Lunde (2005), McMillan and Kambouroudis (2009), and Wang and Wu (2012).

The literature explored several different alternatives with the aim of finding the best model for accurately forecasting volatility. To this end the options market was called upon, which led to the conception of options' "implied" volatility. The Volatility Index (VIX), originally based on the Chicago Board Options Exchange (CBOE) Market Volatility Index, was calculated as an average of the

---

b. As identified by Mandelbrot (1963) and Fama (1965).

c. Please note that the list of ARCH models is an extensive one, and this has been one of the main criticisms of the ARCH genre, but for the purposes of this chapter a small number are mentioned here and a representative model from each category is used in the empirical part of the chapter.

S&P 100 option implied volatilities computed on a real-time basis during the trading day measuring volatility instead of price (Fleming et al., 1995). Later on, the VIX calculation was based on the S&P 500 index because it is a better-known index and also because futures contracts on the S&P 500 are actively traded and S&P 500 option contracts are European-style, making them easier to value (Whaley, 2009). Again the academic literature compared the volatility-forecasting performance of historical measures to that of the VIX, and as a consequence a large number of studies appeared in support of implied volatility measures and the VIX: for example, Fleming et al. (1995), Blair et al. (2001), Carr and Wu (2006), and Yang and Liu (2012). However, alternatives to implied volatility and the VIX were supported by Martens and Zein (2004) and Canina and Figlewski (1993). More recent studies (Ahoniemi, 2008; Konstantinidi et al., 2008; Fernandes et al., 2014) have looked into the forecastability of implied volatility itself.

An additional factor taken into account when forecasting volatility is the data frequency used in the data sets employed. At first daily, weekly, and monthly data were used; however, due to advances in information technology, intraday and high-frequency data became available, this way introducing the concept of "realized" volatility. Volatility-forecasting models incorporating factors based on realized measures have been used in ARCH specification; see, for example, Hansen et al. (2010).

As can be seen, the academic literature, in an attempt to find the best model for forecasting volatility, has considered a number of different factors, some of which have been looked into in the preceding paragraphs. In this chapter, taking into account the recent developments in information technology that allow us to consider a sample of frontier economies, a type of market least explored in the literature, as well as taking into account the characteristics and features found in data sets (such as clustering, leverage, and persistence), a forecasting exercise is performed. The data and methodology are described in the following sections.

3 DATA

All the data are obtained by the Datastream market information service. For all the countries, daily closing price data from Jan. 1, 2008 to Dec. 31, 2013, are selected and the price indices are converted to returns by the standard method of calculating the logarithmic differences.[d] The sample chosen is after the 2007 global financial crisis, mainly due to data availability. The sample consists of four European and four African frontier markets, namely, Bulgaria, Croatia, Romania, Ukraine, Kenya, Mauritius, Nigeria, and Tunisia, for which the main country index is selected.[e] The data for each country are partitioned into the in-sample

---

d. Returns are calculated as $R_t = \log(p_t/p_{t-1})$.
e. The main index of each country is selected: Bulgaria—SE SOFIX (PI), Croatia—CROBEX (PI), Romania—BET COMP Index Euro (PI), Ukraine—PFTS (PI), Kenya—Nairobi SE NSE20 (PI), Mauritius—SE SEMDEX (PI), Nigeria—All Share (PI) and Tunisia—TUNINDEX (PI).

estimation period from Jan. 1, 2008 to Dec. 31, 2011 (ie, 3 years of daily data) and the out-of-sample estimation period from Jan. 1, 2012 to Dec. 31, 2013 (2 years of daily observations). The aforementioned in-sample period is deemed adequate as indicated in Kambouroudis and McMillan (2015), where a large in-sample period is not always necessary and often 3 years of daily observations suffice. The descriptive statistics of the returns are presented in the Table 3.1.

The mean and median of the returns are broadly consistent and close to zero, with most countries giving negative mean returns over the whole sample period, with the exception of Kenya and Mauritius. Overall, the European frontier markets appear to be more volatile, with Ukraine reporting the highest standard deviation of returns, and Tunisia being the least volatile. The Jarque–Bera tests for normality are consistent with the skewness and kurtosis values, and normality is rejected for all series.

4 METHODOLOGY

In this section the models used in the forecasting exercise are presented. The models belong to the GARCH genre of models, which have the ability to capture the stylized effects found in data sets, as described in the previous sections, such as volatility clustering, information asymmetry, and long memory. For this reason three representative models are chosen that capture these stylized effects: the GARCH(1,1) model (the first generation of ARCH models, the generalized ARCH symmetric model); a representative second-generation asymmetric model, the exponential GARCH (EGARCH) by Nelson (1991); and a representative third-generation GARCH-type model capturing the long memory effect, namely the component GARCH (CGRACH) by Engle and Lee (1999).

After using the standard method of calculating the logarithmic returns, the returns process r_t is presented as:

$$r_t = m_t + \varepsilon_t \tag{3.1}$$

where m_t is the conditional mean process, which could include autoregressive (AR) or moving average (MA) terms, and the error term can be decomposed as:

$$\varepsilon_t = \sigma_t z_t \tag{3.2}$$

where z_t is an idiosyncratic zero-mean and constant-variance noise term, and σ_t is the volatility process to be estimated and forecast, with forecast values denoted h_t^2.

4.1 ARCH Effects

The first step in the GARCH-type methodology is to test for the presence of "ARCH effects," making sure that the GARCH-type methodology is relevant. The two tests performed are the Lagrange multiplier (LM) test of Engle (1982)

TABLE 3.1 Descriptive Statistics for All Sample Countries and Results of ARCH Effects Test

Countries	Mean	Median	Maximum	Minimum	Std. dev.	Skewness	Kurtosis	Jarque–Bera	ARCH effects
Bulgaria	−0.00082	0.00000	0.07292	−0.08316	0.01424	−1.05094	12.6586	637	Yes
Croatia	−0.00068	0.00000	0.14779	−0.10764	0.01452	0.06306	18.0132	14,699	Yes
Romania	−0.00058	0.00000	0.10912	−0.12342	0.01834	−0.67349	6.19700	3,520	Yes
Ukraine	−0.00086	0.00000	0.13518	−0.15183	0.01921	−0.21619	12.6701	6,110	Yes
Kenya	6.39E-05	0.00000	0.06948	−0.05234	0.00904	0.68882	12.7682	6,346	Yes
Mauritius	7.89E-05	0.00000	0.07655	−0.06383	0.00833	0.01872	20.5472	20,078	Yes
Nigeria	−0.00022	0.00000	0.03843	−0.04747	0.01063	−0.04335	5.0652	279	Yes
Tunisia	0.00033	6.45E-05	0.04109	−0.05004	0.00642	−0.67838	14.7444	9,114	Yes

Notes: The descriptive statistics are calculated over the whole sample period. The null hypothesis for the ARCH effects test is "no ARCH effects"; for all indices and for all countries the null hypothesis of "no ARCH effects" is rejected.

and White's heteroscedasticity test (White, 1980), having the null hypothesis of "no ARCH effects."[f] For all our sample countries the null hypothesis of "no ARCH effects" is rejected.[g]

4.2 Generalized Autoregressive Conditional Heteroscedasticity (GARCH)

The GARCH model of Bollerslev (1986) and Taylor (1986) requires joint estimation of the conditional mean model (3.1) and the variance process. On the assumption that the conditional mean stochastic error, ε_t, is normally distributed with zero mean and time-varying conditional variance, h_t^2, the GARCH(1,1) model is given by:

$$h_{t+1}^2 = \omega + \alpha \varepsilon_t^2 + \beta h_t^2 \tag{3.3}$$

where all the parameters must satisfy the nonnegativity constraints $\omega > 0$ and $\alpha, \beta \geq 0$, while the sum of $\alpha + \beta$ quantifies the persistence of shocks to volatility. The GARCH(1,1) model generates one-step-ahead forecasts of volatility as a weighted average of the constant long-run or average variance, ω, the previous forecast variance, h_t^2, and previous volatility reflecting squared "news" about the return, ε_t^2. In particular, as volatility forecasts increase following a large return of either sign, the GARCH specification captures the well-known volatility clustering effect.

4.3 Exponential GARCH (EGARCH)

The GARCH model, although nonlinear in the conditional mean error, postulates a linear dependence of conditional variance upon squared past errors and past variances; as a consequence, opposite shocks of the same magnitude will appear to have the same effect on the variance. The "leverage effect," as it is known, refers to the asymmetry effect where the effect between positive and negative shocks upon conditional variance is accounted for. Therefore this negative relationship, in which a negative shock increases the conditional variance by a greater amount than an equal positive shock, is successfully captured by the exponential GARCH model (EGARCH) of Nelson (1991):

$$\log(h_{t+1}^2) = \omega + \alpha \left| \frac{\varepsilon_t}{h_t} \right| + \gamma \frac{\varepsilon_t}{h_t} + \beta \log(h_t^2) \tag{3.4}$$

where the coefficient γ captures the asymmetric impact of news with negative shocks having a greater impact than positive shocks of equal magnitude if $\gamma < 0$, while the volatility clustering effect is captured by a significant α. Finally, the use of the logarithmic form allows the parameters to be negative without the conditional variance becoming negative.

---

f. These tests are residual tests for which a lag length of 5 due to the data frequency is chosen.
g. The results are presented in Table 3.1 with the descriptive statistics.

4.4   Component GARCH (CGARCH)

On the other hand, the component GARCH (CGARCH) model by Engle and Lee (1999) separates long-run and short-run volatility effects by decomposition of conditional mean ARMA models. Thus, while the GARCH model and its asymmetric extensions exhibit mean reversion in volatility to ω, the component GARCH model allows mean reversion to a time-varying trend, q_t. The component model specification is:

$$h_{t+1}^2 = q_{t+1} + \alpha(\varepsilon_t^2 - q_t) + \beta(h_t^2 - q_t) \tag{3.5}$$

where $q_{t+1} = \omega + \rho q_t + \phi(\varepsilon_t^2 - h_t^2)$ represents long-run (or trend) volatility provided $\rho > (\alpha + \beta)$. The forecasting error $(\varepsilon_t^2 - h_t^2)$ serves as the driving force for the time-dependent movement of the trend, and the difference between the conditional variance and its trend $(h_t^2 - q_t)$ is the transitory component of the conditional variance. Stationarity is achieved provided $(\alpha + \beta)(1 - \rho) + \rho < 1$, which in turn requires $\rho < 1$ and $(\alpha + \beta) < 1$. The transitory component then converges to zero with powers of $\alpha + \beta$, while the long-run component converges on q_t with powers of ρ.

4.5   Comparisons of Forecast Performance

There are numerous methods for evaluating and comparing the accuracy of the different forecasting models, as can be seen in the academic literature (Diebold and Lopez, 1996; Poon and Granger, 2003). For the purposes of this exercise, two popular methods are selected: the error-based statistic from which the methods of mean absolute error (MAE) and root mean square error (RMSE) are considered and the second regression-based efficiency tests that are implemented by calculating the coefficient of determination (R^2) of the Mincer–Zarnowitz (MZ) regression where the true volatility value is regressed on a constant and the estimated forecast value (Mincer and Zarnowitz, 1969). Both of these techniques require the estimation of "true" (or "actual") volatility against which the forecast performance of volatility is compared. This issue itself has been widely debated in the academic literature for which differing opinions exist. One solution to the problem is the use of the squared error term from a conditional mean model of the returns estimated over the full data set, as proposed by Pagan and Schwert (1990); this is the method adopted in this study. This method usually gives very low coefficients of determination, often below 10%, as discussed in Andersen and Bollerslev (1998), because squared returns are noisy estimates of true volatility. Realized volatility (calculated using a higher frequency of data) is often the alternative measure of true volatility;[h] however, due to data unavailability we are unable at this stage to consider this option.

---

h. See, for example, Patton (2011).

The MAE statistic measures the average absolute forecast error, which does not permit the offsetting effects of overprediction and underprediction, and the RMSE penalizes large forecast errors:

$$\text{MAE} = \frac{1}{J}\sum\nolimits_{t=1}^{J} |\sigma_t^2 - h_t^2| \tag{3.6}$$

$$\text{RMSE} = \frac{1}{J}\sum\nolimits_{t=1}^{J} (\sigma_t^2 - h_t^2)^2 \tag{3.7}$$

where J is the forecast period, true volatility is σ_t^2, and h_t^2 is the forecast. The lowest MAE and RMSE indicate the best forecast.

The MZ regression is presented here (Mincer and Zarnowitz, 1969):

$$\sigma_t^2 = \alpha + \beta h_t^2 + \varepsilon_t \tag{3.8}$$

The coefficient of determination (R^2) is obtained for comparison purposes, and in this case a higher value for the coefficient of determination will indicate the best forecast.

5   FINDINGS AND DISCUSSIONS

In this section the results of the forecasting exercise are presented. The purpose of this chapter is to enter the ongoing debate within the academic literature on the topic of volatility modeling and forecasting using a sample of eight frontier markets, four from Europe and four from Africa. So far very little is known on how models used in developed and emerging economies perform when data from frontier markets are used. In order to draw conclusions, a selection of models that capture the characteristics found in stock market returns, those of clustering, asymmetry, and long memory, is used in this chapter. After establishing the presence of "ARCH effects" in the data with the use of two tests, the LM test of Engle (1982) and the heteroscedasticity test of White (1980), the exercise uses three representative models from the ARCH family of models which capture the stylized effects, the GARCH(1,1), EGARCH, and CGARCH models, which are frequently used in comparison exercises. Next, three different measures of volatility accuracy, the MAE, the RMSE, and the coefficient of determination of the MZ regression, are employed in order to draw conclusions on the use of well-established volatility forecasting models and to make comparisons which are of interest not only for academics but also for practitioners and policy makers. Table 3.2 presents the findings of this exercise.

Looking at the results in Table 3.2, it appears that the CGARCH model, capturing the long memory effect, does a better overall job irrespective of the country/index and the statistical measure of volatility accuracy chosen. More specifically, when the MAE measure is used, in all countries, with the exception of Croatia, a smaller value is reported when the CGARCH model is used.

TABLE 3.2 Results for the Forecasting Performance of All the Sample Countries Using the Mean Absolute Error (MAE), the Root Mean Square Error (RMSE), and the Coefficient of Determination of the MZ Regression

Statistic	MAE			RMSE			Coefficient of determination (R^2)		
Country/model	G	EG	CG	G	EG	CG	G	EG	CG
Bulgaria	8.76E-05*	8.66E-05	7.95E-05†	0.00015*	0.00014	0.00013†	0.06755	0.07874†	0.06702*
Croatia	5.04E-05*	4.88E-05†	5.04E-05	8.27E-05*	8.16E-05†	8.26E-05	0.01223*	0.01344†	0.01247
Romania	0.00011*	0.00012	8.76E-05†	0.00017	0.00018*	0.00016†	0.04473*	0.04956	0.04984†
Ukraine	0.00020*	0.00019	0.00018†	0.00046*	0.00046*	0.00045†	0.03810*	0.03948	0.04434†
Kenya	3.79E-05*	3.63E-05	3.62E-05†	9.77E-05*	9.76E-05	9.57E-05†	0.03835	0.03251*	0.07213†
Mauritius	1.31E-05*	1.26E-05	9.94E-06†	1.78E-05	1.79E-05*	1.58E-05†	0.00151	0.00108*	0.00726†
Nigeria	7.84E-05	7.86E-05*	7.82E-05†	0.00013	0.00013	0.00012†	0.03532	0.03489*	0.03756†
Tunisia	2.67E-05	2.98E-05*	2.55E-05†	7.38E-05†	7.83E-05*	7.74E-05	0.00196†	0.00181	0.00047*

Notes: For the MAE and RMSE, the lowest value gives the best-performing model and the highest the worst-performing model. When the coefficient of determination of the MZ regression is used, the best-forecasting model is indicated by the highest value and the worst-performing by the lowest value. The best forecast is indicated by † and the worst by *.

When the RMSE measure is applied, apart from the case of Croatia, for which the EGARCH model appears to do a better job (this finding is reported for both measures MAE and RMSE), Tunisia gives the smallest RMSE value when the forecasting model used is the GARCH(1,1) model. A similar story is given also by the coefficient of determination of the MZ regression. The highest R^2s are reported when the CGARCH model is used in the forecasting exercise, with three exceptions out of eight countries: with Bulgaria and Croatia giving the highest coefficient of determination for the EGARCH model and Tunisia for the GARCH(1,1) model. In the case of Croatia, the EGARCH model is consistently found to be the best-performing model irrespective of which measure of volatility accuracy is used, and in the case of Tunisia in two out of three cases the GARCH(1,1) model gives a better result. On the other hand, in trying to identify the model that gives the least accurate forecast, the picture is mixed. When the MAE measure is used, the GARCH(1,1) model gives the highest value in six out of the eight countries, whereas when the RMSE measure is used in the same number of countries, the GARCH(1,1) and EGARCH models give the highest values. Finally, when the R^2 of the MZ regression is used for three countries, the lowest values are reported for the GARCH(1,1) and EGARCH models and for the CGARCH model in two cases.

Finding the winner of the forecasting exercise is not difficult, as it appears that the best forecasts are achieved when the long memory GARCH model, the CGARCH model, is used. This finding is different from what the academic literature has found in previous studies when similar volatility forecasting exercises were carried out; however, unlike in this study, the data sets used were from developed and emerging economies. For developed and emerging markets the asymmetric GARCH models have often provided the best forecasts, as seen in Brailsford and Faff (1996), Brooks et al. (2000), Hansen and Lunde (2005), Alberg et al. (2008), and Kambouroudis and McMillan (2015).

6 CONCLUSIONS AND FURTHER RESEARCH

The purpose of this chapter was to enter the ongoing debate within the topic of volatility forecasting regarding the best model for accurately forecasting volatility in frontier markets. A plethora of academic studies have been entering this debate, and for this reason several modeling aspects and factors have been considered over the years. However, the common element within those studies is that data from developed and emerging economies was considered with little or no consideration for frontier markets. Advances in information technology as well as investor interest have raised awareness for frontier markets, for which research is still at an early stage compared to research conducted on developed and emerging economies.

First, after establishing a sound theoretical framework and addressing the major developments within the volatility forecasting literature, a "horse race" exercise is performed using well-established forecasting models from the

ARCH genre of models known for their ability to capture the stylized characteristics found in stock market returns (more specifically, the GARCH model capturing the clustering effect, the EGARCH model capturing the asymmetry effect, and the CGARCH model taking into account the volatility persistence) on a sample of four European and four African frontier markets. With the use of three statistical measures of forecasting accuracy, the MAE, the RMSE, and the coefficient of determination of the MZ regression, after regressing true volatility on a constant and a forecast, the conclusion reached is that the CGARCH model is the best-performing model with very few exceptions. The academic literature in similar exercises has favored the asymmetric GARCH models, but these findings were based on data from developed and emerging economies.

This chapter sets the foundations and advocates the need for further research to be carried out using data from frontier markets. More volatility forecasting models and techniques should be considered, along with different sample periods as well as more frontier markets, so that better overall conclusions can be reached.

REFERENCES

Ahoniemi, K., 2008. Modelling and forecasting the VIX index, Unpublished working paper, Helsinki School of Economics and HECER.

Alberg, H., Shalit, D., Yosef, R., 2008. Estimating stock market volatility using asymmetric GARCH models. Appl. Financial Econ. 18, 1201–1208.

Andersen, T.G., Bollerslev, T., 1998. Answering the skeptics: yes, standard volatility models do provide accurate forecasts. Int. Econ. Rev. 39, 889–905.

Andersen, T.G., Bollerslev, T., Lange, S., 1999. Forecasting financial market volatility: sample frequency vis-à-vis forecast horizon. J. Empir. Finance 6, 457–477.

Antoniou, A., Ergul, N., Holmes, P., Priestley, R., 1997. The impact of regulatory changes on stock market volatility and the cost of equity capital: evidence from an emerging market. Eur. Financial Manag. 3 (2), 175–190.

Arestis, P., Demetriades, P., 1997. Financial development and economic growth: assessing the evidence. Econ. J. 107, 783–799.

Becketti, S., and Sellon, G.H., 1989. Has financial market volatility increased? Fed. Bank Ks. Econ. Rev. (June).

Berger, D., Punthuanthong, K., Yang, J.J., 2011. International diversification with frontier markets. J. Financial Econ. 101, 227–242.

Blair, B., Poon, S.H., Taylor, S.J., 2001. Forecasting S&P 100 volatility: the incremental information content of implied volatilities and high frequency index returns. J. Econometrics 105, 5–26.

Bollerslev, T., 1986. Generalised autoregressive conditional heteroskedasticity. J. Econometrics 31, 307–327.

Brailsford, T.J., Faff, R.W., 1996. An evaluation of volatility forecasting techniques. J. Bank. Finance 20, 419–438.

Brooks, R., Faff, R., McKenzie, M., Mitchell, H., 2000. A multi-country study of power ARCH models and national stock market returns. J. Int. Money Finance 19, 377–397.

Canina, L., Figlewski, S., 1993. The informational content of implied volatility. Rev. Financial Stud. 6, 659–681.

Carr, P., Wu, L., 2006. A tale of two indices. J. Deriv. 13 (3), 13–29.

Cumby, R., Figlewski, S., Hasbrouck, J., 1993. Forecasting volatilities and correlations with EGARCH models. J. Deriv. 1, 51–63.

Cunado, J., Biscarri, J., Gracia, F., 2006. Changes in the dynamic behaviour of emerging market volatility: revisiting the effects of financial liberalisation. Emerg. Markets Rev. 7, 261–278.

Diebold, F.X., and Lopez, J., 1996. Forecast evaluation and combination. In: Maddala, G.S., Rao, C.R., (Eds.), Handbook of Statistics. North-Holland, Amsterdam, pp. 241–268.

Economou, F., Gavriilidis, K., Kallinterakis, V., and Yordanov, N., 2015. Do fund managers herd in frontier markets—and why? Int. Rev. Financ. Anal. 40 (issue C), 76–87.

Engle, R.F., 1982. Autoregressive conditional heteroscedasticity with estimates of the variance of UK inflation. Econometrica 50, 987–1008.

Engle, R.F., Bollerslev, T., 1986. Modelling the persistence of conditional variances. Econometric Rev. 5, 1–50.

Engle, R.F., Lee, G.G.J., 1999. A permanent and transitory component model of stock return volatility. In: Engle, R.F., White, H. (Eds.), Cointegration, Causality and Forecasting: A Festschrift in Honour of Clive W J Granger. Oxford University Press, Oxford, UK.

Engle, R.F., and Patton, A.J., 2001. What good is a volatility model?, NYU. Archive from: http:// archive.nyu.edu/handle/2451/26881

Fama, E.F., 1965. The behavior of stock market prices. J. Bus. 38, 34–105.

Fernandes, M., Medeiros, M., Scharth, M., 2014. Modeling and predicting the CBOE market volatility index. J. Bank. Finance 40, 1–10.

Fifield, S.G.M., Lonie, A.A., Power, D.M., March 1998. A review of research into emerging stock markets. Econ. Issues 3 (1).

Figlewski, S., 1997. Forecasting volatility. Financ. Mark. Inst. Instrum. 6 (1), 1–88.

Fleming, J., Ostdiek, B., Whaley, R.E., 1995. Predicting stock market volatility: a new measure. J. Futures Markets 15 (3), 265–302.

Franses, P.H., Dijk, D., 1996. Forecasting stock market volatility using (nonlinear) GARCH models. J. Forecasting 15, 229–235.

Glosten, L., Jagannathan, R., Runkle, D., 1993. On the relation between the expected value and the volatility of nominal excess return on stocks. J. Finance 46, 1779–1801.

Grabel, I., 1995. Assessing the impact of financial liberalisation on stock market volatility in selected developing countries. J. Dev. Stud. 31, 903–917.

Hansen, P.R., Lunde, A., 2005. A forecast comparison of volatility models: does anything beat a GARCH(1,1)? J. Appl. Econom. 20, 873–889.

Hansen, P.R., Huang, Z., Shek, H.H., 2010. Realised GARCH: a joint model for returns and realised measures of volatility. J. Appl. Econom. 27 (6), 877–906, Available from: http://ssrn.com/abstract=1533475.

Jayasuriya, S., 2005. Stock market liberalisation and volatility in the presence of favourable market characteristics and institutions. Emerg. Mark. Rev. 6, 170–191.

Jorion, P., 1995. Predicting volatility in the foreign exchange market. J. Finance 50, 381–400.

Kambouroudis, D.S., 2012. Essays on volatility forecasting, PhD thesis, University of St Andrews. Available from: https://research-repository.st-andrews.ac.uk/handle/10023/3191

Kambouroudis, D.S., McMillan, D.G., 2015. Is there an ideal in-sample length for forecasting volatility? J. Int. Financ. Mark. Inst. Money 37, 114–137.

Kim, E.H., and Singal, V., 1993. Opening up to stock markets by emerging economies: effect on portfolio flows and volatility stock prices. In: Claessens, S., and Gooptu, S. (Eds.), Portfolio Investment in Developing Countries, World Bank Discussion Paper 228, September, pp. 383–403.

Kim, E., Singal, V., 2000. The fear of globalising capital markets. Emerg. Mark. Rev. 1, 183–198.

Konstantinidi, E., Skiadopoulos, G., Tsagkaraki, E., 2008. Can the evolution of implied volatility be forecasted? evidence from European and US implied indices. J. Bank. Finance 32, 2401–2411.

Mandelbrot, B., 1963. The variation of certain speculative prices. J. Bus. 36, 394–419.

Martens, M., Zein, J., 2004. Predicting financial volatility: high-frequency time-series forecasts vis-à-vis implied volatility. J. Futures Mark. 24 (11), 1005–1028.

McMillan, D.G., Kambouroudis, D., 2009. Are RiskMetrics forecasts good enough? evidence from 31 stock markets. Int. Rev. Financ. Anal. 18, 117–124.

McMillan, D.G., Speight, A., Ap Gwilym, O., 2000. Forecasting UK stock market volatility. Appl. Financ. Econ. 10, 435–448.

Mincer, J., Zarnowitz, V., 1969. The evaluation of economic forecasts. In: Mincer, J. (Ed.), Economic Forecasts and Expectations. Columbia University Press, New York, pp. 3–46.

Nelson, D.B., 1991. Conditional heteroscedasticity in asset returns: a new approach. Econometrica 59 (2), 347–370.

Pagan, A.R., Schwert, G.W., 1990. Alternative models for conditional stock volatility. J. Econometrics 45, 267–290.

Patton, A.J., 2011. Volatility forecast comparison using imperfect volatility proxies. J. Econometrics 160, 246–256.

Poon, S., Granger, C.W.J., 2003. Forecasting volatility in financial markets: a review. J. Econ. Lit. 41 (2), 478–539.

Richards, A.J., 1996. Volatility and predictability in national stock markets: how do emerging and mature markets differ? IMF Staff Papers 43 (3), 461–501.

Samarakoon, L.P., 2011. Stock market interdependence, contagion, and the U.S. financial crisis: the case of emerging and frontier markets. J. Int. Financ. Mark. Inst. Money 21, 724–742.

Schwert, G.W., 1990a. Stock market volatility. Financ. Anal. J. 46, 23–34.

Schwert, W.G., 1990b. Stock volatility and the crash of '87. Rev. Financ. Stud. 3 (1), 77–102.

Spyrou, I.S., Kassimatis, K., 1999. Did equity market volatility increase following the opening of emerging markets to foreign investors? J. Econ. Dev. 24 (1), 39–51.

Taylor, S.J., 1986. Modelling Financial Time Series. John Wiley & Sons, Chichester, UK.

Walsh, D.M., Tsou, G.Y.-G., 1998. Forecasting index volatility: sampling interval and non-trading effects. Appl. Financ. Econ. 8 (5), 477–485.

Wang, Y., Wu, C., 2012. Forecasting energy market volatility using GARCH models: can multivariate models beat univariate models? Energy Econ. 24, 2167–2181.

Whaley, R.E., 2009. Understanding VIX. J. Portfolio Manag. 35, 98–105.

White, H., 1980. A heteroscedasticity-consistent covariance matrix estimator and direct test for heteroscedasticity. Econometrica 48, 817–838.

Yang, M.J., Liu, M.-Y., 2012. The forecast of the volatility index in emerging markets: evidence from the Taiwan stock market. Int. J. Econ. Finance 4 (2), 217–231.

Chapter 4

Herd Behavior in Frontier Markets: Evidence from Nigeria and Morocco

F. Economou
Centre of Planning and Economic Research, Athens, Greece

Chapter Outline

1 INTRODUCTION

Financial crises and stock market crashes have clearly demonstrated the impact of investors' sentiment on asset pricing and stock markets' efficiency. Herd behavior, which is behavioral similarity based on individuals' interaction that leads to convergence of action and correlated trading (Hirshleifer and Teoh, 2003), is one of the most important behavioral biases that is more likely to occur during periods of market stress when individual investors prefer to follow the market consensus, being reluctant to follow their own knowledge or beliefs (Christie and Huang, 1995). Herding has been widely studied in financial markets (including the stock market, bond market, foreign exchange market, exchange-traded funds market, etc.), and it is evident in both retail and institutional investors' behavior.[a]

Herding can be rational when it relates to payoff externalities, informational learning, principal–agent, and reputation-based problems, or it can derive from behavioral factors (Devenow and Welch, 1996). In any case, this behavior has important implications for market efficiency and portfolio diversification. However, there is also spurious herding (ie, correlated decision making based

---

a. See Spyrou (2013) for a review regarding theory and empirical results of herding behavior in financial markets.

Handbook of Frontier Markets. http://dx.doi.org/10.1016/B978-0-12-803776-8.00004-5

on the same set of fundamental information rather than imitation), which does not cause market inefficiency (Bikhchandani and Sharma, 2000).

Even though empirical evidence of herding in developed and emerging markets is mixed based on the period and the market under examination, herding is expected to be more pronounced in emerging markets since their special characteristics (thin trading, incomplete regulatory framework and corporate information disclosure, low transparency, information asymmetries, etc.) may facilitate herding behavior (Kallinterakis and Kratunova, 2007).

In the same spirit, frontier markets are also expected to display herding behavior. Frontier markets are less developed and less liquid markets that are too small to be considered as emerging (Balcilar et al., 2015; De Groot et al., 2012) and are characterized by low trading volume, high concentration, difficult access, inexperienced market participants, incomplete institutional framework, and limited information disclosure (Economou et al., 2015b; Speidell and Krohne, 2007). Quisenberry (2010) employs the definition of Merrill Lynch, according to which a frontier market is characterized as an "emerging emerging market" (ie, a market that is expected to become emerging). There is growing interest in these markets since their low correlations both among them and with developed markets offer market diversification benefits for international portfolios (Berger et al., 2011; Cheng et al., 2009; Jayasuriya and Shambora, 2009; Speidell and Krohne, 2007). As a result, their stock market behavior should be further analyzed in order to enhance the understanding of frontier markets.

While there is a growing strand of literature about herd behavior in developed and emerging stock markets, the existing literature dealing with frontier markets is limited. Balcilar et al. (2014) examine the cash- and oil-rich Gulf Cooperation Council (GCC) markets, indicating strong and persistent evidence of herding in Dubai, Kuwait, Qatar, and Saudi Arabia, while there is less frequent herding in Abu Dhabi. The authors also establish a direct link between herding and market volatility, and document the impact of shocks due to global factors on herding. A previous study of the GCC frontier markets indicates the presence of three market regimes regarding volatility as well as crossmarket herding effects driven by common factors in the GCC, especially during periods of extreme volatility (Balcilar et al., 2013). The retail investors–dominated Saudi Arabia stock market has also been studied by Rahman et al. (2015). The authors find evidence of herding irrespective of market conditions, which is more pronounced during periods of positive market returns and higher trading activity. Apart from retail investors, herding is also evident in institutional investors in frontier markets. Economou et al. (2015b) indicate that fund managers in Bulgaria and Montenegro herd significantly and intentionally, with herding being stronger during periods of positive market returns and high volume as well as during low-volatility periods for Montenegro. Moreover, Bulgarian and Montenegrin fund managers herded significantly both before and after the outbreak of the global financial crisis.

In this chapter we extend the limited herding literature in frontier markets by examining herd behavior in two African frontier markets, namely Nigeria and

Morocco from 2004 to 2014 employing the cross-sectional dispersion of returns approach of Chang et al. (2000). Moreover, we test for possible asymmetries in herding estimations under different market states (up/down market returns, market volatility, and volume) as well as for the impact of additional explanatory variables, such as the oil price return, the US stock market return, and the US sentiment captured by the Chicago Board Options Exchange (CBOE) VIX index. The impact of the global financial crisis on the two markets under examination also provides interesting insight into the international stock markets dynamics.

The rest of the chapter is structured as follows: Section 2 presents the methodology and the data set employed in order to examine herding in frontier markets, Section 3 reports the empirical results and finally Section 4 offers conclusions.

2   METHODOLOGY AND DATA

2.1   Methodology

Herding has been examined in many different contexts in the financial markets employing different methodological approaches based either on portfolio holdings or on stock market returns. In this chapter we employ the cross-sectional dispersion approach, which is based on the seminal work of Christie and Huang (1995) and Chang et al. (2000). The authors propose an intuitive measure to capture herding and argue that in the presence of herding the cross-sectional dispersion of individual asset returns tends to decrease. The cross-sectional dispersion of returns is calculated as follows:

$$CSAD_t = \frac{\sum_{k=1}^{N}|R_{i,t} - R_{m,t}|}{N} \tag{4.1}$$

where $R_{i,t}$ is the return of stock i on day t, $R_{m,t}$ is the stock market return on day t, and N is the number of all listed stocks in the market on day t. The stock market return is defined as the equally weighted average return of all the individual stocks on day t.

Rational asset pricing models predict an increasing linear relationship between the cross-sectional absolute deviation (CSAD) and stock market return since the individual stocks differ in their sensitivity to the market return. On the other hand, Christie and Huang (1995) suggest that investors are more likely to act in a correlated manner during periods of extreme market returns and market stress resulting in reduced cross-sectional dispersion of returns.

The nonlinear model of Chang et al. (2000) (CCK model) is used in order to capture the relationship between the CSAD and the market return as follows:

$$CSAD_{m,t} = a + \gamma_1|R_{m,t}| + \gamma_2 R_{m,t}^2 + u_t \tag{4.2}$$

where all variables are already defined. Rational pricing models predict a linear relationship with a positive and statistically significant coefficient γ_1. In the presence of herding, the relationship is nonlinear and coefficient γ_2 is expected to be negative and statistically significant; that is, the CSAD increases but at a decreasing rate.

We further examine whether herding displays an asymmetric behavior under different market states as it is usually reported by previous literature (Economou et al., 2011; Chiang and Zheng, 2010; Chiang et al., 2010). To this end we employ a single equation with a dummy variable that enables us to reestimate the model for up/down market days, high/low market volatility days, and high/low trading volume days as follows:

$$
\begin{aligned}
CSAD_{m,t} = a + \gamma_1 D^{\text{up}} \left| R_{m,t} \right| + \gamma_2 D^{\text{up}} R_{m,t}^2 + \gamma_3 (1 - D^{\text{up}}) \left| R_{m,t} \right| \\
+ \gamma_4 (1 - D^{\text{up}}) R_{m,t}^2 + u_t
\end{aligned}
\tag{4.3}
$$

where D^{up} is a dummy variable that takes the value 1 on days with positive market returns/high market volatility/high volume and the value 0 otherwise. In order to identify high market volatility and high volume days, we compare market volatility/volume on day t with the 30-day moving average, and if it is higher D^{up} takes the value 1 and the value 0 otherwise.

Empirical results on asymmetric herd behavior are mixed, depending on the period and market under examination. However, herding is expected to be more pronounced during periods of market stress that are usually characterized by negative market returns (Chang et al., 2000; Chiang and Zheng, 2010; Mobarek et al., 2014), increased market volatility, and increased trading volume (Tan et al., 2008; Economou et al., 2011). As a result, we examine whether coefficient γ_2 is greater than coefficient γ_4 in Eq. 4.3 and whether the difference is statistically significant.

Moreover, since the sample period is quite long, ranging from 2004 to 2014, the global financial crisis that started from the US market may considerably affect herding estimations. Samarakoon (2011) provides empirical evidence of interdependence and contagion in frontier markets to US shocks which is more pronounced during crises, also indicating that the global financial crisis was more contagious for frontier markets (especially for markets with nonoverlapping trading activity with the United States, which respond with 1-day lag) than for emerging markets. In the same spirit, Chen et al. (2014) documented that leading stock markets (US and regional leading markets) Granger-cause frontier equity markets, a relationship that is largely influenced by the global financial crisis. The results are less significant after the crisis, and each individual frontier market differs in its relationship with the leading market. These findings indicate reduced diversification benefits during the global financial crisis period even when investing in frontier markets. In this case we would also expect herding to be more pronounced under extreme US market conditions. In order to test this hypothesis, we reestimate the benchmark model as follows:

$$
\begin{aligned}
CSAD_{m,t} = a + \gamma_1 D^{\text{crisis}} \left| R_{m,t} \right| + \gamma_2 D^{\text{crisis}} R_{m,t}^2 + \gamma_3 (1 - D^{\text{crisis}}) \left| R_{m,t} \right| \\
+ \gamma_4 (1 - D^{\text{crisis}}) R_{m,t}^2 + u_t
\end{aligned}
\tag{4.4}
$$

where D^{crisis} is a dummy variable that takes the value 1 during the global financial crisis of 2007–09 and the value 0 otherwise.

Finally, following Balcilar et al. (2014), we augment the benchmark model with several global market factors that may have an impact on the stock markets under examination such as the oil price return and the US stock market return captured by the S&P 500 index. Additionally, we test for the impact of the US sentiment captured by the CBOE VIX index in the same spirit with Economou et al. (2015a) and Philippas et al. (2013). In order to test these hypotheses, the benchmark model is restated as follows:

$$CSAD_{m,t} = a + \gamma_1 |R_{m,t}| + \gamma_2 R_{m,t}^2 + \gamma_3 R_{i,t}^2 + u_t \qquad (4.5)$$

where $R_{i,t}$ is the return of the crude oil, S&P 500, and CBOE VIX indices, respectively. Eq. 4.5 enables us to test whether herding is more pronounced in the stock markets under examination under extreme changes in the crude oil prices, the US stock market, and the US sentiment (ie, whether coefficient γ_3 is negative and statistically significant).

2.2   Data

Several African countries with developing financial markets have attracted research interest, being also likely to attract investors' interest as part of a second generation of emerging markets (Nellor, 2008). Fig. 4.1 depicts the considerable increase of the MSCI Frontier Markets Africa Index from May 2002 to the first quarter of 2008 and from 2011 to 2014. The index captures mid-cap and

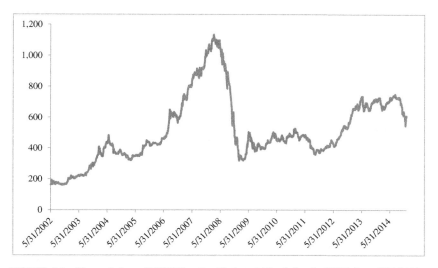

FIGURE 4.1   The evolution of MSCI Frontier Markets Africa Index (in USD) from 5/31/2002 to 12/31/2014. *(Source: Thomson-Reuters Datastream.)*

TABLE 4.1 Descriptive Statistics

	Nigeria		Morocco		Other factors		
	CSAD	Market	CSAD	Market	S&P 500	CBOE VIX	Crude oil Brent
Mean	1.0212	−0.0009	0.6823	0.0093	0.0099	−0.0149	0.0123
Median	0.9676	−0.0114	0.6556	0.0188	0.0319	−0.2341	0.0286
Maximum	11.1977	5.3372	4.7429	2.4099	4.7587	21.5414	5.8649
Minimum	0.0990	−6.5567	0.1515	−1.9719	−4.1126	−15.2259	−4.8326
Std. dev.	0.5606	0.4795	0.2302	0.3561	0.5386	2.9455	0.8618
Observations	2655	2655	2748	2748	2655	2655	2655

large-cap representations of five African frontier markets (Nigeria, Morocco, Kenya, Mauritius, and Tunisia). Nigeria and Morocco represented 74.17% of the index country weights (52.73% Nigeria and 21.44% Morocco) in Dec. 2014.

In this chapter we constructed a survivor-bias-free data set including both active and dead stocks at any time during the period 2004–14. We employ percentage log-differenced returns calculated as follows for all listed equities in Nigeria and Morocco:

$$R_{i,t} = 100 \times [\log(P_{i,t}) - \log(P_{i,t-1})] \tag{4.6}$$

where $P_{i,t}$ is the daily closing price of every stock i on day t, derived from the Thomson–Reuters Datastream database.

Trying to reduce the impact of thin trading on our estimations, we employ only stocks that displayed trading activity[b] on day t, and their number ranged between 8 and 161 for Nigeria and between 12 and 63 for Morocco. Table 4.1 reports the descriptive statistics for the markets under examination as well as for the additional explanatory variables employed in Eq. 4.5. The sample consists of 2655 daily observations for Nigeria and 2748 daily observations for Morocco.

3 EMPIRICAL RESULTS

Table 4.2 reports the empirical results of the benchmark CCK model estimation (Eq. 4.1). Coefficient γ_1 is positive and statistically significant for both Nigeria and Morocco, whereas coefficient γ_2 is positive and statistically significant

---

b. Stocks that did not display any trading activity on day t were removed from the sample in order to avoid biased herding estimations.

TABLE 4.2 Estimates of the Standard CCK (2000) Model

	Constant	$|R_{m,t}|$	$R^2_{m,t}$	R^2 adj.
Nigeria	0.8134 (38.70)***	0.5242 (6.39)***	0.2126 (7.38)***	71.47%
Morocco	0.5669 (34.53)***	0.4085 (3.14)***	0.0747 (0.46)	27.08%

Notes: This table reports the estimated coefficients of the CCK (2000) model. $CSAD_{m,t} = a + \gamma_1|R_{m,t}| + \gamma_2 R^2_{m,t} + u_t$, where $CSAD_{m,t}$ is the cross-sectional absolute deviation of the individual stock returns and $R_{m,t}$ is the return for each market m The sample consists of daily data from 2004 to 2014. t-statistics are given in parentheses using Newey–West (1987) heteroscedasticity- and autocorrelation-consistent standard errors. ***, **, and * represent statistical significance at the 1, 5, and 10% levels, respectively.

only for Nigeria. As a result, there is no evidence of herding employing the benchmark model for the entire sample period. The estimated relationship for Morocco is linear and increasing, consistent with the predictions of the rational pricing models. On the other hand, the relationship for Nigeria is positive and nonlinear, providing evidence of antiherding.

However, herd behavior may exist under different market states. Table 4.3 reports the results of the CCK model during up and down market returns. Overall, there is no evidence of asymmetric herding behavior during up and down market days. Coefficients γ_2 and γ_4 are both positive and statistically significant for Nigeria and statistically insignificant for Morocco.

Testing for possible asymmetries during up and down market volatility days indicates the existence of herding during down market volatility days for Nigeria (Table 4.4), while there is no evidence of asymmetric herding during up and down volume days (Table 4.5). Coefficients γ_2 and γ_4 remain statistically insignificant for Morocco in all the model specifications for possible herding asymmetries.

Moreover, we examine the impact of the global financial crisis of 2007–09 on herding estimations (Table 4.6). The results for Nigeria do not indicate herding either before, during, or after the crisis. However, there is evidence of herding in Morocco during the global financial crisis, with coefficient γ_2 being negative and statistically significant at the 10% significance level. This is the only evidence of herding for Morocco for the whole sample period.

Table 4.7 reports the results of augmenting the benchmark model with several explanatory variables that may relate to pronounced herding (ie, crude oil returns, the US stock market returns captured by the S&P 500, and the US "fear index," the CBOE VIX index). Overall, it seems that there is herding toward the US market only in Nigeria, while we do not report any statistically significant result for the rest of the examined variables. This finding is in line with previous literature regarding Nigeria indicating that US investor sentiment is more important than local factors (Todorov and Bidarkota, 2013). There is no evidence of herding for Morocco, and the addition of several explanatory variables does not affect our initial conclusions.

TABLE 4.3 Estimates of the CCK (2000) Model During Up and Down Periods of the Market

	Constant	$D^{up}\lvert R_{m,t}\rvert$	$D^{up} R^2_{m,t}$	$(1-D^{up})\lvert R_{m,t}\rvert$	$(1-D^{up}) R^2_{m,t}$	R^2 adj.
Nigeria	0.8200 (41.67)***	0.4910 (6.32)***	0.2572 (9.80)***	0.4961 (6.11)***	0.1916 (7.49)***	72.11%
Morocco	0.5665 (36.30)***	0.3240 (2.70)***	0.1404 (0.92)	0.5100 (3.65)***	−0.0022 (−0.01)	27.67%

Wald tests for equality of herding coefficients

	Nigeria	Morocco
$\gamma_1 - \gamma_3$ t-statistic, H_0: $\gamma_1 = \gamma_3$	−0.0051 (−0.07)	−0.1859 (−2.06)**
$\gamma_2 - \gamma_4$ t-statistic, H_0: $\gamma_2 = \gamma_4$	0.0656 (1.87)*	0.1425 (0.98)

Notes: This table reports the estimated coefficients of the CCK model during up and down periods of the market:
$$CSAD_{m,t} = a + \gamma_1 D^{up}\lvert R_{m,t}\rvert + \gamma_2 D^{up} R^2_{m,t} + \gamma_3 (1 - D^{up})\lvert R_{m,t}\rvert + \gamma_4 (1 - D^{up}) R^2_{m,t} + u_t,$$ where $CSAD_{m,t}$ is the cross-sectional absolute deviation of the individual stock returns, $R_{m,t}$ is the return for each market m, and D^{up} is a dummy variable that takes the value 1 on days with positive market returns and the value 0 otherwise. The sample consists of daily data from 2004 to 2014. t-statistics are given in parentheses using Newey–West (1987) heteroscedasticity- and autocorrelation-consistent standard errors. ***, **, and * represent statistical significance at the 1, 5, and 10% levels, respectively. t-statistics and the Wald tests for the null hypothesis $\gamma_1 = \gamma_3$ and $\gamma_2 = \gamma_4$ in the estimated model are reported in the lower panel.

TABLE 4.4 Estimates of the CCK (2000) Model During Up and Down Periods of Market Volatility

	Constant	$D^{up vol}|R_{m,t}|$	$(1 - D^{up vol})|R_{m,t}|$	$D^{up vol} R^2_{m,t}$	$(1 - D^{up vol}) R^2_{m,t}$	R^2 adj.
Nigeria	0.7557 (32.57)***	0.5968 (6.69)***	1.2239 (8.72)***	0.2017 (6.92)***	−0.8252 (−4.85)***	72.14%
Morocco	0.5685 (37.42)***	0.3911 (2.96)***	0.3705 (2.83)***	0.0858 (0.52)	0.2661 (1.06)	27.22%

Wald tests for equality of herding coefficients

	Nigeria	Morocco
$\gamma_1 - \gamma_3$	−0.6271	0.0205
t-statistic, H_0: $\gamma_1 = \gamma_3$	(−7.79)***	(0.25)
$\gamma_2 - \gamma_4$	1.0269	−0.1803
t-statistic, H_0: $\gamma_2 = \gamma_4$	(6.54)***	(−0.92)

Notes: This table reports the estimated coefficients of the CCK model during up and down periods of the market:
$CSAD_{m,t} = a + \gamma_1 D^{up vol}|R_{m,t}| + \gamma_2 D^{up vol} R^2_{m,t} + \gamma_3 (1 - D^{up vol})|R_{m,t}| + \gamma_4 (1 - D^{up vol}) R^2_{m,t} + u_t$, where $CSAD_{m,t}$ is the cross-sectional absolute deviation of the individual stock returns, $R_{m,t}$ is the return for each market m, and $D^{up vol}$ is a dummy variable that takes the value 1 on days with high market volatility and the value 0 otherwise. The sample consists of daily data from 2004 to 2014. t-statistics are given in parentheses using Newey–West (1987) heteroscedasticity- and autocorrelation-consistent standard errors. ***, **, and * represent statistical significance at the 1, 5, and 10% levels, respectively. t-statistics and the Wald tests for the null hypothesis $\gamma_1 = \gamma_3$ and $\gamma_2 = \gamma_4$ in the estimated model are reported in the lower panel.

TABLE 4.5 Estimates of the CCK (2000) Model During Up and Down Periods of Market Volume

	Constant	$D^{up\,vo}|R_{m,t}|$	$D^{up\,vo}R^2_{m,t}$	$(1-D^{up\,vo})|R_{m,t}|$	$(1-D^{up\,vo})R^2_{m,t}$	R^2 adj.
Nigeria	0.8145 (38.56)***	0.4679 (6.31)***	0.2426 (8.30)***	0.5542 (5.74)***	0.2018 (6.34)***	71.66%
Morocco	0.5633 (46.75)***	0.4017 (2.97)***	0.1011 (0.54)	0.4746 (7.12)***	−0.0287 (−0.35)	27.37%

Wald tests for equality of herding coefficients

	Nigeria	Morocco
$\gamma_1 - \gamma_3$		
t-statistic, H_0: $\gamma_1 = \gamma_3$	−0.0863 (−1.15)	−0.0729 (−0.68)
$\gamma_2 - \gamma_4$		
t-statistic, H_0: $\gamma_2 = \gamma_4$	0.0407 (1.03)	0.1298 (0.74)

Notes: This table reports the estimated coefficients of the CCK model during up and down periods of the market: $CSAD_{m,t} = a + \gamma_1 D^{up\,vo}|R_{m,t}| + \gamma_2 D^{up\,vo}R^2_{m,t} + \gamma_3(1 - D^{up\,vo})|R_{m,t}| + \gamma_4(1 - D^{up\,vo})R^2_{m,t} + u_t$, where $CSAD_{m,t}$ is the cross-sectional absolute deviation of the individual stock returns, $R_{m,t}$ is the return for each market m, and $D^{up\,vo}$ is a dummy variable that takes the value 1 on days with high market volume and the value 0 otherwise. The sample consists of daily data from 2004 to 2014. t-statistics are given in parentheses using Newey–West (1987) heteroscedasticity- and autocorrelation-consistent standard errors. ***, **, and * represent statistical significance at the 1, 5, and 10% levels, respectively. t-statistics and the Wald tests for the null hypothesis $\gamma_1 = \gamma_3$ and $\gamma_2 = \gamma_4$ in the estimated model are reported in the lower panel.

TABLE 4.6 Estimates of the CCK (2000) Model During the Global Financial Crisis

	Constant	$D^{crisis}|R_{m,t}|$	$D^{crisis} R_{m,t}^2$	$(1-D^{crisis})|R_{m,t}|$	$(1-D^{crisis}) R_{m,t}^2$	R^2 adj.
Nigeria	0.8190 (40.69)***	0.5602 (6.43)***	0.1805 (7.30)***	0.4636 (5.65)***	0.2602 (10.06)***	72.05%
Morocco	0.5693 (42.78)***	0.4446 (6.42)***	−0.0854 (−1.76)*	0.3505 (2.81)***	0.2138 (1.19)	29.38%

Wald tests for equality of herding coefficients

	Nigeria	Morocco
$\gamma_1 - \gamma_3$	0.0966	0.0941
t-statistic, $H_0: \gamma_1 = \gamma_3$	(1.11)	(0.92)
$\gamma_2 - \gamma_4$	−0.0796	−0.2992
t-statistic, $H_0: \gamma_2 = \gamma_4$	(−2.39)**	(−1.83)*

Notes: This table reports the estimated coefficients of the CCK model during the global financial crisis and before/after the crisis period:
$CSAD_{m,t} = a + \gamma_1 D^{crisis}|R_{m,t}| + \gamma_2 D^{crisis} R_{m,t}^2 + \gamma_3 (1-D^{crisis})|R_{m,t}| + \gamma_4 (1-D^{crisis})R_{m,t}^2 + u_t$, where $CSAD_{m,t}$ is the cross-sectional absolute deviation of the individual stock returns, $R_{m,t}$ is the return for each market m, and D^{crisis} is a dummy variable that takes the value 1 during the global financial crisis of 2007–09 and the value 0 otherwise. The sample consists of daily data from 2004 to 2014. t-statistics are given in parentheses using Newey–West (1987) heteroscedasticity- and autocorrelation-consistent standard errors. ***, **, and * represent statistical significance at the 1, 5, and 10% levels, respectively. t-statistics and the Wald tests for the null hypothesis $\gamma_1 = \gamma_3$ and $\gamma_2 = \gamma_4$ in the estimated model are reported in the lower panel.

TABLE 4.7 Estimates of the Standard CCK (2000) Model Augmented with Additional Variables

Panel A	Constant	$|R_{m,t}|$	$R^2_{m,t}$	$R^2_{oil,t}$	R^2 adj.
Nigeria	0.8897 (49.48)***	0.2906 (5.20)***	0.2048 (13.28)***	−0.0006 (−0.12)	64.94%
Morocco	0.5667 (32.93)***	0.4126 (3.18)***	0.0736 (0.45)	−0.0013 (−0.43)	27.21%
Panel B	**Constant**	$|R_{m,t}|$	$R^2_{m,t}$	$R^2_{S\&P500,t}$	R^2 adj.
Nigeria	0.8188 (39.98)***	0.5398 (6.54)***	0.2099 (7.29)***	−0.0340 (−5.36)***	72.13%
Morocco	0.5659 (33.17)***	0.4058 (3.08)***	0.0762 (0.46)	0.0038 (0.68)	27.01%
Panel C	**Constant**	$|R_{m,t}|$	$R^2_{m,t}$	$R^2_{VIX,t}$	R^2 adj.
Nigeria	0.8162 (39.31)***	0.5290 (6.36)***	0.2117 (7.33)***	−0.0005 (−1.34)	72.13%
Morocco	0.5642 (33.98)***	0.4057 (3.08)***	0.0775 (0.47)	0.0003 (1.53)	27.06%

Notes: This table reports the estimated coefficients of the CCK (2000) model: $CSAD_{m,t} = a + \gamma_1|R_{m,t}| + \gamma_2 R^2_{m,t} + \gamma_3 R^2_{i,t} + u_t$, where $CSAD_{m,t}$ is the cross-sectional absolute deviation of the individual stock returns, $R_{m,t}$ is the return for each market m, and $R_{i,t}$ is the return of the crude oil, S&P 500, and VIX indices in panels A, B, and C, respectively. The sample consists of daily data from 2004 to 2014. t-statistics are given in parentheses using Newey–West (1987) heteroscedasticity- and autocorrelation-consistent standard errors. ***, **, and * represent statistical significance at the 1, 5, and 10% levels, respectively.

Finally, since the employed sample covers a long period, apart from the impact of the global financial crisis, we have also tested for structural breaks that would affect herding estimations. We have endogenously identified the structural breaks for the two markets under examination using the Quandt–Andrews break point test, and the results indicate Oct. 28, 2008, for Nigeria and Dec. 1, 2005, for Morocco as structural breaks. Even though the results remain qualitatively the same before and after the structural break for Nigeria,[c] there is evidence of herding in Morocco during the second subperiod from Dec. 1, 2005, to Dec. 31, 2014. The results of the estimated coefficients and t-statistics of the benchmark model for the period from Dec. 2005 to Dec. 2014 are the following:

$$CSAD_{m,t} = \underset{(63.57)}{0.57} + \underset{(17.37)}{0.58}|R_{m,t}| - \underset{(-7.26)}{0.18}R^2_{m,t} + u_t, \quad R^2 \text{ adj. } 24.01\% \quad (4.7)$$

c. The empirical results for Nigeria are qualitatively the same for the two subperiods, and we do not report them in the chapter in the interest of brevity. The results are available on request.

Coefficient γ_2 is negative and statistically significant, indicating the presence of herding behavior for the subperiod under examination. When we reestimate all model specifications for Morocco for possible asymmetric herding behavior, herding is evident on days with both up and down market returns as reported in Eq. 4.8, and on days with high market volatility Eq. 4.9) and trading volume (Eq. 4.10). Adjusted R^2 is close to 24% for all model specifications.[d]

$$
\begin{aligned}
CSAD_{m,t} = \underset{(62.93)}{0.57} + \underset{(13.48)}{0.57^{\text{up}}}\left|R_{m,t}\right| \underset{(-4.82)}{-0.20 D^{\text{up}}} R^2_{m,t} \\
+ \underset{(15.01)}{0.61}(1 - D^{\text{up}})\left|R_{m,t}\right| - \underset{(-6.65)}{0.20}(1 - D^{\text{up}})R^2_{m,t} + u_t
\end{aligned}
\tag{4.8}
$$

$$
\begin{aligned}
CSAD_{m,t} = \underset{(52.75)}{0.57} + \underset{(16.30)}{0.57 D^{\text{up vol}}}\left|R_{m,t}\right| \underset{(-6.55)}{-0.18 D^{\text{up vol}}} R^2_{m,t} \\
+ \underset{(5.93)}{0.53}(1 - D^{\text{up vol}})\left|R_{m,t}\right| \underset{(-0.26)}{-0.05}(1 - D^{\text{up vol}})R^2_{m,t} + u_t
\end{aligned}
\tag{4.9}
$$

$$
\begin{aligned}
CSAD_{m,t} = \underset{(61.84)}{0.57} + \underset{(16.88)}{0.63 D^{\text{up vo}}}\left|R_{m,t}\right| \underset{(-9.78)}{-0.24 D^{\text{up vo}}} R^2_{m,t} \\
+ \underset{(9.79)}{0.50}(1 - D^{\text{up vo}})\left|R_{m,t}\right| \underset{(-1.28)}{-0.08}(1 - D^{\text{up vo}})R^2_{m,t} + u_t
\end{aligned}
\tag{4.10}
$$

4   CONCLUSIONS

Even though investor psychology and its impact on asset allocation and pricing have been examined in developed markets, frontier markets have not been widely analyzed. The documented international portfolio diversification benefits that are related to investments in frontier markets necessitate an in-depth examination of herding behavior in these markets since correlated trading patterns that exist in the presence of herding may reduce diversification benefits.

In this chapter we examine herding in two African frontier markets that have not been analyzed earlier, using daily data for the period 2004–14. The empirical results employing the benchmark Chang et al. (2000) model do not indicate evidence of herding. However, when testing for asymmetries in herding estimations, we identified herding during down market volatility days for Nigeria. Moreover, there is evidence of herding during the global financial crisis only in Morocco. Finally, testing for the impact of additional variables on herding estimations indicates that there is herding toward the US market in Nigeria (ie, CSAD in Nigeria is reduced under extreme market returns in the US market). Finally, testing for structural breaks reveals significant evidence of herding in Morocco for the subperiod from Dec. 2005 to Dec. 2014, with herding being more pronounced during days of high market volatility and volume.

---

d. There is no evidence of herding being made more pronounced by extreme changes in oil prices, the S&P 500, or the CBOE VIX index under the model specification of Eq. 4.5; the results are not reported in the chapter in the interest of brevity but are available upon request.

The empirical results offer useful insight for both retail and institutional investors who consider asset allocation in these stock markets to be particularly beneficial due to the international portfolio diversification benefits they bear. Correlated return patterns that exist in the presence of herding along with higher transaction costs charged in frontier markets (Marshall et al., 2015) may significantly reduce diversification benefits and investment performance.

Future research should further examine additional explanatory variables that may induce herding and that are not related to the market returns. For example, the impact of domestic market sentiment and crossmarket herding with neighboring (or other) stock markets should also be tested in order to better understand domestic market investors' behavior as well as the magnitude of international diversification benefits.

REFERENCES

Balcilar, M., Demirer, R., Hammoudeh, S., 2013. Investor herds and regime-switching: evidence from Gulf Arab stock markets. J. Int. Financ. Mark. Inst. Money 23, 295–321.

Balcilar, M., Demirer, R., Hammoudeh, S., 2014. What drives herding in oil-rich, developing stock markets? Relative roles of own volatility and global factors. N. Am. J. Econ. Financ. 29, 418–440.

Balcilar, M., Demirer, R., Hammoudeh, S., 2015. Regional and global spillovers and diversification opportunities in the GCC equity sectors. Emerg. Mark. Rev. 24, 160–187.

Berger, D., Pukthuanthong, K., Yang, J.J., 2011. International diversification with frontier markets. J. Financ. Econ. 101, 227–242.

Bikhchandani, S., Sharma, S., 2000. Herd behavior in financial markets. IMF Staff Papers, 279–310.

Chang, E.C., Cheng, J.W., Khorana, A., 2000. An examination of herd behavior in equity markets: an international perspective. J. Bank. Financ. 24, 1651–1679.

Chen, M.P., Chen, P.F., Lee, C.C., 2014. Frontier stock market integration and the global financial crisis. N. Am. J. Econ. Financ. 29, 84–103.

Cheng, A., Jahan-Parvar, M., Rothman, P., 2009. An empirical investigation of stock market behavior in the Middle East and North Africa. J. Empir. Financ. 17, 283–538.

Chiang, T.C., Li, J., Tan, L., 2010. Empirical investigation of herding behavior in Chinese stock markets: evidence from quantile regression analysis. Global Financ. J. 21, 111–124.

Chiang, T.C., Zheng, D., 2010. An empirical analysis of herd behavior in global stock markets. J. Bank. Financ. 34, 1911–1921.

Christie, W.G., Huang, R.D., 1995. Following the pied piper: do individual returns herd around the market? Financ. Anal. J. 51, 31–37.

De Groot, W., Pang, J., Swinkels, L., 2012. The cross-section of stock returns in frontier emerging markets. J. Empir. Financ. 19, 796–818.

Devenow, A., Welch, I., 1996. Rational herding in financial economics. Eur. Econ. Rev. 40, 603–615.

Economou, F., Kostakis, A., Philippas, N., 2011. Cross-country effects in herding behavior: evidence from four south European markets. J. Int. Financ. Mark. Inst. Money 21, 443–460.

Economou, F., Gavriilidis, K., Goyal, A., Kallinterakis, V., 2015a. Herding dynamics in exchange groups: evidence from Euronext. J. Int. Financ. Mark. Inst. Money 34, 228–244.

Economou, F., Gavriilidis, K., Kallinterakis, V., Yordanov, N., 2015b. Do fund managers herd in frontier markets—and why? Int. Rev. Financ. Anal. 40, 76–87.

Hirshleifer, D., Teoh, S.H., 2003. Herd behaviour and cascading in capital markets: a review and synthesis. Eur. Financ. Manage. 9, 25–66.

Jayasuriya, S., Shambora, W., 2009. Oops, we should have diversified! Appl. Financ. Econ. 19, 1779–1785.

Kallinterakis, V., Kratunova, T., 2007. Does thin trading impact upon the measurement of herding? Evidence from Bulgaria. Ekonomia 10, 42–65.

Marshall, B.R., Nguyen, N.H., Visaltanachoti, N., 2015. Frontier market transaction costs and diversification. J. Financ. Mark. 24, 1–24.

Mobarek, A., Mollah, S., Keasey, K., 2014. A cross-country analysis of herd behavior in Europe. J. Int. Financ. Mark. Inst. Money 32, 107–127.

Nellor, D., 2008. The rise of Africa's "frontier" markets, finance and development. IMF Magazine 45, 30–33.

Newey, W., West, K., 1987. A simple, positive semi-definite, heteroskedasticity and autocorrelation consistent covariance matrix. Econometrica 55, 703–708.

Philippas, N., Economou, F., Babalos, V., Kostakis, A., 2013. Herding behavior in REITs: novel tests and the role of financial crisis. Int. Rev. Financ. Anal. 29, 166–174.

Quisenberry, C., 2010. Exploring the frontier emerging equity markets. CFA Inst. Conf. Proc. Quart. 27, 40–53.

Rahman, M.A., Chowdhury, S.S.H., Sadique, M.S., 2015. Herding where retail investors dominate trading: the case of Saudi Arabia. Quart. Rev. Econ. Financ. 57, 46–60.

Samarakoon, L.P., 2011. Stock market interdependence, contagion, and the US financial crisis: the case of emerging and frontier markets. J. Int. Financ. Mark. Inst. Money 21, 724–742.

Speidell, L., Krohne, A., 2007. The case for frontier equity markets. J. Investing 16, 12–22.

Spyrou, S., 2013. Herding in financial markets: a review of the literature. Rev. Behav. Financ. 5, 175–194.

Tan, L., Chiang, T.C., Mason, J.R., Nelling, E., 2008. Herding behavior in Chinese stock markets: an examination of A and B shares. Pacific-Basin Financ. J. 16, 61–77.

Todorov, G., Bidarkota, P., 2013. On international financial spillovers to frontier markets. Int. J. Econ. Bus. Res. 5, 433–452.

Chapter 5

Effects of Interest Rates and Exchange Rates on Bank Stock Returns

E. Katsikas*, S. Brahma**, S.M. Wangeci[†]
*Kent Business School, University of Kent, United Kingdom; **Glasgow Caledonian University Business School, Glasgow, United Kingdom; [†]Adam Smith Business School, University of Glasgow, Glasgow, United Kingdom

Chapter Outline

1 INTRODUCTION

Banks are believed to be more sensitive to interest rates (IR) risk because of a mismatch of maturities between assets and liabilities (Lloyd and Shick, 1977; Faff and Howard, 1999; Kasman et al., 2011). Faff et al. (1999) stated that banks are more sensitive to IR because IR are directly fed into input costs, operating margins, and the demand for services by customers. Globalization is another factor that increases exposure to IR risk (Choi et al., 1992; AtindeÂhou and Gueyie, 2001; Kutty, 2010; Kurmann, 2014; Kasman et al., 2011).

The empirical literature documents mixed evidence on the effects of IR on BSR (Lloyd and Shick, 1977;Lynge and Zumwalt, 1980; Sweeney and Warga, 1986; Kane and Unal, 1988; Faff et al., 1999). In the context of developed countries, some studies have attributed the relationship between IR and bank stock returns (BSR) to economic policies such as deregulation (Flannery and James, 1984; Faff et al., 1999). Empirical literature on the relationship between FX and BSR reports the relationship as being negative (Choi et al., 1992; AtindeÂhou and Gueyie, 2001). Recent studies state that BSR are

Handbook of Frontier Markets. http://dx.doi.org/10.1016/B978-0-12-803776-8.00005-7

becoming less sensitive to IR and FX risk due to improved risk mitigation strategies such as IR derivative markets and expansion of corporate bond markets (Alam and Uddin, 2009; Kurmann, 2014). Kurmann (2014) found that European bank returns were less sensitive to changes in IR risk as compared with BSR in the US market. However, this risk declined over time due to improved risk management methods, such as the use of derivatives. Kurmann (2014) also documented that US banks were more sensitive to foreign exchange rates (FX) risk than European banks for the whole sample period. However, the sensitivity of BSR to FX was reported to be insignificant only after the introduction of the euro in the late 1990s (Kurmann, 2014; Francis and Hunter, 2004). This was attributed to counterparty risk the banks were exposed to due to hedging through currency swaps.

In the context of developing countries, Kasman et al. (2011) and Alam and Uddin (2009) found that banks were exposed to IR and FX risks due to lack of mitigation techniques in these countries. Hooy et al. (2004) showed that during the postcrisis period IR and FX had a significant relationship with BSR, attributing this to unsystematic risk due to government policies such as mandatory consolidation programs for all large banks. Uddin and Alam (2007) and Mukit (2012) found a negative and significant relationship between IR and BSR and a positive and significant relationship between FX and BSR in the context of Asian markets. Similar evidence was also obtained by Kutty (2010) in the context of the Mexican economy. Kurmann (2014) documented a negative relationship between IR and BSR. Overall, empirical studies of both developed and developing countries provide mixed evidence about the effects of IR and FX on BSR. In addition, very few studies are based on developing countries.

Since 2000, Kenya has witnessed significant FDI (foreign direct investment) from several countries. For instance, China has embarked on roughly 65 projects in Kenya with a total cost in the range of $108 million. Two such projects are the construction of the North and East Ring Road sections in Nairobi and the Kenyatta University Teaching, Research and Referral Hospital (Strange et al., 2013). This also makes this research timely in investigating the relationship between Kenyan BSR and IR and FX.

This research is motivated by the portfolio adjustment approach theory, which states that BSR are positively related to exchange risk (Kutty, 2010; Tabak, 2006). This theory also documents that cash flows of foreign capital are dependent on stock prices. Higher stock prices lead to an inward flow of foreign capital into the economy and vice versa. When the latter occurs, there is a decline in the demand for money that then leads to a reduction of IR in an effort to increase demand. As a result, foreign country investment increases to take advantage of lower IR, consequently leading to depreciation of the local currency.

The key contributions of this research are the following: this is the first research in a Kenyan context to empirically examine the effects of both IR and FX on BSR. This is also the first research that examines this relationship during the 2007–08 election violence period.

1.1 Data and Methodology

Two types of IR from the Kenya National Bureau of Statistics have been selected for the study to represent short-term and long-term IR, respectively: 91-day Treasury bill returns and 182-day Treasury bill returns. Their use follows the example of studies by Choi et al. (1992), AtindeÂhou and Gueyie (2001), and Faff and Howard (1999). Monthly inflation rates for the same period used in these studies—Jan. 2004 to Dec. 2013—were obtained for the purpose of calculating real IR returns. In addition, a simple basket of two equally weighted major currencies, the US dollar and the Kenyan shilling, was used as the FX variable. A directly quoted FX—that is, the price of the US dollar expressed in Kenya shillings—was used. The Nairobi Stock Exchange 20-Share Index (NSE 20) was used to represent the market index. The NSE 20 is a price-weighted index of 20 blue-chip companies that has been in use since 1964 (Nairobi Stock Exchange, 2014). The NSE is the leading securities exchange in East Africa.

For the bank data, last day stock prices of eight major commercial banks in Kenya were collected, namely:

Barclays Bank (BB)
CFC Bank (CFC)
Diamond Trust Bank (DTB)
Kenya Commercial Bank (KCB)
National Bank of Kenya (NBK)
National Industrial Credit Bank (NIC Bank)
Standard Chartered Bank (SCB)
Housing Finance (HF)

These banks were selected based on the fact that they were the only banks listed in the NSE 20 with data for the selected period; they are locally owned and are among the top 200 banks in Africa (Central Bank of Kenya, 2013). In total, 120 values were observed for each of the independent and dependent variables from Jan. 2004 to Dec. 2013. Information on bank stock prices, FX, and the market index were obtained from Bloomberg's financial software, while information on short-term IR and inflation rates was obtained from the Central Bank of Kenya website.

Another aim of the research was to investigate how the relationship between IR, FX, and the BSR was affected by the 2007–08 election violence. Hence, the period under study was further subdivided into three other periods, namely: Jan. 2004 to Nov. 2007, Dec. 2007 to Aug. 2010, and Sep. 2010 to Dec. 2013. They represent the periods of preelection violence, election violence, and postelection violence, respectively. While the period of election violence lasted till Feb. 28, 2008, this research extends that period until Aug. 2010, when the new constitution was inaugurated and received the support of 67% of the population. The period after the election violence marked the next significant period for Kenya.

The IR were converted from annualized returns to monthly returns using the following formulas. This was done so as to match them with the rest of the monthly data.

$$SIR = \left[(1 + SIR_{\text{ANNUAL}})^{1/12} - 1 \right] \qquad (5.1)$$

$$LIR = \left[(1 + LIR_{\text{ANNUAL}})^{1/12} - 1 \right] \qquad (5.2)$$

Furthermore, their returns were calculated using the following formulae:

$$RSIR = \text{Log}\left(\frac{SIR_t}{SIR_{t+1}} \right) \qquad (5.3)$$

$$RLIR = \text{Log}\left(\frac{LIR_t}{LIR_{t+1}} \right) \qquad (5.4)$$

where SIR_t and LIR_t are the short-term and long term interest rates at time t, respectively, while SIR_{t+1} and LIR_{t+1} the short-term and long-term interest rate at time $t + 1$.

Moreover, monthly logarithmic returns on bank i at time t BSR_{it} were calculated using the following formulas:

$$BSR_{it} = \text{Log}\left(\frac{P_t}{P_{t+1}} \right) \qquad (5.5)$$

where P_t and P_{t+1} are the prices of the bank stock at time t and time $t + 1$, respectively. In addition, a simple average of all bank returns was calculated to generate a proxy for a portfolio of bank stock returns, BSR_{At}. Next, returns for the market index $RNSE20_t$ and returns on the exchange rate RFX_t were calculated, as shown in the formulas, respectively,

$$RM_t = \text{Log}\left(\frac{NSE20_t}{NSE20_{t+1}} \right) \qquad (5.6)$$

$$RFX_t = \text{Log}\left(\frac{FX_t}{FX_{t+1}} \right) \qquad (5.7)$$

where $NSE20_t$ and $NSE20_{t+1}$ are the prices of NSE20 index at time t and $t + 1$, respectively, while FX_t and FX_{t+1} are the exchange rates at time t and time $t + 1$, respectively. It is important to point out that in this research, a gain in the US dollar results in an increase in the exchange rate; hence positive returns on the exchange rate (RFX) means a depreciation of the Kenyan shilling (Kshs), and vice versa.

Table 5.1 shows the summary statistics for individual BSR, and graphical representations of returns on the portfolio of bank stock, FX, the market, and both short- and long-term IR are also presented later.

TABLE 5.1 Descriptive Statistics on Individual Bank Stock Returns

Returns	Mean	Median	Max	Min	Std. dev.	Jarque-Bera	Probability
Barclays	0.0038	0.0140	0.3257	−0.2877	0.1005	18.0667	0.0001
KCB	0.0151	0.0175	0.3131	−0.2975	0.0981	10.0521	0.0066
SCB	0.0046	0.0073	0.2050	−0.2918	0.0709	50.6453	0.0000
CFC	0.0043	0.0000	0.3942	−0.4610	0.1122	44.0535	0.0000
DTB	0.0156	0.0213	0.2066	−0.3437	0.0886	59.8699	0.0000
HF	0.0043	0.0028	0.4185	−0.3972	0.1448	2.6854	0.2611
NBK	0.0031	−0.0064	0.3692	−0.5884	0.1305	59.1711	0.0000
NIC	0.0124	0.0095	0.3663	−0.2281	0.1000	8.2043	0.0165

Notes: Barclays Bank, CFC Bank (CFC), Diamond Trust Bank (DTB), Kenya Commercial Bank (KCB), National Bank of Kenya (NBK), National Industrial Credit Bank (NIC), Standard Chartered Bank (SCB), Housing Finance (HF).

The Jarque-Bera (JB) test statistic has been used to test normal distribution of the data.[a] Table 5.1 shows that all the banks are normally distributed except Housing Finance that has a probability value greater than 0.05. Generally, average returns for the banks shown are low, ranging from Diamond Trust Bank's return of 0.0156 (1.56%) to National Bank of Kenya's return of 0.0031 (0.31%). Interestingly, the average stock returns of Housing Finance and CFC Bank are the same: 0.43%.

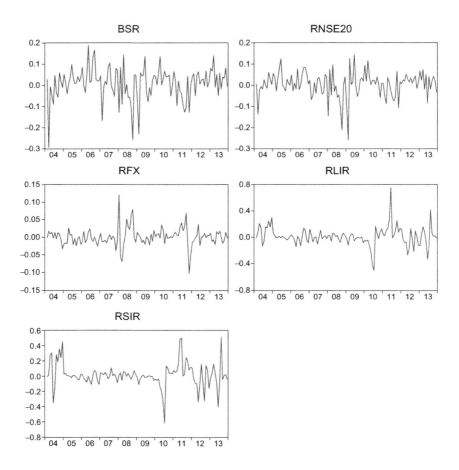

The variable returns are plotted graphically as shown. These graphs suggest that BSR and market index returns (RNSE20) generally followed the same trend over the years. Similarly, both short- and long-term IR followed the same trend

---

a. The JB test statistic measures the difference between the skewness and kurtosis of the series and those from a normal distribution.

for the whole period. Between 2007 and early 2009, all returns—apart from IR—rose and fell sharply. In addition, this was the period in which the Kenyan shilling was at its weakest (note that positive RFX implies depreciation in the Kenyan shilling and vice versa) and the market returns were at their lowest. This can be attributed to the election violence of 2007–08. Additionally, looking at the period between 2010 and 2013, returns on IR shifted up and down greatly in 2010 and reached their lowest point average of 0.4% then, probably due to the Aug. 2010 inauguration of the new constitution, while in 2011 and 2013 they reached their highest point. The year 2004 is also marked by low bank, market, and FX returns. It is evident from Table 5.1 that all of the average returns on all variables and averages for real IR and FX were positive. All of the variables except the actual FX were normally distributed variables. This is evident from the JB test statistic.

Following the empirical literature, this study adopted a multivariate ordinary least squares (OLS) regression. First, returns on BSR and portfolio of banks returns were regressed against returns on the market index, the nominal IR, and nominal FX:

$$BSR_{it} = \alpha_1 + \beta_m RM_t + \beta_{rs} RSIR_t + \beta_{rl} RLIR_t + \beta_{rf} RFX_t + U_t \cdot \qquad (5.8)$$

where α_1 is the slope coefficient, β_m represents the sensitivity of BSR to market returns, β_{rs} the sensitivity of BSR to returns of short-term IR, β_{rl} the sensitivity of BSR to long-term interest rate returns, and finally, β_{rf} the sensitivity of BSR to returns on FX. Next, BSR and portfolio of bank returns were regressed against real short-term interest rates (*SIR*), real long-term interest rates (*LIR*), and real FX, as represented in Model 2:

$$BSR_{it} = \alpha_1 + \beta_m RM_t + \beta_{as} SIR_t + \beta_{al} LIR_t + \beta_{af} FX_t + U_t \qquad (5.9)$$

The various βs represent the different sensitivities of different variables to BSR: β_{as} to actual short-term IR, β_{al} to actual long-term IR, and β_{af} to actual FX, while the other variables are as discussed in Model 1. It was discussed in the review of the literature that inflation rates can change the relationship of IR and BSR. Hence, changes in inflation rates were added into Models 1 and 2. Model 3 shows the adjusted Model 1:

$$BSR_{it} = \alpha_1 + \beta_m RM_t + \beta_{rs} RSIR_t + \beta_{rl} RLIR_t + \beta_{rf} RFX_t + \beta_{ri} RINF_t + U_t \qquad (5.10)$$

The variable β_{ri} represents the sensitivity of BSR to changes in inflation rates (*RINF*), while all other variables remain unchanged. Next, Model 4 shows the adjusted Model 2:

$$BSR_{it} = \alpha_1 + \beta_m RM_t + \beta_{as} SIR_t + \beta_{al} LIR_t + \beta_{af} FX_t + \beta_{ai} INF_t + U_t \qquad (5.11)$$

The variable β_{ai} represents the sensitivity of bank returns to inflation rates (*INF*). As before, all other variables remain unchanged. The variable BSR_{it} represents the portfolio of banks returns.

First a normality test was carried out.

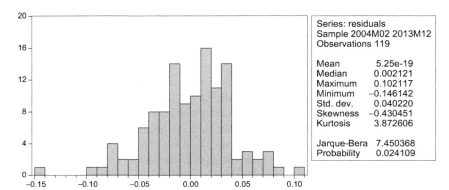

GRAPH FOR MODEL 1

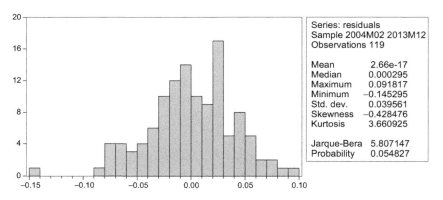

GRAPH FOR MODEL 2

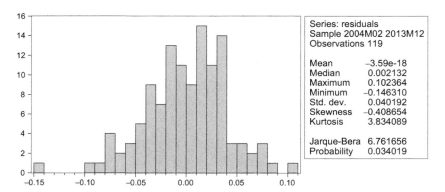

GRAPH OF MODEL 3

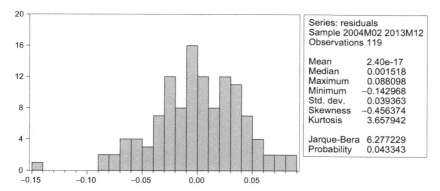

GRAPH OF MODEL 4

The JB probabilities for Models 1, 3, and 4 are 0.0241, 0.034091, and 0.043343, respectively. This suggests that all the residuals are normally distributed. Model 2 had a JB probability of 0.054827, again implying that the residuals were normally distributed and that the t- and F-tests can be used in inference. The mean of the residuals from Models 1, 3, and 4 were small: 5.25e-19, −3.259e-18, and 2.40e-17. This make the OLS estimators unbiased and improved the validity of inferences made from the F- and t-tests of the models' regressions (Burke, 2010).

As mentioned before, in order to examine how BSR were affected by the 2007–08 election violence in Kenya, the sample has been divided into three subperiods. They are: the preelection violence period of Jan. 2004 to Nov. 2007, which gave a total of 47 observations; the election violence period of Dec. 2007 to Aug. 2010, which gave 34 observations; and the postelection violence period of Sep. 2010 to Dec. 2013, which had a total of 41 observations. Even though the number of observations for the various periods varied, each had a significant number of observations to run a regression that would elaborate the relationship between the BSR and both the IR and FX. This was done by regressing Models 1 and 2 for each of the subperiods. Models 3 and 4 are excluded, as inflation rates showed a general lack of significance in changing the relationship between bank stock, the IR, and the FX.

1.2   Results and Analysis

Table 5.2 shows the regression in Eq. 5.8 that tested the relationship between individual BSR and the portfolio of banks returns, and returns of short-term nominal IR, long-term nominal IR, and nominal FX. The coefficients of exchange rate β_{rf} and interest rates β_{rs} and β_{ls} are significant in explaining both the returns of individual banks and the portfolio of banks returns. The coefficient of short-term IR is positive and significant, while the coefficient of long-term IR is negative and significant with respect to the overall portfolio of bank

TABLE 5.2 Results From Estimating Regression Model 1 Using Returns of Short-Term Interest Rates, Long-Term Interest Rates, and Exchange Rates (Jan. 2004 to Dec. 2013)

Banks	α_t	β_m	β_{rs}	β_{rl}	β_{rf}	R^2
Barclays Bank	−0.0011***	1.2565	0.022***	−0.0008	−0.0003**	0.5706
	(−0.0062)	(−0.1071)	(−0.098)	(−0.1094)	(−0.0025)	
Kenya Commercial Bank	0.0111***	1.1890	−0.08*	0.0749	−0.002***	0.5592
	(−0.0061)	(−0.106)	(−0.0964)	(−0.1082)	(−0.0025)	
Standard Chartered Bank	0.0030***	0.6877*	0.0531*	−0.1599*	0.0024***	0.3645
	−0.0053	−0.0919	−0.0836	−0.0939	−0.0021	
CFC Bank	0.0027***	0.7265	0.0225	−0.1017	−0.0023***	0.1762
	−0.0096	−0.1657	−0.1507	−0.1692	−0.0039	
Diamond Trust Bank	0.0131**	0.9183	−0.0269*	−0.0168	−0.0031***	0.4342
	−0.0063	−0.1085	−0.0987	−0.1108	−0.0025	
Housing Finance	0.001***	1.3891***	−0.0295	−0.1158	0.0000***	0.3527
	−0.0109	−0.1895	−0.1724	−0.1936	−0.0044	
National Bank of Kenya	−0.0027***	1.4185***	−0.0112	0.0517	0.0008***	0.4238
	−0.0093	−0.1613	−0.1467	−0.1647	−0.0038	
NIC Bank	0.0084***	1.0177	0.0559	−0.0554	0.0003***	0.373
	−0.0074	−0.1289	−0.1173	−0.1317	−0.003	
Portfolio Bank Returns	0.0044***	1.0754**	0.0007*	−0.0405*	−0.0005***	0.725
	−0.0038	−0.0655	−0.0595	−0.0669	−0.0015	

Notes: Significance at 1%, ***; at 5%, **; at 10%, *; standard errors are enclosed in parentheses.

Model: $BSR_{it} = \alpha_t + \beta_m RM_t + \beta_{rs} RSIR_t + \beta_{rl} RLIR_t + \beta_{rf} RFX_t + U_t$

where BSR_{it} is bank stock returns for bank i and the portfolio of banks at time t, RM_t is market returns of the NSE 20 index, $RSIR_t$ is returns on short-term interest rates at time t, $RLIR_t$ is returns on long-term interest rates at time t, RFX_t is returns on exchange rates at time t, and U_t is the error term.

returns. The coefficient of nominal FX is negative and significant with respect to portfolio bank returns. The market index coefficient β_m is positive and significant with respect to portfolio bank returns. This supports results from previous research that stated that the market index is most significant in explaining banks stock returns (Kasman et al., 2011). There was no significant difference in the relationship between the individual bank returns and portfolio of banks returns and the independent variables. The major difference was that the portfolio returns model had the highest R^2 (0.725), which implies that this model is a better fit to the data, compared to the other models.

The relationships between individual bank returns and the portfolio of bank returns, and real short-term IR, real long-term IR, and real FX are shown in Table 5.3.

Consistent with Model 1, market returns are positive and significant with respect to portfolio bank returns. However, the coefficients of short-term and long-term IR are insignificant with respect to portfolio bank returns. Also consistent with Model 1, the coefficient of real exchange is negative and significant with respect to portfolio bank returns.

Tables 5.4 and 5.5 show the results after adding the inflation rate variable. Consistent with Tables 5.2 and 5.3, the coefficient of market returns is positive and significant while the coefficient of the exchange rate is negative and significant with respect to bank portfolio returns. Both IR were still insignificant. The coefficients of changes in inflation rates in Table 5.4 and inflation rates in Table 5.5 are both positive and significant.

Regressions in Tables 5.6–5.8 were run to investigate how the relationships between individual BSR and the portfolio of banks returns, and real short-term and long-term IR and real FX were affected during the 2007–08 election violence period. Results from Table 5.6 for the preelection violence period showed that in this period, the market index was positive but insignificant. The coefficients of both real short- and long-term IR were also insignificant. The exchange rate coefficients were positive and highly significant with respect to average bank returns.

Table 5.7 shows the results for the election violence period. It was evident that in this period, the coefficients of both short-term IR and long-term IR were insignificant, as in the previolence period. The coefficients of FX were again positive and highly significant with respect to average bank returns.

Table 5.8 shows the results in the postelection violence period. The results are similar to Tables 5.6 and 5.7 in relation to IR. However, the FX were negative and significant with respect to average bank returns.

This study also conducted regressions on Model 1 for the three subperiods that began with the preelection violence period. The results are shown in Tables 5.9–5.11.

The regression results of the effects of nominal IR and nominal FX on BSR are similar to the results of effects of real IR and real FX, as depicted in Tables 5.6–5.8, in the sense that neither the market returns nor the nominal

TABLE 5.3 Results From Estimating Regression Model 2 Using Real Short-Term Interest Rates, Real Long-Term Interest Rates, and Real Exchange Rates (Jan. 2004 to Dec. 2013)

Banks	α_1	β_m	β_{as}	β_{al}	β_{af}	R^2
Barclays Bank	0.0337*	1.2597	0.0615	−0.0675	0.0004***	0.5706
	−0.0745	−0.1029	−0.1691	−0.1699	−0.0009	
Kenya Commercial Bank	0.1055*	1.0000	0.1331	−0.1103	−0.0013***	0.5641
	−0.0733	−0.1012	−0.1663	−0.1671	−0.0009	
Standard Chartered Bank	0.0601*	0.6559*	0.0707	−0.0805	−0.0006***	0.3169
	−0.0663	−0.0916	−0.1504	−0.1512	−0.0008	
CFC Bank	−0.0209	0.7574	−0.1158	0.1128	0.0002***	0.1651
	−0.116	−0.1602	−0.2632	−0.2645	−0.0014	
Diamond Trust Bank	0.1293*	0.9495	0.2643	−0.2711	−0.0013***	0.4377
	−0.0752	−0.1039	−0.1707	−0.1715	−0.0009	
Housing Finance	0.206	1.3730	0.7759	−0.7849	−0.0021***	0.3715
	−0.1298	−0.1794	−0.2947	−0.2962	−0.0016	
National Bank of Kenya	0.1793	1.3946	0.2393	−0.2345	−0.0022***	0.4352
	−0.111	−0.1533	−0.2519	−0.2532	−0.0014	
NIC Bank	0.1477*	1.0049	0.2173	−0.2209	−0.0016***	0.3857
	−0.0887	−0.1226	−0.2013	−0.2024	−0.0011	
Portfolio Bank Returns	0.1051**	1.0743**	0.2058	−0.2071	−0.0012***	0.7339
	−0.0448	−0.0618	−0.1016	−0.1021	−0.0006	

Notes: Significance at 1%, ***; at 5%, **; and at 10%, *.
P values are enclosed in parentheses.
Model: $BSR_t = \alpha_t + \beta_m RM_t + \beta_{as} SIR_t + \beta_{al} LIR_t + \beta_{af} FX_t + U_t$,
where BSR_{it} is bank stock returns for bank i and the portfolio of banks at time t, RM_t is market returns of the NSE 20 index at time t, SIR_t is real short-term interest rates at time t, LIR_t is real long-term interest rates at time t, FX_t is real exchange rates at time t, and U_t is the error term.

TABLE 5.4 Results From Estimating Model 3 With the Inclusion of Changes in Inflation Rates (Jan. 2004 to Dec. 2013)

Banks	α_1	β_m	β_{rs}	β_{rl}	β_{rf}	β_{ri}	R^2
Barclays Bank	−0.0012*	1.2578	0.0218	0.0002	−0.0003**	0.0068**	0.5708
	(0.0062)	(0.1077)	(0.0979)	(0.1100)	(0.0025)	(0.0298)	
Kenya Commercial Bank	0.1052*	1.2036	0.1257	−0.1035	−0.0014***	0.0004***	0.5649
	(0.0735)	(0.1019)	(0.1676)	(0.1683)	(0.0009)	(0.0009)	
Standard Chartered Bank	0.0030***	0.6886*	0.0530*	−0.1592*	0.0024***	0.0048**	0.3647
	(0.0053)	(0.0925)	(0.0840)	(0.0944)	(0.0022)	(0.0256)	
CFC Bank	0.0027***	0.7287	0.0221	−0.1001	−0.0024***	0.0113**	0.1766
	(0.0096)	(0.1666)	(0.1513)	(0.1701)	(0.0039)	(0.0461)	
Diamond Trust Bank	0.0130***	0.9202	−0.0272*	−0.0153	−0.0032***	0.0099**	0.4347
	(0.0063)	(0.1091)	(0.0991)	(0.1113)	(0.0026)	(0.0302)	
Housing Finance	0.0009***	1.3942	−0.0302	−0.1121	−0.0001***	0.0262**	0.3541
	(0.0110)	(0.1904)	(0.1730)	(0.1944)	(0.0045)	(0.0527)	
National Bank of Kenya	−0.0028***	1.4248	−0.0122	0.0564	0.0005***	0.0331**	0.4265
	(0.0093)	(0.1618)	(0.1470)	(0.1652)	(0.0038)	(0.0448)	
NIC Bank	0.0084***	1.0154	0.0562	−0.0572	0.0004***	−0.0123***	0.3736
	(0.0075)	(0.1296)	(0.1177)	(0.1323)	(0.0030)	(0.0359)	
Average Bank Returns	0.0044***	1.0768*	0.0005*	−0.0394*	−0.0006***	0.0072**	0.7254
	(0.0038)	(0.0658)	(0.0598)	(0.0672)	(0.0015)	(0.0182)	

Notes: Significance at 1%, ***; at 5%, **; and at 10%, *.
P values are enclosed in parentheses.

Model: $BSR_{it} = \alpha_i + \beta_m RM_t + \beta_{rs} RSIR_t + \beta_{rl} RLIR_t + \beta_{rf} RFX_t + \beta_{ri} RINF_t + U_t$

where BSR_{it} is bank stock returns for bank i and the portfolio of banks at time t, RM_t is market returns of the NSE 20 index at time t, $RSIR_t$ is returns on short-term interest rates at time t, $RLIR_t$ is returns on long-term interest rates at time t, RFX_t is returns on exchange rates at time t, $RINF_t$ is changes in interest rates at time t, and U_t is the error term.

TABLE 5.5 Results From Estimating Model 4 With the Inclusion of Inflation Rates (Jan. 2004 to Dec. 2013)

Banks	α_1	β_m	β_{as}	β_{al}	β_{af}	β_{ai}	R^2
Barclays Bank	0.0331*	1.2683	0.0455	−0.0529	−0.0005***	0.0009***	0.5741
	(0.0745)	(0.1033)	(0.1699)	(0.1706)	(0.0009)	(0.0009)	
Kenya Commercial Bank	0.0112***	1.1848	−0.0794*	0.071683	−0.0019***	−0.0224**	0.5614
	(0.0061)	(0.1063)	(0.0966)	(0.1085)	(0.0025)	(0.0294)	
Standard Chartered Bank	0.0597*	0.6611*	0.0610	−0.0715	−0.0007***	0.0005*	0.3196
	(0.0664)	(0.0921)	(0.1515)	(0.1521)	(0.0008)	(0.0807)	
CFC Bank	−0.0203	0.7484	−0.0989	0.0974	0.0004***	−0.0009***	0.1683
	(0.1163)	(0.1612)	(0.2651)	(0.2662)	(0.0015)	(0.1412)	
Diamond Trust Bank	0.1286*	0.9598	0.2450	−0.2534	−0.0014***	0.0011***	0.4444
	(0.0751)	(0.1041)	(0.1712)	(0.1719)	(0.0009)	(0.0912)	
Housing Finance	0.2046	1.3920	0.7403	−0.7524	−0.0024***	0.0020	0.3800
	(0.1295)	(0.1796)	(0.2954)	(0.2966)	(0.0016)	(0.1573)	
National Bank of Kenya	0.1784	1.4074	0.2153	−0.2125	−0.0024***	0.0013	0.4400
	(0.1110)	(0.1539)	(0.2531)	(0.2542)	(0.0014)	(0.1348)	
NIC Bank	0.1481*	0.9991	0.2281	−0.2308	−0.0015***	−0.0006	0.3874
	(0.0890)	(0.1234)	(0.2029)	(0.2038)	(0.0011)	(0.1080)	
Portfolio Bank Returns	0.1047**	1.0799*	0.195	−0.1975	−0.001***	0.00006*	0.7366
	(0.0447)	(0.0620)	(0.1020)	(0.1024)	(0.0006)	(0.0543)	

Notes: Significance at 1%, ***; at 5%, **; and at 10%, *.
P values are enclosed in parentheses.
Model: $BSR_{it} = \alpha_1 + \beta_m RM_t + \beta_{as} SIR_t + \beta_{al} LIR_t + \beta_{af} FX_t + \beta_{ai} INF_t + U_t$
where SIR_t represents real short-term interest rates at time t, LIR_t represents real long-term interest rates at time t, FX_t represents real exchange rates at time t, INF_t represents inflation rates at time t, U_t is the error term, and β_{ai} represents the sensitivity of bank stock returns of bank i and the portfolio of bank stock returns to inflation rates.

TABLE 5.6 Results From Regressing Model 2 for the Preelection Violence Period (Jan. 2004 to Nov. 2007); 46 Observations for Each Regression

Banks	α_1	β_m	β_{as}	β_{al}	β_{af}	R^2
Barclays Bank	0.3366	1.611	−0.0859	0.0444	−0.0044***	0.5378
	(0.2433)	(0.2458)	(0.2799)	(0.3179)	(0.0028)	
Kenya Commercial Bank	0.0206**	1.3488	0.2302	−0.5797	−0.4402***	0.4402
	(0.0123)	(0.2497)	(0.1983)	(0.2902)	(0.0080)	
Standard Chartered Bank	0.4234	1.1501	0.1032	−0.1758	−0.0052***	0.3836
	(0.2404)	(0.2429)	(0.2766)	(0.3142)	(0.0028)	
CFC Bank	0.0625	1.0691	−0.2642	0.2578	−0.0010***	0.1967
	(0.3527)	(0.3564)	(0.4059)	(0.4610)	(0.0041)	
Diamond Trust Bank	0.2865	0.7968	0.3049	−0.2118	−0.0042***	0.3376
	(0.2668)	(0.2695)	(0.3070)	(0.3486)	(0.0031)	
Housing Finance	1.0677	2.1175	1.6022	−1.8441	−0.0113***	0.4266
	(0.4806)	(0.4856)	(0.5530)	(0.6280)	(0.0055)	
National Bank of Kenya	0.1659	1.6712	0.5822	−0.5883	−0.0018***	0.3273
	(0.4301)	(0.4345)	(0.4949)	(0.5620)	(0.0050)	
NIC Bank	0.8246	1.3341	0.4445	−0.5974	−0.0095***	0.3724
	(0.3080)	(0.3112)	(0.3544)	(0.4024)	(0.0036)	
Average Bank Returns	0.0033***	1.4035	0.2248	−0.4237	0.0001***	0.6919
	(0.0073)	(0.1475)	(0.1171)	(0.1714)	(0.0047)	

Notes: Significance at 1%, ***; at 5%, **; and at 10%, *.
P values are enclosed in parentheses.
Model: $BSR_{it} = \alpha_i + \beta_m RM_t + \beta_{as} SIR_t + \beta_{al} LIR_t + \beta_{af} FX_t + U_t$,
where BSR_{it} is bank stock returns for bank i and the portfolio of banks at time t, RM_t is market returns at time t, SIR_t is real short-term interest rates at time t, LIR_t is real long-term interest rates at time t, FX_t is real exchange rates at time t, and U_t is the error term.

TABLE 5.7 Results of Regression Model 2 for the Election Violence Period (Dec. 2007 to Aug. 2010); 33 Observations for Each Model

Banks	α_t	β_m	β_{as}	β_{al}	β_{af}	R^2
Barclays Bank	−0.1066	1.0223*	−0.1713	0.1463	0.0015***	0.8299
	(0.1411)	(0.0917)	(0.4845)	(0.4416)	(0.0017)	
Kenya Commercial Bank	0.0028***	1.1125	−0.2686	0.4127	−0.0011***	0.7974
	(0.0102)	(0.1274)	(0.2809)	(0.2884)	(0.0031)	
Standard Chartered Bank	0.1020	0.3908*	−0.0501	−0.0950	−0.0001***	0.5969
	(0.1234)	(0.0802)	(0.4237)	(0.3862)	(0.0015)	
CFC Bank	0.1005	0.6314	−1.1865	0.7888	0.0009***	0.3456
	(0.3810)	(0.2475)	(1.3083)	(1.1926)	(0.0045)	
Diamond Trust Bank	−0.0116	1.0478	−0.4514	0.3515	0.0008***	0.7446
	(0.1925)	(0.1250)	(0.6609)	(0.6024)	(0.0023)	
Housing Finance	−0.2365	1.0987	−0.9163	0.7709	0.0036***	0.4635
	(0.3800)	(0.2469)	(1.3049)	(1.1895)	(0.0045)	
National Bank of Kenya	0.2167	1.3136	−0.2285	0.2877	−0.0033***	0.7131
	(0.2596)	(0.1686)	(0.8913)	(0.8125)	(0.0031)	
NIC Bank	0.1601	0.8116	−0.1243	−0.0159	−0.0011***	0.5544
	(0.2391)	(0.1554)	(0.8211)	(0.7485)	(0.0029)	
Average Bank Returns	0.0331	0.9348*	−0.3725	0.2752	0.0001***	0.8460
	(0.1257)	(0.0817)	(0.4316)	(0.3934)	(0.0015)	

Notes: Significance at 1%, ***; at 5%, **; and at 10%, *.
P-values are enclosed in parentheses.
Model: $BSR_{it} = \alpha_i + \beta_m RM_t + \beta_{as} SIR_t + \beta_{al} LIR_t + \beta_{af} FX_t + U_t$
where BSR_{it} is bank stock returns for bank i and the portfolio of banks at time t, RM_t is market returns of the NSE 20 index at time t, SIR_t is real short-term interest rates at time t, LIR_t is real long-term interest rates at time t, FX_t is real exchange rates at time t, and U_t is the error term.

TABLE 5.8 Results From Regressing Model 2 for the Postelection Violence Period (Sep. 2010 to Dec. 2013); 44 Observations for Each Regression

Banks	α_1	β_m	β_{as}	β_{al}	β_{af}	R^2
Barclays Bank	−0.1286	1.7387	0.1189	−0.1516	0.0018***	0.5436
	(0.2569)	(0.2724)	(0.2974)	(0.2941)	(0.0031)	
Kenya Commercial Bank	0.0209***	1.4086	−0.1081	0.0901	−0.0056***	0.6109
	(0.0089)	(0.1951)	(0.1134)	(0.1187)	(0.0034)	
Standard Chartered Bank	0.2613	0.8622	−0.2584	0.2447	−0.0030***	0.4904
	(0.1679)	(0.1780)	(0.1944)	(0.1922)	(0.0020)	
CFC Bank	0.3044	0.2337	−0.0891	0.1415	−0.0040***	0.0897
	(0.3224)	(0.3420)	(0.3733)	(0.3692)	(0.0038)	
Diamond Trust Bank	0.3370	0.6402	−0.0318	−0.0013	−0.0034***	0.3425
	(0.1869)	(0.1982)	(0.2164)	(0.2139)	(0.0022)	
Housing Finance	0.3418	1.3376	0.0870	−0.1086	−0.0037***	0.5131
	(0.2318)	(0.2459)	(0.2684)	(0.2654)	(0.0028)	
National Bank of Kenya	0.0094	1.4480	−0.1210	0.0820	0.0001***	0.4075
	(0.2877)	(0.3052)	(0.3332)	(0.3295)	(0.0034)	
NIC Bank	0.3221	1.2018	−0.0980	0.0900	−0.0036***	0.4673
	(0.2316)	(0.2456)	(0.2682)	(0.2652)	(0.0028)	
Average Bank Returns	0.2470	1.094	−0.0396	0.0281	−0.0027***	0.7573
	(0.1093)	(0.1159)	(0.1265)	(0.1251)	(0.0013)	

Notes: Significance at 1%, ***; at 5%, **; and at 10%, *.
P values are enclosed in parentheses.
Model: $BSR_{it} = \alpha_i + \beta_m RM_t + \beta_{as} SIR_t + \beta_{al} LIR_t + \beta_{af} FX_t + U_t$
where BSR_{it} is bank stock returns for bank i and the portfolio of banks at time t, RM_t is market returns of the NSE 20 index at time t, SIR_t is real short-term interest rates at time t, LIR_t is real long-term interest rates at time t, FX_t is real exchange rates at time t, and U_t is the error term.

TABLE 5.9 Results From Regressing Model 1 for the Preelection Violence Period (Jan. 2004 to Nov. 2007); 46 Observations for Each Regression

Banks	α_1	β_m	β_{rs}	B_{rl}	β_{rf}	R^2
Barclays Bank	−0.0073**	1.5540	0.1770	−0.2504	−0.0070***	0.5275
	(0.0116)	(0.2359)	(0.1872)	(0.2741)	(0.0076)	
Kenya Commercial Bank	0.0206***	1.3488	0.2302	−0.5797	0.0058***	0.4402
	(0.0123)	(0.2497)	(0.1983)	(0.2902)	(0.0080)	
Standard Chartered Bank	0.0092**	1.2719	0.1607	−0.2364	0.0158***	0.3689
	(0.0159)	(0.3168)	(0.2489)	(0.3663)	(0.0107)	
CFC Bank	0.0075**	1.0418	0.1068	−0.0310	0.0153***	0.2356
	(0.0162)	(0.3300)	(0.2619)	(0.3835)	(0.0106)	
Diamond Trust Bank	0.0112	0.9294	0.0550	−0.2165	−0.0063***	0.2428
	(0.0135)	(0.2735)	(0.2171)	(0.3178)	(0.0088)	
Housing Finance	0.0040**	2.2577	0.6128	−1.4255	−0.0048**	0.4315
	(0.0226)	(0.4589)	(0.3643)	(0.5333)	(0.0147)	
National Bank of Kenya	−0.0174**	1.7375	0.2245	−0.2460	−0.0153**	0.3358
	(0.0202)	(0.4098)	(0.3253)	(0.4762)	(0.0131)	
NIC Bank	0.0092**	1.2719	0.1607	−0.2364	0.0158***	0.3290
	(0.0159)	(0.3168)	(0.2489)	(0.3663)	(0.0107)	
Average Bank Returns	0.0033***	1.403531	0.224823	−0.4237	0.0001***	0.6919
	(0.0073)	(0.1475)	(0.1171)	(0.1714)	(0.0047)	

Notes: Significance at 1%, ***; at 5%, **; and at 10%, *.
P values are enclosed in parentheses.
Model: $BSR_t = \alpha_i + \beta_m RM_t + \beta_{rs} RSIR_t + \beta_{rl} RLIR_t + \beta_{rf} RFX_t + U_t$
where BSR_{it} is bank stock returns for bank i and the portfolio of banks at time t, RM_t is market returns of the NSE 20 index at time t, $RSIR_t$ is returns on short-term interest rates at time t, $RLIR_t$ is returns on long-term interest rates at time t, RFX_t is returns on exchange rates at time t, and U_t is the error term.

TABLE 5.10 Results From Regressing Model 1 for the Election Violence Period (Sep. 2010 to Dec. 2013); 33 Observations

Banks	α_1	β_m	β_{rs}	β_{rl}	β_{rf}	R^2
Barclays Bank	-0.0034***	1.0425	-0.1725	0.1030	0.0010***	0.8350
	(0.0080)	(0.1004)	(0.2213)	(0.2273)	(0.0025)	
Kenya Commercial Bank	0.0028***	1.1125	-0.2686	0.4127	-0.0011***	0.7974
	(0.0102)	(0.1274)	(0.2809)	(0.2884)	(0.0031)	
Standard Chartered Bank	0.0004***	0.4736*	-0.1836	0.0266	0.0023***	0.6137
	(0.0070)	(0.0873)	(0.1924)	(0.1976)	(0.0022)	
CFC Bank	-0.0174***	0.6744	0.0119	-0.3376	-0.0034***	0.3387
	(0.0221)	(0.2768)	(0.6101)	(0.6265)	(0.0068)	
Diamond Trust Bank	0.0125***	1.0280	-0.1603	0.1978	-0.0025***	0.7445
	(0.0111)	(0.1391)	(0.3066)	(0.3149)	(0.0034)	
Housing Finance	-0.0123**	1.1101	-1.1229	0.9951	-0.0005***	0.5177
	(0.0208)	(0.2604)	(0.5739)	(0.5893)	(0.0064)	
National Bank of Kenya	0.0228**	1.3135	-0.1867	0.3873	-0.0001***	0.7041
	(0.0152)	(0.1905)	(0.4199)	(0.4311)	(0.0047)	
NIC Bank	0.0070***	0.7302	0.0932	-0.0538	-0.0064***	0.5644
	(0.0136)	(0.1709)	(0.37660)	(0.3867)	(0.0042)	
Average Bank Returns	0.0016***	0.9356**	-0.2487	0.2164	-0.0013***	0.8467
	(0.0072)	(0.0906)	(0.1997)	(0.2051)	(0.0022)	

Notes: Significance at 1%, ***; at 5%, **; and at 10%, *.
P values are enclosed in parentheses.
Model: $BSR_{it} = \alpha_i + \beta_m RM_t + \beta_{rs} RSIR_t + \beta_{rl} RLIR_t + \beta_{rf} RFX_t + U_t$
where BSR_{it} is bank stock returns for bank i and the portfolio of banks at time t, RM_t is market returns of the NSE 20 index at time t, $RSIR_t$ is returns on short-term interest rates at time t, $RLIR_t$ is returns on long-term interest rates at time t, RFX_t is returns on exchange rates at time t, and U_t is the error term.

TABLE 5.11 Results From Regressing Model 1 for the Postelection Violence Period (Sep. 2010 to Dec. 2013); 44 Observations

Banks	α_1	β_m	β_{rs}	β_{rl}	β_{rf}	R^2
Barclays Bank	-0.0051**	1.6994	-0.0252	0.1067	-0.0039***	0.5560
	(0.0119)	(0.2601)	(0.1512)	(0.1582)	(0.0045)	
Kenya Commercial Bank	0.0209***	1.4086	-0.1081	0.0901	-0.0056***	0.6109
	(0.0089)	(0.1951)	(0.1134)	(0.1187)	(0.0034)	
Standard Chartered Bank	0.0069***	0.8784	-0.0137	-0.0778	-0.0001***	0.4712
	(0.0080)	(0.1755)	(0.1020)	(0.1068)	(0.0031)	
CFC Bank	0.0053***	0.3714	-0.0612	-0.0080	-0.0058***	0.0821
	(0.0152)	(0.3323)	(0.1932)	(0.2022)	(0.0058)	
Diamond Trust Bank	0.0207***	0.6378	-0.0076	-0.0553	-0.0002***	0.2544
	(0.0093)	(0.2043)	(0.1187)	(0.1243)	(0.0036)	
Housing Finance	0.0048***	1.3447	0.0217	-0.0712	0.0018***	0.4780
	(0.0113)	(0.2464)	(0.1432)	(0.1499)	(0.0043)	
National Bank of Kenya	-0.0114**	1.4150	-0.1673	0.1615	0.0054***	0.4188
	(0.0134)	(0.2925)	(0.1700)	(0.1780)	(0.0051)	
NIC Bank	0.0110***	1.2381	0.0355	-0.0544	0.0016***	0.4339
	(0.0112)	(0.2451)	(0.1425)	(0.1491)	(0.0043)	
Average Bank Returns	0.0066***	1.1242	-0.0407	0.0114	-0.0008***	0.7178
	(0.0055)	(0.1209)	(0.0703)	(0.0736)	(0.0021)	

Notes: Significance at 1%, ***; at 5%, **; and at 10%, *.
P values are enclosed in parentheses.
Model: $BSR_{it} = \alpha_i + \beta_m RM_t + \beta_{rs} RSIR_t + \beta_{rl} RLIR_t + \beta_{rf} RFX_t + U_t$,
where BSR_{it} is bank stock returns for bank i and the portfolio of banks at time t, RM_t is market returns on the NSE 20 index at time t, $RSIR_t$ is returns on short-term interest rates at time t, $RLIR_t$ is returns on long-term interest rates at time t, RFX_t is returns on exchange rates at time t, and U_t is the error term.

short- and long-term IR could explain the BSR. However, the nominal exchange rate coefficient is positive and significant with respect to average bank returns in the preelection violence period, as shown in Table 5.9, while negative and significant with respect to average bank returns in the election violence and postelection violence periods, as shown in Tables 5.10 and 5.11.

2 CONCLUSIONS

The main hypothesis in this research is that BSR in Kenya are significantly related to changes in IR and FX. This research showed that changes in short-term nominal IR were positive and significant while changes in long-term nominal IR were negative and significant in explaining average BSR (Lloyd and Shick, 1977; Faff and Howard, 1999; Kasman et al., 2011). The FX and inflation rate variables also showed significant relationship in explaining BSR. The inflation rate coefficients were positive and significant, while the FX coefficient generated mixed results in explaining average BSR. These results are consistent with the results in both developed countries (Kutty, 2010; Choi et al., 1992; AtindeÂhou and Gueyie, 2001; Kurmann, 2014; Kasman et al., 2011) and developing countries (Hooy et al., 2004; Kasman et al., 2011; Alam and Uddin, 2009).

This research also examined the relationship between BSR and changes in IR and FX during the 2007–08 election violence period. Results indicated that BSR were insignificant with respect to IR in all three periods: preelection violence, election violence, and postelection violence. The market returns were positive and significantly explained average BSR in the election violence period. The FX coefficients were positive and significant in the preelection and election violence periods, while negative and significant in the postelection violence period.

Individual BSR behaved the same with respect to how their returns were affected throughout the whole study. The fact that the chosen banks were mostly large banks might have led to this similarity in results. Previous studies have stated that stock returns of large and small banks are affected differently by changes in IR and FX (Faff and Howard, 1999; pp. 96–97). This research does not account for differences in the sizes of banks, which is an area for further research. Some results of this research are inconsistent with previous research; for example, Otuori (2013) found IR to be significant in explaining BSR. Hence, it was believed that further research should be conducted in this area so as to come up with results relevant enough for policy-making purposes.

REFERENCES

Alam, M., Uddin, G.S., 2009. Relationship between interest rate and stock price: empirical evidence from developed and developing countries. Int. J. Bus. Manage. 4 (3), 43–51.

AtindeÂhou, R.B., Gueyie, J.P., 2001. Canadian chartered banks' stock returns and exchange rate risk. Manage. Decis. 39 (4), 285–294.

Burke, O., 2010. More Notes for Least Squares. Department of Statistics, Oxford, pp. 1–14.

Central Bank of Kenya, 2013. Eleventh Bi-Annual Report of the Monetary Policy Committee. Central Bank of Kenya, Nairobi, Kenya.

Choi, J.J., Elyasiani, E., Kopecky, K.J., 1992. The sensitivity of bank stock returns to market, interest and exchange rate risks. J. Bank. Financ. 16, 983–1004.

Faff, R.W., Hodgson, A., Kremmer, M.L., 1999. An investigation of the impact of interest rates and interest rate volatility on Australian financial sector stock return distributions, 1–29.

Faff, R.W., Howard, P.F., 1999. Interest rate risk of Australian financial sector companies in a period of regulatory change. Pac. Basin Financ. J. 7 (1), 83–101.

Flannery, M.J., James, C.M., 1984. The effect of interest rate changes on the common stock returns of financial institutions. J. Financ. 39 (4), 1141–1153.

Francis, B.B., Hunter, D.M., 2004. The impact of the euro on risk exposure of the world's major banking industries. J. Int. Money Financ. 23 (7–8), 1011–1042.

Hooy, C.W., Tan, H.B., Nassir, A.M., 2004. Risk sensitivity of bank stocks in Malaysia: empirical evidence across the Asian financial crisis. Asian Econ. J. 18 (3), 261–276.

Kane, E.J., Unal, H., 1988. Change in market assessments of deposit institution riskiness. J. Financ. Serv. Res. 1 (3), 207–229.

Kasman, S., Vardar, G., Tunç, G., 2011. The impact of interest rate and exchange rate volatility on banks' stock returns and volatility: evidence from Turkey. Econ. Model. 28 (3), 1328–1334.

Kurmann, W.B.P., 2014. Bank risk factors and changing risk exposures: capital market evidence before and during the financial crisis. J. Financ. Stabil., 13, 1–41.

Kutty, G., 2010. The relationship between exchange rates and stock prices: the case of Mexico. N. Am. J. Financ. Banking Res. 4 (4), 1–12.

Lloyd, W.P., Shick, R.A., 1977. A test of Stone's two-index model of returns. J. Financ. Quant. Anal., 363–376.

Lynge, M.J., Zumwalt, J.K., 1980. An empirical study of the interest rate sensitivity of commercial bank returns: a multi-index approach. J. Financ. Quant. Anal. 15 (3), 731–742.

Mukit, D.M., 2012. Effects of interest rate and exchange rate on volatility of market index at Dhaka stock exchange. J. Bus. Technol. 7 (2), 1–18.

Nairobi Stock Exchange, 2014. Available from: http:\\nse.co.ke

Otuori, O.H., 2013. Influence of exchange rate determinants on the performance of commercial banks in Kenya. Eur. J. Manage. Sci. Econ. 1 (2), 86–98.

Strange, A., Parks, B., Tierney, M.J., Fuchs, A., Dreher, A., Ramach, V., 2013. China's Development Finance to Africa: A Media-Based Approach to Data Collection. Working Paper 323. Center for Global Development, Washington, DC.

Sweeney, R.J., Warga, A.D., 1986. The pricing of interest-rate risk: evidence from the stock market. J. Financ. 41 (2), 393–410.

Tabak, B.M., 2006. The Dynamic Relationship between Stock Prices and Exchange Rates: Evidence for Brazil. Banco Central do Brasil, Brazil.

Uddin, G.S., Alam, M., 2007. The impacts of interest rate on stock market: empirical evidence from Dhaka Stock Exchange. S. Asia. J. Manage. Sci. 1 (2), 123–132.

Chapter 6

Financial Contagion From US to African Frontier Markets During the 2007–09 Global Financial Crisis

J. Ahmadu-Bello, T. Rodgers
School of Economics, Finance and Accounting, University of Coventry, Coventry, United Kingdom

Chapter Outline

1 INTRODUCTION, AIMS, AND LITERATURE

The term "contagion" became widely used in the financial lexicon following the seminal work of King and Wadhwani (1990) and Forbes and Rigobon (2002) on financial crises in 1987 and the 1990s. The latter authors describe contagion in terms of it being "a significant increase in cross-market linkages resulting from a shock hitting one country or group of countries" (Forbes and Rigobon, 2002, p. 2223). The crises examined in the literature have been predominantly country- or region-focused events—for example, the 1997 Asian financial crisis, the

Handbook of Frontier Markets. http://dx.doi.org/10.1016/B978-0-12-803776-8.00006-9
93

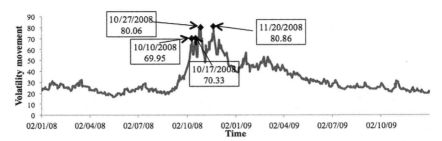

FIGURE 6.1   **Volatility Index (VIX), 2008–09.**

1998 Russian financial crisis, and the Mexican economic crisis in 1994. The 2007–09 crisis was different in that its reach was truly global and in that it unfolded as a series of subevents over a prolonged period. From an African perspective, the 2007–09 crisis was unique as it was the first time that a major financial crisis in another part of the world had a major impact on the continent. In some African markets (eg, Egypt and Nigeria), losses exceeded those in any developed market in percentage terms (African Development Bank, 2009).

The 2007–09 crisis was also different in that it was not a single short sharp shock, but was an event that unfolded in the United States over a period of more than a year. The event can be characterized as being a series of crisis waves (see Section 2, Fig. 6.1). The question that arises from a behavioral finance perspective is: How will markets respond? Will they treat each subevent as separate and unrelated and *anchor* their decisions on the US market in each instance? Or will they become conditioned to crisis-related events in the United States and stop responding to them?

This chapter explores these questions by testing for evidence of financial contagion from the US to African frontier markets. We note that the financial linkages (measured in terms of market correlation) between US and African frontier markets are much weaker than they are between US and developed markets; we believe that this may have implications as to how contagion events unfold in these two sets of countries. A secondary objective of the chapter is therefore to examine any differences found in this respect and to speculate as to whether they have any plausible behavioral-finance-related explanation.

In the remainder of this section we briefly review some of the key literature in respect to the contagion mechanism. Section 2 then presents the data and descriptive statistics. The hypotheses and methodology are described in Section 3 and the results from the study are presented and discussed in Sections 4 and 5. Last, conclusions are drawn in Section 6.

The literature has identified a number of different channels through which contagion events may unfold, with the main focus being on asset market channels, banking channels, and currency channels (Fry-McKibbin et al., 2013; Tonzer, 2013; Lau, 2001). Elsewhere in the literature a distinction is drawn between the relative importance of fundamental causes and investor behavior (Claessens and Forbes, 2004; Dornbusch et al., 2000). Exploring contagion from a behavioral perspective, Calvo and Mendoza (2000) developed a formal model of herding. They argue that the cost of information will lead investors to follow market participants they believe are "well informed" and therefore market rumors will drive large swings in market prices through herding behavior.

A number of papers have attempted to examine the relative importance of behavioral and linkage-related factors. For example, Kaminsky et al. (2003) classify contagion theories into three groups: herding behavior, trade linkages, and financial linkages. They conclude that financial linkages and investor behavior are the most relevant factors in explaining contagion. Elsewhere in the literature a number of papers identify the importance of integration effects and note that during crises integration with global markets increases (Collins and Biekpe, 2003; Kassim, 2013; Cheng and Glascock, 2006).

The relatively low levels of integration may be of particular importance from an African perspective. Berger et al. (2011) analyze frontier market equities with respect to world market integration and diversification. They find little evidence of integration in respect to a number of African countries, including Kenya, Mauritius, and Nigeria. A similar picture is painted by Hatemi-J and Morgan (2007), who find that Nigeria and Zimbabwe have exhibited particularly low levels of integration with global markets.

There are considerable differences in the levels of integration that African and developed markets have with US markets (Table 6.1). There are also considerable differences in the sizes of these markets and the numbers of their respective participants (described in Sections 4 and 5). We believe that our study will show that the combination of these factors will result in considerable differences in the way in which contagion impacts African frontier markets and developed markets.

2 DATA AND DESCRIPTIVE STATISTICS

An issue that every study of contagion faces is that of identifying the crisis starting point and ending point. The 2007–09 crisis was unique among post-1945 financial shocks in that it developed over a relatively long period and contained a number of subevents. This makes identifying the event window potentially problematical.

However, since the crisis originated from the United States, we have the Volatility Index (VIX) of the Chicago Board Options Exchange (CBOE) at our disposal to identify which events produced the greatest "shock" to investors. The index is popularly known as the "fear gauge" given its forward-looking properties. It is presented in Fig. 6.1.

The VIX showed a series of spikes associated with a number of key crisis events. The first spike in the last quarter of 2008 was associated with the lead-up to the Lehman bankruptcy (Sep. 15). Additional spikes were associated with the federal takeover of Fannie Mae and Freddie Mac (Sep. 7), the emergency US$85 billion loan to insurer American International Group (AIG) (Sep. 17) and the crisis-induced sale of Merrill Lynch to Bank of America (Sep. 14).

TABLE 6.1 Descriptive Statistics over the Period 01/01/07–10/15/2009

	Country	Mean Daily Return (%)	Standard Deviation (%)	Correlation with United States[a]	Skewness	Excess Kurtosis
Frontier Africa	United State	−0.036	1.937	1	−0.161	5.799
	Botswana	0.017	0.569	−0.014	1.263	21.198
	Côte d'Ivoire	0.026	25.272[b]	−0.054	0.039	331.493[b]
	Mauritius	0.054	1.295	0.009	0.067	6.713
	Morocco	0.020	1.051	−0.027	−0.570	4.119
	Namibia	−0.022	3.397	0.341	0.882	113.549[c]
	Nigeria	−0.058	1.333	−0.040	0.060	0.603
	Tunisia	0.087	0.656	0.126	−0.586	8.986
	Zambia	0.062	1.280	−0.015	0.475	8.578
Developed	Canada	−0.014	1.854	0.653	−0.526	5.100
	France	−0.053	1.916	0.660	0.207	5.435
	Germany	−0.020	1.870	0.594	0.245	5.999
	Italy	−0.078	1.567	0.484	−0.408	4.825
	Spain	−0.035	1.828	0.578	0.013	4.927
	United Kingdom	−0.028	1.746	0.663	−0.026	4.658

[a]Constant correlations are estimated for the precrisis period of Jan. 1, 2007–Sep. 14, 2008, only. This period is used in order to identify precrisis differences in the level of integration with the US market.
[b]This unadjusted data needs to be treated with caution for reasons identified in the description associated with Figure 6.2b.
[c]This high value is associated with a spike in returns toward the end of the crisis period.

The Lehman bankruptcy was the defining event of the crisis; we therefore use Sep. 15, 2008, to identify the start of what is defined as the *long crisis period*. The VIX remained high well into 2009, which is an indication that this particular crisis was not the type of short, sharp shock modeled previously in the contagion literature by the likes of Forbes and Rigobon (2002). Oct. 2008 saw further crisis measures such as the introduction of the US$700 billion Troubled Assets Relief Program (TARP) in the United States to stave off collapse in the banking system, and we saw further emergency mergers in this sector (eg, Wells Fargo taking over Wachovia). On Nov. 27 the US government had to rescue Citigroup after speculators drove its share price down 60%. Further afield, in the United Kingdom, the Royal Bank of Scotland (RBS) was rescued by the UK government on Oct. 13, and around the same time HBOS plc was forced to merge with Lloyds–TSB, which ultimately led to the partial collapse and bailout of this bank.

Defining the end point of the financial crisis is open to interpretation, but we again use the VIX. Using the mean index value from 2000 as a guide, the index can be identified as reverting back to its average by early Oct. 2009. This gives an indication of market expectations that the crisis was drawing to a close. Based on this, the *long period contagion event* is identified in this study as Sep. 15, 2008, to Oct. 15, 2009.[a]

The individual spikes observed in the VIX suggest that it may be more appropriate to treat the crisis as an *accumulation* of events rather than a single event. This has implications for the study of contagion from the United States to other markets from a behavioral finance perspective. We speculate that we may possibly find evidence of (1) a "decision fatigue" effect given that the crisis developed over such a long period or (2) a representativeness bias (Harman, 2009) where investors respond to each of the subcrises in the same way as they see the impact of the previous subcrisis as representative.

After the Lehman initial shock, there was a series of further fallout events and a whole series of emergency interventions into the financial markets by regulatory authorities. These are well documented in the historical studies of the crisis.[b] We can identify a series of subperiods in the market when fear spiked (Fig. 6.1).

Although individual subperiods are identified, the focus of this study is to examine the cumulative impact of the crisis in terms of changes in correlations as the crisis period lengthened. The *subperiods* identified are therefore: subperiod 1 (09/15/2008–10/10/2008), subperiod 2 (09/15/2008–10/17/2008), subperiod 3 (09/15/2008–10/27/2008), and subperiod 4 (09/15/2008–11/20/2008).

---

a. The mean daily closing value of the VIX over the period 01/03/2000–05/11/2012 was 21.72. The index began to show a significant increase above this level from the middle of 2007, peaking at 79.13 on 10/20/2008. It began to revert to the mean value during 2009 and by 10/15/2009 was at 21.72.
b. See for example: <http://timeline.stlouisfed.org/>. Access date: 01/05/2014.

2.1   Data Sources and Descriptive Statistics

The study is based on the use of daily closing values of stock markets sourced from the Thomson Reuters Eikon Financial Database and shown in local currencies. The indices used are the principal indices from the respective countries. The data run from Jan. 1, 2007 to Sep. 15, 2009.

The daily logarithmic returns of the respective individual-country indices used are presented graphically in Fig. 6.2a–c, and the mean values and associated descriptive statistics are shown in Table 6.1.

The Standard & Poor's (S&P) 500 index is selected as the American index on the basis that it is an index that is reflective of a general cross section of US stocks. The African frontier markets used for the study are identified from the classifications of S&P and MSCI, Inc. The African frontier markets under study include[c] Botswana, Côte d'Ivoire, Mauritius, Morocco, Namibia, Nigeria, Tunisia, and Zambia. The developed markets sampled represent a cross section of developed markets and consist of Canada, France, Germany, Italy, Spain, and the United Kingdom.

Fig. 6.2a provides the chart of daily returns for the US S&P 500 for the full sample period. Volatility in the market can be identified as spiking dramatically in the last quarter of 2008. This corresponded with the Lehman bankruptcy announcement and also the jump in the VIX as observed in Fig. 6.1.

The logarithmic returns in Fig. 6.2b identify that there are significant differences in patterns of volatility between African markets. For example, Morocco and Nigeria exhibit high volatility throughout the period with significant

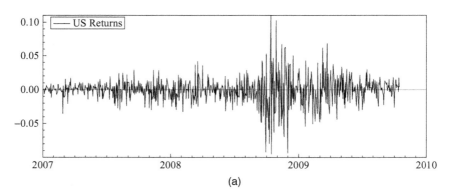

(a)

FIGURE 6.2 Daily returns. (a) US market, over the period 01/01/07–10/15/09; (b) African markets, over the period 01/01/07–10/15/09; and (c) developed markets, over the period 01/01/07–10/15/09

---

c. With the exception of Morocco, all the markets in the sample are classified as frontier markets by S&P. Morocco is classified as a frontier market by MSCI. A number of markets are omitted as the full data required were not available at the time of this study from Thomson Reuters Eikon.

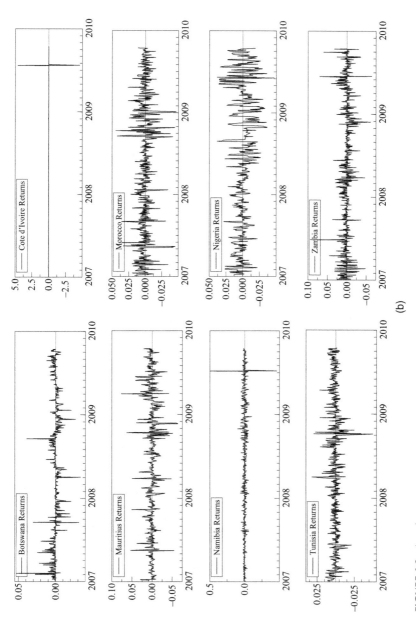

FIGURE 6.2 *(cont.)*

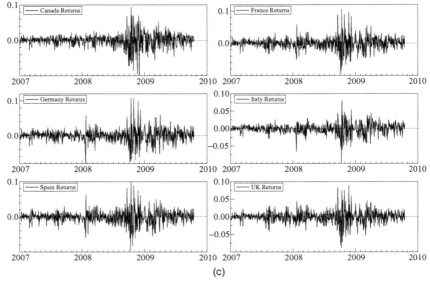

(c)

FIGURE 6.2 (*cont.*)

increases during the crisis period. Botswana, however, appears more volatile before the crisis period, whereas Mauritius shows relatively low precrisis volatility, which increases significantly during the crisis. Côte d'Ivoire shows an important example of why researchers need to be very careful when modeling with this type of frontier market data. The long period of close to zero returns and the sudden spike around the crisis period reflect periods of limited trading in a low-liquidity market.

Fig. 6.2c provides a graphical presentation of the daily returns of the developed markets. It can be identified that volatility in all these markets increased during the crisis period (toward the end of 2008). The similarities in volatility patterns here can be contrasted with those of the African markets identified in Fig. 6.2b. These differences possibly reflect the stronger financial linkages between US and developed markets, as can be identified in the much higher correlation levels illustrated in Table 6.1.

Table 6.1 shows there to be clear differences in the constant correlation estimates between the United States and African countries and between the United States and developed countries in the precrisis period. This can be seen as a reflection of the strength of developed countries' financial linkages with the United States. We argue that African frontier countries, with their relatively weak linkages, can be described as being "low integration" countries and developed countries as "high integration" countries. Under normal market conditions, the standard deviations of returns would be expected to be appreciably higher in the higher-risk frontier markets. The fact that this is not the case is possibly a reflection of the extreme volatility levels in developed markets during the crisis period. It can be noted that mean returns in developed markets were negative during this period, and their standard deviations were very high relative to these returns. The values of the kurtosis and skewness presented in Table 6.1 identify that returns do not follow a normal distribution in either set of markets.

3   HYPOTHESES AND METHODOLOGY

From the analysis of the data in Section 2, a long period and a series of shorter subperiods have been identified. We have also identified considerable differences in terms of precrisis constant correlations, returns, and risk profiles between African and developed markets. On this basis we identify the following sets of hypotheses.

3.1   Hypothesis 1

The hypothesis that contagion occurred in both African frontier and developed markets during the *long crisis period* of 2007–09 is formally tested as:

$H_{1.a}$: There is a statistically significant increase in correlations between US and developed markets over the period 09/15/2008–10/15/2009.
$H_{1.b}$: There is a statistically significant increase in correlations between US and African frontier markets over the period 09/15/2008–10/15/2009.

3.2   Hypothesis 2

The secondary hypothesis is that the crisis developed as a series of subevents and that contagion events occurred in each of these subperiods. This is formally tested as:

$H_{2.a}$: There is a statistically significant increase in correlations between US and developed markets over the cumulative subperiods: 09/15/2008–10/10/2008, 09/15/2008–10/17/2008, 09/15/2008–10/27/2008, and 09/15/2008–11/20/2008.
$H_{2.b}$: There is a statistically significant increase in correlations between US and African frontier markets over the cumulative subperiods 09/15/2008–10/10/2008, 09/15/2008–10/17/2008, 09/15/2008–10/27/2008 and 09/15/2008–11/20/2008.

3.3   Methodology

Contagion literature identifies four commonly used models for investigating contagion and markets' comovement: (1) time-varying correlation techniques such as the dynamic conditional correlation (DCC) model (Engle, 2002; Chiang et al., 2007), (2) correlation coefficient analysis (King and Wadhwani, 1990; Forbes and Rigobon, 2002), (3) cointegration-based techniques (Longin and Solnik, 1995), and (4) the transmission mechanism approach (Eichengreen et al., 1996; Forbes, 2004).

This chapter adopts the DCC–MGARCH model to test for contagion using daily time-varying correlations. The test for contagion is then a one-tailed hypothesis test for a statistically significant increase in the *mean* conditional correlation between the precrisis and crisis periods.

Following Forbes and Rigobon (2002), the first step of the procedure is to develop vector autoregression (VAR)–based equations to estimate the residual returns for pairs consisting of the US market and "a second market." The returns used are 2-day averages; these are used to control for differences in market trading times. It can also be noted that the use of VAR-based mean equations in the MGARCH is necessary to control for high levels of autocorrelation in returns. The equations used take the following format:

$$r_{it} = \mu_i + \sum_{k=1}^{m} \alpha_{ik} r_{it-k} + \sum_{k=1}^{m} \beta_{ik} r_{jt-k} + \varepsilon_{it} \tag{6.1}$$

$$r_{jt} = \mu_j + \sum_{k=1}^{m} \alpha_{jk} r_{jt-k} + \sum_{k=1}^{m} \beta_{jk} r_{it-k} + \varepsilon_{jt} \tag{6.2}$$

Where r represents returns, i identifies the United States, and j is "a second market."

The optimal lag structures for these equation pairs are determined using information criteria. Their residuals are then used to estimate time-varying variance equations, which take a GARCH(1,1) format:[d]

$$\sigma_{it}^2 = \alpha_{i0} + \alpha_{i1} \varepsilon_{it-1}^2 + \beta_{i1} \sigma_{it-1}^2 \tag{6.3}$$

$$\sigma_{jt}^2 = \alpha_{j0} + \alpha_{j1} \varepsilon_{jt-1}^2 + \beta_{j1} \sigma_{jt-1}^2 \tag{6.4}$$

where σ_t^2 is the conditional variance, α_0 the intercept, ε the standardized residuals, α_1 the ARCH parameter, and β_1 the GARCH parameter. The conditional correlation coefficients are estimated from the DCC equation:

$$Q_t = (1 - \alpha - \beta)\bar{Q} + \alpha v_{t-1} v_{t-1}' + \beta Q_{t-1} \tag{6.5}$$

where Q_t is the covariance matrix and v_t represents residuals standardized by the conditional standard deviation. The model is mean reverting as long as the nonnegative scalars satisfy the constraint: $\alpha + \beta < 1$. A significant alpha coefficient value in the DCC equation is also an indication that correlations will vary appreciably over time. The alpha parameter was found to be insignificant for Mauritius, Nigeria, Tunisia, and Zambia. Although other GARCH specifications were tested in respect to these countries, the respective models failed to converge.

The estimated daily time-varying conditional correlations are shown graphically in Appendices 6.1 and 6.2. In order to test for contagion, mean values are calculated for the "precrisis" and "crisis" periods. Comparison-of-means tests

---

d. A number of different functional forms of these equations were tested, including various asymmetric GARCH forms. None of these appreciably outperformed GARCH(1,1).

are then used to test for contagion where the null hypothesis is that mean daily correlations during the crisis are less than or equal to those in the precrisis period. If the null is rejected, contagion is deemed to have been found. If a statistically insignificant increase in correlation is found, the result is interpreted as interdependence rather than contagion (Forbes and Rigobon, 2002).

This hypothesis is illustrated as:

$$H_0 : y2 \leq y1 \, (\text{absence of contagion})$$

$$H_1 : y2 > y1 \, (\text{contagion})$$

where $y2$ and $y1$ are the mean daily correlation values between countries i and j during the crisis and precrisis periods, respectively. If variances are equal, the pooled variance t-test is used:

$$t = \frac{y2 - y1}{s_{\text{pool}} \sqrt{\dfrac{1}{n_1} + \dfrac{1}{n_2}}} \sim t(n_1 + n_2 - 2) \tag{6.7}$$

where $s_{\text{pool}}^2 = \dfrac{\Sigma(y_{1i} - \bar{y}_1)^2 + \Sigma(y_{2j} - \bar{y}_2)^2}{n_1 + n_2 - 2} = \dfrac{(n_1 - 1)s_1^2 + (n_2 - 1)s_2^2}{n_1 + n_2 - 2},$

n_1 = precrisis sample size, and n_2 = sample size during crisis.

If variances are unequal, the Satterthwaite (1946) approximation is used:

$$t = \frac{y2 - y1}{s_{\text{pool}} \sqrt{\dfrac{1}{n_1} + \dfrac{1}{n_2}}} \sim t(df_{\text{Satterthwaite}}) \tag{6.8}$$

where $df_{\text{Satterthwaite}} = \dfrac{(n_1 - 1)(n_2 - 1)}{(n_1 - 1)(1 - c)^2 + (n_2 - 1)c^2}$ and $c = \dfrac{s_1^2 / n_1}{s_1^2 / n_1 + s_2^2 / n_2}$

3.4 Robustness Testing

To add to the robustness of the analysis, an alternative regression-based test is also undertaken to act as a confirmatory test. This takes the form of a test of significance in respect to a regression dummy variable representing the crisis periods.

$$C_{ij,t} = \mu_j + \delta_j \text{Crisis DUMMY}_t + \varepsilon_{ij,t} \tag{6.9}$$

where $C_{ij,t}$ is the conditional correlation at time t between the United States (i) and the second country (j). *Crisis DUMMY$_t$* is a dummy variable taking on a value of 1 over the crisis period. A positive and statistically significant parameter value in respect to the dummy variable is an indication that financial contagion has occurred.

4   RESULTS

The results from a series of tests in respect to hypotheses 1 and 2 are presented in Tables 6.2 and 6.3. These show considerable differences in respect to African frontier and developed countries. The results are presented and described next, and possible reasons for the differences found are then discussed in Section 5.

Table 6.2 identifies evidence of contagion in both data sets over the long period (09/15/2008–10/15/2009). Although evidence of contagion is found in all developed markets, the picture in Africa is mixed. Contagion is found in Botswana, Côte d'Ivoire, and Mauritius. Increases in correlation that were not statistically significant at 5% were also found in respect to Morocco, Nigeria, and Tunisia. Reductions in correlation are found in Namibia and Zambia.

A series of interesting differences between African frontier and developed markets are also found in respect to hypothesis 2. These primarily relate to the issue of timing, as they suggest that, although the crisis had an immediate contagion effect in Africa, contagion to developed markets proceeded at a much slower pace.

The results in respect to the first subperiod (09/15/2008–10/10/2008) appear to suggest that contagion developed faster in the African markets. Contagion was identified in Botswana, Côte d'Ivoire, Morocco, and Namibia. It can be noted that lack of contagion found in the other African markets has to be treated with caution (they showed an insignificant alpha in the DCC–MGARCH model). It is noticeable from Table 6.3 that a number of the developed markets that had initial high levels of correlation with the US market had a reduction in correlation during this first period (Canada, France, Italy, and the United Kingdom). Germany and Spain are the only developed markets to exhibit contagion in this early crisis phase.

The *cumulative* impact of subperiod 1–2 resulted in further increases in correlations for Botswana, Côte d'Ivoire, Morocco, and Namibia. In developed countries there was a considerable increase in Germany and less marked increases in Italy, France, and the United Kingdom.

As the crisis moved to its later phases (cumulative subperiod 1–4), the increases in correlation shown in the African frontier markets was maintained. This manifests itself in contagion terms in Botswana, Côte d'Ivoire, Morocco, and Namibia. In developed markets it can be noted that there is evidence of contagion and interdependence spreading more widely, with Germany, Spain, and the United Kingdom all showing contagion effects and with interdependence also being found in Canada and France.

4.1   Robustness Tests

With the statistical power of comparison-of-means tests questionable under some circumstances, dummy variable regressions were run to test for the robustness of results. There are some marginal differences between Tables 6.3 and 6.4. For example, in respect to subperiod 1 in African markets, the differences found

TABLE 6.2 Comparison-of-Means Based Contagion Tests: Long Crisis Period

	Stable Period		Crisis Period		Test for Equality of Variances[b]		T-test for Equality of Means[c,d]	Evidence of Contagion[e]
African Markets	Mean Corr.[a]	Standard Deviation	Mean Corr.[a]	Standard Deviation	F	Sig		
Botswana	−0.028	0.035	0.011	0.043	30.776	0.000	12.060***	Yes
Côte d'Ivoire	0.028	0.035	0.036	0.074	187.983	0.000	1.659**	Yes
Mauritius	0.043	0.000	0.043	0.000	24.590	0.000	1.881**	Yes
Morocco	0.011	0.036	0.017	0.081	159.192	0.000	1.060	No
Namibia	0.342	0.217	0.318	0.093	164.047	0.000	−1.965	No
Nigeria	0.043	0.000	0.043	0.000	4.982	0.026	0.904	No
Tunisia	0.066	0.002	0.066	0.002	1.811	0.179	0.935	No
Zambia	−0.016	0.000	−0.016	0.000	8.478	0.004	−1.269	No
Developed Markets								
Canada	0.763	0.112	0.828	0.046	121.101	0.000	10.486***	Yes
France	0.713	0.053	0.745	0.053	4.051	0.045	7.795***	Yes
Germany	0.664	0.059	0.769	0.030	67.056	0.000	30.620***	Yes
Italy	0.531	0.101	0.567	0.052	123.984	0.000	6.169***	Yes
Spain	0.602	0.065	0.704	0.046	34.937	0.000	23.574***	Yes
United Kingdom	0.665	0.033	0.720	0.028	3.672	0.056	22.150***	Yes

[a]Mean daily time-varying correlation over the period.
[b]Levine's test of variance equality; where rejection of the null hypothesis indicates inequality.
[c]The t-value reported is the form appropriate for the variance identified.
[d]*Significant at 10%, **significant at 5%, ***significant at 1%.
[e]Contagion is defined as statistical significance at 5% level. Note that the test results for Mauritius, Nigeria, Tunisia, and Zambia need to be treated with caution due to an insignificant alpha in the DCC model.

TABLE 6.3 Comparison-of-Means Based Contagion Tests: Subcrisis Periods

African Markets	Stable Period		Subcrisis Period 1				Cumulative Impact of Subcrisis Periods 1–2				Cumulative Impact of Subcrisis Periods 1–3				Cumulative Impact of Subcrisis Periods 1–4			
	ρ	σ	ρ	σ	t-test[a,b]	Ctn.[c]	ρ	σ	t-test[a,b]	Ctn.[c]	ρ	σ	t-test[a,b]	Ctn.[c]	ρ	σ	t-test[a,b]	Ctn.[c]
Botswana	−0.028	0.035	0.012	0.045	4.697***	Y	0.014	0.041	5.449***	Y	0.020	0.038	7.067***	Y	0.045	0.043	13.139***	Y
Côte d'Ivoire	0.028	0.035	0.103	0.013	21.56***	Y	0.113	0.026	15.02***	Y	0.119	0.026	13.610***	Y	0.110	0.025	19.900***	Y
Mauritius	0.043	0.000	0.043	0.000	0.229	N	0.043	0.000	1.994**	Y	0.043	0.000	2.806***	Y	0.043	0.000	3.813***	Y
Morocco	0.011	0.036	0.131	0.030	13.85***	Y	0.139	0.033	16.55***	Y	0.144	0.031	19.220***	Y	0.152	0.028	25.290***	Y
Namibia	0.342	0.217	0.367	0.037	1.839**	Y	0.366	0.034	1.863**	Y	0.367	0.031	2.083**	Y	0.369	0.026	2.3170**	Y
Nigeria	0.043	0.000	0.043	0.000	1.312*	N	0.043	0.000	2.198**	Y	0.043	0.000	1.719**	Y	0.043	0.000	0.354	N
Tunisia	0.066	0.002	0.067	0.004	1.017	N	0.067	0.004	1.212	N	0.066	0.003	0.849	N	0.066	0.003	0.798	N
Zambia	−0.016	0.000	−0.016	0.000	0.225	N	−0.016	0.000	0.252	N	−0.016	0.000	0.276	N	−0.016	0.000	0.338	N
Developed Markets																		
Canada	0.763	0.112	0.717	0.049	−3.676	N	0.730	0.054	−2.655	N	0.744	0.056	−1.541	N	0.770	0.056	0.719	N
France	0.713	0.053	0.666	0.015	−10.962	N	0.672	0.018	−9.231	N	0.678	0.020	−7.912	N	0.724	0.027	−6.478	N
Germany	0.664	0.059	0.708	0.020	8.195***	Y	0.716	0.025	9.107***	Y	0.724	0.027	10.600***	Y	0.737	0.028	14.88***	Y
Italy	0.531	0.101	0.477	0.026	−6.935	N	0.484	0.029	−5.991	N	0.494	0.033	−4.670	N	0.516	0.039	−1.939	N
Spain	0.602	0.065	0.617	0.020	2.622***	Y	0.617	0.019	3.008***	Y	0.622	0.020	4.080***	Y	0.630	0.019	6.469***	Y
United Kingdom	0.665	0.033	0.665	0.013	−0.111	N	0.669	0.014	1.001	N	0.673	0.015	2.338***	Y	0.681	0.017	5.547***	Y

a As in Table 6.2, the t-value reported is appropriate for the form of variance identified.
b Significant at 10%, **significant at 5%, ***significant at 1%.
c Contagion (Ctn.) is defined as statistical significance at 5% level. Note that the test results for Mauritius, Nigeria, Tunisia, and Zambia need to be treated with caution due to an insignificant alpha in the DCC model. For example, contagion shown in periods 1–2 in respect to Nigeria reflects changes in correlation beyond three decimal places.

TABLE 6.4 Dummy Variable Based Robustness Tests for Contagion: All Periods

	Long Crisis Period			Subcrisis Period 1			Cumulative Impact of Subcrisis Periods 1–2			Cumulative Impact of Subcrisis Periods 1–3			Cumulative Impact of Subcrisis Periods 1–4		
African Markets	Dummy Coefficient	t-value[a]	Ctn.[b]	Dummy Coeff.	t-value[a]	Ctn.[b]	Dummy Coeff.	t-value[a]	Ctn.[b]	Dummy Coeff.	t-value[a]	Ctn.[b]	Dummy Coeff.	t-value[a]	Ctn.[b]
Botswana	0.039	12.642***	Y	0.040	4.697***	Y	0.042	5.449***	Y	0.048	7.067***	Y	0.073	13.139***	Y
Côte d'Ivoire	0.008	1.874**	Y	0.075	8.912***	Y	0.085	11.316***	Y	0.092	13.609***	Y	0.082	15.377***	Y
Mauritius	0.000	2.001**	Y	0.000	0.229	N	0.000	3.746***	Y	0.108	7.346***	Y	0.130	11.229***	Y
Morocco	0.006	1.221	N	0.120	13.846***	Y	0.128	16.553***	Y	0.000	4.861***	Y	0.000	5.699***	Y
Namibia	−0.024	−1.710	N	0.025	0.513	N	0.024	0.548	N	0.132	19.224***	Y	0.141	25.291***	Y
Nigeria	0.000	0.967	N	0.000	2.190**	Y	0.000	2.198**	Y	0.025	0.648	N	0.027	0.856	N
Tunisia	0.000	0.935	N	0.001	2.332***	Y	0.001	2.514***	Y	0.000	1.719***	Y	0.000	0.560	N
Zambia	0.000	−1.449	N	0.000	0.225	N	0.000	0.252	N	0.099	3.731***	Y	0.123	5.896***	Y
Developed Markets															
Canada	0.066	9.090***	Y	−0.046	−1.802	N	−0.033	−1.418	N	−0.018	−0.873	N	0.007	0.427	N
France	0.032	7.795***	Y	−0.046	−3.906	N	−0.041	−3.851	N	−0.035	−3.679	N	−0.025	−3.345	N
Germany	0.106	27.332***	Y	0.045	3.387***	Y	0.053	4.470***	Y	0.060	5.653***	Y	0.073	8.628***	Y
Italy	0.037	5.523***	Y	−0.054	−2.372	Y	−0.046	−2.281	N	−0.036	−2.001	N	−0.015	−1.004	N
Spain	0.102	22.071***	Y	0.014	0.981	N	0.015	1.136	N	0.020	1.660**	Y	0.027	2.919***	Y
United Kingdom	0.054	22.154***	Y	0.000	−0.050	N	0.003	0.486	N	0.007	1.249	N	0.016	3.350***	Y

[a]*Significant at 10%, **significant at 5%, ***significant at 1%.
[b]Contagion (Ctn.) is defined as statistical significance at 5% level. Note that the same caveat needs to be applied as in Tables 6.2 and 6.3; test results for Mauritius, Nigeria, Tunisia, and Zambia need to be treated with caution due to an insignificant alpha in the DCC model.

in relation to Nigeria and Tunisia can, however, be discounted for the statistical reasons described earlier. This leaves Namibia, where, although the comparison- of-means test shows evidence of contagion, the dummy test indicates no contagion. There is also some difference in respect to the developed markets. For example, Spain indicates contagion for subperiod 1 in Table 6.3 but not in Table 6.4.

Although a number of differences can also be identified in the cumulative subperiod data, the general patterns identified are similar. Both tables indicate that contagion impacted African frontier markets quickly around the onset of the crisis and that it took significantly longer for contagion and interdependence effects to gather pace in developed markets.

5 DISCUSSIONS

It was identified in Table 6.1 that the precrisis constant correlations were a lot lower in Africa frontier markets (low integration countries) than in developed markets (high integration countries). We also note that this chapter has found contagion to have occurred relatively early in the crisis period in Africa but that it took longer to develop in developed markets. In this section we explore potential behavioral explanations for these differences. We do not test the hypotheses put forward here, though, which means that they should therefore be treated as speculations.

There are massive differences between African frontier markets in terms of size, number of traders, the education of traders, and information systems. We therefore speculate that differences in trading behavior may reflect *socionomics*-related differences: specifically, *information* effects, *social networking* effects, and *social mood* effects.

Primary information from US financial markets (such as stock prices and volume data) travels almost instantly around the world to both developed and frontier markets. However, before this information is acted upon it has to be interpreted, and this secondary information will often depend on the advice or influence of friends and colleagues, as well as social influences. Social and professional networks are very important in the dissemination and interpretation of this information, and we argue that there are considerable differences between these networks in African and in developed markets. In times of crisis, investors may base their decisions on low-quality information and rumors disseminated through these networks, which can lead to *noise trading* (Thaler, 1993).

The forms of networks found in developed and frontier markets can be very different. Olsen (2004) suggests that when a network takes on an "aristocratic" structure, the speed with which information and informed opinion pass through society can be significantly faster. The structure, according to Olsen (2004), involves few perceived experts and a large number of investors who trust specific experts. We argue that such "aristocratic networks" are a characteristic of investment communities in frontier Africa, and as a result there is a rapid spread of influence and the emergence of trends. The network effect interacts with the *social mood effects* (Forgas, 1995; Nofsinger, 2005), and we wonder whether the aristocratic networks in Africa lead to relatively rapid adjustments in the social mood among African investors.

The results in Table 6.3 suggest that African markets reacted more quickly at the onset of the financial crisis than did their developed markets counterparts. We speculate that the reason for this may lie in the small, illiquid nature of African frontier markets resulting in small, aristocratic social networks. African exchanges generally have few listed companies and relatively low levels of capitalization. This will also be reflected in the relatively low numbers of active locally based traders and therefore, by implication, relatively small social networks of these traders. This can be contrasted with the vast, and liquid, nature of developed markets with large numbers of both active professional and nonprofessional traders. The social networks in these markets are, by implication, going to be much larger than those found in African markets. Whereas in African markets there may be a few dominant opinion formers in the social network, in developed-market social networks there are likely to be a number of competing high-profile opinion formers. This suggests to us that the generation of consensus in African market social networks is likely to be substantially quicker than the generation of consensus in their developed-market counterparts.

It has been suggested that social networking effects can be viewed as a vector of noise trading (Gai and Kapadia, 2010; Olsen, 2004). These processes are of particular importance in Africa, where it has been reported that markets are characterized by the concentration of trading in few stocks and the dominance of a few companies on the exchanges (Allen et al., 2011; Tafirenyika, 2012). Control of these stocks is often dominated by a few individuals or families. This would suggest that these individuals are dominant players within the aristocratic social networks found in Africa, and therefore information coming from them will spread quickly and can act as a vector of noise trading in the markets. This could, in turn, lead to herding behavior.

The implication of these differences in Africa for *herding* behavior within markets is likely to be highly significant. Specifically, it suggests that herding may occur at a *faster speed* in Africa, as secondary-information-based consensus is likely to develop at a faster rate.

The case for herding being found in this study is strong, given the observed increases in correlation (Prechter, 1985, 1999). It can also be noted that Hwang and Salmon (2009) argue that in developed markets the herding process can be relatively slow to develop (looked at in the context of stock market bubbles, which, they argue, can take a number of years to develop). We argue that in the 2007–09 crisis herding occurred more rapidly in African frontier markets than in developed markets and that this is reflected in our results.

Although speed of herding appears to be the most likely reason for the differences in the speed of contagion observed between African frontier and developed markets, other behavioral-related differences may also have been significant as well. We outline these later.

5.1 Decision Fatigue in Africa

From a behavioral perspective we can ask how the attitude of investors changed as subsequent phases of the crises unfolded. Did they become *habituated* to crisis in the United States and stop responding? We contend that the African data show evidence of *decision fatigue*. For instance, the correlations in Botswana, Côte d'Ivoire, and Morocco show increasing levels from the stable period through the cumulative impact of subperiod 1–4. However, it can be noted that the correlations dropped in the long period, which suggests that behavior changed. This, we speculate, was due to decision fatigue. Mood could have played a role in this regard. As the markets are small and moods are shared more quickly as a result of social networks, fatigue effects were likely to develop more quickly in African markets.

5.2 Loss Aversion in Developed Markets

Slow herding in developed markets may also be partly a function of greater loss aversion. Loss aversion can lead to a *disposition effect* whereby investors hold off realizing their losses until a final market capitulation occurs. It may very well be that the combination of the impact of slow decision making in large social networks and a disposition effect may explain the relatively slow process of herding becoming instigated between developed markets.

6 CONCLUSIONS

The key objective of this chapter has been to assess the impact of the 2007–09 financial crisis on financial contagion on African frontier markets. The 2007–09 crisis was unique from a contagion perspective, given that it was a truly global event that had a significant impact on most of the world's financial markets. This has presented us with a unique opportunity to examine the impact of a single event on different types of markets (developed and frontier).

A number of previous papers in the contagion literature have identified herding as contributing to the transmission of crises. However, these have failed to identify the importance of the *speed of the herding process* in the transmission of contagion.

The contribution of this chapter is that we have identified differences in the speed with which contagion developed in African frontier markets and developed markets. We have also outlined a potential herding-related theoretical reason for this difference in speed—namely, that secondary information is processed and applied at a far quicker rate in markets where small social networks are observed.

The findings of this chapter will help African policy makers in their considerations of how to contain, and mitigate the impact of financial contagion on the continent. This research provides insights into the issue of contagion from the African frontier perspective. It is paramount for policy makers to be aware that it is unlikely that Africa will be immune from any future global financial crisis.

REFERENCES

African Development Bank, 2009. Impact of the Global Financial Crisis and Economic Crisis on Africa. Working Paper Series 9.

Allen, F., Otchere, I., Senbet, L., 2011. African financial systems: a review. Rev. Dev. Finance 1 (2), 79–113.

Berger, D., Pukthuanthong, K., Yang, J., 2011. International diversification with frontier markets. J. Financ. Econ. 101 (1), 227–242.

Calvo, G., Mendoza, E., 2000. Rational contagion and the globalization of security markets. J. Int. Econ. 51, 79–113.

Cheng, H., Glascock, J.L., 2006. Stock market linkages before and after the Asian financial crisis: evidence from three greater China economic area stock markets and the US. Rev. Pacific Basin Financ. Mark. Policies 9 (2), 297.

Chiang, T.C., Jeon, B.N., Li, H., 2007. Dynamic correlation analysis of financial contagion: evidence from Asian markets. J. Int. Money Finance 26 (7), 1206–1228.

Claessens, S., Forbes, K., 2004. International financial contagion: the theory, evidence and policy implications. For the conference The IMF's Role in Emerging Market Economics, Amsterdam, Nov. 18–19.

Collins, D., Biekpe, N., 2003. Contagion and interdependence in African stock markets. S. Afr. J. Econ. 71, 1.

Dornbusch, R., Park, C.Y., Claessens, S., 2000. Contagion: understanding how it spreads and how it can be stopped. World Bank Res. Obser. 15 (2), 177–197.

Eichengreen, B., Rose, A., Wyplosz, C., 1996. Contagious currency crises. Scand. J. Econ. 98, 463–484.

Engle, R.F., 2002. Dynamic conditional correlation: a simple class of multivariate generalized autoregressive conditional heteroscedasticity models. J. Bus. Econ. Stat. 20, 339–350.

Forbes, K., 2004. The Asian flu and Russian virus: the international transmission of crises in firm-level data. J. Int. Econ. 63, 59–92.

Forbes, K., Rigobon, R., 2002. No contagion, only interdependence: measuring stock market co-movements. J. Finance 57 (5), 2223–2261.

Forgas, J.P., 1995. Mood and judgment: the affect infusion model (AIM). Psychol. Bull. (117), 39–66.

Fry-McKibbin, R., Martin, V., Tang, C., 2013. Financial Contagion and Asset Pricing. Centre for Applied Macroeconomic Analysis, Australian National University, Canberra.

Gai, P., Kapadia, S., 2010. Contagion in financial networks. Proc. Royal Soc. A-Math. Phys.Eng. Sci. 466 (2120), 2401–2423.

Harman, D., 2009. Judgment and Decision-Making: Psychological Perspectives. John Wiley & Sons, Chichester, UK.

Hatemi-J, A., Morgan, B., 2007. Liberalized emerging markets and the world economy: testing for increased integration with time-varying volatility. Appl. Financ. Econ. 17, 1245–1250.

Hwang, S., Salmon, M., 2009. Sentiment and Beta Herding. SSRN Working Paper Series. No. 299919.

Kaminsky, G.L., Reinhart, C.M., Vegh, C.A., 2003. The Unholy Trinity of Financial Contagion. Working paper, National Bureau of Economic Research, Cambridge, MA.

Kassim, H.S., 2013. The global financial crisis and the integration of Islamic stock markets in the developed and developing countries. Asian Acad. Manag. J. Account. Finance 9 (2), 75–94.

King, M., Wadhwani, S., 1990. Transmission of volatility between stock markets. Rev. Financ. Stud. 3 (1), 5–33.

Lau, L.J., 2001. Lessons from the East Asian Currency Crisis. Stanford University, Stanford, CA.

Longin, F., Solnik, B., 1995. Is the correlation of international equity returns constant: 1960–1990? J. Int. Money Finance 14 (1), 3–26.

Nofsinger, J.R., 2005. The Psychology of Investing, 2nd edn Pearson Education/Prentice Hall, Upper Saddle River, NJ.

Olsen, R., 2004. Trust, complexity and the 1990s market bubble. J. Behav. Finance 5 (4), 186–191.

Prechter, R.R., 1985. Popular culture and the stock market. In: Prechter, R.R. (Ed.), Pioneering Studies in Socionomics. New Classics Library, Gainesville, GA.

Prechter, R.R., 1999. The Wave Principle of Human Social Behaviour and the New Science of Socionomics. New Classics Library, Gainesville, GA.

Satterthwaite, F.E., 1946. Of variance components. Biometrics 2 (6), 110–114.

Tafirenyika, M., 2012. Harnessing African stock exchanges to promote growth [online]. Available from: http://www.un.org/africarenewal/magazine/august-2012/harnessing-african-stock-exchanges-promote-growth

Thaler, R., 1993. Advances in Behavioural Finance. Russell Sage Foundation, New York.

Tonzer, L., 2013. Cross-Border Interbank Networks, Banking Risk and Contagion. FIW Working Paper (129).

APPENDIX 1: TIME-VARYING CORRELATIONS OF US WITH AFRICAN MARKETS

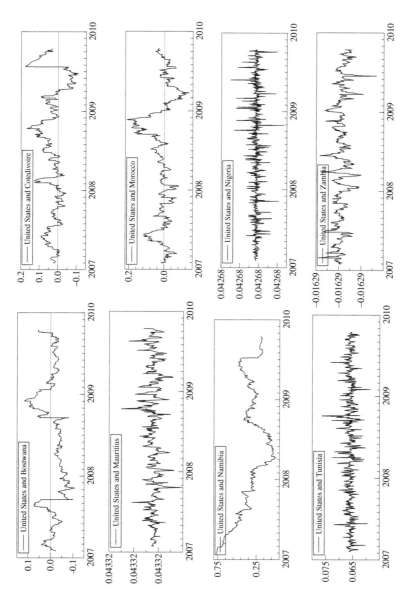

APPENDIX 2: TIME-VARYING CORRELATIONS OF US WITH DEVELOPED MARKETS

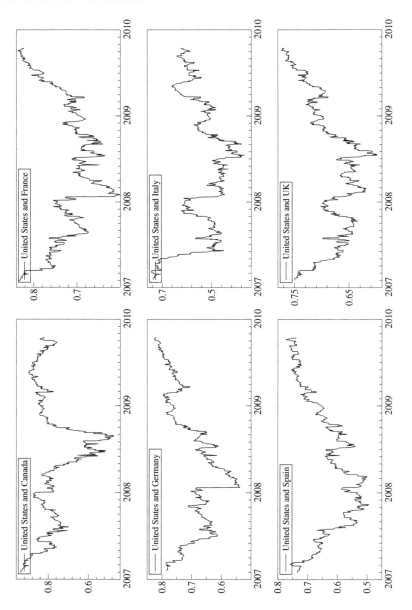

Section B

Europe

Chapter 7

An Assessment of the Real Development Prospects of the EU 28 Frontier Equity Markets

C. Pop*, D. Bozdog**, A. Calugaru†, M.A. Georgescu‡

*Department of Business, Faculty of Business, Babeş-Bolyai University, Cluj-Napoca, Romania; **Financial Engineering Division, Stevens Institute of Technology, Castle Point on Hudson, Hoboken, NJ, United States; †MarketAxess, New York City, NY, United States; ‡Faculty of Public Administration, National University of Political Studies and Public Administration, Bucharest, Romania

Chapter Outline

1 INTRODUCTION

In order to ensure a better differentiation between the wide variety of developing economies and markets, in 1992 the International Monetary Fund introduced the expression "frontier markets" and used the term for describing a subset of smaller, illiquid, less accessible, yet investable (financial) markets, considered to be at an early stage of economic and financial development (Fowler, 2010; Berger et al., 2011). For more than a decade the expression was virtually unknown, and it was brought back into the light by the launch of the first Standard & Poor's (S&P) indices dedicated to frontier markets in Aug. and Oct. 2007. The criteria for monitoring or including a country in the frontier market subset

Handbook of Frontier Markets. http://dx.doi.org/10.1016/B978-0-12-803776-8.00007-0

accompanied the indices. The international investors' growing interest in frontier markets led MSCI Barra to launch a dedicated index in Dec. 2007, followed by the FTSE in Jul. 2008, and by the Russell Frontier Index in 2010. Currently, Standard & Poor's, MSCI Barra, FTSE, and Russell also publish lists of the countries considered to be frontier markets. Moreover, the increasing interest in frontier markets is revealed by the emergence and rise of mutual funds and exchange-traded funds (ETFs) dedicated to these markets, as highlighted by Berger et al. (2011) and De Groot et al. (2012).

The 28 member countries of the European Union (EU) range from developed to frontier markets. The four largest index provider companies include up to 10 EU member countries as frontier markets, as Table 7.1 shows; the present chapter generically refers to EU 10 frontier markets.

The focus on EU 10 frontier markets was induced mainly by these countries' position as EU member states and the influence/impact that the European integration process might have over the development of the respective 10 countries' financial markets. The general expressed idea is that the frontier markets are the next emerging markets and have an important untapped economic potential, providing interesting investment opportunities and diversification benefits (Pop et al., 2013; Chen et al., 2014). Do the EU 10 frontier markets exhibit these characteristics? The answer is a rather complicated one. As of Dec. 2014, the EU 10 frontier markets constituted 3.25% of the EU 28 and only 0.47% of EU 28 equity market capitalization. These figures seem to indicate the growth potential. The

TABLE 7.1 The EU Frontier Markets According to Frontier Index Providers

FTSE (26 frontier countries) as of Mar. 2015	MSCI Barra (32 frontier countries) as of Jun. 2015	Russell (39 frontier countries) as of Mar. 2015	Standard & Poor's (34 frontier countries) as of Jun. 2015
Bulgaria	Bulgaria	Bulgaria	Bulgaria
Croatia	Croatia	Croatia	Croatia
Cyprus	—	Cyprus	Cyprus
Estonia	Estonia	Estonia	Estonia
Lithuania	Lithuania	Lithuania	Lithuania
Malta	—	Malta	—
Romania	Romania	Romania	Romania
Slovakia	—	Slovakia	Slovakia
Slovenia	Slovenia	Slovenia	Slovenia
Latvia (monitored)	—	—	Latvia

Sources: http://www.ftse.com/products/downloads/Europe-Frontier_latest.pdf, https://www.msci.com/market-cap-weighted-indexes, http://www.russell.com/documents/indexes/research/global-guidebook-2015.pdf

EU membership also provides numerous benefits for frontier market economic development, and thus financial development; mainly, the further development of domestic securities markets remains an open question. Eight of the 10 frontier countries come from the former communist bloc, and the reestablishment of their securities exchanges represented an important step toward an open economy. For Malta and Cyprus, the establishment of their respective securities exchanges not until the 1990s was generated mainly by their political situation; both countries gained their independence only during the 1960s. Nevertheless, for all these 10 countries, the national securities exchanges are a source of national pride, as highlighted by O'Hara (2001). As EU member states, all these frontier markets have to face the challenges and the competition pressure generated by the enforcement of the Markets in Financial Instruments Directive (MiFID) in Nov. 2007. The main menaces seemed to derive from the development of alternative trading venues (Skinner, 2007), the potential need to increase the critical size required for an exchange to attract and retain liquidity and to generate the necessary revenues for investments in technology (Haas, 2007), and the possibilities presented to domestic companies to gain access to a variety of trading venues all over Europe. Two reports on Bulgaria and Croatia (World Bank, 2011a,b) show that the alternative trading venues seem not to be of interest for the domestic companies of frontier markets (mainly due to their low liquidity), and the domestic companies' listing process continues to occur on the main regulated market of European frontier countries. Thus for the moment some of the menaces identified in 2007 seem to surround the EU 10 frontier markets, and their reality and their potential dangers should be considered within any future development strategy of European frontier securities markets.

One of the main important strength of any frontier market is represented by the diversification potential it might offer for international investors' portfolios. Nevertheless, this advantage is fading away as the globalization of financial markets is accompanied by the integration process of securities (mainly equity) markets around the world and also generates takeovers of domestic companies by multinationals. For the EU 10 frontier markets, the process of integration with the more developed markets of the EU and the takeovers of domestic companies by European multinationals is expected to be more rapid and to impair the advantage of diversification exhibited by these markets for international investors. Under these conditions, a small, less liquid securities market might not be relevant in the EU context, as pointed out by Iorgova and Ong (2008). On the other hand, the continuance and further development of EU 10 frontier markets seem to be needed to support the growth of smaller domestic companies of local and/or regional interest, as stressed by O'Hara (2001) and Andritzky (2007).

The EU 10 frontier markets are confronted with two extremes: the lack of relevance within the EU and the potential evolution toward an emerging market. Therefore an investigation of their development potential is of importance for the academic world and practitioners alike. The academic literature has concentrated until now on the frontier markets' diversification potential by considering the respective market indices and investigating the integration process with emerging and developed markets. Almost no research has considered the internal diversification potential of the EU frontier markets, a key factor in their future evolution. Moreover, only two papers, by Chen et al. (2014) and Pukthuanthong and Roll (2009), consider all 10 EU frontier markets (included in larger samples) when researching the respective markets' integration level, while no research so far has been dedicated to only the 10 frontier markets of the EU and their internal diversification potential. The results show that, in general, the EU 10 frontier markets exhibit internal diversification potential and therefore can present interesting investing opportunities for domestic and international investors. The internal diversification potential seems to be lower in the cases of Latvia and Malta, with trading concentrated around the pharmaceutical and banking sectors, respectively. Romania has a peculiar position with an apparently limited internal diversification potential.

Further, the present chapter is structured as follows: Section 2 presents a comparative analysis of the EU 10 frontier markets and the existing research results regarding these countries, Section 3 investigates the internal diversification potential of the EU 10 frontier markets using the Granger causality to establish the existence or absence of a domestic index leader and historical domestic, European, and international betas when only one index is reported for the respective frontier market; Section 4 discusses and concludes.

2 A COMPARATIVE ANALYSIS OF THE EU 10 FRONTIER MARKETS

The EU 10 frontier markets represent roughly between one-fifth and one-third of the frontier country lists, as Table 7.1 shows. Therefore, as a group, they have an important position within the frontier market category. How many of the frontier market characteristics or features can be applied to this group of European frontier markets is an interesting question to be answered.

In the absence of a generally accepted definition of frontier (securities) markets, the following set of characteristics or features was identified based on Miles (2005), Speidell and Krohne (2007), Girard and Sinha (2008), Speidell (2008), Wright (2008), Quisenberry and Griffith (2010), Sadorsky (2011), Speidell (2011), Wawrzaszek and Vadlamudi (2011), Gupta et al. (2012), Lin (2011), and Marshall et al. (2015). This set of characteristics refers mainly to the equity segment of frontier securities markets.

First, frontier markets are small, with low market capitalization and/or low ratios of market capitalization to gross domestic product (GDP). Second, frontier markets are illiquid or have limited liquidity seen mainly in thin, infrequent, and irregular trading activity, and have high transaction costs. Third, the trading activity tends to be concentrated around a small number of securities with significant capitalization. Moreover, the sector weight might favor the financial stocks, which, in some cases, compose the vast majority of the frontier equity market universe. Fourth, frontier (securities) markets represent high-risk investments caused by a wide variety of factors, from those specific to the respective securities markets (eg, the absence or limited availability of short selling, a low level of transparency at market level but mainly at company level, weak corporate governance) to security price volatility, exchange rate volatility, inadequate regulatory frameworks, unsatisfactory protection of shareholders and creditors, a shifting attitude toward foreign investors, political risk, and sovereign risk. Fifth, frontier markets usually present a relatively low level of integration with developed and emerging markets, and also provide greater return potential, as recently highlighted by Porwal (2014) for the S&P's frontier markets index between 2008 and 2013. Therefore, frontier markets are perceived to be able to provide important diversification benefits for international/global portfolios.

Four of these five characteristics will be discussed based on Tables 7.2–7.4.

As Table 7.2 shows, all EU 10 frontier markets have had about 20 or 25 years of activity. Their small dimensions and relatively low importance in their respective countries' GDPs is revealed in Table 7.3. Having an average market capitalization of EUR 5759 million and an average ratio of market capitalization to GDP of 22.98%, the EU 10 frontier markets comply with the first characteristic. Two countries, Croatia and Malta, exhibit ratios of market capitalization to GDP similar to those of developed markets—higher than the 25% suggested by Girard and Sinha (2008) as a threshold for developed markets. Thus their market capitalization is low or very low; this phenomenon seems to be characteristic of countries with limited resources and an economic activity dominated by the financial sector. Market capitalization of most of the EU 10 frontier markets follows an upward trend over the 15 years under scrutiny. Romania, Croatia, and Bulgaria exhibit high growth rates, thus continuing to make a modest contribution to their respective countries' GDPs; an exception is Croatia, with a profile closer to an emerging market. The only frontier market that followed a downward trend is Cyprus, with a slight recovery in 2014.

The turnover ratio was used as a proxy for equity market liquidity. As Table 7.3 shows, the liquidity is low, with an average for all markets for the entire period of 11.26%. Between 2000 and 2002 the liquidity of several frontier markets was relatively high, mainly due to the transactions that followed the privatization programs. After the financial crisis in 2008, most of EU 10 frontier markets have seen their liquidity decreasing, mainly due to the exit of institutional foreign investors. The 10 frontier markets under scrutiny comply with the second characteristic also.

The concentration of turnover around the five most traded companies is also presented in Table 7.3. The average for all countries for the entire period is 72.02%. The countries with a lower concentration around the top five companies are Lithuania, Croatia, and Bulgaria. The country with the highest concentration of trades around the top five companies is Slovakia. Only two countries, Croatia and Malta, exhibit a decreasing trend for this concentration, suggesting that an increased number of companies have started to register important trading volumes. It must be pointed out that the EU 10 frontier markets include two extremes: the Baltic countries and Malta with a relatively low number of listed companies (less than 50 on average for the entire period), and Bulgaria, Croatia, and Slovakia with more than 100 listed companies. While for the countries with a

TABLE 7.2 EU 10 Frontier Countries Summary

Country	Stock exchange	Year of stock exchange establishment	Stock market main index	Eurozone member since	Sovereign rating as of Jun. 2015		
					S&P	Moody	Fitch
Bulgaria	Bulgarian Stock Exchange	1997	SOFIX	No	BB+	Baa2	BBB−
Croatia	Zagreb Stock Exchange	1991	CROBEX	No	BB	Ba1	BB
Cyprus	Cyprus Stock Exchange	1996	CSE General Market Index	Jan. 1, 2008	B+	B3	B−
Estonia	NASDAQ-OMX-Baltic Tallinn Stock Exchange	1995	OMX Tallinn	Jan. 1, 2011	AA−	A1	A+
Latvia	NASDAQ-OMX-Baltic Riga Stock Exchange	1993	OMX Riga	Jan. 1, 2014	A−	A3	A−
Lithuania	NASDAQ-OMX-Baltic Vilnius Stock Exchange	1992	OMX Vilnius	Jan. 1, 2015	A−	A3	A−
Malta	Malta Stock Exchange	1990	MSE Index	Jan. 1, 2008	BBB+	A3	A
Romania	Bucharest Stock Exchange	1995	BET-C	No	BBB−	Baa3	BBB−
Slovakia	Bratislava Stock Exchange	1991	SAX Index	Jan. 1, 2009	A	A2	A+
Slovenia	Ljubljana Stock Exchange	1988/1989	SBI 20/SBI Top Index	Jan. 1, 2007	A−	Baa3	BBB+

Notes: Malta started trading only in 1992. The periods each country was an ERM II member are: Bulgaria: no; Croatia: no; Cyprus: May 2, 2005–Dec. 31, 2007; Estonia: Jun. 28, 2004–Dec. 31, 2010; Latvia: May 2, 2005–Dec. 31, 2013; Lithuania: Jun. 28, 2004–Dec. 31, 2014; Malta: May 2, 2005–Dec. 31, 2007; Romania: no; Slovakia: Nov. 28, 2005–Dec. 31, 2008; Slovenia: Jun. 28, 2004–Dec. 31, 2006.
Source: Stock exchanges websites and http://countryeconomy.com/ratings

TABLE 7.3 EU 10 Frontier Securities Markets Summary

Country	2000	2001	2002	2003	2004	2005	2006	2007	2008	2009	2010	2011	2012	2013	2014
Number of listed companies															
Bulgaria	n/a	30	31	31	31	331	346	369	399	399	390	393	387	381	372
Croatia	64	73	73	175	183	194	202	383	377	280	257	254	226	208	204
Cyprus	124	149	159	130	124	119	141	123	119	115	110	106	101	95	94
Estonia	20	17	14	14	13	13	17	18	18	16	15	15	16	18	15
Latvia	22	16	13	13	12	12	11	42	36	35	34	37	31	31	29
Lithuania	54	45	46	45	43	43	44	41	41	41	40	36	33	32	33
Malta	10	12	13	14	14	14	15	16	19	20	21	21	22	24	24
Romania	115	66	65	62	60	64	53	54	64	64	69	79	81	83	83
Slovakia	866	888	510	366	294	224	187	160	193	172	165	147	134	131	125
Slovenia	149	151	135	134	140	116	100	87	84	76	72	66	61	55	51
Equity market capitalization (EUR mil.)															
Bulgaria	661	565	700	1,391	2,062	4,312	7,830	14,821	6,371	6,031	5,498	6,358	5,025	5,093	4,988
Croatia	2,905	3,455	3,826	4,909	8,236	10,909	22,706	48,005	19,666	18,443	19,323	17,566	16,990	15,700	16,533
Cyprus	12,402	6,572	4,505	3,807	3,588	5,580	12,245	20,160	5,733	7,157	5,094	2,198	1,514	1,527	3,331
Estonia	1,932	1,666	2,315	3,005	3,545	2,963	4,522	4,105	1,403	1,850	1,685	1,241	1,769	1,877	1,663
Latvia	593	782	686	902	1,017	1,746	1,643	2,098	1,166	1,317	942	826	842	948	860
Lithuania	1,706	1,360	1,394	2,783	4,755	6,937	7,728	6,892	2,608	3,220	4,220	3,139	2,992	2,907	3,330
Malta	2,169	1,528	1,319	1,467	2,089	3,474	3,416	4,916	2,567	2,844	3,222	2,641	2,754	3,245	3,010

(Continued)

TABLE 7.3 EU 10 Frontier Securities Markets Summary (*cont.*)

Country	2000	2001	2002	2003	2004	2005	2006	2007	2008	2009	2010	2011	2012	2013	2014
Romania	463	1,361	2,646	2,991	8,819	15,311	18,858	21,524	6,474	8,402	9,776	10,818	12,088	17,834	18,385
Slovakia	3,623	3,870	2,462	2,204	3,239	3,729	4,124	4,555	3,907	3,614	3,380	4,183	4,094	4,075	4,444
Slovenia	3,335	3,839	5,355	5,660	7,115	6,697	11,513	19,740	8,468	8,462	7,028	4,873	4,911	5,173	6,214
Market capitalization to GDP (%)															
Bulgaria	4.54	3.52	4.02	7.41	9.87	18.29	29.57	48.16	17.98	17.26	15.25	16.52	12.69	12.75	11.87
Croatia	12.55	13.53	13.61	15.99	24.61	29.88	55.56	110.66	41.37	41.19	43.50	39.75	38.90	36.25	38.37
Cyprus	117.72	57.95	38.18	29.79	25.98	37.43	83.53	126.78	33.41	42.47	29.27	12.22	8.48	9.25	19.03
Estonia	31.31	23.92	29.84	34.55	36.52	26.31	33.77	25.55	8.64	13.44	11.76	7.78	10.46	10.18	8.52
Latvia	8.75	10.52	8.19	8.61	8.67	12.71	10.28	9.98	5.09	7.11	5.22	4.09	3.81	4.06	3.58
Lithuania	13.71	9.96	9.21	16.79	26.07	33.03	32.06	23.98	8.05	12.08	15.29	10.19	9.13	8.40	9.17
Malta	52.43	35.84	29.23	30.60	42.92	67.56	65.61	88.17	43.04	47.62	51.03	40.36	40.54	45.16	38.04
Romania	1.38	3.22	6.08	5.65	14.36	19.09	19.29	17.26	4.63	7.11	7.86	8.24	9.18	12.49	12.25
Slovakia	12.54	11.86	6.85	7.32	9.32	9.48	9.27	8.31	6.07	5.76	5.13	6.05	5.73	5.65	5.91
Slovenia	17.64	18.15	22.67	21.52	25.65	22.91	37.08	57.06	22.74	23.80	19.74	13.47	13.85	14.67	16.68
Turnover ratio (%) as proxy for market liquidity															
Bulgaria	n/a	0.25	1.04	2.23	21.23	23.69	18.10	31.31	20.72	11.14	7.22	3.90	5.46	12.89	5.99
Croatia	6.89	3.75	4.13	4.03	4.24	5.86	8.66	6.39	12.52	5.49	4.10	4.11	2.43	2.57	2.45
Cyprus	88.04	58.64	14.34	5.17	5.08	6.60	23.94	18.43	26.20	18.00	16.47	16.29	15.06	2.04	1.56
Estonia	16.87	14.86	11.22	16.22	n/a	n/a	16.94	37.17	44.05	14.43	14.42	15.07	7.71	10.00	7.66
Latvia	42.72	23.59	27.29	13.60	n/a	n/a	5.11	4.67	2.40	1.06	2.23	3.87	1.96	2.28	2.01
Lithuania	13.36	17.52	13.50	5.78	6.64	n/a	20.79	10.98	12.73	6.65	5.31	5.61	4.32	3.17	2.37

Malta	9.23	3.40	3.35	2.10	3.59	3.48	6.00	1.24	1.91	0.88	1.12	1.44	1.21	1.64	1.69
Romania	20.09	10.83	8.09	8.47	6.72	13.93	12.03	9.20	16.25	7.66	7.20	21.69	13.08	10.12	11.92
Slovakia	16.20	27.30	33.26	26.69	16.33	1.48	1.70	0.48	0.33	3.38	6.80	8.34	3.09	1.96	1.27
Slovenia	9.83	28.35	23.33	11.07	13.12	14.05	12.60	17.13	18.95	12.88	6.50	8.11	6.18	5.79	9.79
Top five companies % of turnover															
Bulgaria	n/a	n/a	n/a	n/a	n/a	n/a	73.66	56.49	52.93	57.21	59.64	52.26	65.11	75.30	61.05
Croatia	91.16	77.36	76.08	79.91	74.09	59.69	58.65	36.42	48.38	57.23	59.46	52.32	47.74	46.88	49.15
Cyprus	41.17	36.18	41.05	50.26	61.16	73.26	79.26	64.34	80.49	90.26	89.43	83.46	85.61	64.06	59.21
Estonia	88.60	94.74	94.32	93.88	96.46	92.26	81.61	71.03	74.52	79.57	78.15	79.65	85.83	85.43	85.86
Latvia	82.34	82.60	66.26	30.77	43.48	73.04	75.54	80.60	77.49	77.86	80.33	79.89	82.00	84.83	89.08
Lithuania	41.26	28.97	21.70	50.44	55.72	51.84	59.69	67.16	73.05	70.11	57.01	56.01	65.43	59.73	58.89
Malta	94.12	88.28	96.38	86.43	94.00	92.52	91.38	88.38	83.45	91.50	83.62	90.05	82.51	73.85	79.20
Romania	n/a	n/a	n/a	67.64	63.25	80.86	77.81	65.04	66.31	69.67	67.95	76.08	73.01	75.75	68.73
Slovakia	n/a	n/a	n/a	87.49	86.26	82.86	90.53	84.09	90.23	88.50	89.55	97.81	96.76	97.81	89.71
Slovenia	45.18	50.96	60.43	53.74	56.10	58.52	68.36	70.08	73.13	78.43	78.20	87.93	86.58	83.96	77.32
Financial sector importance (%) in total equity turnover															
Bulgaria	n/a	n/a	n/a	n/a	n/a	n/a	33.8	49.3	29.5	46.0	47.1	62.1	47.9	41.0	39.5
Croatia	89.8	54.2	48.6	17.5	Financial companies appear only sporadically in top five with low than 10%										
Cyprus	41.4	40.9	48.2	63.4	55.7	81.7	87.8	77.2	81.7	91.5	95.1	93.5	95.4	86.5	78.8
Estonia	60.5	54.4	66.7	61.7	64.7	58.1	No financial companies appear in top five as reported to FESE.								
Latvia	42.3	29.6	No financial companies appear in top five as reported in monthly reports and to FESE.												

(Continued)

TABLE 7.3 EU 10 Frontier Securities Markets Summary (cont.)

Country	2000	2001	2002	2003	2004	2005	2006	2007	2008	2009	2010	2011	2012	2013	2014
Lithuania	21.9	n/a	n/a	n/a	n/a	19.5	29.4	38.4	39.1	27.4	24.3	29.8	16.9	19.9	13.7
Malta	43.2	37.5	44.1	56.6	60.9	65.8	71.7	57.8	47.9	59.2	54.0	64.1	48.2	41.5	51.5
Romania	n/a	n/a	n/a	51.4	54.2	67.3	71.1	70.3	66.6	75.7	73.9	88.5	83.5	72.2	63.5
Slovakia	n/a	n/a	n/a	13.1	32.9	41.8	18.9	28.5	33.5	50.7	64.4	49.6	55.8	47.2	44.1
Slovenia	Financial companies appear only sporadically in top five and with low percentages.														
Equity market performances based on main equity indices (%)															
Bulgaria	29.41	11.27	54.24	150.30	39.60	32.38	48.74	42.14	−79.36	18.82	−15.13	−11.18	8.62	43.00	5.76
Croatia	24.42	16.26	12.27	1.23	20.42	27.26	61.55	62.96	−67.17	13.08	4.33	−18.41	−0.36	1.75	16.26
Cyprus	−65.02	−47.20	−26.78	−16.25	−11.24	52.31	125.38	21.41	−77.43	44.98	33.23	−72.03	−61.16	−12.92	−18.14
Estonia	−0.20	1.48	46.98	34.08	56.11	47.20	29.04	−13.38	−62.98	41.99	69.52	−26.28	34.67	8.62	−8.20
Latvia	49.06	46.93	−14.30	48.36	43.45	65.52	−5.94	−10.21	−54.85	2.96	33.30	−5.63	6.04	15.00	−11.75
Lithuania	−7.30	−18.03	12.47	102.08	67.85	52.66	9.12	4.20	−65.30	44.56	55.93	−26.66	18.76	16.41	4.23
Malta	3.29	−33.66	−15.25	13.39	44.08	62.74	−1.93	3.78	−35.69	7.87	8.86	−17.89	3.49	13.88	−9.40
Romania	7.39	−6.47	123.62	22.62	98.29	31.63	25.07	26.27	−69.68	34.62	13.49	−16.73	6.29	16.28	−1.21
Slovakia	18.64	34.43	16.18	31.21	84.19	26.83	2.10	7.40	−19.78	−25.67	−13.71	−6.47	−10.80	4.20	13.93
Slovenia	0.09	19.01	55.24	65.92	29.56	2.66	56.71	67.79	−66.08	16.31	−14.94	−30.58	7.10	2.53	19.12

Sources: Federation of European Securities Exchanges (FESE), stock exchange websites, and Syriopoulos and Roumpis (2009). In the case of Malta and Slovakia, the percentages are based only on two banks that appear in top five as reported to FESE. In the case of Romania, for the period 2005–10 it reported to FESE the top five without the closed-end funds. For Slovenia for 2000–02 SBI 20 Index was available; since 2004 SBI Top Index was used.

TABLE 7.4 EU 10 Frontier Markets Position Based on Global Competitiveness Report

Financial market development rank

Country	2006/07 (of 125)	2007/08 (of 131)	2008/09 (of 134)	2009/10 (of 133)	2010/11 (of 139)	2011/12 (of 142)	2012/13 (of 144)	2013/14 (of 148)	2014/15 (of 144)
Bulgaria	90	74	74	76	91	75	80	73	60
Croatia	68	68	63	77	88	87	92	78	74
Cyprus	55	39	27	18	15	25	38	64	83
Estonia	25	31	28	29	45	41	39	35	29
Latvia	40	38	39	60	86	60	52	45	33
Lithuania	45	54	56	72	89	89	87	87	65
Malta	46	20	18	13	11	15	15	34	36
Romania	76	78	60	56	81	84	77	72	64
Slovakia	34	33	31	28	37	47	47	42	39
Slovenia	63	47	46	48	77	102	128	134	133
Regulation of securities exchanges rank									
Bulgaria	n/a	n/a	104	108	109	102	109	116	103
Croatia	n/a	n/a	75	73	74	79	82	78	72
Cyprus	n/a	n/a	54	29	34	41	48	75	68
Estonia	n/a	n/a	26	32	44	37	40	40	39
Latvia	n/a	n/a	62	79	99	71	64	64	60
Lithuania	n/a	n/a	41	51	57	50	50	65	70
Malta	n/a	n/a	22	15	12	21	12	17	26
Romania	n/a	n/a	91	88	97	106	111	115	101
Slovakia	n/a	n/a	76	84	89	85	87	93	85
Slovenia	n/a	n/a	70	60	66	73	73	84	88

Source: World Economic Forum Reports (World Economic Forum, 2006, 2007, 2008, 2009, 2010, 2011, 2012, 2013, 2014).

small number of listed companies the turnover concentration around the top five (often representing over 10% of the listed companies) is to be expected, for the second group of countries this concentration indicates that the companies outside the top five are of marginal interest for investors for various motives: from a low free float to lack of transparency and poor levels of corporate governance.

The data for the dominance of the financial sector, as can be seen in Table 7.3, are incomplete. Only for Bulgaria, Cyprus, and Romania were the data extracted from the respective exchanges' monthly reports. For the remaining seven countries the data were estimated based on the top five concentration; in the case of Malta only two banks (Bank of Valletta and HSBC Malta) were considered. Based on these partial data, only Cyprus, Malta, and Romania seem to have the turnover dominated by financial sector companies, while for the other countries, other sectors like manufacturing and telecommunications seem to be dominant, depending on country specifics.

Therefore, the EU 10 frontier markets only partly comply with the third characteristic.

The risks associated with investments in frontier markets are partly presented in Table 7.2 (sovereign risk and exchange rate volatility risk) and Table 7.3 (main equity indices' performances). As Table 7.2 shows, 7 of the 10 EU frontier countries, and partly Bulgaria, present medium grades for sovereign risk and being considered as "investable" economies. Croatia is considered speculative and Cyprus highly speculative. The only country that faced an important downgrade is Cyprus due to the banking crisis the country went through during 2011. The ratings for Croatia, Malta, and Slovenia remained almost at the same level as those of 2000, while Bulgaria, Lithuania, Romania, and Slovakia registered an upgrade from speculative or highly speculative ratings.

The exchange rate volatility risk was also relatively low for the majority of EU 10 frontier markets since 2004/05 when seven countries became members of Exchange Rate Mechanism (ERM) II and agreed to peg their currencies to the euro with the further aim of becoming eurozone members and adopting the euro as their currency. Only Bulgaria, Croatia, and Romania present a potential exchange rate volatility risk. However, this should be considered within the frame that these three countries intend at some time in the future to enter ERM II and also to become eurozone members; therefore their national banks currently ensure a certain level of exchange rate stability.

While the the sovereign and exchange rate risks seem somewhat tamed for the EU 10 frontier markets, the price volatility risk, captured by the annual performances of respective securities exchanges' indices in Table 7.3, tells another story. The average return rate for the entire period for all countries is 12.76%, with Bulgaria and Romania as top performers, while Cyprus is the worst performer of the 10 countries. The values ranging from annual returns as high as 150% and as low as −79% indicate a high level of volatility. Using as a simple proxy for volatility the standard deviation of the annual series, the average standard deviation for the entire period for all 10 countries is 38.03%, which can be considered high. The frontier market with the highest volatility is Cyprus (55.99%), followed by Bulgaria, Romania, and Lithuania with standard deviations higher than 40%, while at the lower end is Malta with a standard deviation of only 25.81%.

The picture of the fourth characteristics is completed by the information in Table 7.4, which shows, according to World Economic Forum ranking, the level of development for the EU 10 frontier markets and the regulation of their respective securities exchanges.

Concerning the financial market development, four countries rank between 25th and 40th position (Estonia, Latvia, Malta, and Slovakia), while the remaining six countries rank below the 50th position, with Slovenia ranking well beyond 100th position. The regulation of the securities markets reveals that only one country, Malta, ranks within or close to the first 25th position, followed by Estonia usually within top 40 positions. The remaining eight countries rank at or well below the 60th position, with Romania having the lowest rank at around 100th position.

The financial development information is completed by the data in Table 7.5, which shows that the EU 10 frontier markets have underdeveloped derivative products and other financial instruments or completely lack those segments, while the turnover concentrates mainly around stock shares and/or bonds, indicating also a low level of market sophistication.

It can be safely inferred that EU 10 frontier markets comply with the fourth characteristic; thus the sovereign risk and exchange rate risk are lower given these countries' positions as EU 28 member states.

TABLE 7.5 EU 10 Frontier Markets' Turnover Structure (%) by Type of Financial Instruments (Annual Averages for the Period 2006–14)

Country	Equities	Bonds	ETFs and UCITs	Structured products	Derivatives	Others (rights, warrants)
Bulgaria	89.87	9.67	0.46	—	—	—
Croatia	43.71	56.01	—	0.17	—	0.11
Cyprus	94.41	2.72	2.87	—	—	—
Estonia	99.99	0.01	—	—	—	—
Latvia	44.58	55.42	—	—	—	—
Lithuania	70.35	29.65	—	—	—	—
Malta	10.39	89.61	—	—	—	—
Romania	87.14	9.70	0.12	2.65	0.39	—
Slovakia	0.87	99.13	—	—	—	—
Slovenia	75.73	19.27	5.00	—	—	—

Sources: FESE and respective securities exchanges websites.

The fifth characteristic is investigated and discussed by a growing body of literature focusing on frontier market integration relative to developed and/or emerging markets. The studies that include a variable number of the EU 10 frontier markets can be split into three categories. The first one incorporates the European frontier markets within medium to large samples of countries (between 15 and 85 countries) and includes the studies of Speidell and Krohne (2007), Speidell (2008), Pukthuanthong and Roll (2009), Berger et al. (2011), Todorov and Bidarkota (2011), Kohlert (2011), Lin (2011), Samarakoon (2011), Guesmi and Nguyen (2011), De Groot et al. (2012), Baumoehl and Lyocsa (2014), Chen et al. (2014), and Marshall et al. (2015). Only the papers of Pukthuanthong and Roll (2009) and Chen et al. (2014) include in their large samples all the EU 10 frontier markets. The second strand of literature is the largest and the oldest, including studies before the countries under scrutiny were labeled "frontier," and concentrates on smaller samples of countries (fewer than 15) grouped based on regional criteria or on congeniality. Within this category the following studies were considered: Schroeder (2000), Patev and Kanaryan (2002), Mateus (2004), Birg and Lucey (2006), Onay (2006), Syllignakis and Kouretas (2006), Vizek and Dadic (2006), Dvorak and Podpiera (2006), Moore (2007), Samitas et al. (2006), Girard and Sinha (2008), Middleton et al. (2008), Syriopoulos and Roumpis (2009), Wang and Moore (2009), Horobet and Lupu (2009), Allen et al. (2010), Todorov and Bidarkota (2010), Demian (2011), Kenourgios and Samitas (2011), Nikkinen et al. (2011), Syriopoulos (2011), Syllignakis and Kouretas (2011), Gupta et al. (2012), Wang and Shih (2013), Guidi and Ugur (2014), and Reboredo et al. (2015). The third group of studies contains research concentrated on only a number of EU 10 frontier markets and is dominated by the studies dedicated to Baltic countries of Maneschioeld (2006), Moroza (2008), Masood et al. (2010), Nikkinen et al. (2012), and Babalos et al. (2014). One study that concentrated on 8 of the 10 EU frontier markets was found, that of Kiviaho et al. (2014).

Despite their variety as to sample, period, or method of research, all these studies document the partial integration of the EU 10 frontier markets with the developed and/or emerging markets; this partial integration evolved from complete segmenta-tion of the respective countries at the beginning of the 2000s to partial integration influenced by the EU englargement announcement, as documented by Dvorak and Podpiera (2006), but not by the accession, as shown by Demian (2011). Moreover, the integration was shown to vary over time, with periods of increase, decrease, and a new increase during the 2007–09 global financial crisis. Berger et al. (2011) and Guesmi and Nguyen (2011) highlight that the EU member countries and respective southeastern European countries exhibit a higher level of integration than the rest of the frontier markets all over the world. Of the EU 10 frontier markets, Romania and Slovakia seem to be the least integrated, while the Baltic countries have an increased level of integration and therefore offer lower diversification benefits, as pointed out by Nikkinen et al. (2011) and Kiviaho et al. (2014).

Based on the vast number of studies mentioned, it can safely be said that the EU 10 frontier markets comply with the fifth characteristic also; however, this fifth characteristic will have the tendency to become weaker as the integration process is expected to continue.

3 HYPOTHESIS, DATA, AND RESEARCH RESULTS

In order to investigate the internal diversification potential of the EU 10 frontier markets, the following two hypotheses were formulated:

Hypothesis 1 (when a stock exchange reports two or more equity indices): if, based on Granger causality, no index leader can be found, the stock exchange exhibits an internal diversification potential and therefore might represent an interesting opportunity for investors. This hypothesis is based on the idea formulated by Canegrati (2008) regarding the leading indices at world level.

Hypothesis 1 modified: if, based on Granger causality, the index leader is an all-share/composite index (including a large portfolio of shares), the stock exchange exhibits an internal diversification potential and therefore might represent an interesting opportunity for investors.

Hypothesis 2 (when a stock exchange reports only one index): if for the selected companies the historic domestic beta is higher than the European beta and international beta, the stock exchange exhibits an internal diversification potential and therefore might represent an interesting opportunity for investors. This second hypothesis is based on the idea formulated by Dvorak and Podpiera (2006) regarding historic beta.

Table 7.6 shows the four countries where multiple equity indices are reported and the remaining six countries with just one reported equity index apiece from which three to four companies were selected.

3.1 The Granger Causality for Testing Hypothesis 1 and 1 Modified

The bivariate Granger causality test is implemented by regressing the respective index on m-lag values of the index and m-lag values of the reference index.

$$R_{\text{Index}}(t) = a_0 + a_1 R_{\text{Index}}(t-1) + \cdots + a_m R_{\text{Index}}(t-m) + \varepsilon_t$$

$$R_{\text{Index}}(t) = a_0 + a_1 R_{\text{Index}}(t-1) + \cdots + a_m R_{\text{Index}}(t-m) + b_1 R_{\text{BET-Fi}}(t-1) + \cdots \\ + b_m R_{\text{BET-Fi}}(t-m) + \varepsilon_t$$

The null hypothesis that the reference index does not Granger-cause the chosen index is accepted if and only if no lagged values of reference are retained in the regression. An F-test is then used to determine whether the coefficients of m-lag values of the reference index are jointly equal to zero. The p-values for each F-test are reported in table format.

The data for the indices were provided by Bloomberg for the available period between Jan. 2000 and May/Jun. 2015. The period under investigation differs for each of the four exchanges. The total return (TR) indices were eliminated due to their short history for all the exchanges. For Croatia only two

TABLE 7.6 The EU 10 Frontier Markets' Equity Indices

Country	Reported equity indices	Selected indices or companies
Bulgaria	SOFIX, BG BX40, BG TR30, BG REIT	SOFIX, BG BX40, BG REIT
Croatia	CROBEX, CROBEX10, CROBEXindustrija, CROBEXkonstruct, CROBEXnutris, CROBEXplus, CROBEXtr, CROBEXtransport, CROBEXturist	CROBEX, CROBEX10
Cyprus	CSE General Index, CSE Main Market Index, CSE Alternative Market Index, CSE Investment Market index, CSE Hotel Index	CSE Main Market Index, CSE Investment Market Index, CSE Hotel Index
Estonia	OMX Tallinn Index (TALSE Index)	Olympic Entertainment Group, Silvano Fashion Group, Tallink Grupp, Tallina Vesi
Latvia	OMX Riga Index (RIGSE Index)	Grindeks, Latvijas Kugnieciba, Olainfarm, SAF-Tehnika
Lithuania	OMX Vilnius Index (VILSE Index)	Apranga, Invalda, Siauliu Banka, TEO LT
Malta	MSE Index (MALTEX Index)	Bank of Valleta, HSBC Bank, Malta International Airport
Romania	BET, BET-TR, BET-Plus/BET-C, BET-Fi, BET-BK, BET-NG, BET-XT, BET-XT-TR	BET, BET-Plus/BET-C, BET-Fi, BET-BK, BET-NG, BET-XT
Slovakia	SBI Top Index	Best Hotels Properties, Slovnaft, Tatry Mountain Resort, Vseobec Uverova Banka
Slovenia	SAX Index	Gorenje, Krka, Mercator, Petrol

Source: Stock market websites.

indices were retained for analysis due to the fact that all the sector indices were launched recently and the data are available only since Feb. 2013. For Cyprus, only the main market indices were considered since it has the largest contribution to the stock market capitalization.

The Granger causality was considered for 1 lag, 5 lags (a typical trading week), and 20 lags (the average number of trading days within a month).

The results of Granger causality test are presented in Table 7.7.

In the case of Bulgaria, the indices show either reciprocal influences or no causality al all. With just one index (BG BX40 of blue chip type) Granger causing the all-share index SOFIX for one lag, these can be safely affirmed that the

TABLE 7.7 Granger Causality Results

Countries	1 lag	5 lags	20 lags	1 lag	5 lags	20 lags
Bulgaria						
	SOFIX Granger causes BG BX40			BG BX40 Granger causes SOFIX		
p-value	0.1855	0.0148	0.0196	0.0039	0.0010	0.0111
	SOFIX Granger causes BG REIT			BG REIT Granger causes SOFIX		
p-value	0.0589	0.2759	0.4725	0.0148	0.2026	0.4170
	BG REIT Granger causes BG BX40			BG BX40 Granger causes BG REIT		
p-value	0.3396	0.4529	0.6202	0.3011	0.6253	0.7665
Croatia						
	CROBEX Granger causes CROBEX10			CROBEX10 Granger causes CROBEX		
p-value	0.0027	0.0004	0.0313	0.2092	0.1238	0.4271
Cyprus						
	CSE Main Market Granger causes CSE Hotel			CSE Hotel Granger causes CSE Main Market		
p-value	0.0024	0.0004	0.0106	0.3629	0.3449	0.4912
	CSE Main Market Granger causes CSE Investment			CSE Investment Granger causes CSE Main Market		
p-value	0.0000	0.0000	0.0000	0.8984	0.9365	0.2157
	CSE Hotel Granger causes CSE Investment			CSE Investment Granger causes CSE Hotel		
p-value	0.0046	0.0123	0.0220	0.1079	0.0367	0.1115
Romania						
	BET Granger causes BET-C/BET-Plus			BET-C/BET-Plus Granger causes BET		
p-value	0.0020	0.0119	0.2358	0.8176	0.8932	0.9998
	BET Granger causes BET-Fi			BET-Fi Granger causes BET		
p-value	0.2196	0.0694	0.0996	0.0053	0.083	0.0812
	BET Granger causes BET-NG			BET-NG Granger causes BET		
p-value	0.3502	0.3751	0.1108	0.1288	0.0213	0.0566
	BET Granger causes BET-XT			BET-XT Granger causes BET		
p-value	0.3498	0.4626	0.2816	0.0929	0.1081	0.0627
	BET Granger causes BET-BK			BET-BK Granger causes BET		
p-value	0.4252	0.4985	0.0651	0.2276	0.1794	0.1820
	BET-C/BET-Plus Granger causes BET-Fi			BET-Fi Granger causes BET-C/BET-Plus		

(Continued)

TABLE 7.7 Granger Causality Results (*cont.*)

Countries	1 lag	5 lags	20 lags	1 lag	5 lags	20 lags
p-value	0.4099	0.7986	0.9879	0.0172	0.1015	0.3681
	BET-C/BET-Plus Granger causes BET- NG			BET-NG Granger causes BET-C/BET-Plus		
p-value	0.3795	0.8695	0.9989	0.0668	0.2291	0.6352
	BET-C/BET-Plus Granger causes BET- XT			BET-XT Granger causes BET-C/BET-Plus		
p-value	0.7393	0.9797	0.9999	0.0491	0.2975	0.6109
	BET-C/BET-Plus Granger causes BET- BK			BET-BK Granger causes BET-C/BET-Plus		
p-value	0.6469	0.8646	0.9899	0.6778	0.8866	0.9698
	BET-Fi Granger causes BET-NG			BET-NG Granger causes BET-Fi		
p-value	0.3085	0.0885	0.1037	0.3274	0.4187	0.1309
	BET-Fi Granger causes BET-XT			BET-XT Granger causes BET-Fi		
p-value	0.0044	0.0416	0.0255	0.3162	0.6460	0.0702
	BET-Fi Granger causes BET-BK			BET-BK Granger causes BET-Fi		
p-value	0.7585	0.1604	0.0705	0.4434	0.5294	0.0178
	BET-XT Granger causes BET-NG			BET-NG Granger causes BET-XT		
p-value	0.8155	0.1073	0.0434	0.2969	0.0218	0.0135
	BET-XT Granger causes BET-BK			BET-BK Granger causes BET-XT		
p-value	0.8063	0.3623	0.1441	0.5892	0.4510	0.0452
	BET-NG Granger causes BET-BK			BET-BK Granger causes BET-NG		
p-value	0.0313	0.0403	0.0097	0.6348	0.5813	0.6114

Source: Authors' calculations based on Bloomberg data.

Bulgarian Stock Exchange does not have a domestic index leader. The Croatian all-share index CROBEX is the index leader for the respective market. The situation is similar for Cyprus, where the CSE Main Market Index Granger-causes the two sector indices. Romania's situation appears to be complicated by the existence of no less than six indices. The BET-Fi index, which includes in portfolio only six closed-end funds, can be considered an index leader for the blue-chip BET index and for BET-XT, which combines the portfolios of BET and BET-Fi. The blue-chip index BET Granger-causes the composite/large portfolio index BET-C/BET-Plus for 1 lag and 5 lags. The energy sector index BET-NG Granger-causes BET-BK, a benchmark index for Romanian mutual funds; it also Granger-causes BET-XT for 5 and 20 lags, with the influence increasing as the lags grow. BET-NG also influences BET for 5 and 20 lags. While no clear index leader emerges for the Romanian market, the fact that several energy companies are included in BET and their shares are in the portfolios of the six closed-end funds of BET-Fi, a relative small number of companies (up to 15, including the six closed-end funds), are leading the Romanian market. Therefore, by concentrating the liquidity, these companies tend to overshadow the remaining majority of 65 listed companies. The results for Romania are partly confirmed by the results of Pop et al. (2013).

The diversification potential is clear for Bulgaria, Croatia, and Cyprus. The result for Romania seems to diminish the country's position as being less integrated than its counterparts. Thus Romania's peculiar position should be briefly mentioned: During 2015, due to the gradual closure of the controversial segment RASDAQ, the main market is expected to receive between 20 and 30 companies transferred from RASDAQ. These new companies might shift the dominance of 15 companies currently concentrating the bulk of Romanian trading.

3.2   Historic Betas for Testing Hypothesis 2

The general formula used to calculate the historic beta is:

$$\text{Beta} = \frac{\text{Covariance (stock}_i, \text{chosen index)}}{\text{Variance (chosen index)}}$$

For the domestic beta, the indices calculated for the respective stock exchanges, as presented in Table 7.6, were used. For European beta, the Euro Stoxx 50 was chosen, while for representing the world, the Russell Global Index was elected. The companies selected for each of the six countries that report a single index were chosen based on how long they were among the top five most traded companies for the respective exchange and the annual average percentage of the total turnover, calculated with the data provided by the Federation of European Stock Exchanges between 2000 and 2014. In the case of Malta, only three companies were selected due to data availability. All data were provided by Bloomberg.

The results are presented in Table 7.8 and, in general, confirm the internal diversification potential for the six stock exchanges. The prevalence of high domestic betas is indirectly confirmed by the conclusions of Girard and Sinha (2008) showing that political, economic, and financial risk factors have great impact in thinly traded markets.

However, while the betas indicate an internal diversification potential for Malta, this potential should be considered with care given the high concentration of trade around just two banks. The situation is similar for Latvia, where the concentration of trade appears around two pharmaceutical companies. Slovakia exhibits an interesting situation, for two of the selected companies exhibit very low domestic betas, suggesting more investigation be undertaken. Moreover, Slovakia is the country with the shortest data availability. Nevertheless, the results for Slovakia and Latvia are in concordance with the findings regarding the lower level of integration of Slovakia and the higher level of integration for Baltic countries. On the other hand, the results for Estonia and

TABLE 7.8 Domestic, European, and International Betas for the Selected Companies

Exchange/company	Domestic beta	European beta (Euro Stoxx 50)	International beta (Russell Global Index)
Estonia			
Olympic Entertainment Group (casino operations and hotel management) Period: Feb. 25, 2002–Dec. 31, 2014	1.4001	0.4501	0.6001
Silvano Fashion Group (production and sale of women lingerie) Period: Feb. 25, 2002–Dec. 31, 2014	0.9411	0.3445	0.1620
Tallink Grupp (maritime transportation) Period: Dec. 9, 2005–Dec. 31, 2014	1.2876	0.3376	0.3721
Tallina Vesi (water supply and waste water treatment) Period: Jun. 2, 2005–Dec. 31, 2014	0.4188	0.1087	0.1620
Latvia			
Grindeks (pharmaceuticals) Period: Jan. 3, 2000–Dec. 31, 2014	0.3204	0.1001	0.1715
Latvijas Kugnieciba (cargo shipping) Period: Jul. 1, 2002–Dec. 31, 2004	1.1971	0.2074	0.2719
Olainfarm (pharmaceuticals) Period: Jan. 3, 2000–Dec. 31, 2014	0.4334	0.2006	0.2423
SAF-Tehnika (telecommunication equipment) Period: Apr. 26, 2004–Dec. 31, 2014	0.4380	0.1954	0.0853
Lithuania			
Apranga (retail trade of apparel) Period: Jun. 10, 2002–Dec. 31, 2014	0.9376	0.3002	0.4271
Invalda (investments) Period: Jun. 10, 2002–Dec. 31, 2014	1.2884	0.2920	0.3367
Siauliu Banka (banking) Period: Jun. 10, 2002–Dec. 31, 2014	0.8731	0.2427	0.2785

Company / Period			
TEO LT (telecommunication) Period: Jun. 10, 2002–Dec. 31, 2014	0.6740	0.1400	0.2097
Malta			
Bank of Valleta (banking) Period: Jan. 3, 2000–Dec. 31, 2014	1.0464	0.0300	0.0075
HSBC Bank (banking) Period: Jan. 3, 2000–Dec. 31, 2014	1.1282	0.0220	0.0251
Malta International Airport (ground services for air transport) Period: Jan. 22, 2003–Dec. 31, 2004 (low trading frequency)	0.4116	0.0418	0.0882
Slovakia			
Best Hotels Properties (hotel ownership) Period: Aug. 3, 2010–Dec. 31, 2014	0.0175	0.0204	0.0324
Slovnaft (oil refining) Period: Aug. 3, 2010–Dec. 31, 2014	1.5175	0.0077	0.1228
Tatry Mountain Resort (mountain resort operator and tourist services) Period: Feb. 12, 2010–Dec. 31, 2014	0.0366	−0.1801	−0.2069
Vseobec Uverova Banka (banking) Period: Aug. 10, 2010–Dec. 31, 2014	1.9369	−0.0345	−0.0997
Slovenia			
Gorenje (home appliance products) Period: Apr. 1, 2003–Dec. 31, 2014	0.6650	0.1887	0.2851
Krka (pharmaceuticals) Period: Apr. 1, 2003–Dec. 31, 2014	0.9248	0.1760	0.1984
Mercator (retailer of fast moving consumer goods) Period: Apr. 1, 2003–Dec. 31, 2014	0.9111	0.1235	0.1892
Petrol (oil refining) Period: Apr. 1, 2003–Dec. 31, 2014	0.9839	0.1415	0.2434

Source: Authors' calculations based on Bloomberg data.

TABLE 7.9 The EU 10 Frontier Markets' Equity Indices

Country	Tested hypothesis	Status	Observations/comments
Bulgaria	Hypothesis 1	Confirmed/accepted	
Croatia	Hypothesis 1 modified	Confirmed/accepted	
Cyprus	Hypothesis 1 modified	Confirmed/accepted	
Estonia	Hypothesis 2	Confirmed/accepted	
Latvia	Hypothesis 2	Partly confirmed	Trade is concentrated on pharmaceutical sector.
Lithuania	Hypothesis 2	Confirmed/accepted	
Malta	Hypothesis 2	Partly confirmed	Trade is concentrated on banking sector.
Romania	Hypothesis 1	Partly confirmed	While no index leader emerges, three indices seem have an influence over the others.
Slovakia	Hypothesis 2	Confirmed/accepted	Two companies need more investigation.
Slovenia	Hypothesis 2	Confirmed/accepted	

Source: Authors' calculations.

Lithuania seem not to converge toward their higher level of integration; thus an increased internal diversification potential represents a strength for these two Baltic countries.

The results for the hypotheses 1, 1 modified, and 2 are integrated in Table 7.9.

The results show that, in general, the EU 10 frontier markets exhibit internal diversification potential and therefore can present interesting investing opportunities for domestic and international investors. The internal diversification potential seems to be lower in the cases of Latvia and Malta, with trading concentrated around the pharmaceutical and banking sectors, respectively. Romania has a peculiar position with an apparent limited internal diversification potential, due to about 15 companies, of which 6 are closed-end funds, being the most traded and overshadowing the remaining majority of listed companies; however, Romania is expected to increase the number of listed companies during 2015 due to the closure of the controversial segment RASDAQ.

These general results complete and enhance, from an inside-out point of view, the findings of partial integration of the EU 10 frontier markets and the overall conclusion that they present diversification opportunities for international portfolios.

4   DISCUSSIONS AND CONCLUSIONS

4.1   Discussions

As member states of the EU 28, the EU 10 frontier markets are confronted with increased competition from the EU developed markets combined with the fast-growing alternative trading facilities within the EU. Moreover, the affiliation to the EU has increased the level of integration of these markets, as highlighted by Guesmi and Nguyen (2011). In order to retain their identity and to remain relevant, at least at a domestic level, within the EU context, the 10 frontier markets should exhibit an internal diversification potential that might represent investment opportunities for investors. The internal diversification potential of the EU 10 frontier markets has been revealed by the current research. Nevertheless, it should be considered with caution since, with the exception of Malta, the remaining frontier markets rank low or very low when financing through local equity markets is considered, as Table 7.10 reveals. The data in Table 7.10 also indirectly indicate, at least for former communist countries, that the listed companies emerged mainly from the privatization programs and only a low number of subsequent initial public offerings of equities and/or bonds reached the exchanges.

Moreover, the environment created by MiFID might induce frontier market companies to search for financing alternatives by accessing other EU exchanges and raising capital from a larger pool of investors potentially at a lower cost, although up to now this has not been a practice among these companies, which

TABLE 7.10 EU 10 Frontier Markets Ranking Based on Financing Through Local Equity Markets

Country	2008/09 (of 134)	2009/10 (of 133)	2010/11 (of 139)	2011/12 (of 142)	2012/13 (of 144)	2013/14 (of 148)	2014/15 (of 144)
Bulgaria	90	85	90	88	84	94	95
Croatia	64	76	96	102	105	105	104
Cyprus	72	60	65	73	86	107	113
Estonia	39	62	68	60	62	59	48
Latvia	91	95	116	104	103	99	96
Lithuania	58	73	83	92	82	73	67
Malta	38	18	9	23	24	25	25
Romania	83	78	89	89	80	98	83
Slovakia	101	93	110	118	117	112	107
Slovenia	76	72	84	108	112	121	122

Source: World Economic Forum Reports (World Economic Forum, 2006, 2007, 2008, 2009, 2010, 2011, 2012, 2013, 2014).

rely on banks rather than securities exchanges for financing sources. Another threat that influences the internal diversification potential of these 10 frontier markets is the potential takeovers and mergers that will engulf the most visible and profitable domestic companies (eg, Romania lost several interesting listed companies such as the carmaker Dacia and the pharmaceutical company Terapia due to takeovers and subsequent delisting); this concentration process might also lead to the relocation or closure of respective economic entities, as highlighted by Evans and Hnatkovska (2007).

In order to overcome the problems related to the equity market segment, all 10 EU frontier markets diversified their securities exchanges through the introduction of the bond segment, although for Estonia this segment is not currently active. Further, 5 of the 10 EU frontier markets (Bulgaria, Croatia, Cyprus, Romania, and Slovenia) aimed for increased diversification by introducing other securities segments, as Table 7.5 shows. These segments are almost negligible within the respective securities exchanges' turnover, and currently the transactions within the Bucharest Stock Exchange are suspended due to lack of investor interest. This situation reveals a low level of sophistication of domestic investors. To a certain degree, this situation also hints toward a growing potential of domestic investors that might support the further development of the respective securities exchanges.

Nevertheless, the combined information from Table 7.4 regarding the financial development of EU 10 frontier markets and Table 7.5 generates a sixth characteristic of these EU 10 frontier markets: the low level of market sophistication due to underdeveloped or absent segments of derivative products and other financial instruments.

Another strategy for further development suggested for the EU 10 frontier markets is to become part of a larger exchange or to form alliances that will enhance their current position. The Baltic countries were taken over between 2002 and 2004 by the OMX Group and subsequently in 2007 were integrated within one of the largest exchanges, NASDAQ-OMX. Thus, the influence of the recent financial crisis seems to cancel the effect of becoming part of a large exchange since the market capitalization remained between 2008 and 2014 at a level similar to the pre-takeover period, with a decreasing trend during the past 3 years, as Table 7.3 shows. In the case of Slovenia, the Ljubljana Stock Exchange was taken over by Wiener Boerse and has been included in the CEE Stock Exchange Group since 2009. In this case, the takeover seemed to work in favor of this exchange; though it could not prevent the sharp decrease in market capitalization during the recent global financial crisis, it ascertained an upward trend during the past 3 years (Table 7.3). The Bulgarian Stock Exchange is another market that tried to enhanced its position through international collaboration, which resulted in the introduction of Deutsche Boerse's Xetra trading platform in Jun. 2008. The World Bank (2011a) considers that this introduction did not yield the expected results for Bulgaria. However, Table 7.3 suggests at least a positive influence, that of stabilizing the market capitalization after the global financial crisis.

The remaining five EU frontier markets, although having various collaboration protocols with other European exchanges that bring little visibility and are virtually unknown to investors, seem to favor the stand-alone position supported by the idea that a domestic securities exchange represents a source of national pride, as highlighted by O'Hara (2001). However, the stand-alone position might not be sustainable if the domestic companies and government institutions will not use the local exchanges for raising, financing, and, providing investors with attractive and adequate securities. Moreover, the stand-alone position might not be credible from a transparency point of view. On the other hand, the diversity of the affinities and congenialities of these remaining five markets will not favor regional alliances or partnerships; for example, for Romania a natural path would be to become part of the CEE Stock Exchange Group, yet Romania's Bucharest Stock Exchange has few affinities and congenialities with the stock exchanges of this group; Slovakia is notably absent from the CEE Stock Exchange Group with which it seems to have affinities.

The EU 10 frontier markets form a heterogeneous group of countries, including a homogeneous subgroup formed by the Baltic countries. As Allen et al. (2010) and Berger et al. (2011) show, the EU 10 frontier markets exhibit low pairwise correlations, hence providing geographical diversification benefits, as stressed by Middleton et al. (2008). The identified internal diversification potential enhances the position of these markets as investment opportunities, as mentioned by Girard and Sinha (2008) that small and value stocks are less risky within a frontier market. Moreover, the extension of MiFID through MiFID2 might enhance further the EU 10 frontier markets' internal diversification (and growth) potential by favoring the development of market segments dedicated to small and medium-sized enterprises (SMEs). Some of these EU frontier markets may not have the potential to evolve to the status of emerging markets. However, they might remain small niche markets providing a trading platform for local and regional companies and remain partly segmented from the mainstream exchanges, therefore continuing to provide (risky yet interesting) diversification opportunities and benefits.

4.2   Conclusions

The present research is the first to concentrate only on the EU 10 frontier markets and their internal diversification potential for the equity market segments.

The EU 10 frontier markets exhibit all five characteristics identified by the academic literature for the (equity) frontier markets. A sixth characteristic was identified and added for the EU 10 frontier securities market: the low level of market sophistication due to underdeveloped or absent segments of derivative products and other financial instruments.

The results show that, in general, the EU 10 frontier markets exhibit internal diversification potential and therefore can present interesting investing opportunities for domestic and international investors. The internal diversification potential seems to be lower in the cases of Latvia and Malta, where trading is concentrated around their pharmaceutical and banking sectors, respectively. Romania has a peculiar position with an apparently limited internal diversification potential, due to about 15 companies, of which 6 are closed-end funds, being the most traded and overshadowing the remaining majority of listed companies.

The internal diversification potential at the equity market level might be further enhanced by the extension of MiFID through MiFID2 by favoring the development at the domestic stock exchange level of segments dedicated to SMEs trading. This evolutionary path might favor the stand-alone position for the five EU frontier markets (Croatia, Cyprus, Malta, Romania, and Slovakia) that are not yet included in an alliance or partnership with other EU securities markets.

These general results complete and enhance, from an inside-out point of view, the findings of partial integration of the EU 10 frontier markets and the overall conclusion that they present diversification opportunities for international portfolios either individually or as a group.

Nevertheless, some of these EU 10 frontier markets, given their economic development limitations, might not evolve to the stage of an emerging market. They may remain small domestic markets, providing financing opportunities for local and regional economic entities and governments. As niche markets, they might retain the diversification advantages given the undervaluation of quality companies as highlighted by Griffith (2014). Each of the EU 10 frontier markets has its own unique opportunities and challenges, as also highlighted by Speidell (2011). Further investigations for a better understanding of these EU 10 frontier markets in their respective regional contexts and the linkages with the emerging and developed markets of the respective regions are needed.

The investigated and highlighted internal diversification potential for the EU 10 frontier markets is only one aspect of their potential future development. The ownership structure of the listed frontier companies is another line of investigation that should be pursued in order to better understand the risk profiles of the respective companies. The growth potential of the domestic investor base is another facet that should be researched since no securities exchange should rely mostly on the diversification opportunities it might offer to foreign investors for further growth and development.

REFERENCES

Allen, D.E., Powell, R.J., Golab, A., 2010. Volatility and correlations for stock markets in the emerging economies of Central and Eastern Europe: implications for European investors. Available at SSRN: http://ssrn.com/abstract=1611472 or http://dx.doi.org/10.2139/ssrn.1611472

Andritzky, J.R., 2007. Capital Market Development in a Small Country: The Case of Slovenia. IMF Working Paper WP/07/229. International Monetary Fund, Washington, DC, USA.

Babalos, V., Balcilar, M., Loate, T.B., Chisoro, S., Gupta, R., 2014. Did Baltic Stock Markets Offer Diversification Benefits during the Recent Financial Turmoil? Novel Evidence from Nonparametric Causality in Quantiles Test. University of Pretoria, Department of Economics Working Paper 2014-71, Pretoria, South Africa. http://www.up.ac.za/media/shared/61/WP/wp_2014_71.zp39317.pdf

Baumoehl, E., Lyocsa, S., 2014. Volatility and dynamic conditional correlations of worldwide emerging and frontier markets. Econ. Model. 38, 175–183.

Berger, D., Pukthuanthong, K., Yang, J.J., 2011. International diversification with frontier markets. J. Financ. Econ. 101 (1), 227–242.

Birg, G., Lucey, B.M., 2006. Integration of smaller European equity markets: a time-varying integration score analysis. Appl. Financ. Econ. Lett. 2 (6), 395–400.

Canegrati, E., 2008. In search of market index leader: evidence from world financial markets. MPRA Paper 11292 (posted Oct. 29). Available online at: http://mpra.ub.uni-muenchen.de/11292/

Chen, M.-P., Chen, P.-F., Lee, C.-C., 2014. Frontier stock market integration and the global financial crisis. N. Am. J. Econ. Finance 29, 84–103.

De Groot, W., Pang, J., Swikels, L., 2012. The cross-section of stock returns in frontier emerging markets. J. Empir. Finance 19, 796–818.

Demian, C.-V., 2011. Contagion in Central and East European markets in light of EU accession. J. Int. Financ. Mark. Inst. Money 21 (1), 144–155.

Dvorak, T., Podpiera, R., 2006. European Union enlargement and equity markets in accession countries. Emerg. Mark. Rev. 7 (2), 129–146.

Evans, M.D.D., Hnatkovska, V.V., 2007. International financial integration and the real economy. IMF Staff Papers 54 (2), 220–269.

Fowler, H., 2010. Frontier markets: the changing face of risk. Emerg. Mark. (9/10). Available from: http://www.emergingmarkets.org/Article/2690705/FRONTIER-MARKETS-The-changing-face-of-risk.html

Girard, E., Sinha, A., 2008. Risk and return in the next frontier. J. Emerg. Mark. Finance 7 (1), 43–80.

Griffith, B., 2014. Examining fundamental quality on the frontier of equity investing. J. Investing 23 (4), 23–36.

Guesmi, N., Nguyen, D.K., 2011. How strong is the global integration of emerging market regions? An empirical assessment. Econ. Model. 28 (6), 2517–2527.

Guidi, F., Ugur, M., 2014. An analysis of South-Eastern European stock markets: evidence on cointegration ad portfolio diversification benefits. J. Int. Financ. Mark. Inst. Money 30, 119–136.

Gupta, R., Jithendranathan, T., Sukumaran, A., 2012. Looking at new markets for international diversification: frontier market perspective. Frontier J. (February 16). http://efrontierjournal.com/2012/02/16/looking-at-new-markets-for-international-diversification-frontier-markets-perspective/

Haas, F., 2007. The Market in Financial Instruments Directive and the Transformation of Europe's Capital Markets. IMF Country Report 07/ 259, International Monetary Fund, Washington, DC, USA.

Horobet, A., Lupu, R., 2009. Are capital markets integrated? a test of information transmission within the European Union. Rom. J. Econ. Forecast. 10 (2), 64–80.

Iorgova, S., Ong, L.L., 2008. The Capital Markets of Emerging Europe: Institutions, Instruments and Investors. IMF Working Paper WP/08/103, International Monetary Fund, Washington, DC, USA.

Kenourgios, D., Samitas, A., 2011. Equity market integration in emerging Balkan markets. Res. Int. Bus. Finance 25 (3), 296–307.

Kiviaho, J., Nikkinen, J., Piljak, V., Rothivius, T., 2014. The co-movement dynamics of European frontier stock markets. Eur. Financ. Manag. 20 (3), 574–595.

Kohlert, D.M., 2011. International diversification in a troubled world: do frontier assets still improve the efficient frontier? J. Investing 20 (2), 42–49.

Lin, W., 2011. International equity diversification: small-cap versus small-market effects, SSRN. Available from: http://ssrn.com/abstract=1742119 or http://dx.doi.org/10.2139/ssrn.1742119

Maneschioeld, P.-O., 2006. Integration between the Baltic and international stock markets. Emerg. Mark. Finance Tr. 42 (6), 25–45.

Marshall, B.M., Nguyen, N.H., Visaltanachoti, N., 2015. Frontier market costs and diversification. J. Financ. Mark. 24, 1–24.

Masood, O., Bellalah, M., Chaudhary, S., Mansour, W., Teulon, F., 2010. Cointegration of Baltic stock markets in the financial tsunami: empirical evidence. Int. J. Bus. 15 (1), 119–132.

Mateus, T., 2004. The risk and predictability of equity returns of the EU accession countries. Emerg. Mark. Rev. 5 (2), 241–266.

Middleton, C.A.J., Fifield, S.G.M., Power, D.M., 2008. An investigation of the benefits of portfolio investment in Central and Eastern European markets. Res. Int. Bus. Finance 22 (2), 162–174.

Miles, W., 2005. Do frontier equity markets exhibit common trends and still provide diversification opportunities? Int. Econ. J. 19 (3), 473–482.

Moore, T., 2007. Has entry to the European Union altered the dynamic links of stock returns for the emerging markets? Appl. Financ. Econ. 17 (17), 1431–1446.

Moroza, J., 2008. Dynamic linkages between Baltic and international stock markets. Master's thesis, Department of Economics, School of Economics and Management, Lund University, Lund, Sweden. http://lup.lub.lu.se/luur/download?func=downloadFile&recordOId=1334907&fileO Id=1646555

Nikkinen, J., Piljak, V., Rothovius, T., 2011. The impact of the 2008–2009 financial crisis on the external and internal linkages of European frontier stock markets. Proceedings of the 15th Annual International Conference on Macroeconomic Analysis and International Finance, and Proceedings of the 18th Conference on the Theories and Practices of Securities and Financial Markets. http://www.uva.fi/materiaali/pdf/isbn_978-952-476-454-4.pdf

Nikkinen, J., Piljak, V., Aijo, J., 2012. Baltic stock markets and the financial crisis of 2008–2009. Res. Int. Bus. Finance 26 (3), 398–409.

O'Hara, M., 2001. Designing markets for developing countries. Int. Rev. Finance 2 (4), 205–215.

Onay, C., 2006. A co-integration analysis approach to European Union integration: the case of acceding and candidate countries. European Integration online Papers (EIoP) 10 (7). http://eiop. or.at/eiop/texte/2006-007a.htm

Patev, P., Kanaryan, N., 2002. Behavior and characteristics of Balkan stock markets. http://content. csbs.utah.edu/~ehrbar/erc2002/pdf/P191.pdf

Pop, C., Bozdog, D., Calugaru, A., 2013. The Bucharest Stock Exchange case: is BET-FI an index leader for the oldest indices BET and BET-C? Int. Bus. Res. Teach. Practice 7 (1), 35–56.

Porwal, P., 2014. Achieving diversification in global portfolio through frontier markets. Int. J. Manag. Res. Bus. Strat. 3 (1), 209–226.

Pukthuanthong, K., Roll, R., 2009. Global market integration: an alternative measure and its implications. J. Financ. Econ. 94 (2), 214–232.

Quisenberry, Jr., C., Griffith, B., 2010. Frontier equity markets: a primer on the next generation of emerging markets. J. Wealth Manag. 13 (3), 51–58.

Reboredo, J.C., Tiwari, A.K., Albulescu, C.T., 2015. An analysis of dependence between Central and Eastern European stock markets. Econ. Syst. 39 (3), 474–490.

Sadorsky, P., 2011. Financial development and energy consumption in Central and Eastern European frontier economies. Energy Policy 39, 999–1006.

Samarakoon, L.P., 2011. Stock market interdependence, contagion, and the U.S. financial crisis: the case of emerging and frontier markets. Int. Financ. Mark. Inst. Money 21, 724–742.

Samitas, A., Kenourgios, D., Paltalidis, N., 2006. Short and long run parametric dynamics in the Balkans stock markets. Int. J. Bus. Manag. Econ. 2 (8), 5–20.

Schroeder, M., 2000. Investment opportunities in Central and Eastern European equity markets. ZEW-Discussion Paper 00-42, Center for European Economic Research (ZEW), SSRN. Available from: http://ssrn.com/abstract=373943

Skinner, C., 2007. The Future of Investing in Europe's Markets after MiFID. Wiley Finance Series. John Wiley & Sons, Chichester,West Sussex, England, UK.

Speidell, L.S., 2008. Diversification snapshot: frontier markets in a troubled world. J. Investing 17 (4), 7–10.

Speidell, L., 2011. Frontier Market Equity Investing: Finding the Winners of the Future. Research Foundation of CFA Institute, Charlottesville, Virginia, USA.

Speidell, L.S., Krohne, A., 2007. The case for frontier equity markets. J. Investing 16 (3), 12–22.

Syllignakis, M.N., Kouretas, G.P., 2006. Long and short-run linkages in CEE stock markets: implications for portfolio diversification and stock market integration. William Davidson Institute Working Paper 832, SSRN. Available from: http://ssrn.com/abstract=910507

Syllignakis, M.N., Kouretas, G.P., 2011. Dynamic correlation analysis of financial contagion: evidence from the Central and Eastern European markets. Int. Rev. Econ. Finance 20 (4), 717–732.

Syriopoulos, T., 2011. Financial integration and portfolio investments to emerging Balkan equity markets. J. Multinatl. Financ. Manag. 1 (1), 40–54.

Syriopoulos, T., Roumpis, E., 2009. Dynamic correlations and volatility effects in the Balkan equity markets. J. Int. Financ. Mark. Inst. Money 19 (4), 565–587.

Todorov, G., Bidarkota, P., 2010. On international financial spillovers to frontier markets. Working paper, Florida International University. http://economics.fiu.edu/events/2011/20110119/international_financial_spillovers.pdf

Todorov, G., Bidarkota, P.V., 2011. Time-varying risk and risk premiums in frontier markets, SSRN. Available from: http://ssrn.com/abstract=1947412

Vizek, M., Dadic, T., 2006. Integration of Croatian, CEE and EU equity markets: cointegration approach. Ekonomski Pregled 57 (9–10), 631–646.

Wang, P., Moore, T., 2009. Sudden changes in volatility: the case of five central European stock markets. J. Int. Financ. Mark. Inst. Money 19 (1), 33–46.

Wang, M.-C., Shih, F.-M., 2013. Time-varying world and regional integration in emerging European equity markets. Eur. Financ. Manag. 19 (4), 703–729.

Wawrzaszek, J., Vadlamudi, H., 2011. Frontier markets: an emerging opportunity for diversifying risk and returns. J. Invest. Consult. 12 (1), 31–38.

Wright, C., 2008. Investors are going beyond emerging markets and blazing new trails: what are the potential risks and rewards? CFA Inst. Mag. (Sep.–Oct.), 30–35.

Reports

World Bank, 2011a. Capital market integration and MiFID implementation: the Bulgarian experience. Report no. 65823-Bg. World Bank, Washington, DC, USA. http://documents.worldbank.org/curated/en/2011/11/16406287/capital-market-integration-mifid-implementation-bulgarian-experience

World Bank, 2011b. Croatia—advisory service on the implementation of the Markets in Financial Instruments Directive (MiFID) in EU candidate and new member states: technical advisory report. Report no. 69879. World Bank, Washington, DC, USA. http://documents.worldbank.org/curated/en/2011/04/16403913/croatia-technical-advisory-report-advisory-service-implementation-markets-financial-instruments-directive-mifid-eu-candidate-new-member-states-case-study-croatia-croatia-technical-advisory-report-advisory-service-implementation-markets-financial-instruments-directive-mifid-eu-candidate-new-member-states-case-study-croatiabr

World Economic Forum, 2006. The Global Competitiveness Report 2006–2007. World Economic Forum, Geneva, Switzerland.

World Economic Forum, 2007. The Global Competitiveness Report 2007–2008. World Economic Forum, Geneva, Switzerland.

World Economic Forum, 2008. The Global Competitiveness Report 2008–2009. World Economic Forum, Geneva, Switzerland.

World Economic Forum, 2009. The Global Competitiveness Report 2009–2010. World Economic Forum, Geneva, Switzerland.

World Economic Forum, 2010. The Global Competitiveness Report 2010–2011. World Economic Forum, Geneva, Switzerland.

World Economic Forum, 2011. The Global Competitiveness Report 2011–2012. World Economic Forum, Geneva, Switzerland.

World Economic Forum, 2012. The Global Competitiveness Report 2012–2013. World Economic Forum, Geneva, Switzerland.

World Economic Forum, 2013. The Global Competitiveness Report 2013–2014. World Economic Forum, Geneva, Switzerland.

World Economic Forum, 2014. The Global Competitiveness Report 2014–2015. World Economic Forum, Geneva, Switzerland.

Chapter 8

Are European Frontier Markets Efficient?

D. Bond, K. Dyson
Ulster Business School, Ulster University, Londonderry, United Kingdom

Chapter Outline

1 INTRODUCTION

The concept of frontier markets is a nebulous term and can carry many meanings. This chapter uses (2013, pp. 3) definition of frontier markets, namely that they are a subset of emerging markets, with lower market capitalization and liquidity or more investment restrictions than more established emerging markets, or both, depending on the country under consideration. Within Europe, the countries that broadly fit these definitions are predominantly the Eastern European, former Soviet bloc, excommunist countries.

As such, these Eastern European frontier markets, by their nature, are smaller in size and lower in liquidity than other comparable markets in the rest of Europe (and indeed the world) and are therefore not highly correlated with other markets, or indeed each other, thus increasing their attraction to investors searching for higher potential yield while lowering the overall volatility of their investment portfolios. Crucially, all such frontier markets exhibit high growth potential and consequently higher expected returns. Partially, these qualities

Handbook of Frontier Markets. http://dx.doi.org/10.1016/B978-0-12-803776-8.00008-2
147

arise from the fact that frontier markets remain relatively local in character, often shaped primarily by internal economic and political dynamics, as these countries have embraced capitalism after the fall of the Soviet bloc in the 1990s; (Speidell and Krohne, 2007; Shadbolt, 2013, eg, for a full exposition of the case for—and against—investing in such frontier markets.)

As more and more international investors have moved into these Eastern European frontier markets, a natural question is: are the financial markets in these countries informationally efficient, or are there inefficiencies from which investors might profit? A corollary question is: have bubbles developed in these markets as they rush to attract investment and "hot money floods in," without investors performing the necessary and appropriate due diligence? This study therefore examines these two questions for Eastern European frontier markets in the period between the late 1990s and mid-2015.

The study is structured as follows: Section 2 examines the theory of informational market efficiency; Section 3 examines the literature in the area of frontier markets and informational efficiency; Section 4 discusses the methodology; while Section 5 examines the data used in the study; the results are discussed in Section 6; and finally, the conclusions and recommendations for further study are summarized in Section 7.

2 THE THEORY OF INFORMATIONAL MARKET EFFICIENCY

While, on the face of it, the concept of informational market efficiency appears relatively simple, the realities are somewhat different, a point made clear by Timmerman and Granger (2004).

Research into the informational efficiency of markets originated with the paper of Samuelson (1965) and the study of Bachelier into commodity markets in the early 1900s (Cootner, 1964). A problem with all of this literature is that the definition of what comprises an efficient market has changed subtly through time (Fama, 1965a,b; for two early definitions). These differences in definition simply compound the problem of investigating whether markets are informational efficient.

To provide a foundation for both his, and future, research into the concept of information efficiency, Fama (1970) refined and defined what is meant by "information." He did so by classifying the information on the basis of three "levels" of availability—namely historical, present, and insider information—in his efficient market hypothesis (EMH). These three levels of information comprise information sets and are self-encompassing, with the higher levels incorporating the lower sets. Therefore, evidence in support of a higher level of informational efficiency provides evidence that the lower level(s) hold(s) also. Thus, by definition, evidence against a lower level of efficiency also topples the level(s) above.

In a weak-form efficient market, the information set comprises prior (historical) share prices or returns. Investors cannot earn excessive returns from detecting patterns in share prices or returns, and consequently from developing trading rules that attempt to exploit the perceived patterns, as no such patterns should exist; thus technical analysis should not yield consistent excess profits.

In a semistrong-form efficient market, the information set comprises all publicly available information, including historical information, thus encompassing weak-form efficiency. Investors cannot earn excess returns from trading in such publicly available information, as it is incorporated instantaneously into the share price once made public, leaving no time to profitably trade from such information; thus fundamental analysis should not yield consistent excess profits.

In a strong-form efficient market, the information set comprises information privy only to the company insiders, as well as all historical and publicly available information. Investors cannot earn excessive returns from trading in such information, as it will also, as with the other information sets, be incorporated instantaneously into the share price.

The empirical study of share prices, their returns and volatility, and consequential levels of informational efficiency mirrors the development of statistical analysis of time series. The traditional view of share prices has been that they follow some variant of a martingale/random walk process (Granger, 1992); for inference purposes, see Campbell et al. (1997) for variants on the random walk process. As more powerful tests have rejected the simple random walk models in empirical studies, more complex econometric models have allowed for the incorporation of some sort of "memory" in the share price formation process. Such models contradict the weak-form variant of the EMH (Gil-Alana, 2006; Floros et al., 2007).

The mounting contradictory evidence, and doubts as to the efficacy of simple martingale/random walk models, have combined and resulted in a reappraisal of what can be defined as an informationally efficient market (Jensen, 1978; Malkiel, 1992; Timmerman and Granger, 2004). As such, these works shift the definition of an informationally efficient market away from an economic framework to a set-theoretic one. This is best summarized by Timmerman and Granger (2004), who, building on the earlier research, provide the following definition:

> *A market is efficient with respect to the information set, Ω_t, search technologies, S_t, and forecasting models, M_t, if it is impossible to make economic profits by trading on the basis of signals produced form a forecasting model in M_t defined over predictor variables in the information set Ω_t and selected using a search technology in S_t.*

This definition requires that prices fully reflect all information to the point that the marginal returns from acquiring the information equal the marginal costs. All of these definitions do not permit profitable arbitrage: a requirement under the earlier definitions of informational efficiency. Fama (1991, 1998) argues that this is a more acceptable approach than that espoused by the likes of Grossman (1976), Grossman and Stiglitz (1980), and Keiber (2007): namely, that truly informationally efficient markets are impossible. Their counterargument is a deceptively simple one: namely, that if arbitrage opportunities do not exist, then there is no profit to be gained from gathering information and trading on it (because if share prices fully reflect all information, then information and trading costs must equal zero). If this is the case, then there will be little motivation to trade and, in the extreme, markets will collapse. The reason why this does not occur, they argue, is that the degree of informational inefficiency determines the level of effort that investors are willing to expend to garner, and then trade, on the information. The profits earned by these investors accrue, according to Black (1986), because of "noise traders" where "noise traders" are those individuals who trade on what they consider to be relevant market information but which, in reality, is simply "noise" in the market and thus irrelevant to the price formation process.

The doubts that have been raised as to whether financial markets are informationally efficient have led to a number of theoretical alternatives to the EMH being proposed. Among these are the theory of fair markets (TFM) and the adaptive markets hypothesis (AMH).

The TFM (Frankfurter, 2006) proposes that informational markets should be considered fair, rather than efficient. The AMH proposes a reconciliation of the EMH with the behavioral alternatives, as proposed by the likes of Shefrin (2000), Statman et al. (2008), and others, by applying evolutionary theory to financial markets.

The groundwork in AMH begins with Farmer and Lo (1999), with formalization of the theory by Lo (2004), who couples bounded rationality and "satisfying" theory (Schwartz, 2004) with evolutionary dynamics to create a more realistic model of the price formation process. Market prices under the AMH reflect as much information as is dictated by the combination of environmental conditions and the number, and nature, of market participants. Thus, profitable opportunities in such markets will be a time-varying function of environmental market conditions. The AMH will therefore permit behavioral biases to exist, with the following implications for market participants: (1) The risk–reward relationship will be inherently unstable through time; (2) arbitrage opportunities will evolve and disappear through time; (3) the profitability of investment strategies will vary through time; (4) markets will continuously innovate; and (5) the prime objective of all firms—in Darwinian terms—is survival.

In summary, the AMH, by permitting arbitrage, provides justification for the activities of traders who, by their activities, ensure that markets remain relatively efficient through time. Thus, the Grossman–Stiglitz–Keiber explanation for the persistent existence of traders is compatible, and consistent, with AMH. Further, by permitting informational efficiency in markets to be a time-varying function, a natural explanation is provided for those studies that find conflicting evidence regarding market efficiency over varying time periods; Timmerman and Granger (2004) and Floros et al. (2007) for a concise summary of such studies.

The AMH is therefore a theory which would seem to be more consistent with the actual evidence of how financial markets operate than is the EMH, which has been amended over the past 40 or so years by subtly redefining what is meant by the term "efficiency" in the light of new, and contradictory, empirical evidence.

3   THE EMPIRICAL LITERATURE ON FRONTIER MARKETS AND INFORMATIONAL EFFICIENCY

The striking feature of the empirical literature on informational efficiency and frontier markets is the paucity of material available. Very little research—whether on a European or other basis—has been carried out into frontier markets and specifically the efficiency of how these markets process information; an example of such an early study, albeit of an emerging market, namely Russia, can be found in Kratz (1999).

3.1   Informational Efficiency and Frontier Markets

Three studies have examined the informational efficiency of stock markets in the Indian subcontinent and surrounding areas. The first study, by Mobarek and Keasey (2000), examines the stock market in Bangladesh, while the second and third studies (Akbar and Baig, 2010; Rehman and Khidmat, 2013) examine the stock market in Pakistan. All three studies, to varying degrees, have issues with respect to data availability, relatively small sample size, thin trading, and methodologies employed, and therefore must be treated with a degree of caution.

Mobarek and Keasey (2000) examine the Bangladesh stock exchange for weak-form market efficiency from 1988 to 1997. The study uses both indices and the returns on 30 actively traded companies, testing using both parametric [autocorrelation, autoregression, and autoregressive integrated moving average (ARIMA)] and nonparametric (runs test) techniques. Irrespective of test and sample used, the authors find evidence that the Bangladesh stock market, for the period examined, is not weak-form efficient. Akbar and Baig (2010), for the neighboring Pakistan stock market from 2004 to 2007, again find evidence supportive of informational inefficiencies at the semistrong-form level. However, evidence contrary to this is provided by Rehman and Khidmat (2013), albeit for a larger sample period: 2001–11.

A number of studies have examined whether African markets are weak-form efficient, the majority of which have focused on the South African market. The evidence, based on weekly data, supports the argument for this market being weak-form efficient in the 1980s and 1990s (Dickinson and Muragu, 1994; Smith et al., 2002; Jefferis and Smith, 2005; Magnusson and Wydick, 2002). Interestingly, one study, that of Appiah-Kusi and Menyah (2003), finds that the South African market appears not to be weak-form efficient from 1990 to 1995. This study also provides results that would appear to indicate that the markets of Botswana, Ghana, and the Ivory Coast all seem to exhibit evidence that weak-form efficiency did not hold during the early and mid-1990s. The findings for Ghana and Botswana are consistent with those of Magnusson and Wydick (2002).

Evidence supportive of weak-form efficiency in other African markets has been provided for Kenya, Zimbabwe, Egypt, Morocco, and Mauritius during the 1990s (Appiah-Kusi and Menyah, 2003), and for Kenya during the 1980s (Kiweu, 1991; Dickinson and Muragu, 1994). However, evidence contrary to weak-form efficiency in African markets has been provided for Egypt, Morocco, and Mauritius during periods in the 1990s (Smith et al., 2002; Bundoo, 2000; Asal, 2000).

A criticism of the African studies discussed is that there are questions as to the quality of available data, the issue of thin trading, and the use of weekly return data in many of the studies. These issues are partially addressed by Miambo and Biekpe (2007), who examine weak-form efficiency in 11 African stock markets (Egypt, Kenya, Zimbabwe, Morocco, Mauritius, Tunisia, Ghana, Namibia, Botswana, BVRM [Bourse Régionale des Valeurs Mobilières regional stock exchange], and Ivory Coast) using daily data from 1997 to 2002, with sample size varying between 9 and 54 stocks. The issue of thin trading is addressed by calculating the returns on a trade-to-trade basis, and adjusting for the variability in trade interval lengths. This adjustment is achieved by weighting the trade-to-trade returns by the number of days between trades. Miambo and Biekpe (2007) observe thin trading in all markets, particularly in Namibia and Botswana, with all but a few of the markets exhibiting evidence contrary to weak-form market efficiency (the exceptions are Kenya and Zimbabwe). However, methodologically, the econometric procedures used to examine whether the markets exhibit evidence of weak-form efficiency are the usual serial correlation and runs tests used in the prior studies.

Jarrett (2010) examines whether four small Pacific-Basin markets (Singapore, Malaysia, South Korea, and Indonesia) exhibit evidence of weak-form efficiency. The data for the study covers the period 1985–2000, with sample size ranging from 390 stocks (Indonesia) to 900 (Malaysia). The study uses a simple autoregressive conditional heteroscedasticity (ARCH) model to examine the returns for each market, and the author concludes that the markets examined exhibit predictable properties, contrary to the weak-form definition of efficiency.

De Groot et al. (2012) investigate the returns of more than 1400 stocks in 24 frontier markets (including Eastern Europe) for the period 1997–2008, examining the impact of value, momentum, and size-based investment strategies in each market.

The value strategy involves grouping the stocks in each market into portfolios based on three characteristics: namely, historical ratios: (1) book-to-market ratio, (2) earnings-to-price ratio, and (3) dividend-to-price ratio. For the value strategy to be successful, stocks with high ratios should, on average, have higher returns than stocks with low ratios.

The momentum strategy involves grouping the stocks into portfolios based on past returns. Stocks with higher past returns are expected to have higher future returns.

The size effect involves grouping the stocks into portfolios based on market capitalization of equity. Stocks with relatively low market capitalization should, based on the strategy, have higher returns than stocks with relatively large market capitalizations.

Each of the strategies outlined is inconsistent with both weak-form and semistrong-form market efficiency, as defined earlier.

De Groot et al. (2012) find that portfolios constructed on either a value or a momentum basis, even after adjusting for transaction costs, generate statistically significant excess returns of between 5% and 15%, depending on the frontier market portfolio examined. Evidence is also found for a significant size effect. The study further investigates whether the excess returns can be explained by risk factors, but finds no supportive evidence for such an effect. Such evidence is therefore contrary to information efficiency holding in the frontier markets investigated.

Okicic (2014) examines the stock returns, and associated volatility, for a number of indices in Eastern European frontier and emerging markets (Bosnia and Herzegovina, Bulgaria, Croatia, Czech Republic, Hungary, Macedonia, Montenegro, Poland, Romania, Serbia, Slovakia, and Slovenia) from 2005 to 2013, employing a simple ARIMA and ARCH methodology. The results of the ARCH analysis provide evidence that there is a "leverage effect," namely that negative shocks in the market increase volatility proportionality more than positive shocks do—a result inconsistent with semistrong-form efficiency. Further, based purely on the ARIMA analysis and associated Ljung-Box statistics, the author rejects the null hypothesis that there is no autocorrelation in the returns, and concludes that the markets exhibit signs of weak-form inefficiency.

To summarize, a number of frontier market studies have found evidence supportive of informational inefficiencies in frontier markets, depending on the time period examined, both in Eastern Europe and elsewhere. However, all of these studies, to varying degrees, have issues with respect to data sources, samples, thin trading, and/or methodologies employed. With respect to data, many of the studies which examine the African markets, for instance, do not use standardized validated data sets, but instead rely on material supplied directly by the relevant stock market, without external validation. However, most of these studies do recognize the issue. With respect to methodology, a number—but not all—of the studies that test for weak-form efficiency use statistical approaches with relatively low power; and, as far as the authors of this present study are aware, there are no studies that examine the relative time series available for evidence of long memory. This study, therefore, attempts to address these issues by using more recently developed econometric techniques and a standardized and externally validated database.

4 METHODOLOGY

The concept of market efficiency is initially explored using the standard tests for basic martingale behavior of the various stock market indices in each of the frontier economies. The tests aim to establish the value of d, the size of the lag operator L^d [eg, $L^1(X_t) = X_{t-1}$] needed to transform the index into a stationary ergodic series. The EMH implies that d should be 1 for the level series of the indices and zero for their returns. If d is 1, the level series follow a random walk and the movement of their returns is completely random. If this is the case, then no advantage can be gained by studying the past movements of the index.

First, the hypothesis that the level indices follow a random walk is explored by using the ADF–GLS test of Elliott et al. (1996). This is a more powerful test than the traditional augmented Dickey–Fuller (ADF) test. The null hypothesis is H_0: $d = 1$ against the alternative H_1: $d = 0$. The test allows for two possibilities: nonzero mean and trend stationarity. In both cases, for the market to be efficient, the null hypothesis should not be rejected. The probability distribution of the test statistic without a trend follows that derived in MacKinnon (1996) and can easily be found. For the trend-stationary version of the test, the probability distribution of the statistic is more complex, and ready figures are not available except for the standard 10, 5, and 1% values. As the power of unit root tests is generally low, the alternative of testing the null hypothesis that H_0: $d = 0$ against the alternative that H_1: $d = 1$ is conducted using the traditional Kwiatkowski–Phillips–Schmidt–Shin (KPSS) test (Kwiatkowski et al., 1992). For the markets to be efficient, the null hypothesis should not be acceptable for the level series and should not be rejected for the returns.

Given the knife-edge nature of the traditional $I(0)/I(1)$ testing processes, this study then considers whether the series might be fractionally integrated. That is, $d \in \mathbb{R}[0,1]$ and can take noninteger values; thus:

$$(1 - L^d) = 1 - dL + d(d-1)L^2/2! - \dots$$

When $d \in \left(0, \frac{1}{2}\right)$, the series is mean reverting and is said to have long memory. That is, the current value of the series depends on previous values of the series going back many time periods. Thus, within a market, knowledge of previous values can give an advantage and the market would not be efficient. When $d \in \left(0, \frac{1}{2}\right)$, it has been shown that the test of whether a series has long memory is either a simple z-score test or t-test of the hypothesis H_0: $d = 0$ against the alternative, H_1: $0 < d < 0.5$. It is the first if the local Whittle estimator (Robinson, 1995) of d is used in the construction of the test statistic, and the second if the GPH estimator (Geweke and Porter-Hudak, 1983) is used. If the markets are efficient, then the value of d should be zero.

It is well known that tests concerning the size of d can give misleading results if the series exhibit either structural breaks or bubble behavior (Smith, 2005; Qu, 2011). In particular, the tests might suggest that the series is $I(1)$ or I; $0 < d < 1$ when actually the series is $I(0)$ with either a structural break or bubble behavior for the period. Identifying what is happening offers many challenges methodologically. For example, if there is bubble behavior, d is likely to be greater than 1 and deriving a test statistic becomes problematic.

Recent approaches to the identification of bubbles have included techniques based on fractional integration (Cunado et al., 2005; Frammel and Kruse, 2011; for details) and on sequential unit roots testing (Phillips et al., 2011). In the first approach, the return series is tested for nonstable fractional integration $(0.5 < d)$. This is an implication of bubble behavior in the levels series. In the second approach, the levels series is tested for a mildly explosive root using a right-tailed unit root test.

In Phillips and Yu (2011) the issue of dating the time line of financial bubbles is explored. They modify the technique proposed by Phillips et al. (2011) and provide a methodology for identifying bubble behavior with consistent dating of bubbles' origination and collapse. The paper also provides a methodology for testing for bubble migration, which could be used to examine possible contagion of individual stock prices. The methodology is based on the analysis of the mildly explosive stochastic process developed in Phillips and Magadalinos (2007a,b). The methodology is to recursively estimate:

$$X_t = \mu + \delta X_{t-1} + \varepsilon_t \qquad \varepsilon_t \sim \text{i.i.d. } (0, \sigma^2)$$

To test for an explosive root, the critical values of the standard Dickey–Fuller test are obtained for the right-tailed alternative hypothesis H_1: $\delta > 1$ rather than the normal left-tailed test H_1: $\delta < 1$. The regression in the first recursion uses $\tau_0 = \lfloor nr_0 \rfloor$ observations for some fraction r_0 of the total sample, where $\lfloor \dots \rfloor$ denotes the integer part of the argument. Subsequent regressions build on this original data using successive observations giving a sample of size $\tau = \lfloor nr \rfloor$ $r_0 \le r \le 1$. The standard Dickey–Fuller t-test can be written as:

$$DF_r^t = \left(\frac{\sum_{j=1}^{\tau} \tilde{X}_{j-1}^2}{\hat{\sigma}_\tau^2} \right)^2 (\hat{\delta}_\tau - 1)$$

where $\hat{\delta}_\tau$ is the least squares estimate of δ based on the first τ observations, $\hat{\sigma}_\tau^2$ is the corresponding estimates of σ, and $\tilde{X}_{j-1}^2 = \left(X_{j-1} - \tau^{-1} \sum_{i=1}^{\tau} X_i \right)^2$.

To test for the existence of a bubble, Phillips and Yu (2011) suggest the maxDF_r^t test that compares the supremum statistics sup$_r DF_r^t$ with the right-tail critical values obtained from the limit distribution $\sup_{r \in [0,1]} r \int_0^r \tilde{W} \, dW / \left(\int_0^r \tilde{W}^2 \right)^{-1/2}$ where W is a standard Wiener process, and $\tilde{W}(r) = W(r) - \int_0^1 W$ is a demeaned Wiener process. Using simulation, they obtain a 5% critical value of 1.5073 for a sample size of 100.

To explore the time line of the bubble, they suggest that the start of the bubble can be identified by $\hat{\tau}_e = \lfloor n\hat{r}_e \rfloor$:

$$\hat{r}_e = \inf \left\{ s : DF_s^t > cv_{\beta_n}^{df} \text{ and } s \geq r_0 \right\}$$

$cv_{\beta_n}^{df}$ is the right-sided $100 \beta_n\%$ critical value of the limit distribution of DF_s^t statistic based on $\tau_s = \lfloor ns \rfloor$ observations and β_n the size of the one-sided test. Similarly, assuming the existence of $\hat{r}_e$, they date the collapse of the bubble by $\hat{\tau}_f = \lfloor n\hat{r}_f \rfloor$ where:

$$\hat{r}_f = \inf \left\{ s : DF_s^t > cv_{\beta_n}^{df} \text{ and } s \geq \hat{r}_e + \gamma \ln(n)/n \right\}$$

$\gamma \ln(n)/n$ is used so that the duration of the bubble is nonnegligible. For practical implementation, they set the critical value sequence for $cv_{\beta_n}^{df}$ using an expansion rule: $cv_{\beta_n}^{df} = -0.8 + \ln(nr)/C$. The value of the constant C can be varied to make the test more or less conservative. In Phillips and Yu (2011) a value $C = 5$ is used to give a conservative test; they suggest that a value of about 100 gives the asymptotic 5% level.

5 OVERVIEW OF EASTERN EUROPEAN MARKETS AND SAMPLE SELECTION

5.1 Eastern European Markets

As many of the prior studies of frontier markets have found, access to quality data can be problematic. This arises for a number of reasons, including nascent stock markets, questions as to the veracity of the data, and issues of incomplete data, often due to remoteness of the market. In an attempt to minimize these issues, this study focuses on Eastern European frontier markets, which came into existence after the fall of the Berlin Wall in 1989 and the subsequent collapse of the Communist system in Eastern Europe. These markets have changed radically over the subsequent 25 years, in terms of their political and economic systems, geopolitical relations, living standards, and degree of foreign direct investment (FDI). Several of these former Communist countries are now members of the European Union (EU), a move which has accelerated their integration into the broader capitalist system. These countries are Bulgaria, Croatia, the Czech Republic, Estonia, Hungary, Latvia, Lithuania, Poland, Romania, Slovakia, and Slovenia. Three of these former Communist countries, the Czech Republic, Hungary, and Poland, are defined as emerging markets by the principal index providers (Dow Jones, Morgan Stanley, FTSE, and Russell) as of 2015, and are therefore excluded from this study. The majority of the former Communist countries have attempted to build their comparative advantage primarily in manufacturing, and secondarily in services. All of them have well-educated labor forces, with relatively low pay scales compared to other Western European economies. One country not mentioned but also classified as a frontier market by all of the index providers is Ukraine, which has had—and sadly, continues to have—a troubled relationship with its former neighboring Communist partner, Russia. Ukraine is therefore also included within this study, along with two other European frontier markets that never fell within the domain of the Communist system, namely Cyprus and Malta. This, therefore, brings the total sample size to 12 countries, 10 of which are former Communist countries (Bulgaria, Croatia, Estonia, Latvia, Lithuania, Romania, Serbia, Slovakia, Slovenia, and Ukraine), and 2 noncommunist countries (Cyprus and Malta). The study includes the two former noncommunist states for comparative purposes.

5.2   Sample Selection

The sample for the study is taken from the widely available Bloomberg financial database. Bloomberg provides coverage of all developed, emerging, and frontier markets globally, with data from a number of verified sources. For the Eastern European frontier markets, data are available for most countries from the host stock market, Dow Jones, Morgan Stanley (MSCI), Nomura, and/or FTSE. In selecting our sample, we strove to obtain the data source with the longest period of complete coverage. To minimize issues of thin trading in individual companies, the study examines broad market indices for each of the countries, comprising large-cap, mid-cap, and small-cap companies. The final sample and periods covered are illustrated in Table 8.1.

Data availability for the each of the Eastern European frontier markets studied varies. The maximum amount of continuous data is available for Latvia, Lithuania, and Ukraine, with 17 years each. Following these markets, the remaining Eastern European frontier markets predominantly have data availability beginning in the early 2000s until 2015. For Malta and Cyprus, the two non–former Communist countries, the time series available run from 1996 to 2015 (Malta) and from 2000 to 2015 (Cyprus). Therefore, all of these times series, for all of the frontier markets examined, cover the period running up to, during, and after the financial crisis that began in 2007.

6   RESULTS

The time series plots in Fig. 8.1a and b suggest that the series have all exhibited either bubble behavior or major shocks in the period pre-2010. It was therefore decided to carry out the analysis for the total time periods and for the period from Jun. 2010 to 2015. Table 8.2 gives the results of the ADF–GLS and KPSS tests for the total time period of each series. As explained in the methodology, the sample distribution is available for the ADF–GLS test only without trend. For the other test statistics, only the 10, 5, and 1% critical values are available. The tables all use the following notation to highlight significant results: *, **, ***, meaning that given the current test statistic the null hypothesis cannot be supported at the 10, 5, and 1% levels, respectively. Therefore, for the level series, all except

TABLE 8.1 Sample Derived From Bloomberg Financial Database

Country	Series	Bloomberg code	Number of firms in index	Start	Finish
Bulgaria	MSCI Bulgaria local	MSEIBGLP	12	05/31/2002	06/22/2015
Croatia	MSCI Croatia daily net TR USD	MSEICRUN	15	05/31/2002	06/22/2015
Cyprus	FTSE/Cyprus Stock Exchange 20	CYSMFTSE	20	12/01/2000	06/23/2015
Estonia	MSCI Estonia daily gross TR USD	MSEIESUG	7	05/31/2002	06/22/2015
Latvia	NOMURA Central Eastern local	NCEELAL	9	01/16/1996	07/22/2013
Lithuania	NOMURA Central Eastern local	NCEELITD	15	01/01/1996	07/22/2013
Malta	Malta Stock Exchange	MALTEX	43	01/02/1996	06/22/2015
Romania	MSCI Romania daily gross TR USD	MSEIROUG	15	11/30/2005	06/20/2015
Serbia	SRX SERBAIN traded Intex EUR	SRXEUR	7	12/08/2005	06/23/2015
Slovakia	Dow Jones total stock market	DWSKD	8	11/30/2006	06/22/2015
Slovenia	MSCI daily gross TR USD	MSEISVUG	10	05/31/2002	06/22/2015
Ukraine	PFTS Stock Exchange Index	PFTS	18	01/12/1998	06/22/2015

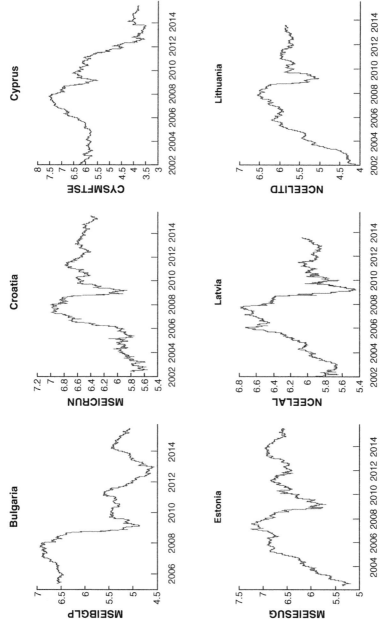

FIGURE 8.1 Time series plots of the logged values of the indices. (a) Bulgaria to Lithuania; (b) Malta to Ukraine

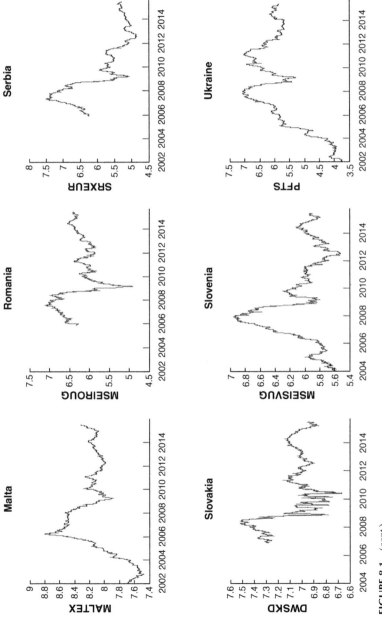

FIGURE 8.1 (cont.)

TABLE 8.2 Integer *d* Level of Integration Tests for Full Period

Country	Levels				Returns			
	ADF-GLS		KPSS		ADF-GLS		KPSS	
		Trend		Trend		Trend		Trend
Bulgaria	−0.01 (0.68)	−1.63 (>0.1)	19.28*** (0.00)	2.98*** (0.00)	−0.92 (0.32)	−2.26 (>0.10)	0.27 (>0.10)	2.98*** (0.00)
Croatia	−0.36 (0.55)	−1.2 (>0.1)	14.80*** (0.00)	4.37*** (0.00)	−5.87*** (0.00)	−7.91*** (0.00)	0.21 (>0.10)	0.07 (>0.10)
Cyprus	0.90 (0.90)	−1.03 (>0.1)	19.83*** (0.00)	7.10*** (0.00)	−0.89 (0.33)	−2.24 (>0.10)	0.32 (>0.10)	0.21** (0.02)
Estonia	0.19 (0.74)	−0.66 (>0.1)	8.08*** (0.00)	3.18*** (0.00)	−4.00*** (0.00)	−5.91*** (0.00)	0.44* (0.06)	0.16* (0.05)
Latvia	−0.07 (0.66)	−1.06 (>0.1)	11.02*** (0.00)	3.22*** (0.00)	−15.69*** (0.00)	−15.4*** (0.00)	0.25 (>0.10)	0.11 (>0.10)
Lithuania	−0.35 (0.56)	−1.59 (>0.1)	27.42*** (0.00)	3.87*** (0.00)	−9.42*** (0.00)	−11.4*** (0.00)	0.18 (>0.10)	0.19** (0.03)
Malta	033 (0.78)	−1.05 (>0.1)	15.69*** (0.00)	4.28*** (0.00)	−6.85*** (0.00)	−8.65*** (0.00)	0.57** (0.03)	0.21* (0.02)
Romania	−1.96** (0.05)	−1.99 (>0.1)	6.00*** (0.00)	3.28*** (0.00)	−4.92*** (0.00)	−7.69*** (0.00)	0.13 (>0.10)	0.11 (>0.10)
Serbia	−0.65 (0.43)	−1.57 (>0.1)	19.69*** (0.00)	2.43*** (0.00)	−4.41*** (0.00)	−6.13*** (0.00)	0.29 (>0.10)	0.28*** (0.00)
Slovakia	−1.07 (0.26)	−2.40 (>0.1)	7.81*** (0.00)	2.91*** (0.00)	−2.79*** (0.00)	−5.19*** (0.00)	0.04 (>0.10)	0.03 (>0.10)
Slovenia	−0.27 (0.59)	0.91 (>0.1)	6.54*** (0.00)	5.66*** (0.00)	−3.24*** (0.00)	−4.16*** (0.00)	0.47** (0.05)	0.16** (0.04)
Ukraine	−0.01 (0.68)	−1.23 (>0.1)	13.54*** (0.00)	6.21*** (0.00)	−6.05*** (0.00)	−9.74*** (0.00)	0.64** (0.03)	0.28*** (0.00)

Romania seem to be clearly $I(1)$ series, as the ADF–GLS test statistic is not significant, meaning that the null of $d = 1$ cannot be rejected; and the KPSS test statistic is highly significant, meaning that the null of $d = 0$ cannot be accepted. This result would suggest that all the markets, except perhaps Romania, are efficient. However, Romania could also be seen as efficient if it is accepted that it is trend stationary. Conducting the same inference on the returns series basically provides similar conclusions. At the 5% level of significance, the KPSS test statistic cannot reject the null hypothesis of stationary returns except for Malta, Slovenia, and Ukraine. The ADF–GLS test statistic rejects the null hypothesis that the returns are $I(1)$ for every series except for Bulgaria and Cyprus.

Table 8.3 gives the results of applying the simple z- and t-tests for long memory using the local Whittle and GPH estimates of d, respectively. As the

TABLE 8.3 Simple Fractional Integration Tests on the Returns Series for Full Period

Country	z-test (local Whittle estimate)	t-test (GPH estimator)
Bulgaria	5.39*** (0.00)	4.02*** (0.00)
Croatia	3.02*** (0.00)	2.33** (0.02)
Cyprus	2.31** (0.02)	1.72* (0.08)
Estonia	2.56** (0.01)	2.16** (0.03)
Latvia	1.96** (0.05)	0.67 (0.49)
Lithuania	5.05*** (0.00)	3.48*** (0.00)
Malta	6.23*** (0.00)	5.45*** (0.00)
Romania	5.08*** (0.00)	3.75*** (0.00)
Serbia	6.23*** (0.00)	5.35*** (0.00)
Slovakia	−0.57 (0.56)	−0.04 (0.97)
Slovenia	4.12*** (0.00)	3.54*** (0.00)
Ukraine	4.92*** (0.00)	4.84*** (0.00)

test is valid only if $d < 0.5$, only the return series are tested. The more powerful z-test using the local Whittle estimate suggests that all series, except that for Slovakia, could have long memory. The t-test based on the GPH estimator gives similar results but also suggest that the Latvian series doesn't have long memory.

The results of applying the Phillips–Yu recursive DF test, with =5, are given in Table 8.4 and Fig. 8.2a and b. Apart from Croatia and Latvia, these results suggest that all the other series have experienced bubble activity during the full time period. For all except Cyprus, this activity was around the time of the financial crisis during 2007–09. With this in mind, the $I(1)/I(0)$ and long memory analysis was conducted on the series for the past 5 years only.

Tables 8.5 and 8.6 give the results of the $I(1)/I(0)$ analysis and the long memory analysis for the period 2010–15. These results are quite different from those for the full data period given in Tables 8.2–8.4. The $I(1)/I(0)$ analysis suggests that all the level series are $I(1)$ and the corresponding returns are $I(0)$, with a

TABLE 8.4 Phillips and Yu Recursive ADF Test for Full Period

Country	Max DF_r^t	Start $\hat{r}_e$	Finish $\hat{r}_f$
Bulgaria	4.4 11/20/2008	10/01/2008	07/27/2009
Croatia	n/a	n/a	n/a
Cyprus	2.38 09/04/2012	06/26/2012	10/05/2012
Estonia	1.39 06/04/2003	05/09/2003	06/18/2003
Latvia	n/a	n/a	n/a
Lithuania	5.10 1/20/1997	03/11/2004 04/11/2005	03/18/2005 04/27/2005
Malta	5.08 12/21/1999	05/14/1999	07/26/1999
Romania	3.62 02/18/2009	01/08/2009	04/02/2009
Serbia	2.89 04/19/2007	01/19/2007	05/21/2007
Slovakia	1.46 11/12/2008	11/07/2008	11/14/2008
Slovenia	1.39 08/09/2007	08/09/2007	08/10/2007
Ukraine	2.34 07/26/2007	08/22/2005 01/22/2007	09/14/2005 03/20/2008

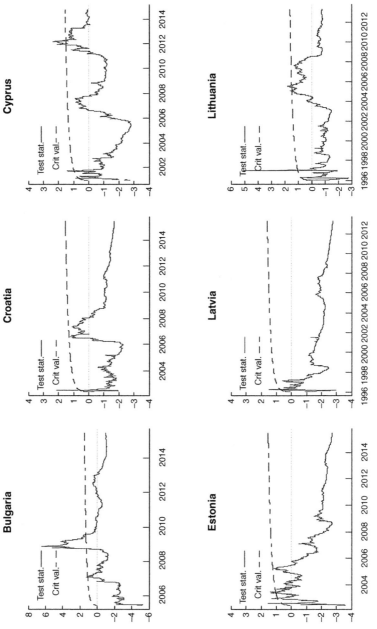

FIGURE 8.2 Time series plots of the Phillips–Yu test statistic. (a) Bulgaria to Lithuania; (b) Malta to Ukraine.

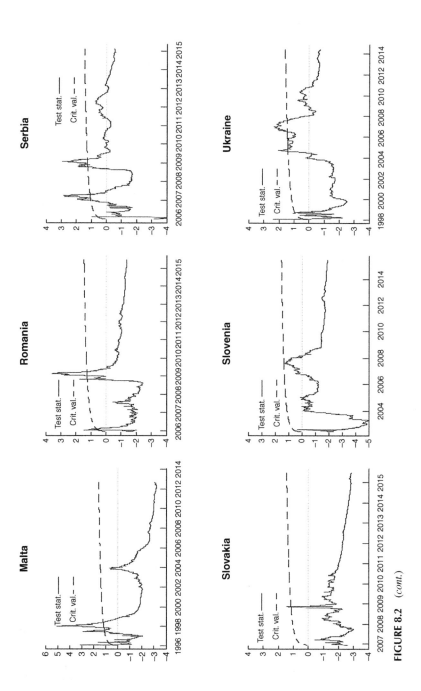

FIGURE 8.2 *(cont.)*

TABLE 8.5 Integer *d* Level of Integration Tests for 2010–15

	Levels				Returns			
	GLS–ADF		KPSS		GLS–ADF		KPSS Cv 0.46	
Country		Trend		Trend		Trend		Trend
Bulgaria	-0.40 (0.54)	-1.63 (>0.1)	3.06*** (0.00)	2.98*** (0.00)	-3.17*** (0.00)	-2.86* (0.09)	-0.32 (>0.10)	0.21** (0.13)
Croatia	-1.42 (0.14)	-1.24 (>0.1)	7.55*** (0.00)	4.38*** (0.00)	-0.64 (0.44)	-7.91*** (0.00)	0.20 (>0.10)	0.07 (>0.10)
Cyprus	0.88 (0.90)	-0.80 (>0.1)	11.62*** (0.00)	3.53*** (0.00)	-3.80*** (0.00)	-4.31*** (0.00)	0.36* (0.09)	0.10 (>0.10)
Estonia	-1.12 (0.23)	-1.18 (>0.1)	2.74*** (0.00)	1.55*** (0.00)	-0.74 (0.40)	-4.22*** (0.00)	0.20 (>0.10)	0.10 (>0.10)
Latvia*	-1.32 (0.17)	-1.49 (>0.1)	2.32*** (0.00)	1.03*** (0.00)	-0.48 (0.51)	-2.46 (>0.10)	0.15 (>0.10)	0.08 (>0.10)
Lithuania	-0.66 (0.43)	-1.26 (0.00)	2.53*** (0.00)	1.13*** (0.00)	-0.77 (0.38)	-1.98 (>0.10)	0.17 (>0.10)	0.16** (0.04)
Malta	-0.60 (0.45)	-0.47 (>0.1)	3.19*** (0.00)	1.96*** (0.00)	-2.4* (0.04)	-6.36*** (0.00)	0.08* (0.08)	-6.36*** (0.00)
Romania	-0.62 (0.45)	-2.01 (>0.1)	9.51*** (0.00)	1.54*** (0.00)	-0.35 (0.56)	-2.09 (>0.10)	0.06 (>0.10)	0.06 (>0.10)
Serbia	-0.48 (0.51)	-1.36 (>0.1)	5.07*** (0.00)	3.00 (0.00)	-4.53*** (0.00)	-1.90 (>0.10)	0.41* (0.07)	0.18** (0.03)
Slovakia	-2.29** (0.02)	-2.28 (0.00)	1.16*** (0.00)	0.96 (0.00)	-0.15 (0.63)	-2.02 (>0.10)	0.31 (>0.10)	0.08 (>0.10)
Slovenia	-1.07 (0.26)	-1.29 (0.00)	2.76*** (0.00)	2.56*** (0.00)	-3.67*** (0.00)	-1.97 (>0.10)	0.14 (>0.10)	0.09 (>0.10)
Ukraine	0.14 (0.72)	-1.30 (>0.1)	10.31*** (0.00)	2.96*** (0.00)	-0.37 (0.55)	-4.70*** (0.00)	0.22 (>0.10)	0.13** (0.09)

*Only to 07/22/2013.

TABLE 8.6 Simple Fractional Integration Tests on the Returns Series for 2010–15

Country	z-test (local Whittle estimate)	t-test (GPH estimator)
Bulgaria	2.76** (0.01)	1.44 (0.15)
Croatia	0.60 (0.55)	0.62 (0.54)
Cyprus	0.51 (0.61)	0.50 (0.62)
Estonia	0.78 (0.43)	0.55 (0.58)
Latvia*	−0.72 (0.47)	−0.51 (0.61)
Lithuania*	0.07 (0.94)	0.73 (0.47)
Malta	1.87* (0.06)	1.22 (0.23)
Romania	0.79 (0.43)	0.08 (0.93)
Serbia	2.45** (0.01)	0.50 (0.61)
Slovakia	−0.31 (0.75)	−0.91 (0.37)
Slovenia	1.39 (0.16)	0.68 (0.50)
Ukraine	1.99** (0.05)	1.96* (0.05)

*Only to 07/22/2013.

slight probability that Cyprus and Serbia might be more complex. The fractional integration analysis of the returns suggests that apart from Bulgaria and Serbia there is little probability that the markets have long memory.

7 CONCLUSIONS AND RECOMMENDATIONS

In this study, 12 frontier financial markets, primarily in Eastern Europe, are investigated to determine whether they are informationally efficient and/or demonstrate evidence of "bubble" activity between the 1990s and 2015. Since the collapse of communism in the early 1990s, all of these markets have adopted a free market agenda and have fully embraced the capitalist system.

The evidence initially presented would appear to indicate that all of the market indices examined follow a random walk process, with the exception of Romania, and can therefore be deemed to be informationally efficient, if one assumes a simple definition of efficiency (ADF–GLS and KPSS tests). This result stands for both the level and returns data. However, when one examines the data for each of the markets from a long memory perspective, it would appear that, with the exception of Slovakia, all of the markets exhibit some evidence of long memory, and thus could be deemed to be showing signs of inefficiency (local Whittle and GPH estimators). A question then arises as to whether this long memory result is actually a result of "bubble" behavior within each of the markets. To test for this, the study applies the Phillips–Yu test and finds evidence of bubble behavior for all of the markets, with the exception Croatia and Latvia. With the exception of Cyprus, this bubble behavior is predominantly to be found around the time of the financial crisis of 2007–09. To determine if the financial crisis has adversely affected the results, the data from 2010 to 2015 are examined in isolation, with results quite different from those of the complete data series. The fractional integration tests for these data indicate that, with the exceptions of Bulgaria and Serbia, the frontier markets examined have little evidence of long memory, but that the initial findings have been strongly influenced by the bubble behavior detected in the 2000s. These findings are more consistent with the tenets of the AMH rather the EMH as espoused by the likes of Fama.

In order to examine the issue more fully, one suggestion for a subsequent study would be to examine the time series for individual share prices in each of the respective frontier markets—although issues of data availability and thin trading in such markets might inhibit such an analysis.

REFERENCES

Akbar, M., Baig, H., 2010. Reaction of stock prices to dividend announcements and market efficiency in Pakistan. Lahore J. Econ. 15 (1), 103–125.

Appiah-Kusi, J., Menyah, K., 2003. Return predictability in African stock markets. Rev. Financ. Econ. 12, 247–270.

Asal, M., 2000. Are There Trends Towards Efficiency? A Case Study of Emerging Markets: The Egyptian Experience. Working paper, University of Goteborg, Sweden.

Black, F., 1986. Noise. J. Finance 41 (3), 529–543.

Bundoo, S., 2000. The Mauritius Stock Exchange: an assessment. Soc. Sci. Hum. Law Manage. Res. J. 3, 67–80.

Campbell, J., Lo, A., MacKinlay, A., 1997. The Econometrics of Financial Markets. Princeton University Press, Princeton, NJ.

Cootner, P., 1964. The Random Character of Stock Market Prices. MIT Press, Cambridge, MA.

Cunado, J., Gil-Alana, L., de Gracia, F.P., 2005. A test for rational bubbles in the NASDAQ stock index: a fractionally integrated approach. J. Bank. Finance 29 (10), 2633–2654.

De Groot, W., Pang, J., Swinkels, L., 2012. The cross-section of stock returns in frontier emerging markets. J. Empir. Finance 19, 796–818.

Dickinson, J., Muragu, K., 1994. Market efficiency in developing countries: a case study of the Nairobi Stock Exchange. J. Bus. Account. 21, 133–150.

Elliott, G., Rothenberg, T.J., Stock, J.H., 1996. Efficient tests for an autoregressive unit root. Econometrica 64 (4), 813–836.

Fama, E., 1965a. The behavior of stock-market prices. J. Bus. 38 (1), 34–105.

Fama, E., 1965b. Random walks in stock market prices. Financ. Anal. J. 21 (5), 55–59.

Fama, E., 1970. Efficient capital markets: a review of theory and empirical work. J. Finance 25 (2), 383–417.

Fama, E., 1991. Efficient capital markets II. J. Finance 46 (5), 1575–1617.

Fama, E., 1998. Market efficiency, long-term returns, and behavioral finance. J. Financ. Econ. 49 (3), 283–306.

Farmer, D., Lo, A., 1999. Frontiers of finance: evolutions and efficient markets. Proc. Natl. Acad. Sci. 96, 9991–9992.

Floros, C., Jaffry, S., Lima, G., 2007. Long memory in the Portuguese Stock Market. Stud. Econ. Finance 24 (3), 220–232.

Frammel, M., Kruse, R., 2011. Testing for a rational bubble under long memory. Quant. Finance 12 (11), 1723–1732.

Frankfurter, G., 2006. The theory of fair markets (TFM): towards a new finance paradigm. Int. Rev. Financ. Anal. 15 (2), 130–144.

Geweke, J., Porter-Hudak, S., 1983. The estimation and application of long-memory time series models. J. Time Ser. Anal. 4, 221–237.

Gil-Alana, L., 2006. Fractional integration in daily stock market indexes. Rev. Financ. Econ. 15 (1), 28–48.

Graham, G., Emid, A., 2013. Investing in Frontier Markets. John Wiley & Sons, Hoboken, NJ.

Granger, C., 1992. Forecasting stock market prices: lessons for forecasters. Int. J. Forecasting 8 (1), 3–13.

Grossman, S., 1976. On the efficiency of competitive stock markets where traders have diverse information. J. Finance 31 (2), 573–585.

Grossman, S., Stiglitz, J., 1980. On the impossibility of informationally efficient markets. Am. Econ. Rev. 70 (3), 393–408.

Jarrett, J., 2010. Efficient markets hypothesis and daily variation in small Pacific-Basin stock markets. Manage. Res. Rev. 33 (12), 1128–1139.

Jefferis, K., Smith, G., 2005. The changing efficiency of African stock markets. S. Afr. J. Econ. 73 (1), 54–67.

Jensen, M., 1978. Some anomalous evidence regarding market efficiency. J. Financ. Econ. 6 (2/3), 95–101.

Keiber, K., 2007. Reconsidering the impossibility of informationally efficient markets. Appl. Financ. Econ. 17 (14), 1113–1122.

Kiweu, J., 1991. The behaviour of share prices in the Nairobi Stock Exchange: an empirical investigation. Thesis. University of Nairobi. Available from: http://erepository.uonbi.ac.ke/xmlui/handle/11295/40162

Kratz, O., 1999. Frontier Emerging Equity Markets Securities Price Behavior and Valuation. Kulwer, London.

Kwiatkowski, D., Phillips, P.C.B., Schmidt, P., Shin, Y., 1992. Testing the null of stationarity against the alternative of a unit root: how sure are we that economic time series have a unit root? J. Econom. 54, 159–178.

Lo, A., 2004. The adaptive markets hypothesis. J. Portfolio Manage. 30 (5), 15–29.

MacKinnon, J.G., 1996. Numerical distribution functions for unit root and cointegration tests. J. Appl. Econom. 11 (6), 601–618.

Magnusson, M., Wydick, B., 2002. How efficient are Africa's emerging stock markets? J. Dev. Stud. 38, 141–156.

Malkiel, B., 1992. Efficient market hypothesis. New Palgrave Dictionary of Money and Finance. Macmillan, London.

Miambo, C., Biekpe, N., 2007. The efficient market hypothesis: evidence from ten African stock markets. Invest. Anal. J. 66, 5–17.

Mobarek, A., Keasey, K., 2000. Weak-Form Market Efficiency of an Emerging Market: Evidence from Dhaka Stock Market of Bangladesh. Paper presented at the ENBS Conference, Oslo, Norway, May.

Okicic, J., 2014. An empirical analysis of stock returns and volatility: the case of stock markets from Central and Eastern Europe. South East Eur. J. Econ. Bus. 9 (1), 7–15.

Phillips, P.C.B., Magadalinos, T., 2007a. Limit theory for moderate deviations from a unit root. J. Econom. 136 (2), 115–130.

Phillips, P.C.B., Magadalinos, T., 2007b. Limit theory for moderate deviations from a unit root under weak dependence. In: Phillips, G.D.A., Tzavalis, E. (Eds.), The Refinement of Econometric Estimation and Test Procedures: Finite Sample and Asymptotic Analysis. Cambridge University Press, Cambridge, pp. 123–162.

Phillips, P.C.B., Wu, Y., Yu, J., 2011. Explosive behavior in the 1990s NASDAQ: when did exuberance escalate asset values? Int. Econ. Rev. 52 (1), 201–226.

Phillips, P.C.B., Yu, J., 2011. Dating the timeline of financial bubbles during the subprime crisis. Quant. Econ. 2 (3), 455–491.

Qu, Z., 2011. A test against spurious long memory. J. Bus. Econ. Stat. 29 (3), 423–438.

Rehman, M., Khidmat, W., 2013. Technical analysis of efficient market hypothesis in a frontier market. Stud. Bus. Econ. 82, 60–67.

Robinson, P., 1995. Gaussian semiparametric estimation of long range dependence. Ann. Stat. 22, 1630–1661.

Samuelson, P., 1965. Proof that properly anticipated prices fluctuate randomly. Ind. Manage. Rev. 6 (1), 41–49.

Schwartz, B., 2004. The Paradox of Choice. Harper Collins, New York.

Shadbolt, P., 2013. Can frontier markets deliver? CFA Inst. Mag. 24 (2), 22–24.

Shefrin, H., 2000. Beyond Greed and Fear: Understanding Behavioral Finance and the Psychology of Investing. Harvard Business School Press, Boston, MA.

Smith, A., 2005. Level shifts and the illusion of long memory in economic time series. J. Bus. Econ. Stat. 23, 321–335.

Smith, G., Jefferis, K., Ryoo, H., 2002. African stock markets: multiple variance ratio tests of random walks. Appl. Financ. Econ. J. 12, 475–484.

Speidell, L., Krohne, A., 2007. The case for frontier equity markets. J. Investing 16 (3), 12–22.

Statman, M., Fisher, K., Anginer, D., 2008. Affect in a behavioral asset-pricing model. Financ. Anal. J. 64 (2), 20–29.

Timmerman, A., Granger, C., 2004. Efficient market hypothesis and forecasting. Int. J. Forecasting 20 (1), 15–27.

Chapter 9

Another Look at Financial Analysts' Forecasts Accuracy: Recent Evidence From Eastern European Frontier Markets

A. Coën*, A. Desfleurs**

*ESG-UQÀM, Graduate School of Business, University of Quebec in Montreal and Ivanhoe-Cambridge Real Estate Chair, Montreal, QC, Canada; **School of Accounting, Faculty of Administration, University of Sherbrooke, Sherbrooke, QC, Canada

Chapter Outline

1 INTRODUCTION

Since the seminal work of De Bondt and Thaler (1990), an important literature has been devoted to the analysis of the behavior of financial analysts (FAs). The crucial role of financial analysts' forecasts (FAFs) in investment decisions on developed and emerging financial markets has been highlighted in numerous

Handbook of Frontier Markets. http://dx.doi.org/10.1016/B978-0-12-803776-8.00009-4

171

studies. Emerging and frontier markets offer significant and promising investment opportunities. If emerging topics are now well acknowledged in the financial literature and in the finance industry, the special issues of frontier markets are still to be explored, especially the role of financial analysts. In this chapter, we suggest focusing on Eastern European frontier markets.

After the economic integration of Eastern European countries with the European Union in 2004, important and significant economic, legal, and political reforms took place. At the same time, the progressive adoption of the International Financial Reporting Standards (IFRS) was led to improve transparency and information disclosure in Eastern Europe. In this challenging context, calling for new investment opportunities, there is a need to improve our knowledge of the role of financial analysts. All around the world the behavior of financial analysts has been severely criticized, especially because of their so-called forecast "overoptimism."

Here, we suggest analyzing the evolution of their forecasts from 2005 to 2013. We use the global financial crisis of 2008 as a potential breakdown. Our main objectives are to analyze whether financial analysts exhibit specific behaviors on these frontier markets. We focus on financial analysts' forecast accuracy and forecast bias to estimate the relative evolution of their performance and level of optimism. We conjecture that the period after the global financial crisis may reasonably have led to an improvement of FAF accuracy and a drop of the level of overoptimism (or a decline of FAF bias). Moreover, it seems to be relevant to show whether financial analysts are pessimistic when they forecast earnings profits and less overly optimistic for loss forecasts. Therefore, we use two specific metrics and compare their evolution with a sample of other European markets standing as benchmarks: European emerging markets, Russia, Germanic countries, and Nordic countries. We also consider three periods: before the global financial crisis (2005–07), during the crisis (2008–10), and after the crisis (2011–13). Our sample of Eastern European frontier markets includes eight countries: Bulgaria, Croatia, Estonia, Latvia, Lithuania, Romania, Slovakia, and Slovenia.

The structure of the chapter is given as follows. In Section 2, we briefly present and motivate our conceptual framework. In Section 3, we describe the data, and precisely define FAF accuracy and FAF bias. In Section 4, we report and analyze the main results. Finally in Section 5, we summarize the main findings and draw our conclusions.

2 CONCEPTUAL FRAMEWORK

Inasmuch as our main objective is to shed light on the evolution of two important topics of financial analysts' forecasts (FAF accuracy and FAF bias), we follow the same methodology already used in previous studies by Coën and Desfleurs (2004, 2014) [for the analysis of FAFs for, respectively, emerging Pacific Rim markets and real estate investment trusts (REITs) on Asian markets]. Here, our contribution is to focus on a sample of Eastern European frontier markets. To our knowledge, no study has ever been done dealing with the performance of financial analysts' forecasts on these promising markets from 2005 to 2013.

The main drawback of frontier markets is the lack of data. Therefore, we have decided to merge the FAF data of eight Eastern European frontier markets in a group consisting of Bulgaria, Croatia, Estonia, Latvia, Lithuania, Romania, Slovakia, and Slovenia. With this approach, we are able to compare the performance of the Eastern European frontier markets group with four other European markets groups made up of 10 countries standing as leading economic partners: Germanic countries (Austria, Denmark, and Germany); Nordic countries (Finland, Norway, and Sweden); European emerging countries (Czech Republic, Hungary, and Poland); and Russia. The main motivation for this choice is to highlight the important and significant economic, political, and legal transition led by Eastern European countries since their integration with the European Union.

2.1   Financial Analysts' Forecast Accuracy

It is well acknowledged in the accounting and financial literature that forecast accuracy (and also FAF bias) is influenced by special topics. We can report that among the main characteristics analyzed are the skills of individual analysts (Mikhail et al., 1997; Clement, 1999); the firm size and analyst coverage (Alford and Berger, 1999; Hong et al., 2000; Lang et al., 2004; Chang et al., 2006; Yu, 2008); the level of diversification (Thomas, 2002); the level of disclosure (O'Brien, 1990); the financing decisions (Bradshaw et al., 2006); the type of earnings (Ciccone, 2005); and country and industry effects (Katz et al., 2000; Capstaff et al., 2001; Patel et al., 2002; Black and Carnes, 2006; Coën et al., 2009; Byard et al., 2011; Tan et al., 2011; Chee et al., 2010). In this exploratory study, we focus on the trend of FAF accuracy during a period marked by the global financial crisis, a significant increase of information disclosure, and a high level of competition. Following the results of Basu et al. (1998), Alford and Berger (1999), or Coën and Desfleurs (2004), we consider that the performance of financial analysts on Eastern European frontier markets during the 2005–13 period should have improved. We also expect important differences for FAF accuracy between Eastern European frontier markets and Germanic and Nordic markets: Russia and European emerging markets may be used as points of reference.

2.2   Financial Analysts' Forecast Bias

As mentioned earlier, earnings forecasts may be biased (too optimistic or too pessimistic), casting serious doubt on the real role of financial analysts, especially during periods of high uncertainty (Das et al., 1998; Ke and Yu, 2006;

Sadique et al., 2010). The literature documents that FAF bias is related to a sentiment of overoptimism on average. Focusing on frontier markets during the global financial crisis, we may expect a positive bias for all groups of countries, with significant differences between subperiods. The adoption of important reforms during the past decade should have induced a decline in FAF bias on Eastern European frontier markets.

3 DATA AND METHODOLOGY

Following Coën and Desfleurs (2004), we use three metrics to analyze FAFs for our sample of Eastern European frontier markets. First, we introduce the metric for FAF accuracy as the absolute difference between the reported and the forecasted earnings. Second, to highlight the specific role of financial analysts and their relative accuracy, we suggest the use of a simple benchmark. With this approach, we are able to compare FAF errors (FAFEs) with forecast errors induced by a naive statistical model. Third, to focus on FAF bias, we analyze the first metric (with the sign positive or negative). A positive value may be interpreted as a kind of overoptimism, whereas a negative value is a sign of pessimism.

3.1 Data

To define earnings FAFs, we use the standard consensus annual forecast data as provided by the International Brokers Estimate System (I/B/E/S) summary database (available on Thomson One 5.0) for a sample of 18 countries from fiscal year 2005–2013. We observe an important heterogeneity among countries and industries (and firms), especially in Eastern European frontier markets. Analyst coverage differs significantly. To shed light on FAFs on Eastern European frontier markets, characterized by a lack of data compared to developed European financial markets, we define five groups of countries with specific legal, fiscal, accounting, or/and economic topics. Thus, the first group gathering Eastern European countries consists of the eight frontier markets: Bulgaria, Croatia, Estonia, Latvia, Lithuania, Romania, Slovakia, and Slovenia. The second group is made up of the new European Economic Community emerging countries: the Czech Republic, Hungary, and Poland. The third is devoted to Russia only, standing as a comparative benchmark to highlight the economic, political, and legal transition. The fourth group consists of the Germanic countries: Austria, Denmark, and Germany. Finally, in the fifth group, we gather together Finland, Norway, and Sweden under the label Nordic countries. We also reduce the influence of extreme outliers: Forecast errors are winsorized at the 5 and 95% levels. We may mention that we use an ordinary least squares (OLS) procedure. After these adjustments, our sample includes 11,420 observations from 2005 to 2013 (also reported in Table 9.1).

TABLE 9.1 Descriptive Statistics of Absolute Analysts Forecast Errors and Naive Errors for Each Country and Each Subperiod

Variables	No. of observations		Mean		T-test: mean = 0		Median		Performance of analysts		Adjusted T-test[a,b]: difference between the subperiods		
	|FAFE|	|NFAFE|	|FAFE|	|NFAFE|	|FAFE|	|NFAFE|	|FAFE|	|NFAFE|	Sup. |FAFE|/|NFAFE|	T-test sup.	Before/after crisis	Before/during crisis	During/after crisis
Frontier markets													
2005–07	145	64	0.540**	0.530**	16.463	11.270	0.479	0.445	0.067	0.154	3.23**	−0.68	4.31**
2008–10	203	131	0.569**	0.661**	20.544	19.114	0.583	0.954	0.999	3.870			
2011–13	229	190	0.410**	0.482**	16.657	17.678	0.245	0.341	0.650	3.083			
2005–13	577	385	0.499**	0.551**	30.534	27.695	0.362	0.479	0.669	4.329			
Emerging markets													
2005–07	190	143	0.242**	0.384**	10.819	14.274	0.112	0.291	1.856	6.178	−3.21**	−2.06*	−1.11
2008–10	292	232	0.304**	0.510**	15.226	21.258	0.136	0.397	2.165	10.484			
2011–13	403	341	0.333**	0.462**	19.123	22.502	0.166	0.340	1.392	8.506			
2005–13	885	716	0.304**	0.462**	26.610	33.772	0.138	0.350	1.737	14.515			
Russia													
2005–07	187	122	0.387**	0.407**	14.872	15.306	0.223	0.324	0.992	3.851	−2.59*	−3.11**	0.79
2008–10	324	221	0.491**	0.535**	23.044	21.590	0.384	0.489	1.166	5.414			
2011–13	408	349	0.468**	0.487**	24.375	24.582	0.323	0.385	0.569	3.972			
2005–13	919	692	0.460**	0.488**	36.520	35.736	0.323	0.400	0.830	7.571			

(Continued)

TABLE 9.1 Descriptive Statistics of Absolute Analysts Forecast Errors and Naive Errors for Each Country and Each Subperiod (cont.)

Variables	No. of observations		Mean		T-test: mean = 0		Median		Performance of analysts		Adjusted T-test[a,b]: difference between the subperiods		
	|FAFE|	|NFAFE|	|FAFE|	|NFAFE|	|FAFE|	|NFAFE|	|FAFE|	|NFAFE|	Sup. |FAFE|/|NFAFE|	T-test sup.	Before/ after crisis	Before/ during crisis	During/ after crisis
Germanic countries													
2005–07	1521	1257	0.277**	0.453**	34.030	47.057	0.140	0.341	2.145	26.579	−1.27	−5.90**	4.51**
2008–10	1571	1459	0.347**	0.595**	39.921	60.814	0.200	0.606	2.348	28.288			
2011–13	1499	1424	0.292**	0.477**	33.881	47.680	0.143	0.352	1.909	23.784			
2005–13	4591	4140	0.306**	0.511**	62.136	88.744	0.158	0.411	2.136	45.281			
Nordic countries													
2005–07	1419	1151	0.294**	0.468**	34.251	46.165	0.143	0.375	2.138	23.785	−0.36	−3.40**	3.10**
2008–10	1467	1341	0.336**	0.562**	37.941	55.085	0.189	0.523	2.205	25.375			
2011–13	1467	1372	0.298**	0.476**	35.834	47.589	0.163	0.360	1.802	22.241			
2005–13	4353	3864	0.309**	0.503**	62.323	85.427	0.165	0.408	2.043	41.170			

Symbols ** and * indicate statistical significance at the 1 and 5% levels, respectively.

[a]FAFE is the mean forecast error at the end of the fiscal year divided by the annual reported earnings and defined by Eq. 9.1.

[b]T-test on mean differences is adjusted using the Satterthwaite procedure if necessary.

3.2 FAF Accuracy on Eastern European Frontier Markets

As well acknowledged in the financial literature, FAF accuracy is defined as the absolute difference between the consensus annual earnings forecast and the reported earnings per share (EPS) for fiscal year t divided by reported earnings: the absolute FAF errors or |FAFE|. To avoid the potential problems induced by market conditions, we deflate FAF errors by reported earnings rather than stock price (as mentioned earlier, see Coën and Desfleurs, 2004; Coën et al., 2009; or Coën and Desfleurs, 2014; among others) as described by the following equation:

$$\left|\text{FAFE}\right| = \left|\frac{e_{j,\,t(h)}}{RE_{j,\,t}}\right| = \left|\frac{F_{j,\,t(h)} - RE_{j,\,t}}{RE_{j,\,t}}\right| \tag{9.1}$$

where $FAFE_t$, the financial analyst forecast error for firm j divided by EPS for fiscal year t; $e_{j,t}$, the forecast error of EPS for firm j for fiscal year t; $F_{j,t}$, the consensus EPS forecast for firm j and fiscal year t; $RE_{j,t}$, the reported EPS for firm j and fiscal year t.

Following Coën and Desfleurs (2004), we also introduce a metric for a naive statistical model based on time series. The naive FAF error (NFAFE) for firm j and fiscal year t is given by the following equation:

$$\left|\text{NFAFE}\right| = \left|\frac{RE_{j,\,t-1} - RE_{j,\,t}}{RE_{j,\,t}}\right| \tag{9.2}$$

The naive model is based on the simple assumption that the earnings forecast for fiscal year t is the previous reported earnings (for fiscal year $t - 1$). To analyze the relative performance of FAF, we also use a second metric initially developed by Brown et al. (1987):

$$SUP_{j,\,t} = \ln\left(\left|\frac{RE_{j,\,t-1} - RE_{j,\,t}}{F_{j,\,t-1} - RE_{j,\,t}}\right|^2\right) \tag{9.3}$$

The interpretation is straightforward. A ratio statistically positive highlights the precision of financial analysts compared to a naive statistical model; financial analysts are more performant.

3.3 FAF Bias on Eastern European Frontier Markets

After the study of FAF accuracy, we now analyze FAF bias. The FAF bias is measured by the relative FAF error (forecast error with its sign) as given by the following equation (the parameters have already been defined in the previous section):

$$\text{FAFE} = \frac{e_{j,\,t(h)}}{\left|RE_{j,\,t}\right|} = \frac{F_{j,\,t(h)} - RE_{j,\,t}}{\left|RE_{j,\,t}\right|} \tag{9.4}$$

FAF error is not biased if FAFE is not statistically different from zero. When FAFE is statistically positive (FAF is higher than reported earnings), financial analysts can be reasonably qualified as overly optimistic. On the contrary, they are considered pessimistic or underpessimistic when the difference is statistically negative.

To analyze the evolution of FAF bias, we follow De Bondt and Thaler (1990) and their methodology previously used by Paudyal et al. (1998), and Coën and Desfleurs (2004) (among others). We regress the variation of earnings forecasts on the difference between the final FAF for year t and the reported earnings for $t-1$:

$$\frac{RE_{j,t} - RE_{j,t-1}}{\left|RE_{j,t-1}\right|} = \alpha + \beta \frac{F_{j,t} - RE_{j,t-1}}{\left|RE_{j,t-1}\right|} + \varepsilon_{j,t} \text{ with } \varepsilon_{j,t} \sim N(0,\sigma^2) \quad (9.5)$$

where $\dfrac{RE_{j,t} - RE_{j,t-1}}{\left|RE_{j,t-1}\right|}$, the variation of reported earnings between fiscal years t and $t-1$; $\dfrac{F_{j,t} - RE_{j,t-1}}{\left|RE_{j,t-1}\right|}$, the difference between FAF of the fiscal year t and the reported earnings of $t-1$.

No bias is detected if $\alpha = 0$ and $\beta = 1$ (at standard statistical level of confidence). We can reject the absence of bias if $\alpha \neq 0$ and/or $\beta \neq 1$. As reported by Coën and Desfleurs (2004) (among others), a negative coefficient estimate for α may be related to overestimation (a so-called optimistic bias). A positive coefficient estimate, by contrast, highlights the presence of underestimation (pessimistic bias). Moreover, a coefficient estimate $\beta < 1$ is interpreted as an overreaction among financial analysts, whereas a coefficient estimate $\beta > 1$ leads to an underreaction as suggested by De Bondt and Thaler (1990). As well acknowledged, financial analysts tend to exhibit overoptimism in their earnings forecasts (Brown et al., 1987; De Bondt and Thaler, 1990; Allen et al., 1997; Brown, 1997; Basu et al., 1998; Chopra, 1998; Alford and Berger, 1999; Ang and Ma, 2001; Ang and Ciccone, 2001; Loh and Mian, 2002; Hope, 2003; Coën and Desfleurs, 2004; Coën et al., 2009; Tan et al., 2011). This phenomenon should be observed for our sample of Eastern European frontier markets.

3.4 FAF by Subperiods and Types of Earnings

To analyze the evolution of FAF on Eastern European frontier markets, we divide our sample into three subperiods using the global financial crisis as a potential breakdown: before the crisis, 2005–07; during the crisis, 2008–10, and after the crisis, 2011–13. Moreover, we suggest adding a dimension to our analysis of FAF accuracy and FAF bias by focusing on the types of earnings. Following Coën and Desfleurs (2004, 2014), we separate earnings profits from earnings losses, on one hand, and earnings increases from earnings decreases, on the other hand. As suggested by Ciccone (2005) and Coën and Desfleurs

(2004, 2014) for Asian financial markets, the crisis may change the behavior of financial analysts and modify FAF accuracy and FAF bias.

4 ANALYSIS OF FAF ON EASTERN EUROPEAN FRONTIER MARKETS

In this section, first, we analyze the evolution of financial analyst forecasts for a large sample of Eastern European frontier markets from 2005 to 2013. Second, we shed light on the impact and consequences of the global financial crisis on FAF accuracy and FAF bias. Third, we compare the FAF on these markets to FAF on European emerging markets, Russia, and Germanic and Nordic financial markets.

4.1 Analysis of FAF Accuracy

We compare the mean of absolute FAF errors with the mean generated by a naive statistical model, as defined by Eq. 9.2, to analyze FAF accuracy. We report descriptive statistics for each group of financial markets and each subperiod in Table 9.1. We note that the mean of absolute FAF errors is statistically different from zero for the full sample period with a value of 0.499 (or 49.9%) and higher than the four other groups of countries: European emerging markets (0.304), Russia (0.460), Germanic countries (0.306), and Nordic countries (0.309). The results reported for Russia reveal that Russia stands as a relevant benchmark with fewer FAF errors and a better FAF accuracy.

As expected, FAF accuracy is better in European emerging markets, Germanic countries, and Nordic countries. As reported, FAF accuracy for Eastern European markets is always better than FAF accuracy induced by a naive model. For the full sample period from 2005 to 2013, the value of the metric is statistically significant: 0.609. To shed light on the analysis of FAF accuracy, we focus now on each subperiod.

4.1.1   Before the Crisis: 2005–07

First, we may report that the FAF accuracy is best in European emerging countries, with an absolute financial analyst forecast error (|FAFE|) of 24.2% (0.242), followed by Germanic countries (27.7%) and Nordic countries (29.4%). The highest |FAFE| is reported, as expected, for Eastern European frontier markets (54%), followed by Russia (38.7%).

While FAF accuracy is statistically better for all groups of countries than is induced by a naive statistical model, this is not the case for our full sample of European frontier markets (0.067). Interestingly, we report a striking result. FAF accuracy has been sharply improving: from 54% before the global financial crisis to 41% afterward. The difference between these subperiods is highly statistically significant, with an adjusted T-statistic of 3.23. For all groups of countries we observe a decline of FAF accuracy, especially for European emerging countries (from 24.2% to 33.3%) and for Russia (from 38.7% to

46.8%). This trend is not statistically significant for Germanic and Nordic countries (from 27.7% to 29.2% and from 29.4% to 29.8%, respectively). The negative effects of the global financial crisis are still to be solved. Nevertheless, with this result we may conclude that there is a significant improvement of the performance of financial analysts on Eastern European frontier markets after the global financial crisis.

4.1.2 During the Crisis: 2008–10

For all groups of countries, including the Eastern European frontier markets, we report a decrease of FAF accuracy introduced by the global financial crisis. The |FAFE| reaches 30.3% in European emerging markets, followed by Nordic countries (33.6%), Germanic countries (34.7%), Russia (49.1%), and frontier markets (56.9%). This decrease in accuracy is statistically highly significant for all groups of countries except for frontier markets.

4.1.3 After the Crisis: 2011–13

After the crisis, we may report an increase of FAF accuracy in all groups except for European emerging markets. |FAFE| declines from 56.9% to 41% for frontier markets. We observe the same trend for Germanic countries (from 34.7% to 29.2%), for Nordic countries (from 33.6% to 29.8%), and for Russia (from 49.1% to 46.8%). For European emerging markets, however, an increase of |FAFE| from 30.4% to 33.3% is reported.

4.2 Analysis of FAF Bias

In this section we study the evolution of the mean of FAF errors. Our main objective is to analyze the forecast bias. Following previous studies (Chopra, 1998; Coën and Desfleurs, 2004; Ciccone, 2005), we expect that the global financial crisis of 2008 has induced a change in the behavior of financial analysts. An increase of FAF accuracy and a decline of overoptimism should be observed. Our results are reported for each group of countries and subperiods in Table 9.2 and 9.3.

The data report that FAFs are systematically optimistic, except for Russia. FAFEs range from 20.4% for frontier markets to 9.6% for Nordic countries (all values are highly statistically significant except for Russia). While we observe a relative decline of this overoptimism for frontier markets (from 29.3% before the crisis to 10.3% after the crisis), we note an inverse trend for European emerging markets (from 10.3% to 11.3%), Germanic countries (from 7.8% to 14.6%), and Nordic countries (from 7.2% to 9.3%), which exhibit an increase of optimistic forecasts.

As reported by Table 9.3, this decline of overoptimism is statistically significant for Eastern European frontier markets. For Russia a statistically significant increase of overoptimism can be reported. From being pessimistic before the crisis (−9.6%), FAFs in Russia are optimistic afterward (8.3%).

TABLE 9.2 Descriptive Statistics of Forecast Errors (FAFE) at the End of the Fiscal Year

FAFE[a] (bias)	Periods	No. of observations	Mean	Student's t	Standard deviation	Median	% Optimism
Frontier markets	2005–07	148	0.293**	5.825	0.612	0.224	64.19
	2008–10	204	0.256**	5.649	0.647	0.171	62.25
	2011–13	233	0.103**	2.819	0.555	0.011	51.07
	2005–13	585	0.204**	8.127	0.608	0.091	58.29
Emerging markets	2005–07	190	0.103**	3.754	0.379	0.011	53.68
	2008–10	292	0.143**	5.636	0.434	0.026	54.79
	2011–13	405	0.113**	4.782	0.474	0.018	53.33
	2005–13	887	0.121**	8.134	0.442	0.019	53.89
Russia	2005–07	195	−0.096*	−2.466	0.545	−0.105	34.36
	2008–10	354	−0.068	−1.937	0.661	−0.043	42.09
	2011–13	433	0.083**	2.727	0.632	0.024	52.66
	2005–13	982	−0.007	−0.351	0.631	−0.031	45.21
Germanic countries	2005–07	1521	0.078**	7.362	0.414	−0.014	46.15
	2008–10	1576	0.139**	11.696	0.472	0.046	57.87
	2011–13	1503	0.146**	13.430	0.421	0.030	57.02
	2005–13	4600	0.121**	18.764	0.438	0.018	53.72
Nordic countries	2005–07	1419	0.072**	6.261	0.431	0.005	51.30
	2008–10	1472	0.124**	10.237	0.464	0.039	57.13
	2011–13	1475	0.093**	8.296	0.431	0.033	56.88
	2005–13	4366	0.096**	14.396	0.443	0.026	55.15

Symbols ** and * indicate statistical significance at the 1 and 5% levels, respectively.
[a]FAFE is the mean forecast error at the end of the fiscal year divided by the annual reported earnings and defined by Eq. 9.4.

TABLE 9.3 Test on the Difference of Forecast Biases (FAFE)

Groups of countries	Bias[a]	Before crisis	During crisis	After crisis	Tests on mean differences	Adjusted T-test[b]
Frontier markets	FAFE	0.293**	0.256**	0.103**	Before/after the crisis	3.07**
					Before/during the crisis	0.55
					During/after the crisis	2.64**
Emerging markets	FAFE	0.103**	0.143**	0.113**	Before/after the crisis	−0.26
					Before/during the crisis	−1.07
					During/after the crisis	0.88
Russia	FAFE	−0.096*	−0.068	0.083**	Before/after the crisis	−3.62**
					Before/during the crisis	−0.54
					During/after the crisis	−3.25**
Germanic countries	FAFE	0.078**	0.139**	0.146**	Before/after the crisis	−4.46**
					Before/during the crisis	−3.82
					During/after the crisis	−0.43
Nordic countries	FAFE	0.072**	0.124**	0.093**	Before/after the crisis	−1.35
					Before/during the crisis	−3.13**
					During/after the crisis	1.85

Symbols ** and * indicate statistical significance at the 1 and 5% levels, respectively.
[a]FAFE is the mean forecast error at the end of the fiscal year divided by the annual reported earnings and defined by Eq. 9.4.
[b]T-test on mean differences is adjusted using the Satterthwaite procedure if necessary.

Following Capstaff et al. (1998), De Bondt and Thaler (1990), and Coën and Desfleurs (2004), we compare FAF variations to reported earnings variations defined by Eq. 9.5. We report interesting and significant results in Table 9.4.

First, for all groups of countries and all subperiods, the coefficient estimate β is below 1 and statistically different from 1. As mentioned earlier, a coefficient estimate $\beta < 1$ clearly indicates that financial analysts tend to overreact with an increase of information flow. Second, the coefficient estimate α is statistically negative for frontier markets for all subperiods (except after the crisis): from -16.7% before the crisis to 0.00% after the crisis. A negative coefficient is interpreted as the presence of overoptimism. This overly optimistic behavior has declined after the global financial crisis. As a comparison, for Germanic and Nordic countries the coefficient estimates are statistically negative after the crisis, but were positive before the crisis. For Russia, the pessimistic behavior before the crisis (18%) has significantly declined afterward; the coefficient estimate is not statistically different from zero.

To improve our analysis, we focus now on profits and loss forecasts on one hand, and on forecasts of earnings increases and decreases on the other hand.

4.3   Analysis of the Evolution of FAFE by Types of Earnings

4.3.1   Earnings Profits Versus Earnings Losses

As reported in Table 9.5, the amplitude of FAF errors is more important for earnings losses than for earnings profits. For the full period, |FAFE| for Eastern European frontier markets is 43.5% for earnings profits compared to 82% for earnings losses. The accuracy tends to improve during the period: from 51.7% before the crisis to 35.2% after (for profits); and from 100% to 75.3% (for losses). For the other groups of countries, we observe a deterioration of FAF accuracy for earnings profits: European emerging markets (from 21.9% to 26.9%), Russia (from 37.5% to 40.5%), Germanic countries (from 21.6% to 21.9%), and Nordic countries (from 22.1% to 24.2%). This decline in accuracy is also observed and more striking for forecasts of earnings losses for European emerging markets (from 71.8% to 83.3%) and Russia (from 80% to 86.5%). However, forecasting errors decline in Germanic countries (from 61.3% to 59%) and Nordic countries (from 59.8% to 48.9%).

When we focus on FAF bias, values are always statistically positive (except for Russia for earnings profits) and higher for losses than for profits. For the full period, the FAFE is 11% for profits compared to 69.2% for losses for the group of Eastern European frontier markets. A decline of FAF bias must be reported during the full period (2005–13): from 25.8% to 3.4% for profits, and from 100% to 51.8% for losses.

4.3.2   Earnings Increases Versus Earnings Decreases

As reported in Table 9.6, |FAFE| is highly statistically significant for all groups of countries and all subperiods. As expected, |FAFE| is higher for earnings

TABLE 9.4 Regression of Reported Earnings Variation on Forecasted Earnings Variation

Countries	Periods	α	T-test: $\alpha = 0$	β	T-test: $\beta = 1$	F	Adjusted R^2 (%)
Frontier markets	2005–07	−0.167**	−2.833	0.584**	4.805	23.09**	35.02
	2008–10	−0.170**	−3.702	0.517**	5.795	33.58**	31.46
	2011–13	0.001	0.025	0.632**	9.819	96.42**	41.96
	2005–13	−0.075**	−3.327	0.587**	12.083	146.00**	37.08
Emerging markets	2005–07	−0.025	0.237	0.836**	13.253	175.64**	60.50
	2008–10	−0.048*	−2.383	0.896**	16.766	281.10**	61.01
	2011–13	−0.026	−1.505	0.771**	15.671	245.58**	43.38
	2005–13	−0.033**	−2.898	0.830**	26.603	707.72**	55.97
Russia	2005–07	0.180**	4.484	0.384**	4.422	19.55**	16.63
	2008–10	0.014	0.394	0.373**	5.573	31.06**	16.51
	2011–13	−0.029	−1.131	0.427**	7.741	59.92**	18.53
	2005–13	0.024	1.280	0.407**	10.643	113.26**	18.16
Germanic countries	2005–07	0.021*	2.337	0.877**	36.818	1355.56**	59.84
	2008–10	−0.043**	−4.594	0.843**	40.035	1602.82**	62.92
	2011–13	−0.038**	−4.613	0.851**	38.377	1472.78**	57.97
	2005–13	−0.021**	−4.185	0.864**	67.801	4596.95**	61.13
Nordic countries	2005–07	0.019*	1.976	0.820**	34.348	1179.81**	58.51
	2008–10	−0.030**	−3.534	0.863**	45.290	2051.15**	68.61
	2011–13	−0.031**	−4.002	0.825**	42.030	1766.50**	62.71
	2005–13	−0.017**	−3.419	0.843**	70.989	5039.49	64.07

Symbols ** and * indicate statistical significance at the 1 and 5% levels, respectively. Regression is given by Eq. 9.5.

TABLE 9.5 Descriptive Statistics of Forecast Errors in Absolute Mean (|FAFE| Measure of Financial Analyst Accuracy) and in Mean (FAFE Measure of Forecast Bias) Distinguishing Reported Earnings Profits From Reported Earnings Losses

Countries	Periods	Reported earnings profits			Reported earnings loss		
		No. of observations	Accuracy |FAFE|	Bias FAFE	No. of observations	Accuracy |FAFE|	Bias FAFE
Frontier markets	2005–07	138	0.517**	0.258**	7	1.000	1.000
	2008–10	148	0.470**	0.071	55	0.837**	0.757**
	2011–13	196	0.352**	0.034	33	0.753**	0.518**
	2005–13	482	0.435**	0.110**	95	0.820**	0.692**
Emerging markets	2005–07	181	0.219**	0.073**	9	0.718**	0.718**
	2008–10	265	0.257**	0.081**	27	0.763**	0.751**
	2011–13	357	0.269**	0.048*	46	0.833**	0.620**
	2005–13	803	0.254**	0.064**	82	0.797**	0.674**
Russia	2005–07	182	0.375**	−0.120**	5	0.800*	0.800*
	2008–10	287	0.456**	−0.139**	37	0.760**	0.544**
	2011–13	352	0.405**	−0.022	56	0.865**	0.786**
	2005–13	821	0.416**	−0.085**	98	0.822**	0.695**
Germanic countries	2005–07	1289	0.216**	0.004	232	0.613**	0.489**
	2008–10	1180	0.271**	0.040**	391	0.577**	0.441**
	2011–13	1204	0.219**	0.069**	295	0.590**	0.459**
	2005–13	3673	0.235**	0.037**	918	0.590**	0.459**
Nordic countries	2005–07	1146	0.221**	0.000	273	0.598**	0.372**
	2008–10	1059	0.254**	0.033**	408	0.549**	0.361**
	2011–13	1135	0.242**	0.038**	332	0.489**	0.284**
	2005–13	3340	0.239**	0.023**	1013	0.543**	0.339**

Symbols ** and * indicate statistical significance at the 1 and 5% levels, respectively.

TABLE 9.6 Descriptive Statistics of Forecast Errors in Absolute Mean (|FAFE| Measure of Financial Analyst Accuracy) and in Mean (FAFE Measure of Forecast Bias) Distinguishing Reported Earnings Increases From Reported Earnings Decreases

Countries	Periods	Reported earnings increase			Reported earnings decrease		
		No. of observations	Accuracy |FAFE|	Bias FAFE	No. of observations	Accuracy |FAFE|	Bias FAFE
Frontier markets	2005–07	115	0.484**	0.203**	30	0.756**	0.648**
	2008–10	116	0.515**	0.138*	85	0.633**	0.424**
	2011–13	147	0.383**	0.019	79	0.452**	0.235**
	2005–13	378	0.454**	0.112**	194	0.578**	0.379**
Emerging markets	2005–07	139	0.202**	0.031	51	0.352**	0.299**
	2008–10	169	0.247**	0.050	123	0.382**	0.272**
	2011–13	228	0.273**	−0.016	171	0.417**	0.285**
	2005–13	536	0.247**	0.017	345	0.395**	0.282**
Russia	2005–07	160	0.358**	−0.155**	25	0.520**	0.374**
	2008–10	212	0.458**	−0.098*	100	0.509**	0.217**
	2011–13	240	0.402**	−0.024	158	0.546**	0.357**
	2005–13	612	0.410**	−0.085**	283	0.531**	0.309**
Germanic countries	2005–07	1157	0.232**	−0.005	358	0.425**	0.347**
	2008–10	838	0.277**	−0.001	722	0.431**	0.304**
	2011–13	862	0.211**	0.021	625	0.404**	0.317**
	2005–13	2857	0.239**	0.004	1705	0.420**	0.318**
Nordic countries	2005–07	998	0.257**	−0.007	416	0.382**	0.257**
	2008–10	783	0.282**	0.011	677	0.398**	0.256**
	2011–13	829	0.281**	0.016	623	0.324**	0.198**
	2005–13	2610	0.272**	0.006	1716	0.367**	0.235**

Symbols ** and * indicate statistical significance at the 1 and 5% levels, respectively.

decreases than for earnings increases. For the full period, |FAFE| related to earnings increases is the highest (45.4%) for frontier markets, followed by Russia (41%), Nordic countries (27.2%), European emerging countries (24.7%), and Germanic countries (23.9%). We may report a significant decrease of |FAFE| before and after the global financial crisis for frontier markets (from 48.4% to 38.3%) and Germanic countries (from 23.2% to 21.1%). We observe an opposite trend for Russia (from 35.8% to 40.2%), European emerging markets (from 20.2% to 27.3%), and Nordic countries (from 25.7% to 28.1%). When we focus on |FAFE| related to earnings decreases, the values are systematically higher. For frontier markets the values range from 75.6% before the crisis to 45.7% after the crisis. Even if this decline highlights an important improvement, the value of is still high. As observed for earnings increases, we note a deterioration of FAF accuracy for earnings decreases for emerging markets (from 35.2% to 41.7%) and Russia (from 52% to 54.6%).

For the FAF bias, the results report an improvement for all groups of countries. For earnings increases, FAF errors decline from 20.3% to 0.19% after the crisis for frontier markets. For earnings decreases, we show a decline in errors from 64.8% to 23.5%. We may note that the values are always statistically positive. This trend can be interpreted as an overestimation of earnings increases and an underestimation of earnings decreases. As a comparison, this phenomenon is not observed in Russia for earnings increases: from −15.5% to −2.4% (a sign of underestimation of earnings increases).

As expected, these results show that financial analysts face more difficulties to forecast earnings decreases and losses. Nevertheless, even if they are still overly optimistic, they tend to revise their forecasts after the crisis. We may conclude that our results report an improvement of FAF accuracy and bias on Eastern European frontier markets.

As well acknowledged on developed financial markets and confirmed here by Germanic and Nordic countries, financial analysts on Eastern European frontier markets tend to be systematically optimistic. They are more accurate in forecasting profits than losses and earnings increases than earnings decreases. After the global financial crisis, a significant improvement must be reported.

5 CONCLUSIONS

In this study, we have shed a new light on the main characteristics of financial analysts' forecasts for a large sample of promising Eastern European frontier markets (Bulgaria, Croatia, Estonia, Latvia, Lithuania, Romania, Slovakia, and Slovenia) during a long period marked by important economic, legal, and political reforms from 2005 to 2013. Our main objective was to analyze the consequences of the global financial crisis of 2008 on financial analysts' behavior in Eastern Europe almost 20 years after the end of the communist era and just after their European Economic Community (EEC) integration in 2004. Therefore we have also taken into account European emerging markets (Hungary, Poland, and the Czech Republic) and Russia as benchmarks. Germanic countries (Austria, Denmark, and Germany) and Nordic countries (Finland, Norway, and Sweden) have also been used as relevant indicators of the road to economic transition. To analyze the evolution of FAF accuracy and bias, we have divided our sample into three subperiods: before the crisis, from 2005 to 2007; during the crisis, from 2008 to 2010; and after the crisis, from 2011 to 2013. We have also defined two metrics for FAF accuracy and bias: |FAFE| and the financial analysts' forecast error, FAFE, with its sign positive or negative. The global financial crisis has been used as a breakdown.

Our results have reported important and significant improvements of FAF accuracy and FAF bias for Eastern European frontier markets. After the global financial crisis and the numerous economic, political, and legal reforms, the performance of financial analysts on these markets can be reasonably compared to that recently observed on European emerging markets. Our approach may be considered an exploratory study introducing and suggesting promising analysis perspectives for future research on FAFs on Eastern European frontier markets.

REFERENCES

Alford, A.W., Berger, P.G., 1999. A simultaneous equations analysis of forecasts accuracy, analysts following, and trading volume. J. Account. Audit. Finance 14, 219–246.

Allen, A., Cho, J.Y., Jung, K., 1997. Earnings forecasts errors: comparative evidence from the Pacific-Basin capital markets. Pacific-Basin Finance J. 5, 115–129.

Ang, J.S., Ciccone, S.J., 2001. International differences in analyst forecast properties. Working paper, Florida State University and University of New Hampshire.

Ang, J.S., Ma, Y., 2001. The behavior of financial analysts during the Asian financial crisis in Indonesia, Korea, Malaysia, and Thailand. Pacific-Basin Finance J. 9, 233–263.

Basu, S., Hwang, L.S., Jan, C.L., 1998. International variation in accounting measurement rules and analysts' earnings forecast errors. J. Bus. Finance Account. 25, 1207–1247.

Black, E.L., Carnes, T.A., 2006. Analysts' forecasts in Asian-Pacific markets: the relationship among macroeconomic factors, accounting systems, bias and accuracy. J. Int. Financ. Manage. Account. 17, 208–227.

Bradshaw, M., Richardson, S., Sloan, R., 2006. The relation between corporate financing activities, analysts' forecasts and stock returns. J. Account. Econ. 42, 53–85.

Brown, L.D., 1997. Analysts forecasts errors: additional evidence. Financ. Anal. J. 53, 81–88.

Brown, L.D., Richardson, G., Schwager, S., 1987. An information interpretation of financial analyst superiority in forecasting earnings. J. Account. Res. 25, 49–67.

Byard, D., Li, Y., Yu, Y., 2011. The effect of mandatory IFRS adoption on financial analysts' information environment. J. Account. Res. 49, 69–96.

Capstaff, J., Paudyal, K., Ree, W., 1998. Analysts' forecast of German firms' earnings: a comparative analysis. J. Int. Financ. Manage. Account. 9 (2), 83–116.

Capstaff, J., Paudyal, K., Rees, W., 2001. A comparative analysis of earnings forecasts in Europe. J. Bus. Finance Account. 28, 531–562.

Chang, X., Dasgupta, S., Hilary, G., 2006. Analyst coverage and financing decisions. J. Finance 61, 3009–3048.

Chee, S.C., Sujin, K., Zurbruegg, R., 2010. The impact of IFRS on financial analysts' forecast accuracy in the Asia-Pacific region: the case of Australia, Hong Kong and New Zealand. Pacif. Account. Rev. 22 (2), 124–146.

Chopra, V.K., 1998. Why so much error in analysts' earnings forecasts? Financ. Anal. J. 54, 35–42.

Ciccone, S., 2005. Trends in analyst earnings forecast properties. Int. Rev. Financ. Anal. 14, 1–22.

Clement, M.B., 1999. Analyst forecast accuracy: do ability, resources, and portfolio complexity matter? J. Account. Econ. 27, 285–303.

Coën, A., Desfleurs, A., 2004. The evolution of financial analysts' forecasts on Asian emerging markets. J. Multinatl. Financ. Manage. 14 (4/5), 335–352.

Coën, A., Desfleurs, A., 2014. The evolution of financial analysts' forecasts for Asian REITs and real estate companies. In: Gregoriou, G., Chuen, D.L.K. (Eds.), Handbook of Asian Finance. Elsevier, Academic Press, Oxford, UK.

Coën, A., Desfleurs, A., Lher, J.F., 2009. The relative importance of determinants of the quality of financial analysts' forecasts: international evidence. J. Econ. Bus. 61, 453–471.

Das, S., Levine, C., Sivarmakrishnan, K., 1998. Earnings predictability and bias in analysts' earnings forecasts. Account. Rev. 73, 277–294.

De Bondt, W.F.M., Thaler, R., 1990. Do security analysts overreact? Am. Econ. Rev. 80 (2), 52–57.

Hong, H., Lim, T., Stein, J.C., 2000. Bad news travels slowly: size, analyst coverage, and the profitability of momentum strategies. J. Finance 55, 265–295.

Hope, O.-K., 2003. Disclosure practices, enforcement of accounting standards and analysts' forecast accuracy: an international study. J. Account. Res. 41 (3), 235–272.

Katz, J.P., Zarzeski, M.T., Hall, H.J., 2000. The impact of strategy, industry and culture on forecasting the performance of global competitors: a strategic perspective. J. Bus. Strat. 17 (2), 119–143.

Ke, B., Yu, Y., 2006. The effect of issuing biased earnings forecasts on analysts' access to management and survival. J. Account. Res. 44, 965–1000.

Lang, M., Lins, K., Miller, D., 2004. Concentrated control, analyst following and valuation: do analysts matter most when investors are protected least? J. Account. Res. 42 (3), 589–623.

Loh, R.K., Mian, M., 2002. The quality of analysts' earnings forecasts during the Asian crisis: evidence from Singapore. J. Bus. Finance Account. 30 (5–6), 715–747.

Mikhail, M.B., Walther, B.R., Willis, R.H., 1997. Do security analysts improve their performance with experience? J. Account. Res. 35, 131–166.

O'Brien, P.C., 1990. Forecast accuracy of individual analysts in nine industries. J. Account. Res. 28, 286–304.

Patel, S.A., Balic, A., Bwakira, L., 2002. Measuring transparency and disclosure at firm-level in emerging markets. Emerg. Mark. Rev. 3, 325–337.

Paudyal, K., Saadouni, B., Briston, R., 1998. Earnings forecasts in Malaysia: an empirical analysis. Adv. Pacific Basin Financ. Mark., 311–334.

Sadique, S., In, F.H., Veeraraghavan, M., 2010. Analyst Bias, Firm Characteristics, and Stock Returns in the Australian Stock Market. Working paper, SSRN. Available from: http://ssrn.com/abstract=158273

Tan, H., Wang, S., Welker, M., 2011. Analyst following and forecast accuracy after mandated IFRS adoptions. J. Account. Res. 49, 1307–1357.

Thomas, S., 2002. Firm diversification and asymmetric information: evidence form analysts' forecasts and earnings announcements. J. Financ. Econ. 64, 373–396.

Yu, F., 2008. Analyst coverage and earnings management. J. Financ. Econ. 88 (2), 245–271.

Chapter 10

Are There Herding Patterns in the European Frontier Markets?

N. Blasco*, P. Corredor**, S. Ferreruela*

*University of Zaragoza, Zaragoza, Spain; **Public University of Navarre, Pamplona, Spain

Chapter Outline

1 INTRODUCTION

The efficient markets hypothesis assumes that investors have homogeneous expectations based on the information available and that they therefore try to maximize utility in a rational way. However, in reality it has been observed that investors may exhibit apparently irrational and predictable biases mainly attributable to psychological factors (Odean, 1998; Barber and Odean, 2000). The close link between rationality and emotion in decision making (Elster, 1998; Lo, 1999; Loewenstein, 2000; Peters and Slovic, 2000, among others) may explain this phenomenon. Rationality and emotions are not antithetical but are in fact complementary in decision making. Behavioral finance includes the emotional component within standard models of financial markets to explain the aggregate effects of decisions made by individual investors who may deviate from full neoclassical rationality (Thaler, 1991; Shefrin, 2000). In this context, the herd behavior of investors has been proposed as an alternative or complementary explanation of their decision-making process.

Handbook of Frontier Markets. http://dx.doi.org/10.1016/B978-0-12-803776-8.00010-0
191

Herding behavior is defined as the apparent attempt by investors to copy the behavior of other investors (Bikhchandani and Sharma, 2000). Rational herding occurs when investors think that others are better informed, so they decide to imitate the decisions observed in other market participants, ignoring their own beliefs or information.

There are various explanations for this phenomenon. In terms of psychology, it has been suggested that the investor may prefer to conform to the market consensus (Devenow and Welch, 1996). Agency theory proposes that the reputation–compensation scheme rewards imitation, as compensation for an investor depends on how his or her performance compares to the performance of other investors, and whether deviations from consensus are costly (Scharfstein and Stein, 1990; Roll, 1992; Brennan, 1993; Rajan, 1994; Trueman, 1994). The type of market which is analyzed also seems to be decisive, as in the case of emerging markets where mimic behavior may be due to imperfect information (Chari and Kehoe, 2004; Calvo and Mendoza, 2000; Bikhchandani et al., 1998). Other explanations arise from differences in factors such as the relative importance of institutional versus individual investors (Lakonishok et al., 1992; Grinblatt et al., 1995; Wermers, 1999) or the level of sophistication of derivatives markets, aspects which could affect the decision-making process of investors. The work of Hirshleifer and Teoh (2003) provides a thorough review of the various explanations that have been offered for this phenomenon in the literature.

However, rational herding behavior is a relative concept that can be hard to verify. It is known that financial markets tend to work with moderate levels of intrinsic herding due to the unconscious impulses of investors to achieve positive returns and avoid negative ones. This makes the characterization and detection of rational herding behavior difficult.

Intuitively, intentional herding (which implies a follow-the-leader type of relationship) could be statistically described as a deviation of the returns of individual assets from market returns smaller than expected in the absence of herding behavior. This is due to the fact that the return of individual assets would not diverge substantially from the overall market return. Based on this idea, the works of Christie and Huang (1995) and Chang et al. (2000) (hereafter referred to as CH and CCK, respectively) are the leaders when it comes to analyzing market herd behavior. They assume that investors will probably ignore their beliefs in favor of market consensus in periods of large price changes, so herd behavior is more likely to appear during such periods.

While previous studies in the literature have examined herd behavior in various markets using this approach, this chapter tries to find further evidence of the presence of such behavior and its patterns in the nine European frontier markets. Frontier markets refer to stock markets in small nations that are at an earlier stage of economic and political development than larger and more mature emerging markets, according to various parameters such as their growth potential, market accessibility, liquidity, and foreign investment restrictions that are usually analyzed by market information providers.

Our study goes some steps further than previous studies. First, we analyze the presence of herding in each individual market using the methodologies developed by CH and CCK in order to provide results comparable with those previously reported in the literature (Chen, 2013). This approach has been widely applied (Demirer and Kutan, 2006; Tan et al., 2008; Chiang et al., 2010; Lao and Singh, 2011; Prosad et al., 2012). It tests for herding by examining whether the cross-sectional return dispersion decreases or increases at a decreasing rate as the market return increases. Authors have traditionally used the ordinary least squares (OLS) regression; however, we have chosen to further include quantile regression (QR) when applying the CCK measure (Koenker and Bassett, 1978), as this seems more suitable for our analysis. Herding is intuitively related to the lower quantiles of the return dispersion distribution, when the returns of most stocks in a market are similar to that of the market itself. However, we cannot ignore the high quantiles of the dispersion distribution, as even with high dispersion herding might be found if the expected positive relationship between return and return dispersion is broken. If we use only OLS, we could overlook herding if it exists only in certain quantiles, as this approach focuses mainly on mean values.

Second, we analyze a period after the onset of the 2008–09 global financial crisis and the ensuing European sovereign debt crisis in which the number of listed stocks in these markets significantly increased. Since the publication of previous results in Chen (2013), Bulgaria and Romania have tripled the number of listed shares; Slovenia and Croatia have doubled; and Estonia, Serbia, and Ukraine have grown by 50%.

Finally, in addition to the analysis of herd behavior in each market, we have used graph analysis tools such as Gephi to try to visualize under which circumstances or at which moments these stock markets or some of them herd around a more global consensus, given their similarity in terms of certain macroeconomic conditions, the economic environment, and market factors.

The chapter is organized as follows. The following section describes the database and the context of the markets under study. The subsequent section is devoted to describing the methodology used. The penultimate section presents the results obtained. The final section presents the main conclusions that can be drawn from the study.

2   DATABASE

Our study analyzes nine frontier markets included in the MSCI EFM Central and East Europe and CIS Index (Bulgaria, Croatia, Estonia, Kazakhstan, Lithuania, Romania, Serbia, Slovenia, and Ukraine) during the period 2011–14. The database, obtained from Thomson Reuters Datastream, comprises the daily prices of the shares which have been listed on these nine markets at least sometime in the sample period.

These nine countries may be classified into two groups according to their membership in the European Union (EU). Slovenia, Estonia, and Lithuania joined the EU in 2004, Bulgaria and Romania in 2007, and Croatia in 2013. The three remaining countries are not yet members of the EU. Such a difference may be a key element for describing the institutional characteristics of these markets.

According to data provided by the World Bank in 2011, the gross domestic product (GDP) of Kazakhstan, Romania, and Ukraine is between 3 and 4 times bigger than that of the other countries analyzed. However, if we look at the ratio of stock market capitalization to GDP, the ranking is as follows: Croatia (38.73), Kazakhstan (28.49), Serbia (22.12), Ukraine (20.09), Slovenia (16.36), Romania (14.99) Bulgaria (14.94), Lithuania (11.86), and Estonia (9.09). The stock market volatility also differs among countries: Ukraine (36%), Romania (26%), and Kazakhstan (24%) have high levels of volatility, whereas Slovenia (13%) and Croatia (15%) generate the lowest levels.

The markets under analysis have institutional and cultural differences compared to other more developed markets. For this reason it is of interest to compare our European frontier markets (EFMs) with other emerging stock markets belonging to their area of influence (Poland, Czech Republic, Hungary, and Russia), as well as with large-cap markets in Europe such as Germany, France, and Great Britain.

The Hofstede Index (Hofstede, 2001) comprises six cultural dimensions that allow different cultures to be compared. The results of a comparison of the mean values of the Hofstede dimensions calculated for the EFMs with the mean values for other more developed markets and for other emerging markets within their area of influence lend support to our analysis of EFMs.

The mean values of power distance and uncertainty avoidance in the Hofstede Index are higher for EFMs (67 and 80, respectively) than the values of developed countries (46 and 62) and very similar to those of other emerging countries (66 and 86). According to these dimensions of the Hofstede Index, European frontier countries are more tolerant of the established power hierarchy and less tolerant of unorthodox ideas and different codes of belief and behavior.

Scores in relation to individualism (38), masculinity (33), and indulgence (24) in these frontier countries are lower than those of developed markets (76, 58, and 53) and also with regard to emerging countries used as a reference (59, 61, and 28). Such low values suggest that in European frontier countries individuals tend to act predominantly as members of a lifelong and cohesive group, family, or organization, within a feminine culture emphasizing modesty and caring and having the perception that their actions are constrained by social rules.

The valuations of these countries for the long-term orientation dimension are close to those of the benchmark countries. Although some differences are found in the individual scores, all the European frontier countries are long-term-oriented societies, and hence the effort to change society and the capacity for adaptation are seen as good qualities for the future.

Institutional factors for EFMs are also different from those of other countries analyzed in the comparative study. We use references provided by the

Worldwide Governance Indicators that summarize the quality of governance. These indicators are voice and accountability, political stability, government effectiveness, regulatory quality, rule of law, and corruption control. In general, it can be said that the nine frontier countries obtain much lower scores than those of emerging countries and very considerably lower than the values shown by the most developed economies in Europe. There are also clear differences among frontier countries. The highest scores belong to Estonia, Slovenia, and Lithuania, and the lowest to Kazakhstan, Ukraine, and Serbia, suggesting the lower institutional development of these markets. As mentioned previously, these results may be closely related to membership or otherwise in the EU.

An additional measure is the Chinn–Ito index (Kaopen) (Chinn and Ito, 2006), which measures a country's degree of capital account openness. The last available index values indicate that while Kazakhstan and Ukraine have negative scores, Estonia, Bulgaria, and Romania show values indicating a degree of openness similar to that of most developed countries.

All the cultural and institutional indicators for the EFMs presented here show a lower degree of development for their stock markets, given their lower degrees of information transparency, economic and social openness, and governance indicators that may influence market trading and liquidity. The herding effect within this framework is not easy to predict since there are elements that encourage gregarious behavior, either individually or toward a global consensus (more collectivism, lack of transparency related to lower institutional development and lower quality of governance, cultural indicators such as uncertainty avoidance, etc.), and others which favor the opposite, particularly against a general consensus (six out of the nine are members of the EU, and EFMs have different capitalization volumes and GDPs and/or different degrees of capital account openness, among others). In these circumstances, the new and updated empirical evidence will be of great interest in order to gain a deeper knowledge of these markets.

3   METHODOLOGY

3.1   CH and CCK Methods

The idea behind the methodologies proposed by CH and CCK is that, in the presence of intentional herding behavior, individuals are likely to leave aside their own beliefs about market behavior in favor of market consensus. Empirically, this would imply that stock returns would be more closely grouped around the overall market return. CH and CCK suggest that this evidence should be particularly intense during periods of large price changes given that, at those moments, investors discriminate individual assets less and treat all stocks in a similar way.

CH's methodological proposal consists of calculating the cross-sectional standard deviation (CSSD) of stock returns relative to the market return for each period t and observing its behavior in times of extreme market movements.

The verification of the existence of herding is performed through the following regression model:

$$CSSD_t = \alpha + \beta_D D_t^L + \beta_U D_t^U + \varepsilon_t \qquad (10.1)$$

where $D_t^L (D_t^U) = 1$ if the aggregate market return on day t is located in the lower (upper) tail of the distribution, and zero otherwise. The β_D (β_U) coefficients, associated with the dummy variables, allow the existence of herd behavior among market participants to be identified.

CCK observe that the model presented by CH is a very restrictive test that requires a high level of nonlinearity to detect the presence of herding, and they therefore propose an alternative. Their proposal uses the cross-sectional absolute deviation (CSAD) of stock returns over the market return as a measure of the dispersion to detect the existence of herding. If market participants imitate each other, there would be a nonlinear relationship between the absolute deviation of returns and market returns. To capture the relationship, they include an additional parameter in the regression. CCK's model takes the following form:

$$CSAD_t = \alpha + \gamma_1 |R_{m,t}| + \gamma_2 [R_{m,t}]^2 + \varepsilon_t \qquad (10.2)$$

Eq. 10.2 introduces a nonlinear item $[R_{m,t}]^2$, as a linearly increasing relationship no longer holds in the presence of herding; more precisely, the dispersion would be lower if herding occurs. Therefore, herding is said to occur if the coefficient γ_2 of the nonlinear item is found to be negative and significant.

Note that the model specification in Eq. 10.2 restricts γ_2 to be the same for both up and down markets, while recent empirical research (Bekaert and Wu, 2000; Hong et al., 2007; Tan et al., 2008) has highlighted the asymmetric characteristics of asset returns. In our context, it is interesting to examine whether the imitative behavior shows an asymmetric response on bullish versus bearish days. Therefore, following Zhou and Anderson (2013), Eq. 10.2 is generalized as follows:

$$CSAD_t = \alpha + \gamma_1(1-D)|R_{m,t}| + \gamma_2 D|R_{m,t}| + \gamma_3(1-D)[R_{m,t}]^2 + \gamma_4 D[R_{m,t}]^2 + \varepsilon_t \qquad (10.3)$$

In Eq. 10.3, we consider asymmetry in both linear and nonlinear terms by setting $D = 1$ if $R_{m,t} < 0$ and $D = 0$ otherwise.

It is worth noting that CCK, and most researchers following them, estimate Eq. 10.2 using OLS. However, there are good reasons to opt for QR as proposed by Koenker and Bassett (1978) when attempting to detect herding in equity markets. Least squares estimators focus on the mean of the distribution of return dispersion, something which is not optimal for detecting stress-related behaviors, as the information contained in the tails of the distribution is lost. QR is a more versatile tool in analyzing extreme quantiles of the return deviation distribution, given that it provides a method to estimate the effects of market return on the dependent variable over its entire distribution.

An additional benefit of using QR is that some statistical problems such as the effect of outliers or nonnormality of the errors can be alleviated (Barnes and Hughes, 2002).

Therefore Eqs. 10.2 and 10.3 would now take the following form:

$$CSAD_t(\tau \mid x) = \alpha + \eta_1 \mid R_{m,t}(\tau) \mid + \eta_2 [R_{m,t}(\tau)]^2 + \varepsilon_t \tag{10.4}$$

$$\begin{aligned} CSAD_t(\tau \mid x) = \alpha &+ \eta_1(1-D) \mid R_{m,t}(\tau) \mid + \eta_2 D \mid R_{m,t}(\tau) \mid \\ &+ \eta_3(1-D)[R_{m,t}(\tau)]^2 + \eta_4 D[R_{m,t}(\tau)]^2 + \varepsilon_t \end{aligned} \tag{10.5}$$

where the τth quantile is that value of the target variable distribution below which the proportion of the population is τ.

3.2   Gephi Proposal

In addition to analyzing each individual market, we have used Gephi software (Bastian et al., 2009) in order to find similarities among different frontier markets in terms of their herding behavior around a global consensus represented by the MSCI EFM Central and East Europe and CIS Index. Gephi is open-source software for graph and network analysis. Its flexible and multitask architecture brings new possibilities for working with complex data sets and producing valuable visual results. The graph consists of a set of nodes and a set of pairs of nodes called edges. The usefulness of a network analysis derives from the data associated to specific nodes and edges, which can be ordered and clustered according to specified criteria.

In our case, we build a network of relationships between markets where each node corresponds to a frontier market and an edge between two nodes corresponds to the frequency with which two stocks listed in two different frontier markets follow the global frontier markets' consensus. That is, a stock in frontier market m_1 is connected to a stock in market m_2 if both stock returns are very close to the global return. The probability of finding such connections between stocks belonging to m_1 and m_2 gives the weight for the edge between m_1 and m_2. Specifically, we carry out the following steps:

1. We calculate the return deviation with respect to the MSCI EFM Central and East Europe and CIS Index (R_{MSCIEFM}) for every stock, in every market, and every day.

$$\mathrm{RD}_{im,t} = (R_{im,t} - R_{\mathrm{MSCIEFM},t})^2 \tag{10.6}$$

$R_{im,t}$ is the daily return on day t of stock i belonging to market m. $m =$ Bulgaria, Croatia, … Ukraine.

2. We set the criteria for identifying the set of minimum deviations, MD. Specifically, we select those daily deviations observed below the critical value corresponding to the first decile of the deviations distribution. The average return deviation is AvRD = 0.00335506, and the cutoff value, leaving aside 10% of the smallest deviations, is DecileRD = 1.28755E-06.

3. Individual stocks included in MD_t are identified, with MD_t being the set of stocks following the global (MSCI EFM Index) market consensus on day t.

$$MD_t = \{im/RD_{im,t} < DecileRD\} \qquad (10.7)$$

4. We select the set of days when the frontier market consensus (minimum deviations) is followed by more than 1000 individual stocks, the aim being to analyze the days with more intense herd behavior.

5. For every day with intense herd behavior (larger number of individual stocks following the global consensus), we compute the number of pairs of stocks (i, j) included in MD_t belonging to two different markets (for every pair of markets m_1 and m_2).

$$E_t(m_1m_2) = \#[(im_1, jm_2) / im_1, jm_2 \in MD_t \text{ with } m_1 \neq m_2] \qquad (10.8)$$

6. We also classify herding days depending on the global return $R_{MSCIEFM}$, so that we can build networks for extreme positive returns (daily $R_{MSCIEFM}$ higher than 1%), extreme negative returns (daily $R_{MSCIEFM}$ lower than -1%) and nonextreme returns (calm days). We aggregate $E_t(m_1m_2)$ for extreme positive return days [denoted as $E_{EPR}(m_1m_2)$], extreme negative return days [$E_{ENR}(m_1m_2)$], and calm days [$E_{NER}(m_1m_2)$], respectively. Using this calculation, in order to avoid market size bias, we scale using the total number of possible combinations of two stocks belonging to each pair of different markets and taking into account the number of intense herding days in every state E (E = extreme positive return, extreme negative return, and nonextreme return). Therefore, we compute the edge between two markets depending on the state as:

$$\text{Edge}_{E(m_1m_2)} = \frac{E_E(m_1m_2)}{\#[(im_1, jm_2) / m_1 \neq m_2] * \#(\text{herding days in state } E)} \qquad (10.9)$$

Using the Gephi software, the graph analysis leads to the visualization of two properties: First, the size of a node gives a measure of the intensity of herd behavior for the stocks of a given market; second, strong edges highlight strong links between markets.

4 EMPIRICAL RESULTS

4.1 Descriptive Statistics

Table 10.1 presents the summary statistics for CSSD, CSAD, and market returns for each market in the sample. As shown in the table, the mean of the aggregate return R_m remains negative for all countries. Both CSSD and CSAD exhibit significant skewness and kurtosis, and are hence not normally distributed.

TABLE 10.1 Summary Statistics of CSSD, CSAD, and R_m

	Bulgaria	Croatia	Estonia	Kazakhstan	Lithuania	Romania	Serbia	Slovenia	Ukraine
CSSD									
Mean	0.0023	0.0025	0.0056	0.0033	0.0075	0.0048	0.0016	0.0067	0.0017
Median	0.0017	0.0022	0.0048	0.0017	0.0047	0.0036	0.0013	0.0043	0.0009
Maximum	0.0172	0.0114	0.0303	0.1168	0.0854	0.0510	0.0377	0.0835	0.0287
Minimum	0.0005	0.0006	0.0014	0.0000	0.0005	0.0009	0.0002	0.0007	0.0001
Std. dev.	0.0019	0.0011	0.0032	0.0069	0.0091	0.0042	0.0017	0.0084	0.0027
Skewness	3.1123	2.3775	2.3370	9.0544	3.9530	4.2934	15.3184	5.0181	5.3687
Kurtosis	13.9817	9.1296	8.9698	112.2516	20.4928	28.8945	300.1422	33.5178	37.8097
Jarque-Bera	6,626.0667	2,527.7456	2,423.9732	502,817.4035	15,431.0011	31,475.9674	3,777,493.3800	43,088.4159	54,849.7749
CSAD									
Mean	0.0091	0.0119	0.0140	0.0075	0.0189	0.0185	0.0050	0.0176	0.0058
Median	0.0076	0.0112	0.0125	0.0043	0.0139	0.0163	0.0045	0.0133	0.0037
Maximum	0.0711	0.0476	0.0538	0.2244	0.1654	0.0987	0.0756	0.1662	0.0954
Minimum	0.0021	0.0028	0.0034	0.0000	0.0012	0.0043	0.0005	0.0018	0.0005
Std. dev.	0.0059	0.0041	0.0068	0.0137	0.0181	0.0105	0.0038	0.0171	0.0072
Skewness	3.4436	1.6104	1.5376	8.4192	3.4652	2.8407	10.2390	4.3340	5.9589
Kurtosis	25.6231	10.2072	6.3061	101.7209	19.6010	16.0824	173.0361	29.1456	55.5625
Jarque-Bera	23,045.2989	2,593.9468	851.1448	407,860.0256	13,416.8844	8,526.9941	1,231,928.9924	31,360.6599	119,220.1335
Observations	989	999	1,002	976	995	1,006	1,008	992	985

(Continued)

TABLE 10.1 Summary Statistics of CSSD, CSAD, and R_m (cont.)

	Bulgaria	Croatia	Estonia	Kazakhstan	Lithuania	Romania	Serbia	Slovenia	Ukraine
R_m									
Mean	−0.0002	−0.0004	−0.0003	−0.0004	−0.0002	−0.0004	−0.0001	−0.0008	−0.0003
Median	−0.0001	−0.0002	0.0001	−0.0002	0.0002	−0.0003	−0.0002	−0.0004	−0.0001
Maximum	0.0372	0.0130	0.0486	0.0851	0.0636	0.0398	0.0335	0.0885	0.0253
Minimum	−0.0221	−0.0335	−0.0663	−0.1160	−0.0855	−0.0448	−0.0080	−0.0831	−0.0496
Std. dev.	0.0039	0.0037	0.0101	0.0078	0.0133	0.0073	0.0023	0.0110	0.0043
Skewness	1.0501	−0.7918	−0.6104	−2.5140	−0.8223	−0.7367	5.6585	−0.4390	−2.8686
Kurtosis	19.6241	9.7598	9.5020	80.4481	11.6307	9.2950	82.0737	19.2671	40.7614
Jarque-Bera	11,570.0986	2,006.4260	1,827.2330	244,955.1000	3,200.2800	1,752.0090	267,990.7000	10,969.3900	59,873.1392
Observations	989	999	1,002	976	995	1,006	1,008	992	985

This table reports the summary statistics of the cross-sectional standard deviations (CSSD), cross-sectional absolute deviations (CSAD), and cross-sectional equally weighted average returns (R_m) for the markets belonging to the MSCI EFM Central and East Europe and CIS Index. The data are obtained from Thomson Reuters Datastream. They range from the start of 2011 to the start of 2015.

TABLE 10.2 Analysis of Herding Behavior in Up and Down Extreme Markets (1–99%) (CH)

Extreme return percentiles 1 and 99%	α	β_D	β_U	R^2 adj.
Bulgaria	0.0022***	0.0076***	0.0077***	0.3150
	(43.09)	(15.15)	(15.34)	
Croatia	0.0039***	0.0024***	−0.0014***	0.0578
	(11.42)	(6.89)	(−4.11)	
Estonia	0.0056***	0.0057***	0.0044***	0.0515
	(55.54)	(5.98)	(4.65)	
Kazakhstan	0.0026***	0.0422***	0.0315***	0.5840
	(18.05)	(29.92)	(22.36)	
Lithuania	0.0075***	0.0000	0.0016	−0.0017
	(25.58)	(0.01)	(0.57)	
Romania	0.0187***	0.0157***	−0.0142***	0.2659
	(17.17)	(14.30)	(−12.98)	
Serbia	0.0014***	0.0024***	0.0089***	0.3202
	(32.67)	(5.76)	(21.20)	
Slovenia	0.0058***	0.0451***	0.0332***	0.4759
	(29.82)	(24.44)	(17.97)	
Ukraine	0.0139***	0.0151***	−0.0124***	0.5169
	(23.37)	(25.26)	(−20.84)	

This table reports the estimation results of herding in the markets belonging to the MSCI EFM Central and East Europe and CIS Index according to Eq. 10.1,

$$CSSD_t = \alpha + \beta_D D_t^l + \beta_U D_t^U + \varepsilon_t$$

where $CSSD_t$ is the equally weighted cross-sectional standard deviation of returns and $R_{m,t}$ is the equally weighted market portfolio return at time t. A significant negative value of β_D and/or β_U suggests the existence of herding. Numbers in parentheses are t-statistics. ***, **, and * represent statistical significance at the 1, 5, and 10% levels, respectively.

4.2 Evidence on Herding: CH and CCK Methods[a]

Table 10.2 presents the estimation results of herding based on Eq. 10.1, which is in the spirit of CH's specification. For clarity reasons only, the results for the extreme 1% are shown on the table. However, extreme 2, 5, and 10% upper and

a. The results shown here correspond in all cases to market returns calculated as the equally weighted market index. However, the estimations were also made considering the benchmark market index returns. Specifically, the stock market indexes used to mirror European frontier markets were respectively: SOFIX, CROBEX, OMX Tallinn, KASE, OMX Vilnius, BET, BELEX, SBI TOP and PFTS. For the CH model, none of the β_D and β_U coefficients was negative. With regard to the model of CCK, the results did not change for the OLS estimation. When using QR with the benchmark market index return as reference, the most relevant change is that herding is additionally detected in Serbia and Ukraine. Complete results are available from the authors upon request.

lower tails have also been set to represent market stress, and the results are available from the authors upon request. The results indicate that herding, as identified by significant and negative β_D and β_U coefficients, is detected only in extreme up markets in Croatia, Romania, and Ukraine, regardless of the extreme percentiles of the returns distribution which have been considered as market stress, although these negative β_U coefficients indicate a stronger herding behavior in the most extreme percentiles. These results are largely in line with Chen (2013), as he does not find any sign of herding in the eight EFMs considered in his sample (Croatia is not included), but differ in reference to Romania and Ukraine.

The results of estimating the herding regression represented by Eq. 10.2, which follows the specification given by CCK, are shown in Table 10.3. As suggested in the literature, a negative value on the coefficient γ_2 is consistent with herding. The coefficient on the market return square is negative and statistically significant only for the Estonian market, suggesting that herding behavior exists only in that market. This holds for the asymmetric herding behavior under market ups and downs as represented in Eq. 10.3, the results of which are shown in Table 10.4. Only the Estonian market exhibits negative γ_3 and γ_4 coefficients for both up and down markets. Chen (2013) also detects herding in the Estonian market when using this approach. However, unlike us, he also observes negative γ_2 coefficients in Kazakhstan, Lithuania, and Romania. As stated earlier, Estonia is the country with the smallest ratio of stock market capitalization to GDP among all the countries in the sample. Moreover, it is the smallest market, with only 15 stocks considered during this period. Both characteristics may affect the behavior of investors in this market and its measurement.

Table 10.5 presents the estimated results for the nine markets using the quantile regression method as represented in Eq. 10.4. We observe that the Estonian market shows a negative coefficient across all quantiles, which is in line with the results of the OLS estimation. Some other interesting results arise in the QR estimation. Croatia and Ukraine, as well as Bulgaria and Kazakhstan, where herding was not detected using previous methodologies, display negative coefficients for some of the quantiles above the 70% level. The phenomenon of herding behavior being more significant for upper quantiles shows that herding activity is more likely to occur under volatile market conditions—that is, when individual asset returns clearly deviate from the market consensus because the market return comprises both very high and very low stock returns. Under these circumstances, in relative terms, additional changes in market return tend to promote the market consensus. On the other hand, Lithuania shows a negative γ_2 coefficient in quantiles up to 10%, indicating a difference between this market and the others and revealing the traditional concept of herding underlying the usual methodologies.

Evidence given in Tables 10.5 and 10.6 clearly indicates that the estimated coefficients vary with the quantile levels. Looking at panels A and B in Table 10.6, the estimated statistics suggest that the results presented in Table 10.5 hold when asymmetry is taken into account, although some differences can be observed between up and down markets. Bulgaria, Estonia,

TABLE 10.3 Analysis of Herding Behavior in European Frontier Markets (CCK)

	α	γ_1	γ_2	R^2 adj.
Bulgaria	0.0045***	1.8149***	0.1461	0.8312
	(37.59)	(39.79)	(0.07)	
Croatia	0.0085***	1.2732***	−0.9709	0.5742
	(59.32)	(23.64)	(−0.29)	
Estonia	0.0090***	0.8492***	−8.7632***	0.3749
	(31.66)	(17.80)	(−7.41)	
Kazakhstan	0.0012***	1.8945***	0.3967*	0.9818
	(15.84)	(114.85)	(1.85)	
Lithuania	0.0074***	1.3081***	4.9070***	0.8256
	(20.33)	(25.73)	(5.30)	
Romania	0.0111***	1.3858***	9.9957***	0.6987
	(36.09)	(18.78)	(3.88)	
Serbia	0.0027***	1.6078***	14.4822***	0.8479
	(36.24)	(34.44)	(8.01)	
Slovenia	0.0067***	1.6165***	3.5631***	0.8798
	(23.84)	(36.97)	(4.74)	
Ukraine	0.0017***	1.8576***	1.5202*	0.9514
	(24.62)	(71.31)	(1.84)	

This table reports the estimation results of herding in the markets belonging to the MSCI EFM Central and East Europe and CIS Index according to Eq. 10.2,

$$CSAD_t = \alpha + \gamma_1 |R_{m,t}| + \gamma_2 [R_{m,t}]^2 + \varepsilon_t$$

where $CSAD_t$ is the equally weighted cross-sectional absolute deviation of returns and $R_{m,t}$ is the equally weighted market portfolio return at time t. A significant negative value of γ_2 suggests the existence of herding. Numbers in parentheses are t-statistics. ***, **, and * represent statistical significance at the 1, 5, and 10% levels, respectively.

Kazakhstan, and Ukraine are again the markets where negative γ_3 and γ_4 coefficients can be found. Bulgaria shows herding in up markets only in some of the higher quantiles, whereas Lithuania shows significant negative coefficients only when the market is down, and again in the lower quantiles, as shown in Table 10.5, where up and down markets are not differentiated.

4.3 Evidence of Herding: Gephi

Figs. 10.1–10.3 show Gephi visualizations of herding relationships among EFMs, both on extreme positive or negative return days and on calm days. The main results can be summarized as follows. Ukraine, Kazakhstan, and Bulgaria

TABLE 10.4 Analysis of Herding Behavior in Up and Down European Frontier Markets

	α	γ_1	γ_2	γ_3	γ_4	R^2 adj.	Wald $\gamma_3 = \gamma_4$
Bulgaria	0.0045***	1.8530***	1.7201***	-1.5204	7.7165	0.8316	0.0750
	(36.50)	(32.69)	(25.53)	(-0.66)	(1.50)		
Croatia	0.0087***	1.0623***	1.1874***	40.1281***	0.5708	0.5788	0.0082
	(56.00)	(9.02)	(19.88)	(2.63)	(0.16)		
Estonia	0.0089***	0.9400***	0.8455***	-13.0256***	-8.0106***	0.3768	0.0310
	(30.48)	(13.99)	(15.88)	(-5.78)	(-6.28)		
Kazakhstan	0.0011***	1.9104***	1.9064***	-0.3836	0.4622*	0.9819	0.0610
	(15.34)	(77.27)	(96.76)	(-0.92)	(1.93)		
Lithuania	0.0078***	1.1406***	1.2746***	11.3823***	4.3265***	0.8292	0.0001
	(21.05)	(15.61)	(21.84)	(6.39)	(4.28)		
Romania	0.0112***	1.3230***	1.3927***	15.0826***	8.8067***	0.6988	0.1809
	(36.02)	(13.94)	(16.58)	(3.44)	(3.04)		
Serbia	0.0027***	1.5930***	1.4670***	14.8317***	48.2214**	0.8480	0.1309
	(33.13)	(26.13)	(14.19)	(6.86)	(2.13)		
Slovenia	0.0067***	1.5754***	1.6356***	2.4277**	4.5284***	0.8820	0.0894
	(24.18)	(28.72)	(32.31)	(2.41)	(4.86)		
Ukraine	0.0017***	1.7999***	1.8057***	8.4986***	2.3577***	0.9519	0.0335
	(24.56)	(38.35)	(56.40)	(2.92)	(2.59)		

This table reports the estimation results of herding in the markets belonging to the MSCI EFM Central and East Europe and CIS Index according to Eq. 10.3

$$CSAD_t = \alpha + \gamma_1(1-D)|R_{m,t}| + \gamma_2 D|R_{m,t}| + \gamma_3(1-D)[R_{m,t}]^2 + \gamma_4 D[R_{m,t}]^2 + \varepsilon_t$$

where $CSAD_t$ is the equally weighted cross-sectional absolute deviation of returns, and $R_{m,t}$ is the equally weighted market portfolio return at time t. D is a dummy variable which takes a value = 1 if $R_{m,t} < 0$, and 0 otherwise. A significant negative value of γ_3 suggests the existence of herding during bullish markets, whereas a significant negative value of γ_4 suggests the existence of herding during bearish markets. Numbers in parentheses are t-statistics. Also reported are the p-values for the hypothesis test $\gamma_3 = \gamma_4$. ***, **, and * represent statistical significance at the 1, 5, and 10% levels, respectively.

TABLE 10.5 Quantile Regression Analysis of Herding Behavior in European Frontier Markets

	Bulgaria	Croatia	Estonia	Kazakhstan	Lithuania	Romania	Serbia	Slovenia	Ukraine
$\tau = 1\%$	4.4305***	-0.8992	-6.5998***	2.5567***	-8.8415***	-1.6493	8.1685***	5.8397***	4.1456***
	(3.79)	(-0.61)	(-4.36)	(11.43)	(-2.82)	(-0.25)	(9.51)	(13.87)	(21.56)
$\tau = 5\%$	4.7286***	0.0223	-11.2364***	1.9324***	-9.7771**	1.8252	8.3324***	4.9871***	4.5994***
	(3.19)	(0.01)	(-6.89)	(11.73)	(-2.56)	(0.26)	(6.89)	(9.71)	(15.62)
$\tau = 10\%$	2.7879**	0.7967	-8.7295***	1.5557***	-7.1221***	4.6722***	8.4334***	4.0497***	4.7169***
	(2.19)	(0.45)	(-4.83)	(7.81)	(-4.48)	(3.14)	(6.22)	(8.34)	(14.76)
$\tau = 30\%$	1.6174	0.2042	-7.0393**	1.0854***	6.6152***	6.7666	11.0633***	4.9403***	6.0421***
	(1.22)	(0.12)	(-2.37)	(4.61)	(8.34)	(0.23)	(6.15)	(4.91)	(8.84)
$\tau = 50\%$	-1.1407	-1.5703	-8.4163***	0.6230***	5.9164***	12.4063***	18.7040***	5.4901***	3.5212***
	(-0.80)	(-0.82)	(-8.60)	(2.81)	(6.91)	(5.98)	(9.36)	(6.33)	(3.91)
$\tau = 70\%$	-1.6238	-4.1170**	-7.3115***	0.6974	6.7458	16.5371***	18.0042***	3.7743***	1.7418
	(-1.01)	(-2.09)	(-7.49)	(0.05)	(1.01)	(5.05)	(11.03)	(4.33)	(0.63)
$\tau = 90\%$	-5.9347*	51.1121	-11.8469***	0.2263	6.5731	24.5026***	19.0583***	15.9079***	-3.6614**
	(-2.30)	(0.72)	(-8.62)	(0.15)	(1.14)	(2.73)	(9.81)	(5.51)	(-1.97)
$\tau = 95\%$	-5.9842*	27.2995	-12.8287***	-2.0698***	7.8789	31.6356	12.4509**	11.8136***	-8.4822***
	(-1.74)	(0.41)	(-5.28)	(-2.61)	(0.32)	(1.52)	(2.32)	(4.04)	(-5.92)
$\tau = 99\%$	-13.4720	8.7867	-18.9427***	-0.7746	21.3858	24.1117	4.5009	10.4323	-11.2948***
	(-1.55)	(0.13)	(-2.83)	(-1.31)	(1.22)	(0.84)	(0.66)	(0.11)	(-5.29)

This table reports the quantile regression estimates for the markets belonging to the MSCI EFM Central and East Europe and CIS Index by different quantile groups according to Eq. 10.4.

$$CSAD_t(\tau\,|\,x) = \alpha + \gamma_1\,|\,R_{m,t}(\tau)\,| + \gamma_2\,|\,R_{m,t}(\tau)\,|^2 + \varepsilon_t$$

where $CSAD_t$ is the equally weighted cross-sectional absolute deviation of returns, and $R_{m,t}$ is the equally weighted market portfolio return at time t. γ_k refers to the kth coefficient conditional on the τth quantile distribution in the estimated equation. For reasons of brevity only the results for γ_2 are shown. α and γ_1 are positive and significant for all countries and quantiles. A significant negative value of γ_2 suggests the existence of herding. Numbers in parentheses are t-statistics. ***, **, and * represent statistical significance at the 1, 5, and 10% levels, respectively.

TABLE 10.6 Quantile Regression Analysis of Herding Behavior in Up and Down European Frontier Markets

Panel A	Bulgaria	Croatia	Estonia	Kazakhstan	Lithuania	Romania	Serbia	Slovenia	Ukraine
$\tau = 1\%$	5.0289**	29.7009**	−4.5098**	2.2772***	−5.5546	10.4678**	8.3398***	7.6931***	6.3577
	(4.21)	(2.18)	(−2.55)	(4.10)	(−1.38)	(2.04)	(7.34)	(10.59)	(0.90)
$\tau = 5\%$	4.8091***	23.2915	−10.7206***	1.8951***	−3.9308	8.9455	8.3777***	6.1993***	8.9578***
	(3.42)	(1.30)	(−9.92)	(11.24)	(−0.30)	(1.26)	(5.52)	(6.87)	(6.16)
$\tau = 10\%$	3.0449	31.0229*	−10.8802***	1.4601***	3.2064	15.8435	7.7447***	5.0202***	9.5469***
	(1.63)	(1.73)	(−9.48)	(3.24)	(0.24)	(1.22)	(4.75)	(6.48)	(5.51)
$\tau = 30\%$	−0.2713	16.4512	−8.2138***	0.2831	9.4790***	20.7352***	11.4217***	3.2269***	11.0198
	(−0.14)	(0.73)	(−4.76)	(0.49)	(7.08)	(9.76)	(4.60)	(5.20)	(1.59)
$\tau = 50\%$	−2.6439	23.6987	−10.9427***	0.4468	13.0215***	17.6642***	18.8716***	3.6113***	14.7470
	(−1.61)	(1.12)	(−5.20)	(1.23)	(10.60)	(8.10)	(7.18)	(2.77)	(0.55)
$\tau = 70\%$	−1.3974	53.0741	−11.1471	−0.2436	11.7339***	15.7558***	16.0865***	1.1808	14.2287***
	(−0.78)	(0.99)	(−0.90)	(−0.48)	(8.90)	(6.45)	(6.52)	(0.68)	(5.31)
$\tau = 90\%$	−6.4821***	67.3296***	−12.8224	−2.5799***	8.8249**	15.7451***	19.3868***	14.1938*	5.0623
	(−3.27)	(2.82)	(−1.61)	(−3.07)	(2.07)	(2.13)	(8.21)	(1.70)	(1.26)
$\tau = 95\%$	−8.4606	44.9005	−12.7934*	−2.9430***	10.1631	4.1344	16.0603***	9.9779	−7.6548
	(−1.41)	(1.19)	(−1.68)	(−3.00)	(0.88)	(0.65)	(2.72)	(0.98)	(−0.23)
$\tau = 99\%$	−13.4720*	133.0665	−32.0886**	−2.3508	3.6815	7.7983	21.0088***	28.0555	−20.7195***
	(−1.74)	(0.55)	(−2.14)	(−0.90)	(0.24)	(1.01)	(3.52)	(0.13)	(−4.19)

Panel B	Bulgaria	Croatia	Estonia	Kazakhstan	Lithuania	Romania	Serbia	Slovenia	Ukraine
$\tau = 1\%$	17.1877***	3.1244	−4.2976**	1.7125	−7.9777**	−1.1460	5.5630	8.6148***	4.2120***
	(4.50)	(1.56)	(−2.49)	(0.08)	(−2.33)	(−0.17)	(0.77)	(12.17)	(18.89)
$\tau = 5\%$	12.8880***	1.2608	−9.2504***	2.0667**	−9.3587**	−4.1883	−1.5119	7.8070***	4.7099***
	(4.44)	(0.68)	(−5.43)	(17.09)	(−2.07)	(−0.48)	(−0.15)	(7.86)	(16.30)
$\tau = 10\%$	10.0774***	3.4258*	−5.2716***	1.7972***	−5.9378***	1.7458	−4.3329	6.2557***	4.8076***
	(3.79)	(1.87)	(−6.88)	(7.51)	(−3.17)	(0.22)	(−0.37)	(5.33)	(15.18)
$\tau = 30\%$	9.3353***	2.3731	−6.6391***	1.1953***	6.3622***	2.0440	73.4671***	6.0456***	4.9816***
	(3.34)	(1.19)	(−7.34)	(4.33)	(3.16)	(1.07)	(2.71)	(8.58)	(11.31)
$\tau = 50\%$	4.2079	0.3095	−8.2993***	0.5640**	5.3047***	12.8872***	54.3073**	5.2546***	5.9790***
	(1.22)	(0.14)	(−7.18)	(2.09)	(6.46)	(6.06)	(2.12)	(6.33)	(5.63)
$\tau = 70\%$	18.3370	−1.7481	−7.0088***	1.8918	3.7300***	13.2907***	42.0015*	6.2546	2.6486**
	(1.41)	(−0.75)	(−5.62)	(0.78)	(3.78)	(2.79)	(1.84)	(0.47)	(2.24)
$\tau = 90\%$	8.1174	1.8146	−9.4331***	1.6738	3.2395	29.9976***	183.8882	14.5899***	−2.5027
	(0.71)	(0.01)	(−9.13)	(0.80)	(0.50)	(2.07)**	(0.73)	(4.71)	(−1.25)
$\tau = 95\%$	24.3789	−1.1197	−11.6174***	−2.2485***	7.8789	41.9129	212.1480**	8.1965	−7.7789
	(1.08)	(−0.00)	(−4.93)	(−2.87)	(0.29)	(2.33)	(2.18)	(1.31)	(−1.35)
$\tau = 99\%$	−37.6980***	−11.9793	−14.0714**	−2.9497***	28.1360	0.1315	220.4379	−8.5124	−9.3564***
	(−2.47)	(−0.10)	(−2.48)	(−18.89)	(0.56)	(0.00)	(0.39)	(−1.15)	(−2.01)

This table reports the quantile regression estimates for the markets belonging to the MSCI EFM Central and East Europe and CIS Index by different quantile groups according to Eq. 10.5.

$$CSAD_t(\tau \mid x) = \alpha + \gamma_1(1-D)|R_{m,t}(\tau)| + \gamma_2 D|R_{m,t}(\tau)| + \gamma_3(1-D)|R_{m,t}(\tau)|^2 + \gamma_4 D|R_{m,t}(\tau)|^2 + \varepsilon_t$$

where $CSAD_t$ is the equally weighted cross-sectional absolute deviation of returns and $R_{m,t}$ is the equally weighted market portfolio return at time t. $\gamma_{k,\tau}$ refers to the kth coefficient conditional on the τth quantile distribution in the estimated equation. D is a dummy variable which takes a value = 1 if $R_{m,t} < 0$, and 0 otherwise. For reasons of brevity only the results for γ_3 (panel A) and γ_4 (panel B) are shown. α, γ_1, and γ_2 are positive and significant for all countries and quantiles. A significant negative value of γ_3 suggests the existence of herding during bullish markets, while a significant negative value of γ_4 suggests the existence of herding during bearish markets. Numbers in parentheses are t-statistics. ***, **, and * represent statistical significance at the 1, 5, and 10% levels, respectively.

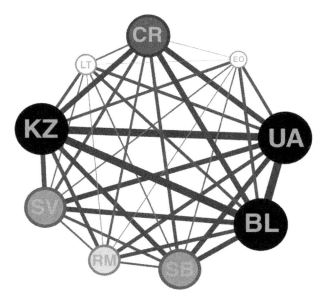

FIGURE 10.1 **Herding relationships among European frontier markets on calm days (non-extreme** R_{MSCIEFM} **days).** *BL*, Bulgaria; *CR*, Croatia; *EO*, Estonia; *KZ*, Kazakhstan; *LT*, Lithuania; *RM*, Romania; *SB*, Serbia; *SV*, Slovenia; *UA*, Ukraine.

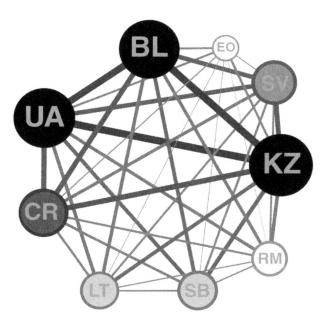

FIGURE 10.2 **Herding relationships among European frontier markets on negative extreme global return days (negative extreme** R_{MSCIEFM} **days).** *BL*, Bulgaria; *CR*, Croatia; *EO*, Estonia; *KZ*, Kazakhstan; *LT*, Lithuania; *RM*, Romania; *SB*, Serbia; *SV*, Slovenia; *UA*, Ukraine.

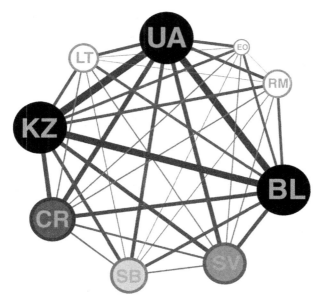

FIGURE 10.3   Herding relationships among European frontier markets on positive extreme global return days (positive extreme R_{MSCIEFM} days). *BL*, Bulgaria; *CR*, Croatia; *EO*, Estonia; *KZ*, Kazakhstan; *LT*, Lithuania; *RM*, Romania; *SB*, Serbia; *SV*, Slovenia; *UA*, Ukraine.

are the markets with the clearest tendency to herd toward the global MSCI EFM Index, followed by Croatia. Lithuania and Estonia are, in contrast, the markets with the least global herding behavior. Romania, Serbia, and Slovenia show an intermediate herding level toward the EFM index. It should be noted that Kazakhstan and Ukraine (the markets with the most intense herding relationships) are the countries outside the EU with higher indicators of economic activity in terms of GDP but a lower degree of economic openness and less institutional development, whereas Lithuania and Estonia (the markets with the least intense herding relationships) are members of the EU, small in terms of economic development, but more open and more developed institutionally. Nevertheless, Bulgaria, one of the markets with more intense global herding behavior, can not be so easily classified together with Kazakhstan and Ukraine except for the fact that these three markets also share individual herd behavior under volatile market conditions together with Croatia, which is the next (fourth) participant of the global consensus.

It is also interesting to note that calm herding days (nonextreme return days with more than 1000 individual stocks following the overall consensus) multiply by 10 the herding on extreme (positive or negative) return days. Thus Fig. 10.1 is, perhaps, the most representative of herd behavior toward the MSCI EFM Index, even though the relationships structure is largely reproduced in periods of extreme returns. Intense herding days represent 10% of the time period under analysis.

Estonia is the market that most clearly deviates from the global consensus and offers its own performance on both calm and extreme return days, suggesting that the market with the clearest evidence of individual herding is the one less prone to follow the area consensus described by the MSCI EFM Index.

In summary, although we have found some evidence of herding in EFMs both at an individual level and at a global level, our results indicate that special attention should be paid to the methodology applied in herding analysis, given that there are many types of imitative behavior and the models and procedures offered by the literature to date detect only a part of them.

5 CONCLUSIONS

This study has examined the herding behavior in nine EFMs at both individual and global levels using the models proposed by CH and CCK and a graphical approach which allows possible relationships among markets to be detected (using Gephi software). The results are not homogeneous among the methodologies: the CH model finds herding only in extreme up markets in Croatia, Romania, and Ukraine, whereas the results of applying the CCK measure are compatible with the existence of herding only in the Estonian market, for both the market as a whole and up and down markets. We further tested for herding by employing a quantile regression approach, and observe that estimated CCK coefficients vary with the quantile levels. Estonia still shows negative coefficients across all quantiles, whereas Bulgaria, Croatia, Kazakhstan, and Ukraine show significant herding only in the higher quantiles of the distribution. Lithuania, in contrast, displays negative coefficients in the lower quantiles.

With respect to the tendency to herd around a global consensus, the results using the Gephi tool indicate that the markets showing a more intense herding tendency are Bulgaria, Croatia, Kazakhstan, and Ukraine, the ones that show significant herding in the highest quantiles. Nevertheless, Estonia and Lithuania, two small markets that provide evidence of individual herding behavior along the entire return dispersion distribution or in the lowest quantiles, respectively, are the markets which do not follow the MSCI EFM Index consensus.

These nonhomogeneous results are difficult to explain solely on the basis of market characteristics or institutional and cultural factors. Besides the differences caused by analysis over different time horizons, as is the case of our chapter compared with Chen (2013), the results also depend on the methodology applied. The usual methodologies look for a specific type of herding and therefore may be useful for detecting such a herd behavior. It should be noted that there is no universally accepted methodology for detecting herding, however or whenever it is present in a market or a set of markets. This may be the reason why the results found in the empirical literature are not homogeneous or comparable.

ACKNOWLEDGMENT

This chapter has received financial support from the Spanish Ministry of Economy and Competitiveness (ECO2012-35946-C02-01 and ECO2013-45568-R) and the Government of Aragón/European Social Fund (S14/2).

REFERENCES

Barber, B.M., Odean, T., 2000. Trading is hazardous to your wealth: the common stock investment performance of individual investors. J. Finance 55, 773–806.

Barnes, M., Hughes, A.W., 2002. A Quantile Regression Analysis of the Cross Section of Stock Market Returns. Working paper, Federal Reserve Bank of Boston, Boston, MA, USA.

Bastian, M., Heymann, S., Jacomy, M., 2009. Gephi: an open source software for exploring and manipulating networks. In: International AAAI Conference on Weblogs and Social Media. Available from: http://gephi.github.io/.

Bekaert, G., Wu, G., 2000. Asymmetric volatility and risk in equity markets. Rev. Financ. Stud. 13, 1–42.

Bikhchandani, S., Hirshleifer, D., Welch, I., 1998. Learning from the behavior of others: conformity, fads and informational cascade. J. Econ. Perspect. 12, 151–170.

Bikhchandani, S., Sharma, S., 2000. Herd Behavior in Financial Markets: A Review. IMF Working Paper WP/00/48. International Monetary Fund, Washington, DC, USA.

Brennan, M., 1993. Agency and Asset Prices. Finance Working Paper No. 6–93, UCLA.

Calvo, G., Mendoza, E., 2000. Rational Contagion and the Globalization of Securities Markets. J. International Economics 51 (1), 79–113.

Chang, E.C., Cheng, J.W., Khorana, A., 2000. An examination of herd behavior in equity markets: an international perspective. J. Bank. Finance 24, 1651–1679.

Chari, V.V., Kehoe, P., 2004. Financial crises as herds: overturning the critiques. J. Economic Theory 119 (1), 128–150.

Chen, T., 2013. Do investors herd in global stock markets? J. Behav. Finance 14 (3), 230–239.

Chiang, T.C., Li, J., Tan, L., 2010. Empirical investigation of herding behavior in Chinese stock markets: evidence from quantile regression analysis. Global Finance J. 21 (1), 111–124.

Chinn, M.D., Ito, H., 2006. What matters for financial development? Capital controls, institutions, and interactions. J. Dev. Econ. 81 (1), 163–192.

Christie, W.G., Huang, R.D., 1995. Following the pier piper: do individual returns herd around the market? Financ. Anal. J. 51, 31–37.

Demirer, R., Kutan, A.M., 2006. Does herding behavior exist in Chinese stock markets? J. Int. Financ. Mark. Inst. Money 16, 123–142.

Devenow, A., Welch, I., 1996. Rational herding in financial economics. Eur. Econ. Rev. 40, 603–615.

Elster, J., 1998. Emotions and economic theory. J. Econ. Lit. 36, 47–74.

Grinblatt, M., Titman, S., Wermers, R., 1995. Momentum investment strategies, portfolio performance and herding: a study of mutual fund behavior. Am. Econ. Rev. 85, 1088–1105.

Hirshleifer, D., Teoh, S.H., 2003. Herd behaviour and cascading in capital markets: a review and synthesis. Eur. Financ. Manage. 9 (1), 25–66.

Hofstede, G., 2001. Culture's Consequences: Comparing Values, Behaviors, Institutions, and Organizations across Nations. Sage Publications, Beverly Hills, CA.

Hong, Y., Tu, J., Zhou, G., 2007. Asymmetries in stock returns: statistical tests and economic evaluation. Rev. Financ. Stud. 20 (5), 1547–1581.

Koenker, R.W., Bassett, Jr., G., 1978. Regression quantiles. Econometrica 46, 33–50.

Lakonishok, J., Shleifer, A., Vishny, R.W., 1992. The impact of institutional trading on stock prices. J. Financ. Econ. 32, 23–43.

Lao, P., Singh, H., 2011. Herding behaviour in the Chinese and Indian stock markets. J. Asian Econ. 22 (6), 495–506.

Lo, A., 1999. The three P's of total risk management. Financ. Anal. J. 55, 12–20.

Loewenstein, G., 2000. Emotions in economic theory and economic behavior. Am. Econ. Rev. 90, 426–432.

Odean, T., 1998. Are investors reluctant to realize their losses? J. Finance 53 (5), 1775–1798.

Peters, E., Slovic, P., 2000. The springs of action: affective and analytical information processing in choice. Pers. Soc. Psychol. Bull. 26, 1465–1475.

Prosad, J.M., Kapoor, S., Sengupta, J., 2012. An examination of herd behavior: an empirical evidence from Indian equity market. Int. J. Trade Econ. Finance 3 (2), 154–157.

Rajan, R.G., 1994. Why credit policies fluctuate: a theory and some evidence. Quart. J. Econ. 436, 399–442.

Roll, R., 1992. A mean/variance analysis of tracking error. J. Portfolio Manage. Summer, 13–22.

Scharfstein, D.S., Stein, J.C., 1990. Herd behavior and investment. Am. Econ. Rev. 80, 465–479.

Shefrin, H., 2000. Beyond Greed and Fear: Understanding Behavioral Finance and the Psychology of Investing. HBS Press, Boston, MA.

Tan, L., Chiang, T.C., Mason, J., Nelling, E., 2008. Herding behavior in Chinese stock markets: an examination of A and B shares. Pacific-Basin Finance J. 16, 61–77.

Thaler, R., 1991. Quasi-Rational Economics. Russell Sage Foundation, New York.

Trueman, B., 1994. Analyst forecasts and herding behavior. Rev. Financ. Stud. 7, 97–124.

Wermers, R., 1999. Mutual fund herding and the impact on stock prices. J. Finance 54, 581–622.

Zhou, J., Anderson, R.I., 2013. An empirical investigation of herding behavior in the US REIT market. J. Real Estate Finance Econ. 47 (1), 83–108.

Section C

Asia

Chapter 11

Is Bankruptcy a Systematic Risk? Evidence From Vietnam

T. Chaiyakul*, K. Bangassa**, M. Iskandrani[†]
**Kasetsart University Sriracha Campus, Faculty of Management Sciences, Chonburi, Thailand;
**University of Liverpool, Management School, Liverpool, United Kingdom; [†]University of
Jordan, Faculty of Business, Amman, Jordan*

Chapter Outline

1 INTRODUCTION

The Vietnamese stock market is an MSCI frontier market. Vietnam has been identified as an investable economy in need of more capital and market liquidity, as opposed to a more developed emerging market. The Vietnamese stock market has been growing aggressively. According to the World Bank, the average Vietnamese stock market capitalization as a percentage of GDP for the period from 2003 to 2012 was 12.25%, with a minimum of 0.36% in 2003 and a maximum of 25.24% in 2007. As a rule of thumb, stock market capitalization of 50% or more as a percentage of GDP indicates a developed market. According to HSBC (2012), the HOSE (Ho Chi Minh City Stock Exchange) is skewed toward financials, whereby 50 companies operate in the financial sector with more than 49% market capitalization, followed by consumer staples (19%), utilities (12%), and materials (6%).

Vietnam is ruled by one political party. The Vietnamese equities market consists of two major stock exchanges, the HOSE and the Hanoi Stock Exchange (HNX). The HOSE was the first stock exchange in Vietnam; it was

Handbook of Frontier Markets. http://dx.doi.org/10.1016/B978-0-12-803776-8.00011-2

started in 2000 with the government's decision to privatize state-owned enterprises (SOEs) and support the raising of capital needed for the economic development of Vietnam. The HOSE has grown up rapidly. In 2006 the HOSE had 34 listed companies with a market capitalization of USD 1.1 billion. In 2012 there were 303 listed companies with a market capitalization of USD 29.9 billion. The HOSE is larger than HNX. The indices tracking the two markets are the VN-INDEX and HNX-INDEX, respectively.

Starting in Jul. 2003, foreign investors became able to invest in up to 30% of the total value of the SOEs that had been privatized. This amount was raised to 49% toward the end of 2005, with the aim of promoting the privatization process. To participate in the market, foreign investors are required to open an account in one of the local brokerage firms. There is currently a quota of 60% foreign room, which limits the maximum amount foreign investors can buy in 1 day.

The products available for trading in both markets include Vietnamese equities, and government and corporate bonds. The HOSE mainly deals with equity trading, whereas the HNX deals with equities, bonds, and over-the-counter (OTC) securities.

As mentioned previously, the first stock market was established in 2000 with the government's decision to privatize SOEs and support raising the capital needed for the economic development of Vietnam. The Vietnamese government aims to build a market economy in Vietnam within the general framework of a socialist sociopolitical system and socialist principles. Nguyen et al. (2014) argue that privatization can be useful in the process of developing the Vietnamese stock market and that providing market access to well-established institutions is important for the long-term development of the market. They also question whether Vietnam has laid down the basic elements needed to establish a sustainable stock market. The position of the World Bank (1992) regarding the privatization which is embraced by many nations around the globe (eg, Western Europe, Latin America, Southeast Asia, Russia, Eastern Europe, Africa, etc.) is that "privatization is not a blanket solution for the problems of the poorly performing SOEs. It cannot in and of itself make up totally for lack of competition, for weak capital markets, or for the absence of an appropriate regulatory framework."

Between 1989 and 2008 Vietnam achieved an average growth rate of 7.4% per annum. However, while the GDP per capita of Vietnam increased to US $1000 in 2008 (which indicated a very favorable achievement), according to the General Statistics Office of Vietnam, 2008 was a gloomy year for the Vietnamese economy (Pincus, 2009), and ended with a significant drop in performance compared to the achievements registered during the previous year. Pincus argues that huge capital inflows in 2007 and early 2008 accelerated economic "overheating," increases in inflation, and the building of a significant current account deficit. The HOSE lost 66% of its value that year, becoming the worst performer at a global level. In 2008 besides domestic challenges to the economy, Vietnam was also affected by the GFC, which started with the US subprime mortgage crisis and was further intensified by the unexpected collapse of Lehman Brothers in 2008. Big economies in the world—such as those of the United States, the United Kingdom, and many euro zone countries—suffered from the financial crisis (Das and Shrestha, 2009). Increases in inflation beyond 25%, rises in the cost of housing, a significant drop in the Vietnamese dong against the US dollar, falling wages in real terms as a result of rallying inflation, employee strikes across the nation, etc., gave further evidence that the Vietnamese economy was hit hard by a national and the global financial crisis. As a result of the GFC, Vietnam's economy was affected mainly in the areas of trade, investment, capital mobility, and the financial markets. The economy of Vietnam was directly and indirectly affected by the financial crisis and economic recession in the economies of its major trading partners, such as the United States, the European Union, Japan, etc.

Inflation figures of double digits were recorded in 2007 and reached 28.32% in Aug. 2008. Furthermore, fiscal and trade deficits of up to 5% and over 20% of GDP, respectively, were recorded. Demand for manufactured export goods, such as footwear and furniture, dropped significantly. Other areas of the Vietnamese economy which were also affected significantly included properties and construction materials, chemicals used in agriculture and industry, etc. Companies listed on the HOSE and HNX were affected by the financial crisis and as a result laid off a number of employees. Multinational corporations were globally affected by the financial crisis, and consequently the level of foreign direct investment (FDI) in Vietnam dropped significantly, leading to delays in and cancelations of investment projects.

Furthermore, investor psychology was affected by the GFC, which in turn had impacts on domestic capital markets. In 2008 the VN-INDEX and the HNX-INDEX lost 66.9 and 67.2% of their values, respectively. According to the figures reported by 41 out of 63 provinces and municipalities in Vietnam, 66,700 workers lost their jobs in 2008, increasing the unemployment rate to 4.65%. Based on these figures, it is estimated that the total number of workers who lost their jobs in 2008 due to the all-around severe effects of the global and national financial crisis on Vietnam's economy could have been well over 80,000. The General Statistics Office of Vietnam reported a fall in the Consumer Price Index (CPI) amounting to 0.68% in Dec. 2008 compared to Nov. 2008, which was preceded by falls of 0.76 and 0.19% in Nov. and Oct. 2008, respectively. As a result of these negative impacts of the financial crisis on the Vietnamese economy, the overall economic growth of the nation declined from 8.48% in 2007 to 6.23% in 2008.

There is an ongoing and unresolved debate over whether bankruptcy risk is a stated variable in explaining equity returns. For example, Fama and French (1996) consider that the existence of anomalous size and value premiums can arise as a result of financial distress. We are going to assess the extent to which, if any, bankruptcy risk explains, in a systematic manner, equity returns above the risk premiums which can be empirically identified as important for market, size, and BM factors.[a] The probability of bankruptcy reflects the extent of a firm's financial distress, while the eventual outcome from severe financial distress can be bankruptcy. Altman (1993) provides an early review of literature on bankruptcy prediction and measures of ex ante bankruptcy risk. Accordingly, the existing evidence that bankruptcy risk is systematic is related to a distress factor explanation for the market, size, and BM effects. Griffin and Lemmon (2002) and Campbell et al. (2008) argue that it is not difficult to identify a mechanism for bankruptcy risk that can be priced if we accept that financially distressed firms have prices that comove and are difficult to diversify due to arbitrage restrictions. Lang and Stulz (1992) and Denis and Denis (1995) report evidence which implies that bankruptcy risk could be positively related to systematic risk. Shumway (1996) finds evidence suggesting that the risk of default is systematic. Vassalou and Xing (2004) also argue that default risk is systematic and therefore can be priced in the cross-section of equity returns.

On the other hand, Asquith et al. (1994) find that bankruptcy is mostly due to idiosyncratic factors, implying that it is unrelated to systematic risk. Vassalou and Xing (2004) report that debt default risk is related to the size and BM characteristics of a firm, but that the evidence regarding its impacts on equity returns is mixed and is likely to be related to the strength of shareholder bargaining power in extracting rents from competing claim holders in a distress situation (Aretz, 2011; Zhang, 2012; Garlappi et al., 2008).

Our contribution in this context can then be straightforwardly stated: we assess bankruptcy risk as a latent risk factor conditioned on economic states which provide a hypothesis for its fleeting existence. In so doing, we attempt to revisit some of the conflicting findings reported to date and offer out-of-sample evidence.

In sum, we are able to more clearly specify the relationship between bankruptcy risk and equity returns. Our test basis is the most recent GFC, which supplies a set of useful economic circumstances that provide the potential to clearly present out-of-sample evidence for the relationship between bankruptcy risk and equity returns.

We are also motivated by the recommendations of Lo and MacKinlay (1990), who argue that empirical findings should be examined out-of-sample to ensure that any findings reported are not a product of data snooping. The Vietnamese market, which is a frontier market, is tested in this study. The data set we examine is not investigated with appropriate scope in existing studies (eg, for studies of the United States see Lang and Stulz, 1992; Opler and Titman, 1994; Asquith et al., 1994; Dichev, 1998; Griffin and Lemmon, 2002; Vassalou and Xing, 2004; for studies of the United Kingdom see Hussain

---

a. For the purposes of drawing together a large literature, we use the terms distress, default, and bankruptcy interchangeably while recognizing that there are significant nuances and steps between each of them. We explain our approach on the grounds that our measurement approaches necessarily do not make this distinction, as discussed elsewhere in the chapter.

et al., 2001; Agarwal and Taffler, 2008).[b] Hence, we examine the relationship between bankruptcy risk and equity returns by conducting both portfolio and cross-sectional analyses.

In this paper we investigate the relationship between bankruptcy risk and equity returns using the GFC and the HOSE as a test basis. This study is organized as follows: Section 2 reviews the existing literature. Section 3 describes research design, data, and methodology. Section 4 discusses the empirical evidence, and Section 5 concludes the study.

2 LITERATURE REVIEW

The relationship between bankruptcy risk and equity returns is examined by small group of prior researchers using different bankruptcy risk measures. For instance, Dichev (1998) employed models developed by both Altman (1968) and Ohlson (1980) to measure bankruptcy risk. Similarly, Griffin and Lemmon (2002) employ the O-score developed by Ohlson (1980) as the proxy for bankruptcy risk. The study from Vassalou and Xing (2004) is the first one to apply the model developed by Merton (1974).[c] They argue that the models designed by Altman (1968) and Ohlson (1980) are naturally backward looking, since financial statements tend to present a firm's past performance rather than its future prospects. The Merton (1974) option-pricing model uses market-value data to compute the bankruptcy risk of firms. Bystrom et al. (2005) also apply the Merton (1974) model to measure bankruptcy risk and investigate the relationship between bankruptcy risk and equity returns.

Existing studies that investigate the relationship between bankruptcy risk and equity returns report dissimilar findings. For instance, Lang and Stulz (1992) study the effect of bankruptcy announcements on the equity value of a bankrupt firm's competitors and conclude that bankruptcy announcements decrease the value of competitors, implying a positive relationship between bankruptcy risk and equity value. Vassalou and Xing (2004) analyze the effects of bankruptcy risk on stock returns by using the Merton (1974) option-based model and conclude that bankruptcy risk in the United States is a systematic risk. More recently, Chava and Purnanandam (2010) reported a positive cross-sectional relationship between default risk and expected stock returns.

On the other hand, there are other studies that disagree with the evidence that bankruptcy risk is a systematic risk. For example, Opler and Titman (1994) study the effect of financial distress on corporate performance and report that the stock returns of more leveraged firms in distressed industries are lower than those of less leveraged firms, and hence, by implication, bankruptcy risk is not a systematic risk. Asquith et al. (1994) analyze financially distressed firms that

---

b. Among the limited number of published studies on this topic relating to Southeast Asia, to the best our knowledge, there is only a study by Bystrom et al. (2005), which uses data from Thailand.
c. The method used in calculating the bankruptcy risk measure developed by Vassalou and Xing (2004) is very similar to the one used by Moody's KMV, the world's leading credit-rating company.

try to avoid bankruptcy through public and private debt restructuring, asset sales, mergers, and capital expenditure reductions. They find no evidence which supports the expectation that the better performing companies in their sample are those that are more successful in dealing with financial distress, since such firms are as likely to go bankrupt as the other firms. Therefore, they argue that bankruptcy risk is an idiosyncratic factor. Dichev (1998) uses the models from Altman (1968) and Ohlson (1980) to investigate whether bankruptcy risk is a systematic risk by using all industrial firms on the New York Stock Exchange (NYSE), American Stock Exchange (AMEX), and OTC markets from 1981 to 1995, and they report that bankruptcy risk is not rewarded by higher returns. In actuality, firms with a high bankruptcy risk are reported to earn substantially lower than average returns.

Hussain et al. (2001) study the behavior of relative financial distress by applying the capital asset pricing model (CAPM) and the Fama and French (1993) three-factor model and using UK data for the period 1980–99. Their results show that there is no difference between returns of financially distressed and nonfinancially distressed firms, implying that bankruptcy risk is not systematic. Griffin and Lemmon (2002) examine the relationship between bankruptcy risk and stock returns. They employ the model from Ohlson (1980) to calculate the probability of bankruptcy and show that bankruptcy risk is negatively related to equity returns. Agarwal and Taffler (2008) use the Taffler (1983, 1984)[d] bankruptcy prediction model to measure bankruptcy risk and test whether bankruptcy risk is a separately priced risk factor. Their study illustrates that financially distressed stocks earn lower returns than nonfinancially distressed stocks. Their findings are consistent with the evidence reported by Dichev (1998). More recently, Da and Gao (2010) argued that the abnormal returns on high default risk stocks found by Vassalou and Xing (2004) are mainly due to short-term return reversals rather than systematic default risk.

Gharghori et al. (2007) employ data from the Australian market during the period from Jan. 1996 to Dec. 2004 to investigate whether default risk is priced in the cross-section of equity returns. They augment the Fama and French (1993) three-factor model with their new default-risk factor (developed by applying the Merton (1974) option-based model) and report that default risk is not priced in equity returns. Bystrom et al. (2005) analyze data of 50 financially distressed companies from the Stock Exchange of Thailand. They also apply the Merton (1974) model to measure the probability of bankruptcy and argue that bankruptcy risk is not a systematic risk. Samad et al. (2009) find a significant inverse relationship between distress risk and the BM equity measure. This is a finding consistent with Lang and Stulz (1992), Denis and Denis (1995), Shumway (1996), and Chen and Zhang (1998). Furthermore, Avramov et al. (2009) find that firms with low credit risks obtain higher returns

---

d. The Taffler (1983, 1984) model was developed from UK data.

compared to high credit risk firms due to mispricing by retail investors and the inability of arbitrageurs to play a role because of prohibitive factors such as illiquidity of low-rated stocks. Also, Gharghori et al. (2009) examine Australian companies and find that default probability is negatively related to returns. They also report that the claim by Fama and French (1996) that size and BM factors explain the cross-sectional variation in equity returns is not consistent with their finding from Australian data, and they thereby recommend further research in different markets to gain more understanding about the default risk hypothesis.

Chen et al. (2010) examine the relationship between financial distress and idiosyncratic volatility. They use the Altman (1968) and Ohlson (1980) models to measure the risk of bankruptcy. Applying the Ferguson and Shockley (2003) approach and the CAPM, they show that the stocks with high volatility and high distress risks have low returns. They argue that the presence of idiosyncratic volatility, which is connected to distress risk, explains why some high distress stocks do not receive high returns, since idiosyncratic risks are not priced but diversified. Gutiérrez et al. (2012) analyze firms' total value performance in relation to different bankruptcy systems and find that the total value of firms in financial distress is low, possibly due to a decline in efficiency. Garlappi and Yan (2011) develop and test a model that explains lower returns for financially distressed stocks, among other findings. Aretz and Shackleton (2011) also argue that asset-return correlations are more important determinants of betas than default risk, since the relation between leverage and beta bias can be diversified away by including a large number of securities in a portfolio.

Lin et al. (2012) employ data from the Taiwan stock market during the period from Jan. 1996 to Dec. 2007 to investigate the relationship between default risk and equity returns. They use both the Merton (1974) and the compound-option models[e] used by Geske (1977, 1979), Delianedis and Geske (2003), and Lin and Chang (2009) to measure the default risk. They apply Fama and French (1993) three-factor model to test the influences of firm's size, BM, and default risk on equity returns. Moreover, Lin et al. (2012) use the two-pass regression of Fama and MacBeth (1973) to test the influences of size, BM, and default factors on equity returns. The portfolio analysis reveals that both the firm's size and its BM ratio cannot proxy the default risk. With respect to the default risk effect, they show that no significant differences exist in average returns of portfolios with high and low default risks. Nevertheless, by employing the Fama and French (1993) three-factor model they find that default risk is part of systematic risk, but that still the firm's size and BM ratio cannot proxy for default risk.

---

e. Lin et al. (2012) stated that under the Merton (1974) model the capital structure of a firm contains equity and a zero coupon bond. However, they mentioned that the compound-option model comprises the corporate debt structure into long and short maturity dates.

Kim (2013) employs data from the US market during the period 1978–2007 to analyze the relationship between bankruptcy risk and subsequent returns. For bankruptcy risk he uses the O-score (Ohlson, 1980) and the BSM-prob model (Hillegeist et al., 2004). Kim (2013) argues that using two proxies of bankruptcy risk increase the possibility to detect the source of anomaly and reduce the bias of results that may occur because of differences in sample periods. His findings reveal that there is a negative relationship between the O-score and subsequent returns, whereas there is no relationship between BSM-prob and subsequent returns. In particular, he finds that funds from operations divided by the total liabilities is the only component that predicts returns, whereas the relationship between funds from operations divided by the total liabilities and subsequent returns diminishes once he controls for cash flows from operations divided by average total assets. He concludes that the funds from operations divided by total liabilities follow those of cash flows from operations divided by average total assets.

Chen and Lee (2013) test the effect of firm's size, BM ratio, liquidity, and default risk on portfolio returns and investigate the impact of a momentum factor on portfolio returns. They use the data from the Taiwanese stock market during the period from Jan. 1986 to Dec. 2008. They follow the methodology of Vassalou and Xing (2004) and Bharath and Shumway (2008) in order to calculate a firm's expected default frequency. For market liquidity, they use the Amihud (2002) illiquidity ratio and Pastor and Stambaugh (2003). Their results reveal three interesting findings, which are as follows:

1. The effect of default risk on equity returns exists only when they control for market liquidity; the opposite is true once they control for the firm's size and BM ratio.
2. Under the asset pricing regression, the results show that there is a relationship between the default risk and equity returns. However, after they control for the firm's size, BM ratio, and momentum, they notice that default risk cannot act as systemic risk in asset pricing.
3. With respect to the timing of the distress, they find that a short-term reversals in portfolios have high default risks.

Simlai (2014) analyzes the variability of average portfolio returns in relation to firm-level characteristics for US distressed firms. He follows Campbell et al. (2008) to build a financial-distress measure. In particular, Simlai (2014) studies the effect of firm size, BM ratio, and momentum on average portfolio returns with application of the Fama and French (1993) three-factor model and the Carhart (1997) four-factor model, using US data for the period 1972–2008. His results show that average excess returns for small firms are negatively associated with systematic risk and high-growth firms are negatively related to the probability of financial distress. With respect to the momentum effect, the results show that high-distressed firms have negative momentum, while the low-distressed firms have positive momentum. Simlai (2014) concludes that firm size and BM ratio effects are not associated with distress risk, and that the momentum factor is not a proxy of distress risk.

3 RESEARCH DESIGN, DATA, AND METHODOLOGY

If the coefficient of the bankruptcy risk factor is statistically significant in a regression analysis, bankruptcy risk can be considered as systematic risk. Hence, the degree of the variability of returns of distressed firms with respect to asset pricing factors is expected to be higher than that for nondistressed firms, if the risk of bankruptcy is a systematic risk. This could be well demonstrated by investigating the relationship between asset returns and the measures for bankruptcy risk over a changing economic environment. The GFC created a suitable condition to investigate the significance of bankruptcy risk in asset pricing. We use the DLI bankruptcy risk measure developed by Vassalou and Xing (2004), which is an application of the Merton (1974) option-pricing model. This measure is based on market-value data, unlike the Altman (1968) and Ohlson (1980) models that use historical data from financial statements.

We apply portfolio and regression analyses to investigate the relationship between equity returns and risk of bankruptcy. In portfolio analyses, quintile portfolio returns are formed based on the DLI bankruptcy-risk measure, size-bankruptcy risk measure, and BM-bankruptcy-risk measure. We look for the presence of a monotonic pattern that displays the level of equity returns as the value of bankruptcy risk increases or decreases. Return differences between high and low bankruptcy portfolios that are controlled by firm characteristics are examined. A null hypothesis $H_0 : \bar{X}_1 - \bar{X}_2 = 0$, where $\bar{X}_1$ is the population mean return for high bankruptcy risk portfolio and $\bar{X}_2$ is the population mean return for low bankruptcy risk portfolio, is tested. The alternative hypothesis is $H_1 : \bar{X}_1 - \bar{X}_2 \neq 0$. The null hypothesis H_0 will be rejected in favor of the alternative hypothesis H_1 if the population means are statistically different. The test statistic for the difference between two mean returns is conducted following Lomax (2007).[f]

In conducting regression analysis we divide the study period into precrisis, crisis, and postcrisis periods. The precrisis period is from Jul. 1, 2007 to Sep. 14, 2008; the crisis period is from Sep.15, 2008 to Mar. 31, 2009; and the postcrisis period is from Apr. 1, 2009 to Dec. 31, 2010.

---

f. The test statistic of the difference between two means is conducted following Lomax (2007): $t = \dfrac{\bar{X}_1 - \bar{X}_2}{s_{\bar{X}_1 - \bar{X}_2}}$, where $\bar{X}_1$ and $\bar{X}_2$ are the means for sample 1 and sample 2, respectively, and $s_{\bar{X}_1 - \bar{X}_2}$ is the standard error of the difference between two means, which is the standard deviation of the sampling distribution of the difference between two means and is computed as $s_{\bar{X}_1 - \bar{X}_2} = S_p \sqrt{\dfrac{1}{n_1} + \dfrac{1}{n_2}}$, where, S_p is a pooled standard deviation. $S_p = \sqrt{\dfrac{(n_1 - 1)S_1^2 + (n_2 - 1)S_2^2}{n_1 + n_2 - 2}}$, where S_1^2 and S_2^2 are sample variances, and n_1 and n_2 are the sample sizes for groups 1 and 2, respectively.

The proxies of market returns, size, and BM ratio are augmented by the bankruptcy risk factors used in the cross-sectional regression analysis. In previous studies on the relationship between bankruptcy risk and equity returns— such as Griffin and Lemmon (2002), Vassalou and Xing (2004), and Gharghori et al. (2007)—the market return, size, and BM ratio factors are incorporated to investigate the explanatory power of bankruptcy risk in pricing equity returns, since these factors have shown significant ability to explain equity returns and are often used in investigations of asset pricing. Following Fama and French (1993, 1996), this study employs excess market returns and the return on a zero-net investment portfolio for size and the BM equity ratio in the cross-sectional regression analysis.

Unlike previous studies (to our knowledge), this study initially uses the ADLI as the proxy for bankruptcy risk. The reason for this is that if assets are priced rationally, bankruptcy risk must proxy as a nondiversifiable risk factor in returns. Following Vassalou and Xing (2004), the DLI formula developed from the Merton (1974) option-pricing model is shown as follows:

$$DLI_t = N(-DD_t) \tag{11.1}$$

$$DD_t = \frac{\ln(V_A / X_t) + (r - (1/2)\sigma_A^2)(T)}{\sigma_A \sqrt{T}} \tag{11.2}$$

where DLI_t is the DLI, N is the cumulative density function of the standard normal distribution, DD_t represents the number of standard deviations that a firm deviates from the mean for bankruptcy to occur, V_A is the market value of the firm's equity, X_t is the total amount of the firm's debts, r is the risk-free rate, σ_A is the volatility of the firm's asset returns, and T is the time to maturity of the firm's debt. The larger the value of DD, the smaller the probability of bankruptcy risk; a higher DLI indicates a higher probability of bankruptcy. The ADLI is constructed from a simple average of the DLI of all firms.

The model choice follows previous studies in the literature, that is, Vassalou and Xing (2004) and Bystrom et al. (2005). Following Vassalou and Xing (2004), the daily data are aggregated in order to obtain monthly observations. Daily market values for firms (V_A) are employed, while annual data are used for the book value of debt (D_t), calculated using "short-term debt and the current portion of long-term debt" (Datastream item WC03051) plus half the "long-term debt" (Datastream item WC03251). This study includes long-term debt in the calculations because firms need to deal with their long-term debts, and these interest payments are part of their short-term liabilities. Following Vassalou and Xing (2004) and Moody's KMV, which is a credit-rating company, this study uses 50% of long-term debt encounters in the calculations. Moody's KMV argues that this choice is sensible and adequately captures the financing constraints of firms. Vassalou and Xing (2004) also found that having a different proportion of long-term debt included in the DLI calculations does not lead to a significant change in the results. Monthly equity volatilities (σ_A) were estimated using 12-month historical sample volatilities. The risk-free rate for each market is the Vietnamese discount rate-middle rate. Following Bystrom et al. (2005), the time to maturity of debt (T) is always assumed to be 1 year.

To investigate whether bankruptcy risk is priced in equity returns, we construct the model as follows:

$$R_t = a + bEMKT_t + sSIZE_t + hBM_t + gADLI_t + \varepsilon_t \qquad (11.3)$$

where R_t and $EMKT_t$ refer to the excess return of a stock and the market, respectively. The Vietnamese discount rate-middle rate is used as a proxy for the risk-free rate. The variable $SIZE_t^g$ refers to return on the zero-investment portfolio, which is long on stocks with a small market capitalization (size) and short on large-sized stocks, as in the Fama and French (1993) model. The variable BM_t refers to the BM equity-value ratio of each stock. The variable $ADLI_t$ is the simple average of the DLI of all firms.

The data in this study come from all firms in the HOSE for the period Jan. 2007 to Dec. 2010. All data were collected from the Datastream database. A return is the monthly average return calculated from the percentage change of the monthly return index. The monthly DLIs (Vassalou and Xing, 2004) are employed as monthly bankruptcy risk variables. Size, or the market capitalization, is the share price multiplied by the number of ordinary shares in issue. The daily market values of firms are employed to calculate the monthly average size of firms. Each month, the BM equity ratio of a firm is the last fiscal year's book value of the equity divided by the current month's market value of the equity. Following previous literature such as Vassalou and Xing (2004) and Griffin and Lemmon (2002), firms with a negative BM are excluded from this study because it is difficult to interpret BM portfolios. The stocks in low BM portfolios refer to those with the highest growth potential; however, many negative BM stocks face financial difficulties.

4 RESULTS OF ANALYSIS AND DISCUSSION OF FINDINGS

In Table 11.1 stocks are sorted into five portfolios based on the Vassalou and Xing's (2004) DLI bankruptcy risk measure. The average returns of each portfolio sorted by the bankruptcy risk measure are calculated. A high DLI bankruptcy risk measure is related to the stocks which carry a high probability of becoming bankrupt, whereas a low bankruptcy risk is related to stocks which have a low probability of becoming bankrupt. A bankruptcy risk premium (discount) prevails when the difference between the returns of the highest and lowest bankruptcy risk portfolios are positive (negative) and statistically significant. The average returns for all portfolios shown in Table 11.1 are negative over the

---

g. The methodology to calculate SMB_t follows Fama and French (1993).

TABLE 11.1 Average Returns of Portfolios Sorted by Bankruptcy Risk Measures

Average returns

DLI-sorted portfolios

Low	2	3	4	High	High–low	t-values
−0.06804	−0.06221	−0.07691	−0.01777	−0.06894	−0.00089	−0.0637

Stocks are sorted into five portfolios by their levels of bankruptcy risk using DLI models (Vassalou and Xing, 2004). The average returns of each portfolio are then computed. When stocks are sorted by DLI, Portfolio 5 contains the stocks with highest bankruptcy risk. "High–low" is the return difference between the high and low bankruptcy risk portfolios. Significance at the 1 and 5% levels is indicated by ** and *, respectively.

whole study period, that is, from Jul. 1, 2007 to Dec. 31, 2010—indicating that the stocks did not perform well during this period of time. The difference in average returns between high DLI–sorted portfolios and low DLI–sorted portfolios is showing that the average returns for high DLI–sorted portfolios are lower than average returns for low DLI–sorted portfolios. However, the difference is statistically insignificant. There is no particular pattern observed in average returns of the bankruptcy risk–sorted portfolios according to the results presented in Table 11.1. We expect a monotonic pattern that displays the changes in the level of equity returns as the value of bankruptcy risk increases or decreases if there exists a relationship between bankruptcy risk and portfolio returns.

Table 11.2 presents average returns of quintile portfolios, which are sorted by the DLI bankruptcy risk measure while being controlled for the size factor

TABLE 11.2 Average Returns of DLI-Sorted Portfolios Controlled by Size

Average returns

DLI-sorted portfolios

Size	Low	2	3	4	High	High–low	t-values
1 Small	−0.07751	−0.02779	−0.07906	0.01357	−0.08318	−0.00567	−0.2677
2	−0.06496	−0.07021	−0.07671	−0.05695	−0.06859	−0.00363	−0.0974
3 Large	−0.06277	−0.10894	−0.07589	−0.06512	−0.03927	0.02350	1.428

Stocks are sorted into three portfolios by their levels of market capitalization (sizes). In each size-sorted portfolio, stocks are then sorted into five portfolios by their DLIs. Next, the average returns of DLI size–sorted portfolios are computed. When stocks are sorted by size, Portfolio 3 contains the biggest stocks. When stocks are sorted by DLI, Portfolio 5 contains the stocks with highest bankruptcy risk. "High–low" is the return difference between the high and low bankruptcy risk portfolios. Significance at the 1 and 5% levels is indicated by ** and *, respectively.

(small, medium, and large). Size is represented by the market capitalization of the stocks. Therefore, fifteen bankruptcy-size sorted portfolios are formed. Fourteen out of fifteen portfolios formed in this way have negative average returns, and there is no particular observable pattern both size and bankruptcy risk-wise. We expect a monotonic pattern that displays the changes in the level of equity returns as the value of bankruptcy risk increases or decreases. The average returns calculated for small and medium portfolios with low bankruptcy risk are greater than returns for small and medium portfolios with high bankruptcy risk. Thus, the high minus low average returns for these portfolios are negative. Though the size-returns dimension of these results is consistent with the existing literature—in which small-sized firms are widely known for greater levels of returns compared to large-sized firms—the findings are inconsistent with the risk-return relationship, wherein higher return is normally expected for higher risk.

Table 11.3 presents average portfolio returns of stocks which are formed by sorting stocks using the levels of their BM ratios (low, medium, and high) and quintile DLI bankruptcy risk measures. BM is calculated as the ratio of the book value of the stock divided by the market value of the stock for the purpose of convenience. Hence, 15 bankruptcy-BM portfolios are formed. The portfolio formed by taking the intersection of medium BM–ratio stocks and high bankruptcy risk (high DLI) stocks produce an interesting finding, whereby the difference in average returns between high and low portfolios in this category generate a value of 6.38%, which is statistically significant at 1% level of significance. However, the average returns for all 15 portfolios are negative. Furthermore, there is no particular pattern observed in average returns of the 15 bankruptcy risk–sorted portfolios which were formed by controlling for the BM factor. We expect a monotonic pattern that displays the changes in the level of equity returns as the value of bankruptcy risk increases or decreases.

TABLE 11.3 Average Returns of DLI-Sorted Portfolios Controlled by BM

Average returns

DLI-sorted portfolios

Size	Low	2	3	4	High	High–low	*t*-values
1 Small	−0.06794	−0.04014	−0.09414	−0.05854	−0.07791	−0.00996	−0.7566
2	−0.06524	−0.05655	−0.11871	−0.02531	−0.00140	−0.06383	5.8359**
3 Large	−0.06636	−0.04218	−0.04209	−0.03213	−0.08160	−0.01524	−0.9402

Stocks are sorted into three portfolios by levels of their BM ratios. In each BM-sorted portfolio, stocks are then sorted into five portfolios by their DLIs. Next, average returns of the DLI BM–sorted portfolios are computed. When stocks are sorted by BM, Portfolio 3 contains the stocks with the highest BM. When stocks are sorted by DLI, Portfolio 5 contains the stocks with the highest bankruptcy risk. "High–low" is the return difference between the high and low bankruptcy risk portfolios. Significance at the 1 and 5% levels is indicated by ** and *, respectively.

TABLE 11.4 Results of Multifactor Regression Analysis During Various Economic States

Market	CONST	EMKT	SIZE	BM	ADLI	R^2 (adj.)
Whole	0.04661*	0.09046*	−0.2549*	−0.00004*	0.0096	40.86%
Precrisis	0.0336	0.09472*	−3.092*	−0.000053*	0.28	47.32%
Crisis	0.0286	0.0529*	−1.541*	−0.000017*	−0.745*	26.24%
Postcrisis	−0.049*	0.11224*	0.1845*	−0.000052*	0.63*	35.64%

This table presents the results from the test of size and BM factors along with bankruptcy risk measures. EMKT refers to the excess return on the stock market portfolio over the risk-free rate. Size refers to returns on the zero-investment portfolio, which is long on stocks with a small market capitalization (size) and short on large-sized stocks. BM refers to the BM ratio of each stock. ADLI presents the average DLI, which is a simple average of the DLIs for all firms. The estimation period is from Jan. 1996 to Dec. 2007. Significance at the 1% level is indicated by *.

Table 11.4 presents results derived by applying regression analysis using the Fama and French (1993, 1996) factors augmented by the bankruptcy risk factor, that is, the ADLI (Vassalou and Xing, 2004). The coefficients for the market portfolio are significantly positive at the 1% level, whereas the coefficients for the size factor are significantly negative during the whole period, and the precrisis and crisis periods, but significantly positive during the postcrisis period. The coefficients for the BM factor are significantly negative during all periods of analysis. The ADLI factor is positively correlated to the stock return series during all four periods, except for the crisis period, but significantly positive only during the postcrisis period. If bankruptcy risk is clearly related to the level of equity returns consistent with the fundamental principle in finance which proclaims direct relationship between risk and return, we expect significantly positive coefficients for the ADLI factor during all periods of analysis.

The findings based on the portfolio analyses do not show an adequate level of support for the existence of a positive and significant relationship between bankruptcy risk and equity returns. The prevalence of below-zero values for portfolio returns of stocks sorted by the DLI measure indicate that these stocks have generally underperformed over the study period. Furthermore, a negative value for the difference between portfolios formed from stocks with a high DLI measure and portfolios formed from stocks with a low DLI measure is unexpected.

No monotonic and expected patterns of average portfolio returns were calculated for those stocks sorted by the DLI measure while being controlled for size and BM factors. According to Fama and French (1996), anomalous size and value premiums are expected to arise as a result of a financial distress factor. The DLI is expected to effectively stand as a proxy for bankruptcy risk, and hence we would expect the average portfolio returns to reveal a monotonic trend due to the fundamental relationship between risk and return, that is, the higher the risk, the higher would be the expected return. The expected relationship is only demonstrated by the medium portfolio sorted by the BM factor, whereby the difference between high BM–sorted and low BM–sorted portfolio return is positive and statistically significant at a 1% level.

The results of regression analysis show that the coefficient for the ADLI is negatively related to stock returns during the financial crisis period, unlike the positive and statistically significant coefficient during the postcrisis period. The coefficients for the ADLI during the whole period and the precrisis period are also consistent with the fundamental theory of finance at least in terms of direction.

5 CONCLUSIONS AND RECOMMENDATIONS

We tested the relationship between bankruptcy risk and equity returns by conducting portfolio and regression analyses for stocks listed on the HOSE in order to expand the boundaries of research in this topical area by including a frontier market. Expected monotonic patterns were observed neither from the average returns of stocks sorted by the DLI measure nor from the average returns of stocks sorted by the DLI and size factors, as well as by the DLI and BM factors. Further analysis was conducted by applying the Fama and French (1993, 1996) three factors augmented by the ADLI in cross-sectional settings. The regression analysis was conducted for the whole study period, as well as for the subperiods, that is, precrisis, crisis, and postcrisis. Except for the crisis subperiod, the coefficients for the ADLI factor indicate a direct relationship between bankruptcy risk and stock returns in the HOSE. The coefficient for the analysis conducted during the postcrisis period is also statistically significant. We recommend repeating the analysis using the Altman (1968) and Ohlson (1980) bankruptcy risk measures.

REFERENCES

Agarwal, V., Taffler, R., 2008. Does financial distress risk drive the momentum anomaly? Financ. Manage. 37 (3), 461–484.

Altman, E.I., 1968. Financial ratios, discriminant analysis and the prediction of corporate bankruptcy. J. Finance 23 (4), 589–609.

Altman, E.I., 1993. Corporate Financial Distress and Bankruptcy, second ed. Wiley, New York.

Amihud, Y., 2002. Illiquidity and stock returns: cross-section and time-series effects. J. Financ. Mark. 5 (1), 31–56.

Aretz, K., 2011. How Does a Firm's Default Risk Affect Its Expected Equity Return? Paper. Manchester Business School, Manchester, United Kingdom. Available from: http://ssrn.com/abstract=1569462

Aretz, K., Shackleton, M.B., 2011. Omitted debt risk, financial distress and the cross-section of expected equity returns. J. Bank. Finance 35 (5), 1213–1227.

Asquith, P., Gertner, R., Scharfstein, D., 1994. Anatomy of financial distress: an examination of junk-bond issuers. Quart. J. Econ. 109 (3), 625–658.

Avramov, D., Chordia, T., Jostova, G., Philipov, A., 2009. Credit ratings and the cross-section of stock returns. J. Financ. Mark. 12 (3), 469–499.

Bharath, S.T., Shumway, T., 2008. Forecasting default with the Merton distance to default model. Rev. Financ. Stud. 21 (3), 1339–1369.

Bystrom, H., Worasinchai, L., Chongsithipol, S., 2005. Default risk, systematic risk and Thai firms before, during and after the Asian crisis. Res. Int. Bus. Finance 19 (1), 95–110.

Campbell, J.Y., Hilscher, J., Szilagyi, J., 2008. In search of distress risk. J. Finance 63 (6), 2899–2939.

Carhart, M.M., 1997. On persistence in mutual fund performance. J. Finance 52 (1), 57–82.

Chava, S., Purnanandam, A., 2010. Is default risk negatively related to stock returns? Rev. Financ. Stud. 23 (6), 2523–2559.

Chen, J., Chollete, L., Ray, R., 2010. Financial distress and idiosyncratic volatility: an empirical investigation. J. Financ. Mark. 13 (2), 249–267.

Chen, C.-M., Lee, H.-H., 2013. Default risk, liquidity risk, and equity returns: evidence from the Taiwan market. Emerg. Mark. Finance Trade 49 (1), 101–129.

Chen, N.f., Zhang, F., 1998. Risk and return of value stocks. J. Bus. 71 (4), 501–535.

Da, Z., Gao, P., 2010. Clientele change, liquidity shock, and the return on financially distressed stocks. J. Financ. Quant. Anal. 45 (1), 27–48.

Das, S.B., Shrestha, O.L., 2009. Vietnam: further challenges in 2009. ASEAN Econ. Bull. 26 (1), 1–10.

Delianedis, G., Geske, R.L., 2003. Credit Risk and Risk Neutral Default Probabilities: Information About Rating Migrations and Defaults. Paper presented at the EFA 2003 Annual Conference.

Denis, D.J., Denis, D.K., 1995. Causes of financial distress following leveraged recapitalizations. J. Financ. Econ. 37 (2), 129–157.

Dichev, I.D., 1998. Is the risk of bankruptcy a systematic risk? J. Finance 53 (3), 1131.

Fama, E.F., French, K.R., 1993. Common risk factors in the returns on stocks and bonds. J. Financ. Econ. 33 (1), 3–56.

Fama, E.F., French, K.R., 1996. Multifactor explanations of asset pricing anomalies. J. Finance 51 (1), 55–84.

Fama, E.F., MacBeth, J.D., 1973. Risk, return, and equilibrium: empirical tests. J. Polit. Econ. 81 (3), 607–636.

Ferguson, M.F., Shockley, R.L., 2003. Equilibrium "Anomalies". J. Finance 58 (6), 2549–2580.

Garlappi, L., Shu, T., Yan, H., 2008. Default risk, shareholder advantage, and stock returns. Rev. Financ. Stud. 21 (6), 2743–2778.

Garlappi, L., Yan, H., 2011. Financial distress and the cross-section of equity returns. J. Finance 66 (3), 789–822.

Geske, R., 1977. The valuation of corporate liabilities as compound options. J. Financ. Quant. Anal. 12 (4), 541–552.

Geske, R., 1979. The valuation of compound options. J. Financ. Econ. 7 (1), 63.

Gharghori, P., Chan, H., Faff, R., 2007. Are the Fama-French factors proxying default risk? Aust. J. Manage. 32, 223–249.

Gharghori, P., Chan, H., Faff, R., 2009. Default risk and equity returns: Australian evidence. Pac. Basin Finance J. 17 (5), 580–593.

Griffin, J.M., Lemmon, M.L., 2002. Book-to-market equity, distress risk, and stock returns. J. Finance 57 (5), 2317–2336.

Gutiérrez, C.L., Olmo, B.T., Azofra, S.S., 2012. Firms' performance under different bankruptcy systems: a Europe–USA empirical analysis. Account. Finance 52 (3), 849–872.

Hillegeist, S.A., Keating, E.K., Cram, D.P., Lundstedt, K.G., 2004. Assessing the probability of bankruptcy. Rev. Account. Stud. 9 (1), 5–34.

HSBC, 2012. Asia-Pacific Equity Research, Vietnam. Available from: www.hsbcnet.com/nutshell/attachment/pdf/asia-pacific-vietnam.pdf

Hussain, S.I., Diacon, S., Toms, J.S., 2001. Equity Returns, Bankruptcy Risk and Asset Pricing Models. SSRN. Available from: http://ssrn.com/abstract=312980

Kim, S., 2013. What is behind the magic of O-Score? An alternative interpretation of Dichev's (1998) bankruptcy risk anomaly. Rev. Account. Stud. 18 (2), 291–323.

Lang, L.H.P., Stulz, R., 1992. Contagion and competitive intra-industry effects of bankruptcy announcements: an empirical analysis. J. Financ. Econ. 32 (1), 45–60.

Lin, Y.L., Chang, T.C., 2009. Modeling corporate credit risk with multiple debt issues. Manage. Rev. 28 (4), 43–68.

Lin, Y.-l., Chang, T.-c., Yeh, S.-j., 2012. Default risk and equity returns: evidence from the Taiwan equities market. Asia-Pac. Financ. Mark. 19 (2), 181–204.

Lo, A.W., MacKinlay, A.C., 1990. Data-snooping biases in tests of financial asset pricing models. Rev. Financ. Stud. 3 (3), 431–467.

Lomax, R.G., 2007. An Introduction to Statistical Concepts, second ed. Lawrence Erlbaum Associates, Mahwah, NJ.

Merton, R.C., 1974. On the pricing of corporate debt: the risk structure of interest rates. J. Finance 29 (2), 449–470.

Nguyen, H., Oates, G., Dunkley, M., 2014. A review of the establishment of the Stock Market in Vietnam-in relation to other transitional economies. Int. J. Econ. Finance 6 (10), 17–25.

Ohlson, J.A., 1980. Financial ratios and the probabilistic prediction of bankruptcy. J. Account. Res. 18 (1), 109–131.

Opler, T.C., Titman, S., 1994. Financial distress and corporate performance. J. Finance 49 (3), 1015–1040.

Pastor, L., Stambaugh, R.F., 2003. Liquidity risk and expected stock returns. J. Polit. Econ. 111 (3), 642–685.

Pincus, J., 2009. Vietnam: sustaining growth in difficult times. ASEAN Econ. Bull. 26 (1), 11–24.

Samad, F., Yusof, M.A.M., Shaharudin, R.S., 2009. Financial distress risk and stock returns: evidence from the Malaysian stock market. J. Int. Finance Econ. 9 (2), 19–38.

Shumway, T.G., 1996. The Premium for Default Risk in Stock Returns. Unpublished PhD thesis, University of Chicago, Chicago, IL.

Simlai, P., 2014. Firm characteristics, distress risk and average stock returns. Account. Res. J. 27 (2), 101–123.

Taffler, R.J., 1983. The assessment of company solvency and performance using a statistical model. Account. Bus. Res. 13 (52), 295–307.

Taffler, R.J., 1984. Empirical models for the monitoring of UK corporations. J. Bank. Financ. 8 (2), 199–227.

Vassalou, M., Xing, Y., 2004. Default risk in equity returns. J. Finance 59 (2), 831–868.

World Bank, 1992, Privatisation: eight lessons of experience. Available from: http://www.worldbank.org/html/prddr/outreach/or3.htm

Zhang, A.J., 2012. Distress risk premiums in expected stock and bond returns. J. Bank. Finance 36 (1), 225–238.

Chapter 12

Investors' Herding in Frontier Markets: Evidence From Mongolia

A. Erdenetsogt*, V. Kallinterakis**

*ABJYA LLC Brokerage Company, Ulaanbaatar, Mongolia; **University of Liverpool, Management School, Liverpool, United Kingdom

Chapter Outline

1 INTRODUCTION

Herd behavior as a trading practice has been studied in the context of both developed and emerging markets for different investor types (individual and institutional) over various periods of time. However, recent years have witnessed the advent of a new category of markets, which have been collectively dubbed "frontier," and for which very little is known concerning the behavior of their investors in general and herd behavior in particular. We aim at contributing in this area by investigating the presence of herding in the Mongolian Stock Exchange (MSE) to gauge whether it is significant, and whether its significance varies with a series of domestic market conditions related to market returns and market volume. What is more, we will investigate whether US market dynamics confer an effect over herding in Mongolia, and finally, we will test whether the 2008 global financial crisis has affected the presence of herding there.

In the wider context of behavioral finance, herding represents the tendency of individuals to mimic the actions of others following the interactive observation of each other's actions (Hirshleifer and Teoh, 2003). The practice of herding presupposes that individuals follow the behavior of others with disregard for their own private signals or the prevailing market fundamentals. Holmes et al. (2013)

Handbook of Frontier Markets. http://dx.doi.org/10.1016/B978-0-12-803776-8.00012-4

and Gavriilidis et al. (2013) have argued that such a practice could be driven by intent or could be completely spurious in nature. Intentional herding is assumed to be motivated by situations entailing asymmetry among market participants. Such asymmetry can be of an *informational* nature (Devenow and Welch, 1996; Teraji, 2003), in which case less informed investors choose to imitate the trades of better informed ones in order to free ride on the informational advantage of the latter. Widespread mimicry of this type can erode the value of the public pool of information, eventually leading to cascading phenomena (Banerjee, 1992; Bikhchandani et al., 1992), whereby people simply mimic the actions of others because they consider others to be informed. Another type of asymmetry prompting herding—specifically among investment professionals (eg, fund managers and financial analysts)—is *professional* (Scharfstein and Stein, 1990; Trueman, 1994; Welch, 2000; Clement and Tse, 2005). Fund managers of below-average skills can be expected to be tempted to mimic the trades of their better-able peers; the reason for this is that fund managers are normally assessed on a relative basis (vs each other), hence imitating "good" peers benefits "bad" managers, as it allows them to improve their professional image when their assessments are due.

While the above asymmetries of their trading environments can prompt investors to herd intentionally (with the purpose of extracting some benefit from herding), unintentional—also known as "spurious" (Bikhchandani and Sharma, 2001)—herding is normally the product of commonalities observed in the trading environment. *Relative homogeneity* among investors, for example, can lead them to exhibit similarities in their trades with no imitative or interactive observations being present. Such relative homogeneity can manifest itself through investors bearing similar educational backgrounds or professional qualifications, thus receiving similar signals or interpreting them similarly while being subject to a uniform regulatory environment (De Bondt and Teh, 1997; Wermers, 1999; Voronkova and Bohl, 2005). *Style investing* (Bennett et al., 2003) can also culminate in spurious herding; if several investors, for example, practice the same investment strategy, their trades can be expected to be correlated without, however, this being the result of direct imitation among them.

Herding was the focus of ample empirical research throughout the past two decades, with research indicating the presence of some patterns across

---

a. Earlier studies (Lakonishok et al., 1992; Grinblatt et al., 1995; Wermers, 1999) reported limited evidence of herding among US funds, with later studies (Sias, 2004; Choi and Sias, 2009) arguing in favor of extensive institutional herding in the US. Wylie (2005) reported limited evidence of herding among UK funds, while similar findings were reported for Germany (Walter and Weber, 2006). Conversely, Choe et al. (1999) documented severe herding among foreign funds in the Korean market prior to the outbreak of the Asian crisis, and Voronkova and Bohl (2005) presented evidence of widespread herding among Polish pension funds, while Holmes et al. (2013) showed that equity funds in Portugal not only herded persistently, but also intentionally. Chang et al. (2000) showed that herding was significant in the emerging, but not the developed, markets of their sample, while Hwang and Salmon (2004) documented significant herding for both the US and South Korea. Economou et al. (2011) found significant herding for southern European markets, controlling for the euro zone sovereign debt crisis, while research has also indicated that investors herd significantly in Asian markets in general (Chiang and Zheng, 2010), and China in particular (Tan et al., 2008; Chiang et al., 2010).

markets. Overall, funds in emerging markets tend to exhibit stronger herding behavior than that of their peers in developed ones,[a] while retail investors have also been found to herd significantly (Kumar and Lee, 2006; Dorn et al., 2008; Kumar, 2009). Herding further appears to be more pronounced for the largest (Wylie, 2005; Walter and Weber, 2006) and the smallest (Lakonishok et al., 1992; Wermers, 1999; Chang et al., 2000) capitalization stocks (ie, there exists a size effect in herding[b]) and has also been documented to exhibit industry effects (see eg, the studies by Gavriilidis et al., 2013; Gebka and Wohar, 2013).

Although researchers have investigated herding in several developed and emerging markets, there has been very little attention to the specific market segment of frontier markets. An interesting feature of frontier markets is the wide heterogeneity characterizing them; indeed, their ranks include high-income countries, such as Qatar and Bahrain, alongside several very poor sub-Saharan countries. Despite the lack of a uniform definition for frontier markets, they tend to entail one or more of the following features: nascent financial development; very small market capitalization and volume; and low but rising per capita income due to rapid economic growth, which is often stimulated by heavy reliance on natural resources (Umland, 2008; Behar and Hest, 2010; De Groot et al., 2012). Most of these markets have restrictions on the entry and trade of foreign investors; however, the relative illiquidity characterizing these markets is a key deterrent to foreign investors' entry even where such restrictions are absent. In general, frontier markets are treated as high-risk destinations, with many of them being in transitional stages of political and/or economic development, having moved since the 1990s either from central planning to market economies or from illiberal regimes to democratic systems.

The early levels of financial development in most frontier markets can be expected to be reflected through the inadequate institutional designs of their stock exchanges, and this is a fact capable of enhancing informational uncertainty in these markets, giving rise to herding among their investors. If investors in such a market feel concerned about the quality of public information or the enforceability of disclosure rules, it is reasonable to expect that they might start mimicking their peers if they consider their peers' actions to be informative. This can be expected to be particularly true for these markets' retail investors, who, due to the relatively young age of most frontier stock exchanges, lack investment experience. However, institutional investors (domestic as well as foreign ones) may

---

b. Large capitalization indices are often used as benchmarks in the investment industry, leading many fund managers to try to track the performance of these indices; to that end, many fund managers end up holding portfolios mimicking the composition of those indices. Thus fund managers may maintain similar portfolios overall; that is, ones dominated by large stocks. For more on this, see Walter and Weber (2006). Herding in small-capitalization stocks can be motivated by the enhanced risk in terms of information and liquidity surrounding them. These stocks tend to enjoy limited analyst coverage, thus maintaining higher levels of informational uncertainty, which in turn renders herding a viable strategy when trading them. What is more, the low volumes associated with these stocks render trading on them feasible only when investors' interest picks up on them (since this will make order execution possible), thus rendering herding more likely in the process.

also consider herding a viable strategy in order to counter this high information risk; what is more, herding by institutional investors may also be motivated by these markets' high liquidity risk, since (as mentioned earlier) frontier markets tend to be characterized by rather low capitalization and trading volume.[c]

This study contributes to research on herding in frontier markets by examining herding in the context of the MSE during the Dec. 1999–May 2012 period. Our study aims at addressing the following research questions:

- Do investors herd in Mongolia?
- Does herding in Mongolia remain significant, controlling for various domestic market variables (market returns; market volume)?
- Does herding in Mongolia remain significant when controlling for the dynamics of the US market?
- Does the significance of herding in Mongolia vary within as opposed to outside the recent 2008 global financial crisis?

In summary, we report that there is evidence supporting the presence of herding in the Mongolian market, irrespective of the market's performance (ie, positive/negative market returns), the level of volume, the day-to-day change in volume, and the US market's dynamics. Controlling for the size of market returns (the market's performance) presents us with a different pattern, as herding is found to be significant only for extreme positive and extreme negative market returns. Finally, investors in Mongolia herded outside, but not during, the period of the 2008 financial crisis.

The rest of our study is structured as follows: the next section provides a brief summary of the evolution of the MSE since the country's transition to a market economy in the 1990s, while Section 3 presents the data used in this study and the empirical design employed, along with some descriptive statistics. Section 4 discusses the results and provides some concluding remarks, coupled with the implications of our study for various market participants.

2 MONGOLIAN STOCK EXCHANGE: A BRIEF OVERVIEW

The MSE was established in 1991 as part of the government's privatization policy amid the country's transition from central planning to a market economy. A total of 96.1 million shares worth a total of $7 million from 475 state-owned enterprises were successfully placed on the primary market during the 1992–95 period; this led to the kick starting of secondary market operations, initially via 29 brokerage firms. By the end of 2011, total market capitalization had expanded to $1.7 billion; at the same time, the value of total transactions on the MSE in that year was $270 million, of which 68% related to government bonds, 31% to equities, and 1% to corporate bonds. Government bonds are not traded regularly; however, when their sale is announced, domestic investors (mainly

---

c. If most stocks are thinly traded, it is reasonable to expect fund managers to target the most liquid stocks in order to be able to sell them in the future with higher likelihood; if so, this suggests that funds in frontier markets would be expected to trade similar stocks—the largest.

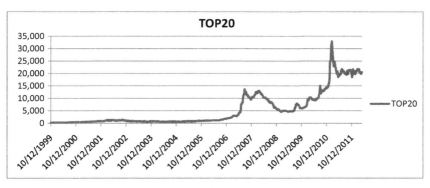

FIGURE 12.1   TOP20 index evolution (9/12/1999–8/5/2012).

commercial banks) dominate their subscriptions. Equity transactions grew by 75% in 2011, and their value is almost evenly split between local (52%) and foreign (48%) investors. Even though Mongolia has a bank-based financial system, its capital market has experienced rapid development over the years, supported by steady economic growth that is courtesy of the country's abundant natural resources and increasing foreign investments. In 2012 a total of 1,519 institutional[d] and 563,000 individual investors were registered with the Securities Clearing House and Central Depository, with the bulk of equity trading (70%) being in the hands of institutional investors.

The overall market is characterized by illiquidity and very high concentration. Assuming the 2011 total transaction value of $270 million above, and given that 31% of it is related to equities, this implies that equity trading had an annual value totaling around $84 million for a total of over 300 listed stocks, that is, the average annual value traded per stock was just under $250,000, a notably low value. Most listed firms on the MSE are actually very small in size[e] (as of May 2012, about 60% of the listed companies' market capitalization was less than $100,000, down from 90% in 1999), while the fact that the average monthly salary in Mongolia is around $150 obviously deters retail investors from substantially participating in their market's trading volume. On top of that, the brokerage industry is also concentrated, with the five largest brokerage firms making up around 71% of total equity transactions and 95% of government and corporate bond transactions.

Fig. 12.1 presents the evolution of the TOP-20 index (the market's main index, encompassing the twenty largest listed stocks) Dec. 9, 1999–May 8, 2012.

---

d. In the absence of domestic funds in Mongolia, the term "institutional investors" is used here to include domestic commercial banks and other companies, as well as foreign companies, banks, and institutional investors.

e. Most of these small companies do not even have a website or an information page and very few analysts follow them in the press. Moreover they also do not provide financial information regularly; in 2011, only 158 companies submitted their balance sheets to the MSE and only 155 companies announced shareholder meetings, out of a total of over 300 listed firms.

As Fig. 12.1 indicates, the index grew slowly during the years up to 2006 (from around 250 units in Dec. 1999 to around 1200 units in Aug. 2006), followed by a dramatic surge afterwards, which (with some fluctuations) was maintained until the spring of 2008 (index value then was around 13,000 units), when it started declining for about a year. By Mar. 2009 the index had begun rallying again, this time reaching a dazzling peak of almost 33,000 units in Feb. 2011, before crashing afterwards to around 20,000 units in May of that year and hovering around that value until the spring of 2012.

3 DATA AND METHODOLOGY

Linking herding to the relationship between the cross-sectional dispersion of equity returns and the return of the market was first empirically calibrated by Christie and Huang (1995), who proposed the following test to detect herding:

$$CSSD_t = \alpha_0 + \alpha_1 \, D_t^U + \alpha_2 \, D_t^L + \varepsilon_t \qquad (12.1)$$

In Eq. 12.1, D_t^U is a dummy variable that assumes a value of 1 if the market return rests in the extreme upper tail of the market-return distribution; otherwise it assumes a value of 0. Similarly, D_t^L is a dummy variable assuming the value of 1 if the market return rests in the extreme lower tail of the market-return distribution; otherwise it assumes the value of 0. $CSSD$ is the cross-sectional standard deviation, calculated as:

$$CSSD_t = \sqrt{\frac{\sum_{i=1}^{n}(r_{i,t} - r_{m,t})^2}{n-1}} \qquad (12.2)$$

In Eq. 12.2, $r_{i,t}$ is the return of security i in day t, $r_{m,t}$ is the equal-weighted return of the market in day t, and n represents the number of stocks traded on day t.

The rationale of the Christie and Huang (1995) model was rather straightforward. On the one hand, the presence of herding in the market would be expected to lead stocks to track the overall market's return, thus leading the cross-sectional dispersion of returns to decline; herding would also be expected to lead to abnormally high absolute market returns. On the other hand, given the differing sensitivity of each stock to market movements, an increase in a market's absolute returns would be expected to lead to a linear increase in the cross-sectional dispersion of returns. If herding is indeed present during extreme periods, the dummies' coefficients (α_1 and/or α_2) should be negative and significant, indicating that the CSSD decreases during extreme market periods.

The issue with the aforementioned approach is threefold. First of all, as Economou et al. (2011) noted, outliers can easily introduce biases in the calculated CSSD. Second, the employment of dummies to capture extreme market periods is rather crude (Hwang and Salmon, 2004), as it restricts the sample upon which herding is tested; herding, for example, may be present during periods of mild market returns and this is something the aforementioned model cannot identify. Third, there is little certainty that the relationship between the cross-sectional dispersion of returns and the absolute returns of the market will remain linear in the presence of herding, given evidence (Lux, 1995; Lux and Marchesi, 1999) indicating that herding is capable of introducing nonlinear dynamics in the market. To account for the aforementioned issues, Chang et al. (2000) proposed the following empirical design to test for the presence of herding:

$$CSAD_{m,t} = \alpha_0 + \alpha_1 \mid r_{m,t} \mid + \alpha_2 r_{m,t}^2 + \varepsilon_t \tag{12.3}$$

In Eq. 12.3, *CSAD* is the cross-sectional absolute deviation of returns, calculated as:

$$CSAD_t = \frac{1}{n} \sum_{i=1}^{N} \mid r_{i,t} - r_{m,t} \mid \tag{12.4}$$

The definition of the variables in Eqs. 12.3 and 12.4 is the same as in Eq. 12.2. The advantage of the Chang et al. (2000) approach over that of Christie and Huang (1995) is that it utilizes the entire market-return distribution (without resorting to dummies to arbitrarily identify extreme periods), while accounting for both the linear (through coefficient α_1) and the nonlinear (through coefficient α_2) part of the relationship between the CSAD and market returns. Rational asset-pricing assumptions would predict a positive value for α_1 and an insignificant value for α_2; however, in the presence of herding, we would expect α_2 to be significantly negative.

To test for the robustness of our findings from Eq. 12.3 under various domestic market conditions, we repeat our estimates, conditioning this equation upon the following two variables:

Market returns. We first reestimate Eq. 12.3 twice, once for days of positive market returns (upmarket days) and once for days of negative market returns (downmarket days)—the latter is proxied through $r_{m,t}$—as follows:

$$CSAD_{m,t}^{UP} = \alpha_0^{UP} + \alpha_1^{UP} \mid r_{m,t} \mid + \alpha_2^{UP} r_{m,t}^2 + \varepsilon_t \tag{12.5}$$

$$CSAD_{m,t}^{DOWN} = \alpha_0^{DOWN} + \alpha_1^{DOWN} \mid r_{m,t} \mid + \alpha_2^{DOWN} r_{m,t}^2 + \varepsilon_t \tag{12.6}$$

The superscripts ^{UP} and ^{DOWN} are used to denote that the equation is run for up and down market days, respectively. The purpose of this is to gauge whether herding varies in significance with the *sign of market returns*, given evidence from the literature suggesting that herding is more prevalent during periods of negative market performance.[f] This may be due to investors' greater risk aversion (selling with other investors when the market falls to minimize losses) or due to professional reasons ("bad" managers mimicking the trades of "good" managers during market slumps can argue that they made the correct investment decisions—essentially those they copied from their "good" peers—and blame the adverse market conditions for their losses). We also rank the values of $r_{m,t}$ in ascending order and split them into five quintiles (Q1–Q5),[g] each with an equal number of observations, and reestimate Eq. 12.3 for each of these quintiles; the rationale for this is to gauge whether herding significance, aside from the sign, also varies with the *size of market returns*.

Market volume. We calculate the total daily market volume as the sum of the daily volumes of trade of all actively traded stocks and reestimate Eq. 12.3 separately for days of increasing and days of decreasing market volume,[h] as follows:

$$CSAD_{m,t}^{\text{UPV}} = \alpha_0^{\text{UPV}} + \alpha_1^{\text{UPV}} \mid r_{m,t} \mid + \alpha_2^{\text{UPV}} r_{m,t}^2 + \varepsilon_t \tag{12.7}$$

$$CSAD_{m,t}^{\text{DOWNV}} = \alpha_0^{\text{DOWNV}} + \alpha_1^{\text{DOWNV}} \mid r_{m,t} \mid + \alpha_2^{\text{DOWNV}} r_{m,t}^2 + \varepsilon_t \tag{12.8}$$

The superscripts [UPV] and [DOWNV] are used to denote that the equation is run for increasing or decreasing market volume days, respectively. We also rank this daily aggregate volume series in ascending order, split it into five quintiles (Q1–Q5),[i] and estimate Eq. 12.3 for each quintile in order to gauge the impact of different volume sizes on herding.

In view of the established (Chiang and Zheng, 2010) impact of US market dynamics over herding worldwide, we employ the following specification to test whether such an impact holds for the Mongolian market:

$$CSAD_{m,t} = \alpha_0 + \alpha_1 \mid r_{m,t} \mid + \alpha_2 r_{m,t}^2 + \alpha_3 r_{\text{S\&P500},t}^2 + \varepsilon_t \tag{12.9}$$

In the previous equation, $r_{\text{S\&P500},t}^2$ is the squared daily return of the S&P 500 index, proxying here for US market dynamics. A significant value for α_3 would suggest a significant effect of the US market over the Mongolian CSAD; if the value of α_3 is both significant and negative, this would essentially suggest that the US market motivates herding in the Mongolian one.

---

f. Evidence on herding being stronger during downmarkets has been reported in Chang et al. (2000), Chen (2013), Gavriilidis et al. (2013), Holmes et al. (2013), Philippas et al. (2013) and Mobarek et al. (2014).

g. Q1 is the highest return quintile (the quintile with the most positive returns) and Q5 is the lowest return quintile (the quintile with the most negative returns).

h. That is, days for which volume has increased/decreased compared to the previous day.

i. Q1 is the highest volume quintile (the quintile with the highest volume values) and Q5 is the lowest volume quintile (the quintile with the lowest volume values).

TABLE 12.1 Descriptive Statistics

	Mean	Standard deviation
$CSAD_{m,t}$	0.0117	0.0150
$r_{m,t}$	0.0268	0.2948
Total number of stocks in sample	341	
Average total market trading volume	225,547	
Average daily number of actively traded stocks	18	

Notes: Table 12.1 presents some descriptive statistics on the variables used in the estimation of the Chang et al. (2000) model and its variants employed in this study. The variable $r_{m,t}$ refers to the Mongolian market's average return, calculated as the equal-weighted average of all listed stocks' returns; the variable $CSAD_{m,t}$ refers to the cross-sectional absolute deviation of returns for the Mongolian market. All returns are calculated as first differences of logarithmic prices. Total market-trading volume is calculated daily as the sum of the daily volumes of individual shares. All data were obtained from the MSE and cover the period Dec. 10, 1999–May 8, 2012.

Finally, we test for the presence of herding in Mongolia during and outside the 2008 global financial crisis period using the following specification:

$$CSAD_{m,t} = \alpha_0 + \alpha_1 D^{CRISIS} \mid r_{m,t} \mid + \alpha_2 (1 - D^{CRISIS}) \mid r_{m,t} \mid \\ + \alpha_3 D^{CRISIS} r_{m,t}^2 + \alpha_4 (1 - D^{CRISIS}) r_{m,t}^2 + \varepsilon_t \quad (12.10)$$

Here, D^{CRISIS} is a dummy that assumes a value of 1 from Aug. 1, 2008 onwards, and 0 otherwise.

Our data covers the period of Dec. 10, 1999–May 8, 2012 and includes daily closing prices and trading volumes of 341 stocks; all stocks—both active and dead/suspended—listed on the MSE during that period are included, thus mitigating the survivorship bias. Data were obtained from the MSE. Table 12.1 presents some descriptive statistics related to CSAD and $r_{m,t}$,[j] as well as the trading activity of the MSE. If there is one thing that is very clearly manifested through this table, it is the very small fraction of actively traded stocks on average: a mere 18, or 5.3% of the total number of listed stocks during that period (341). This is indicative of a market in which about one in 20 stocks trades actively on average every day, something in line with our expectations from frontier stock exchanges.

4   RESULTS AND CONCLUSION

Table 12.2 presents the estimated coefficients from Eq. 12.3, where herding is estimated unconditionally. As the results indicate, α_1 is significantly[k] positive (1.1905), denoting that the cross-sectional absolute deviation of returns bears a

---

j. Both the returns of the S&P 500 series mentioned previously as well as the returns of each individual stock used to calculate $r_{m,t}$ are calculated as the first difference of logarithmic closing prices.
k. For brevity reasons, statistical significance in this study will be defined at the 5% level (ie, any estimate whose p-value is less than 0.05 will be considered statistically significant).

TABLE 12.2 Estimates of Herding in Mongolia for the Full Sample Period
(Unconditional Herding)

α_0	α_1	α_2	Adjusted R^2
0.1107 (0.0000)	1.1905 (0.0000)	−0.2629 (0.0000)	0.5101

Notes: Table 12.2 presents the estimates from the following equation:

$$CSAD_{m,t} = \alpha_0 + \alpha_1 \left| r_{m,t} \right| + \alpha_2 r_{m,t}^2 + \varepsilon_t$$

All estimates' p-values are reported in parentheses. The variable $r_{m,t}$ refers to the Mongolian market's average return, calculated as the equal-weighted average of all listed stocks' returns; the variable $CSAD_{m,t}$ refers to the cross-sectional absolute deviation of returns for the Mongolian market. All returns are calculated as first differences of logarithmic prices.

linearly increasing relationship with average market returns, in line with rational asset-pricing predictions. The coefficient α_2 is significantly negative (-0.2629), suggesting that investors herd significantly in the Mongolian market.

Controlling for market returns confers little effect over our results, since, as Panel A in Table 12.3 shows, the values of α_2 from Eqs. 12.5 and 12.6 are significantly negative during both up- and downmarket days. Since $|\alpha_2^{UP}| > |\alpha_2^{DOWN}|$, this implies that herding is stronger during upmarket days compared to downmarket days, with the difference between the two estimates being statistically significant. The presence of stronger herding during up markets may be the product of investors' optimism, mainly on the part of unsophisticated/inexperienced investors (Grinblatt and Keloharju, 2001; Lamont and Thaler, 2003), whose effect can be quite substantial in frontier markets, as explained earlier. Panel B in Table 12.3 contains the results from estimating Eq. 12.3 for each of the return quintiles discussed in the previous section. As the results indicate, herding is significant only for Quintiles 1 and 5, thus showing that it is only during extreme positive or negative market days that herding appears significant.[1] The value of α_2 for Q1 (-0.6481) is—in absolute terms—larger than that for Q2 (-0.1962), in line with what we witnessed in Panel A about herding being stronger during up markets. Overall, results from Table 12.3 suggest that more than the sign, it is the size of market returns that is crucial for the identification of herding in Mongolia. The fact that investors in that market herd when returns grow extreme can perhaps be attributed either to uncertainty (the case of extreme negative market returns prompting investors to liquidate their positions to mitigate further losses) or euphoria (the case of extreme positive market returns driving investors to jump onto the bandwagon).

Controlling for market volume demonstrates that herding is significant irrespective of whether volume increases or decreases at the aggregate level; as Table 12.4 (Panel A) shows, the values of α_2 from Eqs. 12.7 and 12.8 are significantly negative during both increasing and decreasing volume days. Since

---

1. We also observe that α_2 is significant at the 10% level (p-value = 0.0862).

TABLE 12.3 Estimates of Herding in Mongolia for the Full Sample Period (Conditioning Herding Upon Market Returns)

Panel A: herding conditioned upon the sign of market returns (positive/negative)

	α_0^{UP}	α_1^{UP}	α_2^{UP}	Adjusted R^2
Up markets	0.0679 (0.0000)	1.5743 (0.0000)	−0.6842 (0.0000)	0.5415
	α_0^{DOWN}	α_1^{DOWN}	α_2^{DOWN}	Adjusted R^2
Down markets	0.1306 (0.0000)	1.2083 (0.0000)	−0.2508 (0.0000)	0.5112
F_1 (test statistic) $(\alpha_1^{UP} = \alpha_1^{DOWN})$	117.9750 (0.0000)			
F_2 (test statistic) $(\alpha_2^{UP} = \alpha_2^{DOWN})$	1573.1214 (0.0000)			

Panel B: herding conditioned upon the size of market returns (Q1–Q5)

	α_0	α_1	α_2	Adjusted R^2
Q1	0.0730 (0.0188)	1.5268 (0.0000)	−0.6481 (0.0000)	0.3461
Q2	−0.0677 (0.1859)	5.2133 (0.0009)	−17.5771 (0.0862)	0.1448
Q3	0.0875 (0.0000)	−1.8094 (0.3208)	67.4903 (0.2598)	−0.0010
Q4	0.0750 (0.0000)	2.6716 (0.0745)	−26.9633 (0.2944)	0.0124
Q5	0.2467 (0.0000)	0.9362 (0.0000)	−0.1962 (0.0000)	0.3458

Notes: Table 12.3, Panel A presents the estimates from the following equations:

$$CSAD_{m,t} = \alpha_0^{UP} + \alpha_1^{UP} \mid r_{m,t} \mid + \alpha_2^{UP} r_{m,t}^2 + \varepsilon_t$$
$$CSAD_{m,t} = \alpha_0^{DOWN} + \alpha_1^{DOWN} \mid r_{m,t} \mid + \alpha_2^{DOWN} r_{m,t}^2 + \varepsilon_t$$

The superscript ^{UP} (^{DOWN}) is used to denote that the equation is run for up (down) market days. F_1 and F_2 statistics test, respectively, the following null hypotheses: $\alpha_1^{UP} = \alpha_1^{DOWN}$ and $\alpha_2^{UP} = \alpha_2^{DOWN}$. Table 12.3, Panel B presents the estimates from the following equation:

$$CSAD_{m,t} = \alpha_0 + \alpha_1 \mid r_{m,t} \mid + \alpha_2 r_{m,t}^2 + \varepsilon_t$$

The equation is estimated for Quintiles 1–5, which are constructed as follows: having calculated $r_{m,t}$, we rank its values in ascending order and split them into five quintiles (Q1–Q5) of equal number of observations.
All estimates' p-values are reported in parentheses. The variable $r_{m,t}$ refers to the Mongolian market's average return, calculated as the equal-weighted average of all listed stocks' returns; the variable $CSAD_{m,t}$ refers to the cross-sectional absolute deviation of returns for the Mongolian market. All returns are calculated as first differences of logarithmic prices.

TABLE 12.4 Estimates of Herding in Mongolia for the Full Sample Period (Conditioning Herding Upon Market Volume)

Panel A: herding conditioned upon the day-to-day change of market volume (increasing/decreasing)

	α_0^{UP}	α_1^{UP}	α_2^{UP}	Adjusted R^2
Up-volume markets	0.1120 (0.0000)	1.2745 (0.0000)	−0.2567 (0.0000)	0.5498
	α_0^{DOWN}	α_1^{DOWN}	α_2^{DOWN}	Adjusted R^2
Down-volume markets	0.0806 (0.0000)	1.4708 (0.0000)	−0.6190 (0.0000)	0.5124
F_1 (test statistic) $(\alpha_1^{UPV} = \alpha_1^{DOWNV})$		19.5318 (0.0000)		
F_2 (test statistic) $(\alpha_2^{UPV} = \alpha_2^{DOWNV})$		110.1038 (0.0000)		

Panel B: herding conditioned upon the size of market volume (Q1–Q5)

	α_0	α_1	α_2	Adjusted R^2
Q1	0.0290 (0.0000)	1.6046 (0.0000)	−0.5811 (0.0000)	0.6489
Q2	0.0710 (0.0000)	1.4615 (0.0000)	−0.2796 (0.0000)	0.6458
Q3	0.0787 (0.0000)	1.7696 (0.0000)	−0.9144 (0.0000)	0.5907
Q4	0.1513 (0.0000)	1.3753 (0.0000)	−0.4272 (0.0000)	0.5181
Q5	0.1265 (0.0000)	1.2958 (0.0000)	−0.5601 (0.0000)	0.3815

Notes: Table 12.4, Panel A presents the estimates from the following equations:

$$CSAD_{m,t} = \alpha_0^{UPV} + \alpha_1^{UPV} \left| r_{m,t} \right| + \alpha_2^{UPV} r_{m,t}^2 + \varepsilon_t$$

$$CSAD_{m,t} = \alpha_0^{DOWNV} + \alpha_1^{DOWNV} \left| r_{m,t} \right| + \alpha_2^{DOWNV} r_{m,t}^2 + \varepsilon_t$$

The superscript ^{UPV} $(^{DOWNV})$ is used to denote that the equation is run for increasing (decreasing) market volume days. The F_1 and F_2 statistics test, respectively, the following null hypotheses: $\alpha_1^{UPV} = \alpha_1^{DOWNV}$ and $\alpha_2^{UPV} = \alpha_2^{DOWNV}$
Table 12.4, Panel B presents the estimates from the following equation:

$$CSAD_{m,t} = \alpha_0 + \alpha_1 \left| r_{m,t} \right| + \alpha_2 r_{m,t}^2 + \varepsilon_t$$

The equation is estimated for Quintiles 1–5, which are constructed as follows: having calculated the aggregate (total) daily market volume by summing up the trading volumes of all listed stocks every day, we rank its values in ascending order and split them into five quintiles (Q1–Q5) of equal number of observations.
All estimates' p-values are reported in parentheses. The variable $r_{m,t}$ refers to the Mongolian market's average return, calculated as the equal-weighted average of all listed stocks' returns; the variable $CSAD_{m,t}$ refers to the cross-sectional absolute deviation of returns for the Mongolian market. All returns are calculated as first differences of logarithmic prices.

TABLE 12.5 Estimates of Herding in Mongolia for the Full Sample Period (Controlling for the Effect of US Market Dynamics)

α_0	α_1	α_2	α_3	Adjusted R^2
0.1107	1,907	−0.2630	−0.3754	0.5102
(0.0000)	(0.0000)	(0.0000)	(0.1843)	

Notes: Table 12.5 presents the estimates from the following equation:

$$CSAD_{m,t} = \alpha_0 + \alpha_1 |r_{m,t}| + \alpha_2 r_{m,t}^2 + \alpha_3 r_{S\&P500,t}^2 + \varepsilon_t$$

All estimates' p-values are reported in parentheses. The variable $r_{m,t}$ refers to the Mongolian market's average return, calculated as the equal-weighted average of all listed stocks' returns; the variable $r_{S\&P500,t}$ is the daily return of the S&P 500 index; the variable $CSAD_{m,t}$ refers to the cross-sectional absolute deviation of returns for the Mongolian market. All returns are calculated as first differences of logarithmic prices.

$|\alpha_2^{\text{UPV}}| < |\alpha_2^{\text{DOWNV}}|$, this implies that herding is stronger during decreasing, compared to increasing, volume days, with the difference between the two estimates being statistically significant. This is possibly the result of investors following each other into and out of the same stocks with greater propensity when the overall volume in the market is lower, as a means of avoiding liquidity risk. When viewing the estimates from the volume quintiles (Panel B in Table 12.4), we notice that α_2 is significantly negative for all of them, thus again confirming that herding significance in Mongolia is not a function of the market's total trading activity. This is a very interesting finding and is probably due to the fact that volume in that market is not just low, but also concentrated among very few stocks. With the average daily fraction of actively traded stocks hovering around 5% (around 18 stocks; Table 12.1), it is highly likely that investors in that market trade not whenever they want, but whenever the number of investors willing to trade is sufficient enough to allow order execution. Under such circumstances, herding should come as no surprise, given that the already limited volume is allocated among a very small number of stocks.[m]

Table 12.5 presents the results from Eq. 12.9, from which it is obvious that the US market dynamics bear no effect whatsoever over the Mongolian market. The coefficient α_3 is insignificant, whereas α_2 remains significant and negative, confirming the robustly significant herding in that market. Given that Mongolia is a very small frontier market with limited integration to the global financial

---

m. It is interesting to note here that the average number (18) of actively traded stocks every day is less than the number of stocks comprising Mongolia's main index (TOP-20). The fact that the 20 blue chips of a market with well over 300 listed stocks cannot be traded every day with 100% probability helps illustrate the illiquidity issue plaguing frontier markets—and facing international investors. For more on this, see the Meketa Investment Group (2010) white paper on frontier markets, in which the authors admit that it takes around 2 weeks to build a position in a frontier market—and even longer to exit that position.

TABLE 12.6 Estimates of Herding in Mongolia for the Full Sample Period (Controlling for the Effect of the 2008 Crisis)

α_0	α_1	α_2	α_3	α_4	Adjusted R^2
0.1485	−2.4681	1.1144	3.9059	−0.2458	0.5409
(0.0000)	(0.0000)	(0.0000)	(0.0000)	(0.0000)	

Notes: Table 12.6 presents the estimates from the following equation:

$$CSAD_{m,t} = \alpha_0 + \alpha_1 D^{CRISIS} |r_{m,t}| + \alpha_2(1-D^{CRISIS}) |r_{m,t}| + \alpha_3 D^{CRISIS} r_{m,t}^2 + \alpha_4(1-D^{CRISIS}) r_{m,t}^2 + \varepsilon_t$$

All estimates' p-values are reported in parentheses. The variable $r_{m,t}$ refers to the Mongolian market's average return, calculated as the equal-weighted average of all listed stocks' returns; D^{CRISIS} is a dummy assuming the value of 1 from Aug. 2008 onwards and 0 otherwise; the variable $CSAD_{m,t}$ refers to the cross-sectional absolute deviation of returns for the Mongolian market. All returns are calculated as first differences of logarithmic prices.

system, it should perhaps come as little surprise that the US market's dynamics do not impact upon it.[n]

The 2008 financial crisis does indeed appear to have affected herding in Mongolia, as Table 12.6 indicates; the estimates from Eq. 12.10 show that, whereas α_4 is significantly negative (suggesting the presence of herding pre-crisis), α_3 is significantly positive (ie, herding was absent during the crisis). We experimented with alternative windows to proxy for the 2008 financial crisis (eg, Aug.–Dec. 2008), with results in all cases being similar to those of Table 12.6, thus confirming that investors in Mongolia herded outside, but not during, the 2008 financial crisis. As a result, the onset of this crisis appears to have dampened the herding tendencies of investors in Mongolia, possibly due to the new fundamentals revealed by the crisis, leading investors to trade based on them and away from the precrisis consensus (Borio, 2008).[o]

In summary, we report that there is evidence supporting the presence of herding in the Mongolian market, irrespective of the sign of the market's performance (ie, positive/negative market returns), the level of volume, the day-to-day change in volume, and the US market's dynamics. Controlling for the size of the market's performance presents us with a different pattern, as herding is found to be significant only for extreme positive and extreme negative market

---

n. Eq. 12.9 here was estimated assuming contemporaneous market returns from Mongolia and the United States. However, Mongolia and the United States are not located in the same time zone; hence, to account for the effect of time difference, we reestimated equation 12.9 using lagged US market returns (ie, the lagged returns of the S&P 500 index). Results are qualitatively very similar, again indicating the presence of significant herding in Mongolia and the absence of any effect of the US market over the Mongolian market.

o. We experimented with alternative windows to proxy for the 2008 financial crisis (eg, Aug.–Dec. 2008). Results in all cases were similar to those reported here; namely, that herding in Mongolia is significant (insignificant) outside (during) the crisis.

returns. Finally, investors in Mongolia herded outside, but not during, the 2008 financial crisis.

The evidence presented in this study is of key relevance to the investment community, in particular for those investors with a global outlook. Frontier markets exhibit little correlation with developed ones, and this naturally implies diversification benefits from investing in them. However, as the case of Mongolia indicates, foreign investors targeting these markets should be ready to embrace their liquidity risk and—most importantly—face extensive herding. Although the presence of herding should theoretically provide foreign investors with arbitrage opportunities (in the spirit of De Long et al., 1990), whether they will be able to take advantage of them in view of such low trading activity remains an open question.

Our results are also of particular interest to regulators and policy makers in Mongolia, as they denote a market where investors resort to imitation in their trades to a great extent, and this needs to be addressed in order to avoid the potential side effects of herding, including a rise in systemic risk and price destabilization. Although no explicit "counter-herding" measures have been prescribed in the relevant literature, one way to discourage herding among investors would be to improve the transparency of the market environment. Key to this attempt is the promotion of investors' financial education, so that they are able to gain better understanding of the investment process and rely less on the influence of their peers. Improving disclosure rules (such as, eg, raising the reporting standards demanded in terms of financial statements, auditing, and insider dealing/trading) and their enforceability (via the stringent monitoring of their implementation) could lead to an increase in the quality of the market's informational environment, allowing investors to place greater faith in public information. To this end, regulators should also focus on undertaking measures aimed at encouraging foreign investors' participation, since the sophistication of overseas investors would help boost the market's informational efficiency—and liquidity. Given the aforementioned issue of liquidity risk facing overseas traders, the introduction of indexed products, such as exchange-traded funds and index futures/options, would allow foreign investors to enter the market with greater ease, without having to search through a universe of hundreds of listed stocks with little volume or analysts' coverage. Although the aforementioned observations are related to Mongolia given the focus of our study, they contain useful implications for the rest of the frontier markets, which—to varying degrees—are facing similar issues in their evolutionary process.

REFERENCES

Banerjee, A.V., 1992. A simple model of herd behavior. Quart. J. Econ. 107, 797–817.

Behar, G., Hest, S., 2010. Topics in Frontier Markets: Aligning Portfolios With the Global Economy. Research Report. Northern Trust.

Bennett, J.R., Sias, R., Starks, L., 2003. Greener pastures and the impact of dynamic institutional preferences. Rev. Financ. Stud. 16, 1203–1238.

Bikhchandani, S., Hirshleifer, D., Welch, I., 1992. A theory of fads, fashion, custom, and cultural change as informational cascades. J. Polit. Econ. 100, 992–1026.

Bikhchandani S., Sharma, S., 2001. Herd Behavior in Financial Markets. IMF Staff Papers 473, pp. 279–310.

Borio, C., 2008. The financial turmoil of 2007-?: a preliminary assessment and some policy considerations. Working Paper 251. Bank for International Settlements, Monetary and Economic Department, Basel, Switzerland.

Chang, E.C., Cheng, J.W., Khorana, A., 2000. An examination of herd behavior in equity markets: an international perspective. J. Bank. Finance 24, 1651–1679.

Chen, T., 2013. Do investors herd in global stock markets? J. Behav. Finance 14, 230–239.

Chiang, T.C., Li, J., Tan, L., 2010. Empirical investigation of herding behavior in Chinese stock markets: evidence from quantile regression analysis. Global Finance J. 21, 111–124.

Chiang, T.C., Zheng, D., 2010. An empirical analysis of herd behavior in global stock markets. J. Bank. Finance 34, 1911–1921.

Choe, H., Kho, B.-C., Stulz, R.M., 1999. Do foreign investors destabilize stock markets? The Korean experience in 1997. J. Financ. Econ. 54, 227–264.

Choi, N., Sias, R.W., 2009. Institutional industry herding. J. Financ. Econ. 94, 469–491.

Christie, W.G., Huang, R.D., 1995. Following the pied piper: do individual returns herd around the market? Financ. Analysts J. 51, 31–37.

Clement, M.B., Tse, S.Y., 2005. Financial analyst characteristics and herding behavior in forecasting. J. Finance 60, 307–341.

De Bondt, W.F.M., Teh, L.L., 1997. Herding behavior and stock returns: an exploratory investigation. Swiss J. Econ. Stat. 133, 293–324.

De Groot, W., Pang, J., Swinkels, L., 2012. The cross-section of stock returns in frontier emerging markets. J. Empir. Finance 19, 796–818.

De Long, J.B., Shleifer, A., Summers, L.H., Waldmann, R.J., 1990. Positive feedback investment strategies and destabilizing rational speculation. J. Finance 45, 379–395.

Devenow, A., Welch, I., 1996. Rational herding in financial economics. Eur. Econ. Rev. 40, 603–615.

Dorn, D., Huberman, G., Sengmueller, P., 2008. Correlated trading and returns. J. Finance 63, 885–920.

Economou, F., Kostakis, A., Philippas, N., 2011. Cross-country effects in herding behavior: evidence from four south European markets. J. Int. Financ. Mark. Inst. Money 21, 443–460.

Gavriilidis, K., Kallinterakis, V., Leite-Ferreira, M.P., 2013. Institutional industry herding: intentional or spurious? J. Int. Financ. Mark. Inst. Money 26, 192–214.

Gebka, B., Wohar, M.E., 2013. International herding: does it differ across sectors? J. Int. Financ. Mark. Inst. Money 23, 55–84.

Grinblatt, M., Keloharju, M., 2001. What makes investors trade? J. Finance 56, 589–616.

Grinblatt, M., Titman, S., Wermers, R., 1995. Momentum investment strategies, portfolio performance, and herding: a study of mutual fund behavior. Am. Econ. Rev. 85, 1088–1105.

Hirshleifer, D., Teoh, S.T., 2003. Herd behavior and cascading in capital markets: a review and synthesis. Eur. Financ. Manage. 9, 25–66.

Holmes, P.R., Kallinterakis, V., Leite-Ferreira, M.P., 2013. Herding in a concentrated market: a question of intent. Eur. Financ. Manage. 19, 497–520.

Hwang, S., Salmon, M., 2004. Market stress and herding. J. Empir. Finance 11, 585–616.

Kumar, A., 2009. Dynamic style preferences of individual investors and stock returns. J. Financ. Quant. Anal. 44, 607–640.

Kumar, A., Lee, C.M.C., 2006. Retail investor sentiment and return comovements. J. Finance 61, 2451–2486.

Lakonishok, J., Shleifer, A., Vishny, R., 1992. The impact of institutional trading on stock prices. J. Financ. Econ. 32, 23–43.

Lamont, O.A., Thaler, R.H., 2003. Can the market add and subtract? Mispricing in tech stock carve-outs. J. Polit. Econ. 111, 227–268.

Lux, T., 1995. Herd behavior, bubbles and crashes. Econ. J. 105, 881–896.

Lux, T., Marchesi, M., 1999. Scaling and criticality in a stochastic multi-agent model of a financial market. Nature 397, 498–500.

Meketa Investment Group, 2010. Frontier Markets. White Paper.

Mobarek, A., Mollah, S., Keasey, K., 2014. A cross-country analysis of herd behavior in europe. J. Int. Financ. Mark. Inst. Money 32, 107–127.

Philippas, N., Economou, F., Babalos, V., Kostakis, A., 2013. Herding behavior in REITS: novel tests and the role of financial crisis. Int. Rev. Financ. Anal. 29, 166–174.

Scharfstein, D.S., Stein, J.C., 1990. Herd behavior and investment. Am. Econ. Rev. 80, 465–479.

Sias, R.W., 2004. Institutional herding. Rev. Financ. Stud. 17, 165–206.

Tan, L., Chiang, T.C., Mason, J.R., Nelling, E., 2008. Herding behavior in Chinese stock markets: an examination of A and B shares. Pac. Basin Finance J. 16, 61–77.

Teraji, S., 2003. Herd behavior and the quality of opinions. J. Socio Econ. 32 (6), 661–673.

Trueman, B., 1994. Analyst forecasts and herding behavior. Rev. Financ. Stud. 7 (1), 97–124.

Umland, K., 2008. Frontier Markets: New Investment Opportunities and Risks. Working Paper. Institute of Fiduciary Education.

Voronkova, S., Bohl, M.T., 2005. Institutional traders' behavior in an emerging stock market: empirical evidence on Polish pension fund investors. J. Bus. Finance Account. 32, 1537–1560.

Walter, A., Weber, M., 2006. Herding in the German mutual fund industry. Eur. Financ. Manage. 12, 375–406.

Welch, I., 2000. Herding among security analysts. J. Financ. Econ. 58, 369–396.

Wermers, R., 1999. Mutual fund herding and the impact on stock prices. J. Finance 54, 581–622.

Wylie, S., 2005. Fund manager herding: a test of the accuracy of empirical results using U.K. data. J. Bus. 78, 381–403.

Chapter 13

Structural Breaks, Efficiency, and Volatility: An Empirical Investigation of Southeast Asian Frontier Markets

P. Andrikopoulos*, D.L.T. Anh**, M.K. Newaz*

*Coventry Business School, Coventry, United Kingdom; **School of Banking and Finance, National Economics University, Hanoi, Vietnam

Chapter Outline

1 INTRODUCTION

This study investigates stock price behavior of the Southeast Asian (SEA) frontier markets of Vietnam, Laos, and Cambodia. To do so, we are testing stock market efficiency of these markets, and especially the extent to which stock prices follow a random walk. The contribution of this paper is therefore twofold. First, from an academic perspective, it complements prior evidence on the issue of informational efficiency for these markets using out-of-sample data, especially covering the period following the 2007–09 global financial crisis. Second, from a professional investment viewpoint, assessing the level of stock market efficiency of these countries allows better understanding of their economies and of the soundness of their financial systems, as in the presence of market efficiency stock market prices should accurately reflect companies'

Handbook of Frontier Markets. http://dx.doi.org/10.1016/B978-0-12-803776-8.00013-6

actual performance. Furthermore, the understanding of how securities markets perform allows relevant governments to adopt appropriate policies to stimulate growth and capital investments, leading to the improvement of the country's economic environment.

In brief, using alternative testing procedures, our results suggest that all three markets under examination are currently weak-form inefficient. Furthermore, the degree of informational inefficiency (or not) varies on the basis of the methodology adopted and the frequency of the examined stock return series. For example, although all markets appear to be influenced by long memory dynamics and symmetric volatility, testing for randomness in the return series indicate a marginal degree of efficiency in the case of the newer stock markets of Cambodia and Laos.

The rest of the chapter is structured as follows. Section 2 presents a review of key prior literature on market efficiency and empirical evidence from emerging and frontier markets. Data and methodology are provided in Section 3; Section 4 reports the findings of the empirical tests. Finally, conclusions are drawn in Section 5.

2 LITERATURE REVIEW

According to the efficient market hypothesis (Fama, 1965), stock returns in a weak-form efficient market follow a random walk model, meaning that they are unpredictable and uncorrelated to past price information. Although the concept of random walk was first mentioned in a study by Pearson (1905), it was Maurice Kendall (1953) who demonstrated these mathematical properties in a number of stock market indices. Subsequent studies (Cowles, 1960; Osborne, 1962) further confirm these findings, leading to the development of the *random walk hypothesis* (Samuelson, 1965) that emphasizes the impossibility of investors forecasting stocks' rates of return in a market with fully available information. Working intensely on the concept of stock market efficiency since the early 1960s, Eugene Fama introduced this groundbreaking hypothesis in his seminal paper in 1970, by defining the term "efficient market" as "a market at which prices always "fully reflect" available information" (Fama, 1970, p. 383). Therefore, under this condition all new information should be instantly reflected in stock prices.

The concept of market efficiency has been extensively investigated in different countries under different market conditions and alternative test procedures. Nonetheless, findings are not always conclusive. For example, in a study of the US market over the period 1963–73, Sharma and Kennedy (1977) show that US equity prices follow a random walk, evidence that was further corroborated by Szakmary et al. (1999) for NASDAQ. On the other hand, by running specification tests using weekly return series for the period 1962–85, Lo and MacKinlay (1988) produce evidence of serial correlation during the whole period and within all subperiods. These findings corroborated an earlier study by Fama and French (1987), who reject the presence of random walks in the US stock market during the period 1926–40. In a subsequent study, Fama and French (1988) suggest that equity returns can be predicted from their factor components.

Outside the US market, and especially for Europe, Worthington and Higgs (2004) report the existence of randomness in the stock markets of Germany, Ireland, Portugal, Sweden, and the United Kingdom but not in the markets of Austria, Belgium, Denmark, Finland, France, Greece, Italy, Netherlands, Norway, Spain, and Switzerland. These findings are also supported by later studies (Borges, 2011; Mishra, 2012; Smith, 2012).

In a follow-up study, Worthington and Higgs (2005) confirm that the markets of Hong Kong, New Zealand, and Japan are weak-form efficient, but their findings are refuted by Suleman et al. (2010), who show that all stock prices of Hong Kong, Singapore, Japan, and Australia do not follow a random walk. Similar findings are documented for all the emerging markets of Pakistan, India, Sri Lanka, China, Indonesia, Malaysia, Philippine, Thailand, and Bangladesh (Suleman et al. 2010; Nisar and Hanif, 2012). Finally, a similar picture is reported for the emerging and frontier markets of Latin America, with all equity markets of Argentina, Brazil, Chile, Columbia, Mexico, Peru, and Venezuela being weak-form inefficient (Worthington and Higgs, 2003; Righi and Ceretta, 2011).

In contrast to other emerging and frontier markets in various regions, research on randomness in equity prices of SEA frontier markets is limited. Notably, there are no prior studies in the literature on weak-form efficiency in the Laos and Cambodia stock markets. Regarding Vietnam, there are few studies that provide consistent results. In an examination of the market index (VN Index) and five individual stocks listed on Ho Chi Minh Stock Exchange (HOSE) for the period 2000–04, Loc (2006) provides evidence of positive autocorrelation in the share price, hence rejecting the random walk hypothesis. This evidence was further corroborated by later studies using a number of testing methodologies and time periods (Guidi and Gupta, 2011; Aumeboonsuke, 2012; Vinh and Thao, 2013). Nonetheless, in a more recent study by Phan and Zhou (2014) the authors conclude that the Vietnamese stock market does not follow a random walk during the whole period, but in contrast to prior studies, there is a significant improvement in efficiency during the period 2009–13. Our study adds to this literature by examining the newly formed markets of Laos and Cambodia for the first time.

3 DATA AND METHODOLOGY

3.1 The Data

All three markets under examination are relatively new. Vietnam's stock market officially came into operation on Jul. 20, 2000, with the establishment of the HOSE, while 5 years later the Hanoi Stock Exchange (HNX) was inaugurated. The indicators for stock price volatility in the HOSE and the HNX are the VN Index and the HNX Index, respectively. While the VN Index is a collection of large-cap listed companies with more than VND 120 billion of equity capital, the HNX Index consists of medium and small-cap companies with a minimum capital of VND 30 billion. Over the years, the Vietnamese stock market has seen a remarkable surge of new companies listed, mostly driven by the simple registration procedures and the small capital requirements. The number of listed companies in the market has risen from only 5 equities in 2000 to 1240 securities at the end of 2014. In contrast, the other two markets are considerably smaller in size and in magnitude. The Laos Securities Exchange (LSX) was the first capital market in the Lao PDR and officially opened in Oct. 2010. Although the purpose of opening the LSX was to attract foreign capital to fund the long-term capital requirements of local companies, 5 years after its establishment there are still only four securities listed on the market. Finally, one of the most recent and smallest markets in the SEA region is the Cambodia Securities Exchange (CSX), which was launched in Apr. 2012 with only two securities [Phnom Penh Water Supply Authority and Grand Twins International (Cambodia) Plc] that were listed at the end of 2014. For the purposes of this study, we use daily and weekly prices of the four market indices (VN, HNX, LSX, and CSX) from the period of their establishment up to the end of 2014. All price series are obtained from Thomson's Datastream database. As shown in Table 13.1, the study analyzes a total of 3432 (VN Index) and 2194 (HNX Index) daily observations for the Vietnamese market. As regards the stock markets of Laos and Cambodia, our time series for returns is considerably smaller, consisting of 983 and 616 daily observations, respectively, covering the period from Jan. 2011 to Dec. 2014 (Laos) and Mar. 2012 to Dec. 2014 (Cambodia).

Daily and weekly returns are estimated as

$$R_t = \log p_t - \log p_{t-1} = \log \frac{p_t}{p_{t-1}} \tag{13.1}$$

TABLE 13.1 Summary of Sample Size for the Index of Each SEA Frontier Stock Market

Index	Frontier market	Sample period	No. of daily observations	No. of weekly observations
VN Index	Vietnam	Jul. 28, 2000 to Dec. 31, 2014	3432	741
HNX Index	Vietnam	Jan. 4, 2006 to Dec. 31, 2014	2194	462
LSX Index	Lao PDR	Jan. 12, 2011 to Dec. 31, 2014	983	170
CSX Index	Cambodia	Apr. 19, 2012 to Dec. 31, 2014	616	141

where R_t is the index return at time t, while p_t and p_{t-1} are the closing prices at time t and $t-1$, respectively.

3.2   Tests for Randomness

In line with prior literature, we examine randomness in stock returns using a series of alternative test procedures, such as the presence of unit roots, the autocorrelation Q-statistic test, the runs test, and the variance ratio test. In detail, we employ an ADF unit root test to check whether the return series are stationary or not.[a] By subtracting Y_{t-1} from both sides of a first-order autoregressive model we have:

$$Y_t - Y_{t-1} = \rho Y_{t-1} - Y_{t-1} + u_t = (\rho - 1)Y_{t-1} + u_t \qquad (13.2)$$

If $\Delta Y_t = Y_t - Y_{t-1}$ and $\delta = \rho - 1$, we then have $\Delta Y_t = \delta Y_{t-1} + u_t$, where $\delta = 0$ and $\rho = 1$ indicates that the time series follow a random walk. Alternatively, if $\delta < 0$ or $\rho < 1$, the time series is stationary. Statistical significance is measured using the *tau statistic*, as suggested by Dickey and Fuller (1981), for testing for the existence of a unit root.[b] The presence of autocorrelation is then tested by calculating the correlation coefficient of current stock returns and their lags using the mathematical notation:

$$\rho_k = \frac{\sum_{t=1}^{N-k}(r_t - \overline{r})(r_{t+k} - \overline{r})}{\sum_{t=1}^{N}(r_t - \overline{r})^2} \qquad (13.3)$$

where ρ_k is the correlation coefficient of the stock return at lag k, N is the number of observations, r_t is the stock return in period t, r_{t+k} is the stock return in period $t + k$, and $\overline{r}$ is the mean of the stock returns. If ρ_k is approximately equal to zero, stock returns are normally distributed with a zero mean, indicating independence in the time series for returns. Alternatively, if ρ_k is different from zero, there is a relation between current stock returns and lagged returns, violating the conditions of the random walk hypothesis. To test the joint hypothesis that all correlation coefficients equal zero, we

---

a. A time series process is characterized as stationary if its mean and variance are constant and the covariance between two different time periods depends upon the lag between them. The mean and variance of the time series are estimated as $(Y_t) = \mu$ and $Var(Y_t) = E(Y_t-\mu)^2$, respectively. The covariance of Y values at times t and $t + k$ is estimated as $\gamma_k = E[(Y_t-\mu)(Y_{t+k}-\mu)]$, while a unit root is defined by using the first-order autoregressive model of $Y_t = \rho Y_{t-1} + \mu_t$ with $(-1 \le \rho \le 1)$. If $\rho = 1$, there is a unit root in the time series process.

b. Dickey and Fuller (1981) show that the coefficient after transformation to δ does not follow a normal distribution when the size of the sample is large. This results in conventional *t-statistic* results being erroneous.

employ the Ljung–Box portmanteau statistic Q (Ljung and Box, 1978), calculated as

$$Q_{LB} = N(N+2)\sum_{j=1}^{k} \frac{p_j^2}{N-j} \tag{13.4}$$

where Q_{LB} is the Ljung–Box statistic Q following a chi-square distribution, p_j is the correlation coefficient term at lag jth, and N is the number of observations. If the value of Q exceeds the value of *chi-square* for k degrees of freedom, there should be at least one p_j *value* indifferent to zero, rejecting the null hypothesis of randomness in the time series.

The last two alternative test procedures that we employ for the assessment of randomness are the runs test (Bradley, 1968) and the variance ratio (Lo and MacKinlay, 1988; Wright, 2000). The former test is a nonparametric test for examining possible autocorrelation. In general, a run is a sequence of the same movements or signs. By counting the number of runs in the selected sample the existence of autocorrelation can be detected, with a large number of runs indicating a random walk. Under the null hypothesis that stock returns are independent, the number of runs should follow a normal distribution with mean and variance calculated as

$$E(R) = \frac{2n_1 n_2}{n_1 + n_2} + 1 \tag{13.5}$$

$$\sigma_R^2 = \frac{2n_1 n_2 (2n_1 n_2 - n_1 - n_2)}{(n_1 + n_2)^2 (n_1 + n_2 - 1)} \tag{13.6}$$

where $E(R)$ is the statistical mean, σ_R^2 is the variance of runs, n_1 is the number of returns with a positive sign (+), n_2 is the number of returns with a negative sign (−), and R is the number of runs. In line with prior literature, we assume $n_1 > 10$ and $n_2 > 10$. Following the estimation of the mean and variance of the runs, our decision rule is to accept the null hypothesis (at a 95% level of significance) if the number of runs (R) stays within the interval of $Prob[E(R) - 1.96\sigma R \leq R \leq E(R) + 1.96\sigma R] = 0.95$.

The variance ratio test is employed to assess whether or not stock market returns are independently and identically distributed with a constant mean and finite variance.[c] If the stock returns follow a random walk, the variance of the kth *difference* at a specific period would be equal to the k time variance of that period's first difference. We calculate the variance ratio at lag k by multiplying

---

c. This will indicate that the variance is a linear function of the relevant holding periods.

$1/k$ by the ratio of variance at the kth difference to the variance at the first difference, algebraically formulated as

$$V(k) = \frac{1}{k} \times [var(x_t + x_{t-1} + \ldots + x_{t-k+1})] / [var(x_t)]$$

$$= \frac{1}{k} \times [var(y_t + y_{t-k})] / [var(y_t - y_{t-1})] \qquad (13.7)$$

$$= 1 + 2\sum_{i=1}^{k-1} \frac{(k-i)}{k} \times \rho_i$$

where ρ_i is the autocorrelation coefficient at lag i for x_t. Thus, if stock returns follow a random walk, ρ_i must equal 0 and the variance ratio for any lag must be equal to 1. We test the null hypothesis of H_0: $\rho_i = 0$ for every value of i by considering the following equation:

$$VR(k) = [\hat{\sigma}^2(k)] / [\hat{\sigma}^2(1)] \qquad (13.8)$$

where $\hat{\sigma}^2(1)$ is the variance of the return in period 1 and $\hat{\sigma}^2(k)$ is the variance of the return in *period k*. We estimate $\hat{\sigma}^2(1)$ as:

$$\hat{\sigma}^2(1) = (T-1)^{-1} \sum_{t=1}^{T} (x_t + \hat{\mu})^2 = (T-1)^{-1} \sum_{t=1}^{T} (y_t - y_{t-1} - \hat{\mu})^2 \quad (13.9)$$

where $\hat{\mu}$ is the sample mean ($\hat{\mu} = T^{-1} \sum_{t=1}^{T} x_t$). Similarly, we calculate $\hat{\sigma}^2(k)$ for overlapping long-horizon returns as:

$$\hat{\sigma}^2(k) = m^{-1} \sum_{t=1}^{T} (x_t + x_{t-1} + \ldots + x_{t-k+1} - k\hat{\mu})^2$$

$$= m^{-1} \sum_{t=1}^{T} (y_t - y_{t-k} - k\hat{\mu})^2 \qquad (13.10)$$

where $m = (T - k + 1)(1 - kT^{-1})$.

To account for possible deviation of stock market returns from the normal distribution assumption, we adopt the rank-based statistical procedure introduced by Wright (2000),[d] with the rank-based statistic calculated as:

$$R_1(k) = \left(\frac{\frac{1}{Tk}\sum_{t=k}^{T}(r_{1t} + \cdots + r_{1t-k+1})^2}{\frac{1}{T}\sum_{t=1}^{T}r_{1t}^2} - 1 \right) \times \varnothing(k)^{-1/2} \qquad (13.11)$$

---

d. Wright (2000) has extended the Lo and MacKinlay test (1988) by introducing rank differences, so that the variance ratio test could be applied in cases in which the distribution of returns is not normally distributed.

$$R_2(k) = \left(\frac{\dfrac{1}{Tk}\sum_{t=k}^{T}(r_{2t}+\cdots+r_{2t-k+1})^2}{\dfrac{1}{T}\sum_{t=1}^{T}r_{2t}^2} - 1 \right) \times \varnothing(k)^{-1/2} \qquad (13.12)$$

where $r_{1t} = \dfrac{r(y_t)-(T+1)/2}{\sqrt{(T-1)(T+1)/12}}$, $r_{2t} = \varnothing^{-1}[r(y_t)/(T+1)]$, T is the number of observations of first differences of y_t, $\varnothing_t$ is the asymptotic variance, $r(y_t)$ is the rank of y_t, and $\varnothing^{-1}$ is the inverse of the $\varnothing$-standard normal cumulative distribution function.

3.3 Structural Breaks, Long Memory Dynamics, and Test for Volatility

SEA frontier markets have been subjected to major political and economic policy changes in the past few decades. In order to identify these structural changes (eg, such as the tax reforms, banking sector reforms, crisis and regime shifts), we use the multiple structural break model of Bai and Perron (1998, 2003). They consider the following multiple linear regression with m breaks:

$$y_t = X_\beta' + Z_t'\delta_j + \varepsilon_t \qquad t = T_{j-1}+1,\ldots,T_j \quad \text{for } j = 1,\ldots,m+1 \quad (13.13)$$

In this model y_t is the dependent variable, x_t ($p*1$) and z_t ($q*1$) are vectors of covariates, β and δ_j are corresponding vectors of coefficients, and ϵ_t is an error term. The break points ($T_1 \ldots T_m$) are treated as unknown, while, conventionally, $T_0 = 0$ and $T_{m+1} = T$. As β is not subject to structural change whilst δ_j is, the model is a pure structural break model when $p = 0$ and a partial structural break model when otherwise. For a specific set of m breakpoints we have $\{T\}_m = (T_1,\ldots,T_m)$, where the sum of squared residuals is minimized by

$$S(\beta,\delta|\{T\}) = \sum_{j=0}^{m}\left\{\sum_{t=T_j}^{T_{j+1}-1} y_t - X_t'\beta - Z_t'\delta_j\right\} \qquad (13.14)$$

To obtain estimates of (β, δ), we use a least squares regression. In order to select the number of breaks, the Bai–Perron testing procedure first considers the F-statistic to test the null of no structural breaks ($m = 0$). It then considers the UDmax and WDmax tests, both testing the null of no structural breaks against an unknown number of breaks, given some upper bound M. We adopt the most general specification (eg, trimming point 0.15 and a maximum of three breaks) to allow for all features that the Bai–Perron model offers.

Due to globalization, policy makers in multinational and transnational companies face new challenges in managing their global financial resources so that countries can take full advantage of these opportunities while reducing the potential risk. To tackle this issue, volatility forecast plays a vital role. We applied GARCH (generalized autoregressive conditional heteroscedasticity) family models to investigate the volatility of SEA frontier markets. The volatility modeling process generates mean and conditional variance equations for the series being investigated. Generally, a standard ARIMA (autoregressive integrated moving average) model or a regression model is used to generate the mean equation for the analysis of volatility. Whichever method is used, it includes a term (ε_t) to represent error or residual over time. In this study, we apply an ARIMA model to generate the mean equation for the adopted volatility model. The ARIMA(p, q) process considers linear models of the form shown in Eq. 13.15:

$$Z_t = \mu + \theta_1 Z_{t-1} + \theta_2 Z_{t-2} + \ldots + \theta_p Z_{t-p} - \varphi_1 \varepsilon_{t-1} \\ - \varphi_2 \varepsilon_{t-2} - \ldots - \varphi_q \varepsilon_{t-q} + \varepsilon_t \tag{13.15}$$

where ε_t, ε_{t-1},... are present and past forecast errors, and μ, θ_1, θ_2, ..., φ_1, φ_2... are parameters to be estimated. The notation Z_t is used for the stationary data at time t. When differencing has been used to generate stationarity, the model is said to be *integrated* and is written as ARIMA(p, d, q), in which p and q represent the order of the autoregressive terms and moving average, respectively. The middle parameter d is simply the number of times that the series needs to be differenced before trend stationarity is achieved.

Engle (1982) presents a basis for formal theory of volatility modeling. At the root of volatility modeling is the distinction between conditional (stochastic) and unconditional (constant) errors. The *conditional variance* of the error terms is denoted by σ_t^2 and is time varying. Volatility modeling involves adding a variance equation to the original mean equation, which in turn models the conditional variance. Engle (1982) introduces the ARCH (autoregressive conditional heteroscedasticity) model. The ARCH(p) models conditional variance as

$$\sigma_t^2 = \omega + \sum_{t=1}^{p} \alpha_i \varepsilon_{t-i}^2 \tag{13.16}$$

where $\omega > 0$ and $\alpha_i > 0$.

Many modifications of the basic ARCH(p) model have been developed over time. One of the most widely used volatility models is the GARCH (referenced earlier) developed by Bollerslev (1986). Unlike ARCH, it models the conditional variance as

$$\sigma_t^2 = \omega + \sum_{t=1}^{p} \alpha_i \varepsilon_{t-i}^2 + \sum_{j=1}^{q} \beta_j \sigma_{t-j}^2 \tag{13.17}$$

where $\omega > 0$ and $\alpha_i \geq 0$ and $\beta_j \geq 0$ to eliminate the possibility of a negative variance.[e] The GARCH specification in Eq. 13.17 allows for the conditional variance to be dependent on past information. It is explained by past short-run (α_i) shocks represented by the lag of the squared residuals (ε_i^2) obtained from the mean equation and by past longer-run (β_j) conditional variances (σ_j^2). This is referred to as the GARCH(p, q) process. In GARCH models, $\sum_{i=1}^{p} \alpha_i + \sum_{j=1}^{q} \beta_j$ should be less than unity to satisfy stationarity conditions. If β_j are all zero, the equation reduces to the ARCH(p) process described in Eq. 13.16—the earliest form of the volatility model developed by Engle (1982). It is rare for the order (p, q) of a GARCH model to be high, while a GARCH(p, q) can be extended to allow for the inclusion of exogenous or predetermined regressors (z) in the variance equation, mathematically notated as

$$\sigma_t^2 = \omega + \sum_{t=1}^{p} \alpha_i \varepsilon_{t-i}^2 + \sum_{j=1}^{q} \beta_j \sigma_{t-j}^2 + Z_t' \pi \qquad (13.18)$$

The EGARCH(p, q) model (exponential GARCH) of Nelson (1991) can also accommodate asymmetric effects, therefore solving important shortcomings of hitherto symmetric models. This is done by specifying the conditional variance in the manner:

$$\log_e(\sigma_t^2) = \omega + \sum_{i=1}^{p} (\alpha_i \left| \frac{\varepsilon_{t-i}}{\sigma_{t-i}} \right| + \gamma \frac{\varepsilon_{t-i}}{\sigma_{t-i}}) + \sum_{j=1}^{q} \beta_j \log_e(\sigma_{t-j}^2) \quad (13.19)$$

Note that the left-hand side of equation is the logarithm of the conditional variance. This indicates that the leverage effect is exponential; hence, guaranteeing that the forecasts of the conditional variance will be nonnegative. One reason that EGARCH has been popular in financial applications is that the conditional variance, σ_t^2, is an exponential function, thereby removing the need for a constraint in the parameters to ensure a positive conditional variance (Longmore and Robinson, 2005). The model also permits asymmetries via the γ term. The presence of leverage effects is tested by the hypothesis that $\gamma < 0$. If $\gamma < 0$, negative shocks increase volatility, while if $\gamma = 0$, the model is symmetric. Two additional advantages from using the EGARCH family models are that the values of p and q are very rarely high, and that these models tend to be parsimonious. Furthermore, before generating an optimal model for our return series, we also test possible misspecification using the Ljung–Box Q-statistic. The Q-squared (Q_{SQ}) statistic is employed to check the ARCH in the residuals,

---

e. Nonetheless, prior literature suggests that in practice this $\beta_j \geq 0$ constraint can be overrestrictive (Nelson and Cao, 1992; Tsai and Chan, 2008).

while if more than one volatility model with significant parameters is found, the model with the maximum *log likelihood* (LL) criterion is selected as the most optimum.

4   EMPIRICAL RESULTS

4.1   Results From Randomness Tests

Panels A and B in Table 13.2 present the results of the augmented Dickey–Fuller (ADF) unit root examination using three alternative specifications: (1) with intercept, (2) with intercept as a linear trend, and (3) without intercept.

According to the results, we have to reject the existence of a unit root for all specifications and for all daily (Panel A) and weekly (Panel B) return time series. The values of ρ are all consistently negative and significant at the 1% level, irrespective of the model applied. On this basis, we have to reject the null hypothesis of stock market returns following a random walk for the countries of Vietnam, Laos, and Cambodia. This finding corroborates prior literature on the informational efficiency of the Vietnamese market and it is very similar to the ADF unit root test results of Guidi and Gupta (2011). A very similar picture is portrayed by the autocorrelation tests presented in Table 13.3. As mentioned in the previous section, the autocorrelation Q-statistic test of Ljung and Box

TABLE 13.2 Unit Root Test Results for the Index of Each SEA Frontier Stock Market

Panel A: daily returns				
Index	VN Index	HNX Index	LSX Index	CSX Index
Intercept	−21.103***	−38.943***	−16.344***	−23.526***
Intercept, linear trend	−21.126***	−38.949***	−16.337***	−23.568***
None	−21.076***	−38.952***	−16.346***	−23.311***
Panel B: weekly returns				
Index	VN Index	HNX Index	LSX Index	CSX Index
Intercept	−15.347***	−17.273***	−10.354***	−11.071***
Intercept, linear trend	−15.367***	−17.281***	−10.363***	−11.010***
None	−15.316***	−17.292***	−10.402***	−10.930***

Notes: The VN Index represents large-cap stocks (>VND 120 billion), while the HNX Index consists of medium and small-cap companies listed on the Vietnamese stock exchange. The LSX Index and the CSX Index are the composite indices of the Laos Securities Exchange and the Cambodia Stock Exchange, respectively. *** signifies the rejection of the null hypothesis of having a unit root at a 1% level of significance.

TABLE 13.3 Autocorrelation Test Results for Daily SEA Frontier Stock Market Indices

Panel A: daily returns								
Index	VN Index		HNX Index		LSX Index		CSX Index	
Lag	AC	Q-stat	AC	Q-stat	AC	Q-stat	AC	Q-stat
1	0.30	308.51***	0.18	72.16***	0.18	30.80***	0.056	1.92
3	0.02	318.70***	0.04	77.36***	0.04	39.85***	0.017	3.52
5	0.12	395.94***	0.07	101.01***	0.09	52.20***	0.071	6.84
7	0.05	430.39***	−0.01	101.30***	0.02	58.16***	0.003	7.35
9	0.03	436.23***	0.05	109.57***	0.04	68.00***	−0.009	7.52
11	0.05	451.55***	0.02	110.60***	0.03	70.09***	0.082	12.62
13	0.04	458.43***	0.04	115.25***	−0.03	70.99***	0.024	18.42
15	0.06	487.26***	0.01	120.39***	−0.08	80.12***	0.055	20.35
Panel B: weekly returns								
Index	VN Index		HNX Index		LSX Index		CSX Index	
Lag	AC	Q-stat	AC	Q-stat	AC	Q-stat	AC	Q-stat
1	0.16	20.07***	0.21	20.61***	0.35	21.32***	0.16	3.86**
3	0.11	47.56***	0.09	28.63***	−0.08	22.57***	−0.03	4.56
5	0.16	71.56***	0.06	36.77***	−0.09	24.53***	0.11	6.82
7	0.07	76.29***	0.06	39.47***	0.01	25.19***	−0.04	7.05
9	0.06	78.91***	0.03	39.82***	0.03	25.53***	−0.08	8.18
11	0.00	79.14***	−0.01	39.89***	0.07	26.90***	0.02	8.53
13	−0.02	80.12***	−0.04	41.81***	0.04	28.47***	−0.06	11.04
15	−0.11	88.63***	−0.07	45.34***	−0.04	28.92**	0.02	11.29

Notes: The VN Index represents large-cap stocks (>VND 120 billion), while the HNX Index consists of medium and small-cap companies listed on the Vietnamese stock exchange. The LSX Index and the CSX Index are the composite indices of the Laos Securities Exchange and the Cambodia Stock Exchange, respectively. *** and ** signify the rejection of the null hypothesis of no autocorrelation at the 1 and 5% levels of significance, respectively.

(1978) examines the null hypothesis of no autocorrelation among return series. According to both Panels A and B, there is a statistically significant autocorrelation for all return series and up to 15 lags for the stock markets of Vietnam and Laos, but surprisingly not for the case of Cambodia. The strongest autocorrelation (AC) is observed in the case of the VN Index for both the daily and weekly returns (for lag = 1, AC values of 0.30 and 0.16 with a Q-statistic of 308.51 and 20.07, respectively). All values are significant at the 1% level.

In contrast, apart from the case of the weekly return series for the Cambodian market using one lag, which is positive and significant at the 5% level, all other values are statistically insignificant for all selected lags. This finding suggests that the Cambodian stock market is weak-form efficient. However, the presence of randomness and informational efficiency in this case should always be assumed with caution, as the market is relatively new with a limited number of securities listed on it.

Overall, these results are consistent to those presented in Aumeboonsuke (2012), Vinh and Thao (2013), and Phan and Zhou (2014) for the Vietnamese stock market, and the first-ever empirical evidence reported for the stock markets of Cambodia and Laos.

Testing possible randomness using the nonparametric runs test and the variance ratio further strengthens these findings. According to Panel A in Table 13.4, the runs test report z-statistics of -11.984 and -4.677 for the two indices of VN and HNX are statistically significant at the 1% level for the daily data. The negative values in this case indicate that daily upward (downward) return movements are followed by subsequent upward (downward) movements, violating the assumption of randomness. Hence, the results suggest that the Vietnamese stock market exhibits clear evidence of autocorrelation, rejecting the null hypothesis of randomness, and further corroborating the prior findings of Guidi and Gupta (2011), Vinh and Thao (2013), and

TABLE 13.4 Runs Test Results for Daily SEA Frontier Stock Market Indices

Panel A: daily returns				
Index	VN Index	HNX Index	LSX Index	CSX Index
E(R)	1715.765	1097.482	473.230	259.699
var(R)	856.7655	547.981	226.839	108.577
StDev(R)	29.271	23.409	15.061	10.420
Z-stat	−11.984***	−4.677***	−0.480	−2.178**
Panel B: weekly returns				
Index	VN Index	HNX Index	LSX Index	CSX Index
E(R)	370.903	231.499	82.657	68.586
var(R)	184.652	114.998	39.203	32.376
StDev(R)	13.589	10.724	6.261	5.689
Z-stat	−4.703***	−3.497***	−0.424	−0.454

Notes: The VN Index represents large-cap stocks (>VND 120 billion), while the HNX Index consists of medium and small-cap companies listed in the Vietnamese stock exchange. The LSX Index and the CSX Index are the composite indices of the Laos Securities Exchange and the Cambodia Stock Exchange, respectively. *** signifies the rejection of the null hypothesis of no autocorrelation at a 1% level of significance.

TABLE 13.5 Variance Ratio Test Results for Daily SEA Frontier Stock Market Indices

Panel A: daily returns				
Index	VN Index	HNX Index	LSX Index	CSX Index
Ranks	19.032***	17.737***	14.533***	11.606***
Rank scores	20.559***	18.765***	14.701***	12.246***
Signs	12.943***	12.944***	10.313***	8.297
Panel B: weekly returns				
Index	VN Index	HNX Index	LSX Index	CSX Index
Ranks	11.636***	8.484***	5.574***	4.953***
Rank scores	12.708***	8.889***	5.421***	5.467***
Signs	7.982***	5.875***	4.320***	2.799**

Notes: The VN Index represents large-cap stocks (>VND 120 billion), while the HNX Index consists of medium and small-cap companies listed in the Vietnamese stock exchange. The LSX Index and the CSX Index are the composite indices of the Laos Securities Exchange and the Cambodia Stock Exchange, respectively. *** and ** signify the rejection of the null hypothesis of random walk at the 1 and 5% levels of significance, respectively.

Phan and Zhou (2014). On the contrary, the results for Laos suggest no presence of autocorrelation in the return series (z-statistic of -0.480), while for the Cambodian stock market the null hypothesis of a random walk is rejected at the 5% level (z-statistic of -2.178).

In the case of the weekly data (Panel B), the runs test further confirms the previous findings with a z-statistic of -4.703 and -3.497 for the Vietnamese market. Nonetheless, the test fails to reject the null hypothesis of a random walk in the cases of Laos and the Cambodian stock market indices.

To shed more light into these surprising findings, we assess their robustness using the more rigorous variance ratio test of Wright (2000). All results for daily and weekly returns for the four indices are presented in Table 13.5 in Panels A and B, respectively.

According to Panel A, all rank-based test results and rank scores are positive and statistically significant at the 1% level, rejecting the null hypothesis of weak-form efficiency in the examined SEA frontier markets. As regards the sign-based results, the tests on the daily returns further confirm what had been reported previously in the case of Vietnam and Laos, but provide conflicting results from the Cambodian stock market, as the S-value reported is 8.297, which is insignificant in statistical terms.

The results from the examined weekly returns presented in Panel B further confirm the case of informational inefficiency for the examined markets, in which the null hypothesis of random walks is rejected in both the rank-based and sign-based tests. All values are positive and significant at the 1% level. This conclusion supports prior findings in the literature (Guidi and Gupta, 2011; Vinh and Thao, 2013; Phan and Zhou, 2014).

4.2 Results on Structural Breaks and Volatility

The results from Bai and Perron (2003) structural break test for the daily and weekly return series are presented in Table 13.6. Three break dates are identified in each series, and these are statistically significant.[f] These break dates are then incorporated as variance regressors in the modeling of stock market volatility.

The mean and conditional variance equations for daily and weekly series are presented in Tables 13.7 and 13.8, respectively. The choice of ARIMA for the data is based on the model (1) being parsimonious, (2) having significant parameters, (3) having errors that are white noise, and (4) reporting a minimum

TABLE 13.6 Bai-Perron (2003) Structural Break Test Results

Panel A: daily returns

		Global L breaks versus none			
Country	F-stat and scaled F-stat	Weighted F-stat	*UD*Max stat**	*WD*Max stat**	Break dates
VN Index	6.635	6.635	6.635	7.594	Oct. 27, 2003
	4.983	5.922			Feb. 28, 2007
	5.275	7.594			Jan. 4, 2009
HNX Index	5.592	5.592	5.592	5.849	Oct. 17, 2007
	4.816	5.723			Feb. 25, 2009
	4.063	5.849			Jun. 17, 2010
LSX Index	0.352	0.352	3.467	4.291	Feb. 20, 2012
	3.467	4.120			Jan. 22, 2013
	2.981	4.291			Jan. 27, 2014
CSX Index	1.857	1.857	4.073	3.427	Mar. 16, 2012
	3.427	4.072			Mar. 22, 2013
	2.031	2.924			Feb. 08, 2014

(Continued)

f. These breaks in the return time series are triggered by important political or economic events in the countries in question. For example, the structural break of Oct. 27, 2003, for Vietnam follows immediately after the signing of an agreement between the governments of Vietnam and the United States to start—for the first time since the end of the Vietnam War—commercial flights between the two countries. Meanwhile, the break of Feb. 28, 2007, is driven by the Vietnamese government's announcement to invest US$33bn in infrastructure projects, for example, a high-speed rail link between Hanoi and Ho Chi Minh City.

TABLE 13.6 Bai-Perron (2003) Structural Break Test Results (*cont.*)

Panel B: weekly returns					
	Global L breaks versus none				
Country	F-stat and scaled F-stat	Weighted F-stat	*UD*Max stat**	*WD*Max stat**	Break dates
VN Index	5.972 4.185 4.17	5.972 4.973 5.927	5.972	5.972	Oct. 17, 2003 Jan. 19, 2007 Mar. 6, 2009
HNX Index	4.434 3.956 3.215	4.434 4.698 4.629	4.434	4.698	Oct. 19, 2007 Feb. 13, 2009 Jun. 18, 2010
LSX Index	0.684 3.147 4.164	0.685 3.740 5.995	4.164	5.995	Jul. 22, 2011 Jan. 27, 2012 Feb. 1, 2013
CSX Index	2.922 3.049 2.002	2.922 3.623 2.882	3.049	3.624	Sep. 21, 2012 May 31, 2013 Oct. 25, 2013

Notes: The VN Index represents large-cap stocks (>VND 120 billion), while the HNX Index consists of medium and small-cap companies listed in the Vietnamese stock exchange. The LSX Index and the CSX Index are the composite indices of the Laos Securities Exchange and the Cambodia Stock Exchange, respectively.

TABLE 13.7 Results From Volatility Models (Daily Returns)

Panel A: mean equation			
VN Index	**AR(1)**	**MA(1)**	**MA(2)**
ARIMA(1,0,2) (0,0,0) *z*-statistic	0.994 452.870***	−0.745 −39.238***	−0.237 −12.513***
HNX Index	AR(1)	MA(1)	
ARIMA(1,0,1) (0,0,0) *z*-statistic	0.669 5.989***	−0.556 −4.648***	
LSX Index	AR(1)	MA(1)	
ARIMA(1,0,1) (0,0,0) *z*-statistic	0.869 22.023***	−0.887 −26.312***	
CSX Index	AR(1)	MA(1)	
ARIMA(1,0,1) (0,0,0) *z*-statistic	0.957 52.092***	−0.982 −102.824***	

TABLE 13.7 Results From Volatility Models (Daily Returns) (*cont.*)

Panel B: conditional variance equations

	ω	α_1	β_1	D_2
VN Index				
EGARCH	−0.789	0.434	0.949	0.263
(1,1)	−10.493***	14.101***	131.426***	2.320**
z-statistic	LL = 10,329.73	SBC = −6.007	$Q_{SQ}(12)$ = 32.192 (0.650)	
HNX Index				
EGARCH	−0.651	0.397	0.956	
(1,1)	−7.235***	10.995***	102.933***	
z-statistic	LL = 5,688.361	SBC = −5.173	$Q_{SQ}(12)$ = 4.616 (0.948)	
LSX Index				
EGARCH	0.000	0.361	0.373	
(1,1)	3.861***	5.524***	3.531***	
z-statistic	LL = 3,036.301	SBC = −6.155	$Q_{SQ}(12)$ = 26.065 (0.889)	
CSX Index				
EGARCH	−1.293	0.370	0.879	
(1,1)	−2.970***	4.519***	19.312***	
z-statistic	LL = 1,828.873	SBC = −5.941	$Q_{SQ}(12)$ = 40.825 (0.267)	

Notes: The VN Index represents large-cap stocks (>VND 120 billion), while the HNX Index consists of medium and small-cap companies listed in the Vietnamese stock exchange. The LSX Index and the CSX Index are the composite indices of the Laos Securities Exchange and the Cambodia Stock Exchange, respectively. *D_2 is a dummy variable representing structural breaks. *** and ** signify the rejection of the null hypothesis of random walk at the 1 and 5% levels of significance, respectively.

TABLE 13.8 Results From Volatility Models (Weekly Returns)

Panel A: mean equation

VN Index	AR(1)	AR(2)	MA(1)	MA(2)
ARIMA(2,0,2)(0,0,0)	−0.360	−2.303	0.520	−0.455
z-statistic	−2.303**	4.028***	2.944***	−2.624***
HNX Index	AR(1)	MA(1)		
ARIMA(1,0,1)(0,0,0)	0.669	−0.556		
z-statistic	5.990***	−4.648***		
LSX Index	AR(1)	MA(1)		
ARIMA(1,0,1)(0,0,0)	−0.943	0.983		
z-statistic	−63.156***	223.576***		
CSX Index	AR(1)	MA(1)		
ARIMA(1,0,1)(0,0,0)	0.544	−0.530		
z-statistic	2.540**	−2.678**		

(Continued)

TABLE 13.8 Results From Volatility Models (Weekly Returns) *(cont.)*

Panel B: conditional variance equations

	ω	α_1	β_1	D_1	D_2	D_3
VN Index						
EGARCH	−0.585	0.407	0.959	0.685	−0.455	
(1,1)	−4.101***	5.625***	62.687***	3.075***	−2.624***	
z-statistic	LL = 1426.6	SBC = −3.8	$Q_{SQ}(12)$ = 27.2 (0.854)			
HNX Index						
EGARCH	−6.259	0.360		−5.021	1.283	
(1,0)	−46.159***	4.193***		−15.582***	3.968***	
z-statistic	LL = 725.3	SBC = −3.1	$Q_{SQ}(12)$ = 19.8 (0.975)			
LSX Index						
EGARCH	−0.557	−0.409	0.891			
(1,1)	−5.24***	−5.460***	68.347***			
z-statistic	LL = 407.3	SBC = −4.7	$Q_{SQ}(12)$ = 45.8 (0.128)			
CSX Index						
EGARCH	−7.530	0.517		−1.383	−4.494	1.641
(1,0)	−28.748***	2.541**		−2.362**	−9.045***	2.438**
z-statistic	LL = 310.1	SBC = −4.2	$Q_{SQ}(12)$ = 10.3 (0.999)			

Notes: The VN Index represents large-cap stocks (>VND 120 billion), while the HNX Index consists of medium and small-cap companies listed in the Vietnamese stock exchange. The LSX Index and the CSX Index are the composite indices of the Laos Securities Exchange and the Cambodia Stock Exchange, respectively.
* D_1, D_2, and D_3 are dummy variables represent the structural breaks. *** and ** signify the rejection of the null hypothesis of random walk at the 1 and 5% levels of significance, respectively.

Schwarz Bayesian criterion (SBC) (Schwarz, 1978). The mean equations act as a basis for generating the conditional variance equations for each series. To obtain the optimal GARCH(p, q) model, all combinations of (p) = (0,1,2) and (q) = (0,1,2) were considered (except for $p = q = 0$), as suggested by Angelidis et al. (2004). The threshold order determines the impact (or otherwise) of news shocks. The threshold order of zero means that the volatility model is symmetric; for example, the impact of good news equals the impact of bad news in terms of volatility effect. A threshold order of one means the model is asymmetric, that is, the impact of good news does not equal the impact of bad news. All combinations of symmetric and asymmetric volatility models were run. In most instances more than one of the ARCH, GARCH, EGARCH, and/or PGARCH models with significant parameters are found. The model with maximum LL criterion is selected as the optimal model for each series, and according to the Q_{SQ} statistic all models presented are correctly specified ($Q_{SQ} > 0.05$). According to our results, the dummy variable(s) which address(es) structural break(s) is (are) insignificant in most of the cases. For example, according to Table 13.7 Panel B, a significant D_2 is reported only for the case of the Vietnam's VN Index (*z-value of 2.320, significant at the 5% level*). Thus, these findings generally indicate that although there are structural breaks in the return series, they do not significantly influence the volatility of the examined markets.

The empirical results reveal that EGARCH volatility models are optimal for all cases except the daily LSX Index. This supports the findings of Alberg et al. (2008), who investigated the forecasting performance of various volatility models and concluded that the EGARCH volatility model generates better results. The analyses also show that $\beta_i > \alpha_i$ in all daily series. This indicates that there is a relatively long-term impact of shocks on stock markets. Natural disasters, political unrest, unstable economic situations, and decisions concerning macroeconomic fundamentals create these longer effects on stock markets. These results are also consistent with the weekly data. However, the short-term impact of shocks ($\alpha_i > \beta_i$) is found in the cases of the weekly HNX Index and the CSX Index. Symmetric volatility models are statistically significant in both daily and weekly series, implying that the impact of positive and negative news or shocks is the same in magnitude. This indicates that local news announcements (good and bad) regarding macroeconomic fundamentals, politics, and specifics about companies have the same impact on daily and weekly returns. Consequently, on the basis of these findings, we have to reject the null hypothesis of randomness in the return time series.

5   CONCLUSIONS

In this study, a number of econometric procedures are employed to investigate the weak-form efficiency of the three SEA frontier markets of Vietnam, Laos, and Cambodia. According to our results, the earliest and largest market of the three, that is Vietnam—is found to be weak-form inefficient, regardless of the test procedure used. On the other hand, in the case of the LSX there are mixed results. For example, our null hypothesis of a random walk is rejected using unit root, autocorrelation, and variance ratio tests, but it is accepted using a runs test on both daily and weekly data. In the case of the CSX the results are particularly interesting, as the market appears to be weak-form efficient according to the results from the autocorrelation Q-statistic test (using both daily and weekly data), runs tests (weekly data), and the variance ratio test (daily data). Hence, this study brings about a surprising finding: that this younger and considerably smaller SEA frontier market shows some positive signs of weak-form efficiency. Nonetheless, none of the three markets examined demonstrates consistently significant evidence on weak-form efficiency across all methodologies employed.

As regards the empirical results on market volatility and the long memory dynamics of these markets, the EGARCH volatility models appear to be optimal for all cases except that of the daily LSX Index. Results also indicate that there is a relatively long-term impact of shocks on these stock markets. For example, natural disasters, political unrest, unstable economic situations, and decisions concerning macroeconomic fundamentals create these longer effects on stock prices. Our results indicate a short-term impact of shocks in the case of the weekly indices for the HNX and the CSX. Moreover, symmetric volatility models are statistically significant in both daily and weekly series, implying that the impacts of positive and negative news or shocks are the same in magnitude.

Any attempt by relevant governments to increase the informational efficiency of their equity markets so as to promote their business environment and attract foreign invested capital requires above all the creation of an appropriate legislative and regulatory framework. For example, some of the key changes urgently needed in this very early stage in the life of these markets are (1) the strengthening of the role and capacities of the relevant securities commissions to raise awareness and confidence in the market across local and foreign investors; (2) completion of the securities laws and the appropriate regulatory framework to improve information transparency and restrict insider trading, and (3) propagation of an open mechanism and incentive schemes to attract more listings of local companies and additional investors (especially foreign and institutional investors) for the purposes of market development, product diversification, and competition enhancement.

REFERENCES

Alberg, D., Shalit, H., Yosef, R., 2008. Estimating stock market volatility using asymmetric GARCH models. Appl. Financ. Econ. 18 (15), 1201–1208.

Angelidis, T., Benos, A., Degiannakis, S., 2004. The use of GARCH models in VaR estimation. Stat. Methodol. 1 (2), 105–128.

Aumeboonsuke, V., 2012. Weak-form efficiency of six equity exchanges in ASEAN. Eur. J. Sci. Res. 84 (4), 532–538.

Bai, J., Perron, P., 1998. Estimating and testing linear models with multiple structural changes. Econometrica 66 (1), 47–78.

Bai, J., Perron, P., 2003. Computation and analysis of multiple structural change models. J. Appl. Economet. 18 (1), 1–22.

Bollerslev, T., 1986. Generalized autoregressive conditional heteroscedasticity. J. Econom. 31, 307–327.

Borges, M.R., 2011. Random walk tests for the Lisbon stock market. Appl. Econ. 43 (5), 631–639.

Bradley, J.V., 1968. Distribution-Free statistical tests. Manage. Sci. 16 (1), 141–143.

Cowles, A., 1960. A revision of previous conclusions regarding stock price behavior. Econometrica 28 (4), 909–915.

Dickey, D., Fuller, W.A., 1981. Likelihood ratio statistics for autoregressive time series with a unit root. Econometrica 49 (4), 1057–1072.

Engle, R.F., 1982. Autoregressive conditional heteroskedacticity with estimates of the variance of United Kingdom inflation. Econometrica 50 (4), 987–1007.

Fama, E.F., 1965. The behavior of stock market price. J. Bus. 38, 34–105.

Fama, E.F., 1970. Efficient capital markets: a review of theory and empirical work. J. Financ. 25 (2), 283–417.

Fama, E.F., French, K.R., 1987. Permanent and temporary components of stock prices. J. Polit. Econ. 96 (2), 246–273.

Fama, E.F., French, K.R., 1988. Dividend yields and expected stock returns. J. Financ. Econ. 22 (1), 3–25.

Guidi, F., Gupta, R., 2011. Are ASEAN Stock Market Efficient? Evidence From Univariate and Multivariate Variance Ratio Tests. Discussion Papers in Finance, Griffith University.

Kendall, M.G., 1953. The analysis of economic time-series. Part I: prices. J. Roy. Stat. Soc. 116 (1), 11–34.

Ljung, G.M., Box, G.E.P., 1978. On a measure of lack of fit in time series models. Biometrika 65 (2), 297–303.

Lo, A.W., MacKinlay, A.C., 1988. Stock market prices do not follow random walks: evidence from a simple specification test. Rev. Financ. Stud. 1 (1), 41–66.

Loc, T.D., 2006. Equitisation and Stock Market Development: The Case of Vietnam. Unpublished PhD Thesis, University of Groningen.

Longmore, R., Robinson, W., 2005. Modeling and forecasting exchange rate dynamics in Jamaica: an application of asymmetric volatility models. Money Aff. 18 (1), 23–56.

Mishra, P., 2012. Weak-form market efficiency: evidence from emerging and developed world. J. Commer. 3 (2), 26–34.

Nelson, D.B., 1991. Conditional heteroscedasticity in asset returns: a new approach. Econometrica 59 (2), 347–370.

Nelson, D.B., Cao, C.O., 1992. Inequality constraints in the univariate GARCH model. J. Bus. Econ. Stat. 10 (2), 229–235.

Nisar, S., Hanif, M., 2012. Testing weak-form of efficient market hypothesis: empirical evidence from South-Asia. World Appl. Sci. J. 17 (4), 414–427.

Osborne, M.F.M., 1962. Periodic structure in the Brownian motion of stock prices. Oper. Res. 10 (3), 345–379.

Pearson, K., 1905. The problem of the random walk. Nature 72, 294.

Phan, K.C., Zhou, J., 2014. Market efficiency in emerging stock markets: a case study of the Vietnamese stock market. IOSR J. Bus. Manage. 16 (4), 61–73.

Righi, M., Ceretta, P., 2011. Random walk and variance ratio tests for efficiency in the sub-prime crisis: evidence for the U.S. and Latin markets. Int. Res. J. Finance Econ. 72, 25–32.

Samuelson, P.A., 1965. Proof that properly anticipated prices fluctuate randomly. Ind. Manage. Rev. 6 (2), 41–49.

Schwarz, G., 1978. Estimating the dimension of a model. Ann. Stat. 6 (2), 461–464.

Sharma, J.L., Kennedy, R.E., 1977. A comparative analysis of stock price behavior on the Bombay, London, and New York stock exchanges. J. Financ. Quant. Anal. 12 (3), 391–413.

Smith, G., 2012. The changing and relative efficiency of European emerging stock markets. Eur. J. Finance 18 (8), 689–708.

Suleman, M.T., et al., 2010. Testing the weak-form of efficient market hypothesis: empirical evidence from Asia-Pacific markets. Int. Res. J. Finance Econ. 58, 121–133.

Szakmary, A., et al., 1999. Filter tests in Nasdaq stocks. Financ. Rev. 34 (1), 45–70.

Tsai, H., Chan, K.S., 2008. A note on inequality constraints in the GARCH model. Economet. Theor. 24 (3), 823–828.

Vinh V.X., Thao, L.D.B., 2013. Empirical investigation of efficient market hypothesis in Vietnam Stock market. SSRN Electronic Journal 03/2013.

Worthington, A., Higgs, H., 2003. Tests of Random Walks and Market Efficiency in Latin American Stock Markets: an Empirical Note. School of Economics and Finance Discussion Papers and Working Papers Series, No. 157. Queensland University of Technology, School of Economics and Finance, Brisbane, Australia.

Worthington, A., Higgs, H., 2004. Random walks and market efficiency in European equity markets. Global J. Finance Econ. 1 (1), 59–78.

Worthington, A., Higgs, H., 2005. Weak-Form Market Efficiency in Asian Emerging and Developed Equity Markets: Comparative Tests of Random Walk Behavior. School of Accounting and Finance Working Paper Series, No. 05/03. University of Wollongong, Wollongong, Australia. Available from: http://ro.uow.edu.au/commpapers/199

Wright, J.H., 2000. Alternative variance-ratio tests using ranks and signs. J. Bus. Econ. Stat. 18 (1), 1–9.

Index

Printed in the United States
By Bookmasters